D1564211

Permanent Crisis

# Permanent Crisis

## THE HUMANITIES IN A
## DISENCHANTED AGE

*Paul Reitter and Chad Wellmon*

THE UNIVERSITY OF CHICAGO PRESS

CHICAGO AND LONDON

The University of Chicago Press, Chicago 60637
The University of Chicago Press, Ltd., London
© 2021 by The University of Chicago
Published 2021
Printed in the United States of America

30  29  28  27  26  25  24  23  22  21      2  3  4  5

ISBN-13: 978-0-226-73806-2 (cloth)
ISBN-13: 978-0-226-73837-6 (e-book)
DOI: https://doi.org/10.7208/chicago/9780226738376.001.0001

Library of Congress Cataloging-in-Publication Data

Names: Reitter, Paul, author. | Wellmon, Chad, 1976– author.
Title: Permanent crisis : the humanities in a disenchanted age /
Paul Reitter and Chad Wellmon.
Other titles: Humanities in a disenchanted age
Description: Chicago ; London : The University of Chicago Press, 2021. |
Includes bibliographical references and index.
Identifiers: LCCN 2021004009 | ISBN 9780226738062 (cloth) |
ISBN 9780226738376 (ebook)
Subjects: LCSH: Humanities. | Humanities—Germany—History—19th century. |
Education, Higher—Germany—History—19th century. | Humanities—
United States—History. | Germany—Intellectual life—19th century.
Classification: LCC AZ356 .R45 2021 | DDC 001.3—dc23
LC record available at https://lccn.loc.gov/2021004009

*To our children—*
*Cecelia, Vann, Ev, and Whit*

# Contents

# Introduction

The term *permanent crisis* is, of course, an oxymoron, since *crisis* refers, in its classic definition at least, to a decisive moment—a turning point between what came before and what might now follow.[1] A crisis does not persist; it passes. Yet today the desire to declare every moment decisive is common. Crises roil capitalism, but they also sustain it. Long before calling for creative destruction and disruption without end became fashionable, Friedrich Engels and Karl Marx expressed the hope that the periodic crises of modern industrialization would eventually be overcome through "permanent revolution."[2] The idea that crisis was to be welcomed, not feared, has taken more moderate forms as well. Jacob Burckhardt, a contemporary of Engels and Marx, emphasized the productive side of crisis, although, with the reserve he considered appropriate for historians, he preferred gradual crises over the revolutionary kind.[3] Writing in 1873, toward the end of a long, successful career as an art historian at the University of Basel, Burckhardt warned that "historical crises" could be destructive and that "artists and poets" in particular tended to go too far in "glorifying" them. But he thought they were right to claim that crises created new perspectives, new ways of seeing.

Yet Burckhardt didn't apply that logic to his own intellectual domain: the academic humanities. He was not alone in this. Many scholars prize calm and stability—Burckhardt himself preferred the serenity of Basel to the frenetic atmosphere of Berlin—and so resist conceiving of historical crisis and disorder as crucial to their professional success. But whereas Burckhardt never suggested that the humanities were imperiled by crisis, other humanities scholars have, in the subsequent century and a half, freely wielded the language of crisis to describe their institutional circumstances and standing in the broader culture. They have even tended to treat crisis as a threat to the very existence of the humanities. Around the time he commented on crisis, Burckhardt heard his younger colleague Friedrich Nietzsche, whose histrionics he had begun to regard with suspicion, use the discourse of crisis in just this way in a theatrical series of public lectures. While wary of Nietzsche, Burckhardt actually shared his worry that the humanities were being Prussianized: scaled up, standardized, and pressed into state service. Burckhardt would have agreed that if there were good reason to be skeptical of crisis talk in the humanities, the same went for attempts to deflect such talk. The point still applies: in many reckonings with public debates about the humanities, today as in Nietzsche's day, crisis talk has been dismissed too quickly, sometimes by the same critics who employ it.

In a 2018 essay in the *Atlantic* titled "The Humanities Are in Crisis," the historian Benjamin Schmidt explained why, unlike so many other humanities scholars, he had long avoided the word *crisis* when discussing humanities enrollments in colleges and universities in the United States. First, he didn't think the enrollment figures were all that bad. Even in 2013, they were better than ever in absolute terms, and the percentage drops during and after the Great Recession had been gentle, worlds away from the free fall the mid-1970s had seen. But second, Schmidt admitted to a certain categorical reservation about using such language. "One thing I learned earning a history degree," he wrote, "is that people usually announce a 'crisis' so that they can trot out solutions they came up with earlier."[4] By 2018, however, Schmidt had changed his mind. New data suggested that the state of the humanities had deteriorated and, as the title of his essay indicates, now justified the use of *crisis*. History itself had pushed him into the mainstream. And Schmidt's message was clear: it is finally time for supporters of the academic humanities to worry.

The intellectual historian Stefan Collini, one of Britain's most influential commentators on higher education, persists in adhering to his stance as a holdout with regard to crisis talk. In his essay collection *Speaking of Universities* (2017), he stresses that he's no fan of the "it's all going to the dogs" discourse or "Cassandraism" that has been, in his view, a long-standing part of academic culture. As have Schmidt and countless others, past and present, Collini portrays cries of crisis in the humanities as hasty and even counterproductive. He writes that such bewailing often results from an ahistorical perspective, something that is particularly off-putting in people who claim to be historically minded. If academics were aware of how much of their crisis rhetoric repeated old laments, they might adopt a different tone, or come up with more original turns of phrase. This is important, Collini says, because thoughtful rearticulations of the university's core values matter. Edging into crisis discourse himself, Collini emphasizes that such rearticulations are now urgently needed, and he challenges concerned citizens of the university to provide them.[5]

*Permanent Crisis* is not a call to action. Rather, we have written a work of historical scholarship and what we hope will be a clarifying and at times invigoratingly counterintuitive contribution to the debate about the plight of the humanities, particularly at US and European institutions of higher learning. Our book has two primary objects of critique: (a) how the notion of a crisis of the humanities has been invoked and (b) how it has been dismissed. We agree that even if most of the forces besetting the academic humanities aren't new—vocationalism, managerialism, anti-intellectualism—the present moment is a particularly difficult one for humanities scholars and for all who consider themselves the humanities' beneficiaries or defenders. At the same time, we think that crisis talk in the humanities is often peevish, self-serving, lacking in historical perspective, and antithetical to the careful thinking and scholarly virtues to which humanities scholars typically aspire. In uncovering the roots of the persistent sense of crisis surrounding the humanities, we highlight continuities that extend well beyond the twenty-first-century United States. We show that today's humanities scholars experience and react to basic pressures in ways that are strikingly similar to the response of their nineteenth-century German counterparts. In German universities of the 1800s—as in those in the United States, particularly today—humanities scholars felt threatened by the very processes that supplied the means for the modern humanities to flourish, such as institutional rationalization and the democratization of knowledge.

But we also emphasize the constructive side of crisis discourse. Indeed, one of our chief claims is that *the self-understanding of the modern humanities didn't merely take shape in response to a perceived crisis; it also made crisis a core part of the project of the humanities.* The humanities came into their own in late nineteenth-century Germany by being framed as, in effect, a privileged resource for resolving perceived crises of meaning and value that threatened other cultural or social goods as well. The perception of crisis, whether or not widely shared, can focus attention and provide purpose. In the case of the humanities, the sense of crisis has afforded coherence amid shifts in methods and theories and social and institutional transformations. Whether or not they are fully aware of it, for politically progressive and conservative scholars alike, crisis has played a crucial role in grounding the idea that the humanities have a special mission. Part of the story of why the modern humanities are always in crisis is that we have needed them to be.

Even humanities scholars who are determined to avoid crisis talk wind up reinforcing it. Collini, for example, clearly didn't set out to produce a book of the same ilk as Allan Bloom's *The Closing of the American Mind* (1987), and he didn't write that kind of sensationalizing account of the university (and especially the humanities) in decline. Far from it. In *Speaking of Universities*, Collini soberly addresses the tension between research and open-ended or liberal learning, the dynamic that, for him, remains the defining feature of modern universities and the instrumental logic governing university administrations and the societies that sustain universities. He asserts that some of this tension is unavoidable and that academics should learn to live with it—at least up to a point. Only reluctantly, moreover, does Collini admit that liberal higher education and the academic humanities have reached the crisis stage. But when he writes about what the humanities offer society, Collini makes the kind of dramatic, redemptive promises that necessitate crisis and pervade writings in defense of the modern humanities. It's not simply the case that the humanities are worth preserving in the face of pressures that make their continued existence difficult. For Collini those pressures are part of a larger social and cultural crisis that the humanities are uniquely well equipped to help resolve.

Collini suggests that the managerialism harming the academic humanities with its quantitative metrics has also damaged society as a whole, dehumanizing the workplace more broadly. Since managerialism relies on linguistic deformations and clichés, and since humanities scholars are often in the business of deconstructing such things, the humanities can militate against managerialism in their own special way. Up to this point, Collini's argument suggests that the humanities can help address a pressing sociocultural problem. This is likely to come across as a reasonable, even modest claim rather than a promise of redemption.

But as Collini lays out the value of the humanities in a time of crisis, his rhetoric intensifies into hyperbole. Referring to certain forays into public discourse by humanities scholars, he writes of how "the energy released by the collision between, on the one hand, the immovable mass of decayed half-truths and rotting clichés and, on the other, the irresistible force of genuine ethical insight functions like a prose version of the Large Hadron Collider."[6] Overwrought assertions of this kind damage the credibility of the humanities, especially when it is humanities scholars who regularly make such rhetorical intemperance the target of critique. Justifying the modern humanities by depicting them as the agent through which we will overcome modern crises of meaning has led to further problems and pressures in the humanities, beginning with crises of overpromising.

## METHOD, PRACTICE, DISCOURSE

Although we focus on pervasive features of crisis talk in the present volume, we don't believe that everyone who sees the humanities as being in crisis thinks about or experiences crisis in the same way. Yet people who do invoke the notion of crisis often presume the existence of a crisis consensus, a prior agreement on what the humanities are as well as a general account of their current condition. They seldom ask with Kyla Wazana Tompkins, "Is your crisis in the Humanities, my crisis?"[7] For our part, we highlight the heterogeneity of the discourse about the humanities. Scholars and public intellectuals, as well as those who, like Collini, speak in both roles, have offered disparate and sometimes even conflicting definitions of the humanities. The humanities are a set of academic disciplines; the humanities are a form of humanism;[8] the humanities are a unique set of skills or ways of knowing;[9] the humanities are a kind of self-cultivation.[10] We will not offer another definition of what the humanities are; instead, we will show how the signifier "the humanities" came to mean and do what it does.

When a university dean, an op-ed columnist, or an English professor uses the term *the humanities*, whether intentionally or not, she is invoking a whole set of commitments, ideals, and sensibilities: qualitative over quantitative reasoning; a celebration of interpretation and a wariness toward positivism; an interest in and concern with the subject of knowledge, not simply the object of knowledge; valuation of the particular as much as the general.[11] To align oneself with the humanities is implicitly (or even explicitly) to affirm not simply a bureaucratic arrangement of departments or a set of disciplines but a particular disposition. The humanities serve intellectual, cultural, and social functions. They are, as the philosopher Wilhelm Dilthey put it in 1882, a "bulwark," safeguarding something sacred or valuable against forces that threaten their very existence.[12] In the following chapters, then, instead of proceeding from a theoretical statement about what the humanities essentially are, we focus on what people do in the name of the humanities and what they use the humanities to accomplish. We consider the humanities as both practice and discourse. We devote particular attention to how people have used the humanities to stand in for or even constitute a particular ethical project or, again, a way of life. The current institutional arrangement of university-based knowledge—with its particular norms, practices, ideals, and virtues—was not necessary; it could have been otherwise. Our aim is to show how the humanities came to serve distinct functions and particular ends.

## ON THE DISCONTINUITY OF THE HUMANITIES

More specifically, we are interested in the discourses and practices of what we call the *modern* humanities. *Modern* here refers neither to a distinct historical epoch or culture nor to an uncritical claim of contemporary interest but to the persistent present mindedness and situatedness of intellectuals and scholars who have tried to define, defend, and justify something like the humanities. In contrast to prior traditions of humanist knowledge, as we shall see, the modern humanities are consistently cast as a particular project to countervail against specific historical forces and problems that threaten *the human*. The *modern* humanities address not disordered desires, unruly passions, or the presence of evil but historical changes: industrialization, new technologies, natural science, and capitalism. This permanent relationship to the present links the modern humanities to the temporality of crisis. Whereas the temporality of change or development is ongoing, observable, and slow, that of crisis is decisive, exceptional, and particular. Crisis requires a language suitable for the present moment and situation, a language that communicates the transformative potential of now.[13] This is why those who claim to speak on behalf of the modern humanities often do so through exhortation and declaration.

Yet even as their defenders have insisted on the urgency of the humanities, they have just as consistently argued for the humanities' continuity across space and time. In focusing on *the modern humanities*, then, we presume the presence of a historical and cultural distinction that is crucial to our larger story. This distinction represents our interpretive point of departure, and so we want to offer an account, at the onset, of how it works and why it is significant.

Recent efforts among scholars to establish the history of humanities as a distinct field started with a question: "How did the humanities develop from the *artes liberales*, via the *studia humanitatis*, to modern disciplines?"[14] Our question is slightly different: Have the continuities linking the humanist scholarship of the faraway past to that of today been stretched thin? Or have they, or some of them, remained robust? These are, of course, big questions, and we won't treat them comprehensively, let alone try to resolve them. But we do begin with the premise that the continuities between the modern, university-based disciplines collectively known as the humanities and earlier forms of humanist knowledge such as the *studia humanitatis* have been exaggerated.[15] The modern humanities are not the products of an unbroken tradition reaching back to the Renaissance and, ultimately, to Greek and Roman antiquity. There are important discontinuities and dif-

ferences, one of which is the persistent discourse of crisis that has characterized the professionalized humanities of the modern research university
as it has developed in Germany and the United States. We hope to illuminate
the operations and evolution of this discourse as well as its effects on other
humanist practices.

<br>

## DISTANT RELATIVES

On April 26, 1336, the Italian scholar and poet Petrarch wrote a letter to
Father Francesco Dionigi of Borgo describing his ascent of Mont Ventoux, in
southern France. Since the nineteenth century, Petrarch's reflections have
been celebrated as the work of "the first truly modern man," the product of a
modern "individual personality."[16] However, the echoes of Augustine in the
letter are hard to miss: the ascent, the discussion of conversion, the inner
eye, and the role that reading plays in forming a self.[17] Like Augustine's
*Confessions*, Petrarch's letter testifies to a life shaped by reading. He writes
that he was prompted to scale Ventoux by his experience of Livy's *History of
Rome*, which includes a description of the Macedonian king Philip V's climb
of Mount Hemus. The rest of the letter is filled with quotations from and
allusions to Cicero, Virgil, the Gospel of Matthew, Psalms, Job, Ovid—and,
perhaps most famously, the *Confessions*. But unlike Augustine, who confidently took hold of his Bible, Petrarch opened the *Confessions* tentatively. It
simply "occurred to" him, as he leafed desultorily through the pages of the
book, to read whatever passage "chance" might lead him to.[18] For Augustine, reading was an encounter with the traces of a divine will; reading had a
proper and certain end. For Petrarch, it was just as likely to be an encounter
with the "surging emotions" and "vague, wandering thoughts" of an ambivalent and uncertain self—an encounter that is not with the divine but,
rather with the thoughts of human authors.[19]

Augustine could neither have attended a university nor taught at one,
since universities didn't exist in the fourth century, but Petrarch could have,
even though he chose not to. Although he intermittently studied law at the
University of Bologna from 1320 to 1326, Petrarch the humanist scholar was
stridently "anti-institutional."[20] In *On His Own Ignorance and That of Many
Others* (1367), he spun his castigation of university-based scholars and their
slavish devotion to "The Philosopher," Aristotle, into an anti-institutional
broadside against medieval universities. Here Aristotle stands in for a
monolithic curriculum and the medium through which universities repro-
duced themselves: strict adherence to a fixed body of learning.[21] According
to Petrarch, the university was moribund, a victim of its own institutional

success. It was limiting and uncritical, defined by intellectual narrowness and ideological conformity.[22] Universities had become sectarian institutions that mistook erudition, "adventitious ornament," for reason.[23]

Petrarch's criticisms didn't slow the growth of the university, however. By the time he died, in 1374, there were nearly thirty universities across Europe, all sharing a basic set of institutional norms and ideals. Before receiving their official papal charters, these universities had developed almost "spontaneously" out of the densest networks of traveling students and scholars who had settled around particular schools and teachers.[24] Universities declared themselves fixed centers of teaching and learning that nevertheless transcended their physical location. They institutionalized this local-universal dynamic in standard pedagogical practices—especially the lecture with the commentary and the disputation with the questions[25]— and in staples such as the sequence of degrees (bachelor's, master's, doctoral) and structures such as the four faculties: arts or philosophy, medicine, law, and theology, with the arts or philosophy faculty ranking lowest and the theology faculty highest. There were also hierarchical systems of dress (e.g., academic gowns and robes) and various other privileges for the guild-like institution that the university would remain for centuries.[26]

Petrarch and the initial generations of humanists in Italy understood their own humanist forms of reading, writing, speaking, thinking, and sociability as protests against those of the university. They upheld the letter, dialogue, and oration, their preferred forms of communication, as superior to the academic *lectio* and *questiones*. By comparing themselves to the cultures and practices that dominated universities, these original humanists also fashioned the individuals they aspired to become. When fourteenth- and fifteenth-century humanists such as Petrarch, Leonardi Bruni, and Coluccio Salutati complained about the intellectual barrenness of medieval universities, they were, as Christopher Celenza has put it, creating a "posture"—that of outsiders resisting the dominant knowledge institution of the day.[27] When Salutati, humanist scholar and chancellor of the Republic of Florence, wrote at the end of the fourteenth century that the "*studia litterarum* has risen somewhat in our day," he meant that reading and writing in accord with the highest models of classical Latin, above all Cicero, "the prince of eloquence," had become an established practice among Florence's educated elite.[28] At the beginning of the fifteenth century, Florentine citizens, clergy, and even university teachers gathered regularly in private circles outside universities to read and discuss ancient texts, listen to lectures, and practice that most humanist of communicative forms—dialogue. These groups of educated citizens helped establish new modes of socialization that spread to Rome, Naples, Kraków, Heidelberg, Augsburg, Vienna, and elsewhere across Europe. These groups represented an alternative to the model of learned and scholarly socialization that universities provided: scholastic forms of *lectio* and *disputatio*. In this way, these congeries of educated individuals made possible the academies and learned societies that began to flourish in the second half of the sixteenth century.[29]

But humanist scholars gradually abandoned their antiuniversity posture. Over the course of the fifteenth century, they sought out university positions and helped establish the *studia humanitatis* as elements of the faculty of arts in universities across Europe. They became institutional insiders. As the twentieth-century German émigré scholar Paul Oskar Kristeller showed, the term *humanist* (*humanista*) first appeared in the "slang of university students and gradually penetrated into official usage" to name "the professional teacher of the *studia humanitatis*," which comprised grammar, rhetoric, poetry, history, and moral philosophy.[30] One of the first instances of *humanista* occurs in a document dated October 21, 1512, in a reference to a teacher of poetry and rhetoric.[31] As for *studia humanitatis*, the term didn't signify the pursuit of theological, metaphysical, or philosophical knowledge, or, as some contemporary commenters claim about the modern humanities, the cultivation or training of the "soul" as an end in itself,[32] but a more "modest" notion: that the kinds of technical skills and knowledge humanists taught—reading, writing, and speaking about ancient Latin and Greek texts—helped prepare students for study in the higher faculties as well for lives as active citizens, friends, and family members.[33] The fifteenth-century Florentine statesman and teacher Leonardo Bruni, for example, described the *studia humanitatis* as a "combination of literary skill and factual knowledge."[34] They were less an explicitly ideological, philosophical, or religious undertaking than, as Kristeller describes them, an "educational program" concerned primarily with "literature."[35] The aims of early humanist scholars and teachers like Bruni were more quotidian, more practical, more technical—in short, more tightly circumscribed—than later scholars have made them out to be.[36] By the middle of the fifteenth century, the *studia humanitatis* were fixed features of the arts faculties in almost every Italian university. Kristeller called Italian humanists of the Renaissance "the ancestors of modern philologists and historians," thus implying that the latter were related to the former but also distant from them.[37]

Yet Bruni's commitment to the knowledge and skills of the *studia humanitatis* was motivated by something not simply technical: a faith that the literature of a now lost world of antiquity could have an effect in the present. To read, speak, and write well meant to do as the ancient Romans did, especially Cicero and Virgil. Renaissance humanists named certain ancient texts *literae humaniores* because they believed that these exemplary written works could make people morally better.[38]

As universities and other schools of higher education absorbed the *studia humanitatis*, they also set the conditions for their transformation. When the fifteenth-century humanist scholar Lorenzo Valla sought to systematize the *studia humanitatis* by introducing and refining technical methods, he implicitly reconceptualized the basic purpose of this endeavor.[39] Valla wanted to establish the *studia humanitatis* as a legitimate alternative to the scholastic curriculum that trained students to think in a Latin that he argued was abstract, formal, and unmoored from any historical reality.[40] Rejecting common scholastic-Aristotelian categories, Valla recast the humanist scholars' intellectual horizons of possibility. Instead of mere preparatory activities—aids that facilitated the real knowledge work in law, medicine, or theology—he held up the *studia humanitatis* as entailing more concrete ways of thinking than those currently available in universities. As the medium of all relationships—human/human, human/divine, present/ past—language, especially the classical Latin of Cicero and Quintilian, provided a common practice through which people not only could interact and communicate but also think about the world. Latin, Valla wrote, was the "great sacrament, indeed, the great divinity";[41] it was not just a means of communication but a medium and resource for the highest forms of human reason and action. Many contemporaries lambasted Valla's efforts to legitimate the *studia humanitatis* as both futile and amoral. His obsession with method and system would, it was thought, sever the link between scholarly practice and moral formation that Petrarch, Salutati, and Bruni had simply assumed was the proper and ultimate end of the *studia humanitatis*.

Over the next two centuries, as Anthony Grafton and Lisa Jardine have shown, humanist scholars followed Valla in justifying the *studia humanitatis* in terms of method rather than moral formation.[42] As scholars such as Georgius Agricola, Peter Ramus, Justus Lipsius, and Philipp Melanchthon developed increasingly detailed and explicit methods that could be repeated and successfully applied without the guidance of a charismatic teacher, they also began to treat texts as material objects to be mined for meaning in new ways.[43] Instead of merely pointing to or recounting the truth, texts could now, as Walter Ong put it, "contain truth, like boxes."[44] The fifteenth- and sixteenth-century humanists who followed Valla treated the works of Cicero and other classics of antiquity as "clouded windows, which proper treatment could restore to transparency, revealing the individuals who had written them" and transmitting the knowledge they and generations of intermediaries had entrusted to texts.[45] Humanists such as

Valla conceived of knowledge as erudition. Knowledge was something that already existed, and it was the task of the historical and textual arts, the *studia humanitatis*, to cultivate, collect, and organize it.[46] The Renaissance humanists' conception of knowledge as erudition, as bound to human language and the material forms it assumed in texts, distinguished it from the then predominant theological conception of knowledge as metaphysical inquiry.[47] The *studia humanitatis* considered human things, which included, as we have noted, a vast array of arts recovered from ancient texts, from poetry and painting to natural philosophy and mining.[48] The *studium divinitatis*, or scholastic theology, considered the divine and reason itself. Until at least the seventeenth century, the fault line separating the study of "divinity" from, as one English writer put it in 1483, "humanity," remained the most important institutional and intellectual division of knowledge.[49]

Yet even as humanist scholars continued to justify their scholarship in terms of method, the desire to maintain the moral promise of humanist learning persisted. When Erasmus outlined the proper method for teaching students how to read a text in *De ratione studii* (On the right method of study, 1512), he assumed that adherence to and rigorous application of a humanist method would produce a reader who was not only accurate but morally sound. After conducting students through a series of exercises, the teacher, Erasmus wrote, should "finally" bring out the "moral implications" of the text at hand. Neither here nor elsewhere did Erasmus fully articulate how humanist reading practices necessarily led to virtue. Still, like the scholars who preceded him, he took for granted that humanist forms of writing and sociability, as well as humanist methods—the act of reading rigorously, carefully, methodically—produced salutary moral effects.[50] But fifteenth-century humanist scholars also raised a basic question about the ends of reading: Should readers be concerned primarily with "getting the text objectively right," or using it, as Augustine might have put it, for "obtaining what you love"?[51] These scholars' doubts about the power of reading to enable communication between minds and worlds—to relay the kinds of intention and purpose that Augustine understood to be at the core of reading and books—would only grow stronger.[52] The notion that books constituted an order or world of their own would, accordingly, grow stronger too.

By the early sixteenth century, the *studia humanitatis* had become established features of university curricula.[53] This was because their practitioners and defenders had adapted them to institutional norms and expectations: designing curricula, establishing professorships, producing textbooks, developing related institutions.[54] But as the *studia humanitatis* attained the institutional authority and legitimacy to inspire and transform individual readers—and to socialize and train European elites to enter civil society as lawyers, doctors, politicians, notaries, and bureaucrats of state and church—they also opened themselves to wounding attacks. From the fifteenth-century skepticism toward Valla's attempts to reform dialectic to early eighteenth-century German complaints about pedantic university philologists, critics blasted textually disposed scholars for failing to model virtue and cultivate it in their students.[55]

Deteriorating institutional conditions exacerbated the problem of purpose and justification. After an initial "golden age" that lasted in some places until the end of the fifteenth century, the *studia humanitatis* suffered through more than two centuries of decline, their institutional fate being bound up with the tumult of the arts (or sometimes philosophy) faculties in universities across Europe.[56] Until at least the late eighteenth century, professors in the arts faculties were subjected to the indignities of sitting at the bottom of a hierarchy atop which, especially in northern European universities, reigned the theology faculty. Arts faculties' offerings appeared last in course catalogs; the professors themselves marched last in academic parades, and their academic robes were generally less grand.[57] As secondary schools gradually assumed the preparatory function of the arts faculties in training students in rhetoric and other areas of humanist study over the course of the seventeenth and eighteenth centuries, enrollments in these faculties declined precipitously. This was so much the case in German-speaking lands that enrollments approached zero at some universities.[58]

## ON THE VALUE OF USELESS KNOWLEDGE

The entry for "humaniora or studia humanitatis" in Zedler's *Grosses vollständiges Lexicon* (a German-language "universal" lexicon published between 1731 and 1754) crystalizes the humanities' peculiar position in the middle of the eighteenth century: "Those free arts that prepare one for study in the higher faculties. Those typically thought to be included under the *Humanioribus* include philosophy, history, antiquities, poetry, oratory, grammar, and languages, as though they distinguished humans from other animals. Cicero pro Archia I. 3. Pro Mur. 29. *Gellius* XIII. 15. *Nouins* I. 160. *Walch* de Litteris Humanioribus. These are now understood as the sciences necessary to master the higher faculties."[59] The entry clearly identifies the *studia humanitatis* as preparatory elements in a broader university curriculum, technical skills and capacities considered necessary for all higher, professional study. The entry also notes, however, in an aside tinged with skepticism—"as though they distinguished humans from other animals"—that they are commonly thought to have a moral or transformative effect. The references to the then standard glosses of the *studia humanitatis* in Cicero,

Aulus Gellius, and others function less as evidence for the claim of efficacy and more as adages recognizable from the barest of bibliographic information. But these references also point to a series of conflations and contradictions, which, the entry suggests, characterize the *studia humanitatis* themselves. In *Pro Archia*, Cicero defends the Greek poet Licinius Archias (121–61 BCE) by expounding on the ways in which the "study of the humanities and literature" (studiis humanitatis ac litterarum) forms character and binds humans together.[60] The reference to the commonplace book of the Roman author Gellius is to *Humanitas*, which, we read, means not so much *philanthropia* (common sympathy with all humans) as *paideia* (the marker of a particular formation or education).[61] The *studia humanitatis*, then, represent not something universal but rather inculcation in a distinct cultural tradition (a canon of ancient Greek and Roman texts), a moral ideal (Cicero as exemplar), and a curriculum.[62] *Humanitas* is a virtue developed through a particular form of education and in accord with its ideal character. Yet the entry in the Zedler lexicon tells readers that a growing "prejudice" against studying anything that doesn't meet an immediate need has led people to dismiss the *studia humanitatis* "as impractical arts." For this reason, the entry continues, almost grudgingly, those who dedicate themselves "exclusively and solely" to studying them deserve "praise."[63]

In suggesting that these historical technical arts could be ends in themselves, the Zedler entry anticipates the transformation of the problem of the *studia humanitatis* (i.e., justification by method or moral edification) into that of the modern humanities. That is, it points to the growing gap between the *studia humanitatis* as a limited but necessary preparatory training for cultured elites on the one hand and the humanities as a self-sufficient moral resource on the other. Over the next half century, intellectuals and scholars, especially in German-speaking lands, sought to transform the *studia humanitatis* and all those arts that had settled into the lower faculty of the university into an explicitly moral and philosophical project, tying them to the human and reason as universals, as ends in themselves. "The human being," wrote Immanuel Kant in 1798, "is destined by his reason to be in a society with other human beings and to cultivate himself, to civilize himself, and to moralize himself by means of the arts and sciences."[64] Kant and the pantheon of German philosophers, theorizers, and bureaucrats who followed him identified the university, and the philosophy faculty in particular, as the primary institution of this human development project. Whereas the higher faculties of law, medicine, and theology relied, as Kant wrote, on the "command of an external legislator" (the state and its statutory authority), the lower, philosophy faculty relied on and had access to reason itself. Its professors and students were only interested in securing the "interests of knowledge"—in other words, in pursuing knowledge for its own sake.[65] By drawing an analogy between human intellection and the divine mind, Kant and the neo-humanists, idealists, and Romantics who followed him ascribed the capacity for spontaneous, creative reason to humans, conceiving of it in terms traditionally limited to the mind of God. In so doing, they elevated the activities and creations of the human mind above the merely technical, useful, or necessary. These intellectual activities and the objects to which they gave form became ends in themselves.

Yet around the same time, as German scholars began labeling themselves as university-based philosophers (that identity itself being a new scholarly persona), humanist doubts and assumptions about reading reached an apotheosis in German classical philology. Scholars turned practices and techniques honed in biblical criticism into advanced methods and applied them to ancient pagan texts. From the beginning, they assumed that modern philology's demand for technical mastery was compatible with ethical cultivation. "By mastering and criticizing the variant readings and technical rules offered by the grammatical books and scholia," the philologist Friedrich August Wolf wrote in his epochal *Prolegomena to Homer* (1795), "we are summoned into old times, times more ancient than those of many ancient writers, and, as it were, into the company of those learned critics."[66] The careful study of ancient manuscripts, scholia, and commentaries according to preestablished methodological conventions enabled a better understanding of the ancient world, which, in turn, facilitated an encounter with the moral exemplars of antiquity. But such study could also undercut the authority of the ancient texts, as did Wolf's conclusion that the *Odyssey* was not the work of one author, Homer, but the product of textual accretion over time—a conclusion similar to the one biblical scholars had reached about the authorship of the Old Testament. Modern readers were bound not by books or even the love of books but by technical methods. The objects of the application of these methods were fungible or even incidental.

While biblical and classical philologists were worrying about the authority of ancient texts, a new generation of scholars began to raise similar concerns about more modern ones. An important factor in this development was the destabilizing effects of the proliferation of print.[67] In 1803 August Wilhelm Schlegel, a German Romantic and one of the first scholars to approach literature—not just drama or poetry but a much broader range of printed writing, including novels—as an art, lamented the pitiful state of German reading and writing, invoking what he termed "literature proper."[68] Given the ready availability of printed texts, German readers no longer read with "devotion but rather with a thoughtless distraction." To remedy this situation, Schlegel proposed that literature be distinguished as a particular kind of writing that had been filtered and sorted from among the surfeit of all that had been printed. In his view, literature wasn't simply a "raw aggregate of books" but the material expression of a universal *Geist* (spirit)—the expression of a common life, even a common humanity. And it was this common human spirit that gave literature its unity and made it a "store of works that are complete as a type of system." If Kant had located the historical development of human being and reason itself in "the arts and sciences," Schlegel was more specific. The "spirit," human being and reason, worked itself out in literature.

It is not incidental, then, that one of the first documented uses of the word *humanism* occurred at this time. In 1808 the philosopher and educational reformer Friedrich Niethammer coined *Humanismus* in a polemic against school reformers seeking more practical pedagogical training. "Humanism," he wrote, referred not simply to the "study of the so-called *humaniora* in the learned schools" but also to the pedagogy of antiquity whose essential feature was the elevation of a student's "humanity over his animality."[69] In a conflation that would eventually characterize the modern humanities, Niethammer further defined humanism as both a curricular program (the study of ancient texts via humanist scholarly traditions) and a moral project with an underlying philosophical anthropology. He envisioned the transformation of the *studia humanitatis* into a pedagogical project oriented toward the "idea of the human in itself as well as its vocation."[70] No longer subordinate to the professionalizing interests of the higher faculties (law, medicine, and theology) or to the confessional ends of the *studium divinitatis*, the newly conceived humanities would constitute their own institutional and pedagogical "system" that would safeguard reason over instrumental rationality, the human mind over the animal body. The modern humanities would "defend the human's spiritual nature in its autonomy, its independence from the material world, and thus assert something that is very true."[71]

Just as importantly, Niethammer, as one reviewer enthused in 1808, juxtaposed the new humanities with those "branches of knowledge such as mathematics, physics, chemistry, which are more immediately related to material production" and better suited for "material use and practical utility."[72] In a "German culture" consumed by the "drive for money and profit" and devoted to "big agriculture and forestry, manufacturing, commerce, and industrialization," knowledge as an end in itself was worth nothing, Niethammer wrote.[73] "Technical and mechanical know-how" triumphed over "pure," noninstrumental knowledge. These instrumental sciences and the technologies and historical processes they unleashed did not simply transform knowledge; they corrupted educational institutions, religion, traditions, and every element of human "moral development" (*Bildung*).[74] In the context of such cultural and spiritual loss, the new humanities, he asserted, were needed to "exercise and form" human reason and thus ensure the "general education of individual humans" as well as the "development" of all of humanity.[75] Niethammer underscored this compensatory role by redrawing the divisions of knowledge. Instead of comparing the humanities to theology as the *studia humanitatis* or *literae humaniores* (the study of things more human than divine), as had historically been done, he pitted the humanities against the natural and physical sciences. In this sense, the new humanities were fundamentally modern because they served not some antiquarian curiosity but the explicit needs of both present and future; they provided practical moral succor for a new age. Yet Niethammer still sought to legitimate the humanities as newly understood by asserting their continuity not only with the "so-called *humanioren* as taught in the schools of the learned" but in a "more distinguished sense with the entire pedagogy of antiquity."[76] Against the onslaught of industrial and technical revolutions, the new, modern humanities would, he claimed, emerge as keepers of "humanity."[77]

Seventy-five years later, in 1883, Wilhelm Dilthey offered a more systematic account of Niethammer's claim when he argued that the modern humanities satisfied a "need" by compensating for the alienating effects of an industrial and technical modern society.[78] More recently, the German philosopher Odo Marquand has argued that the humanities compensate for the "losses" of modernization, which have been largely effected by the natural sciences and associated technological advances.[79]

Niethammer, Dilthey, and Marquand make several important assumptions and claims that recur in the following chapters as we recount the narratives that justify and defend the modern humanities. First, they presume the continuity and identity over space and time of a human essence or being that a monolithic Western modernity threatens to render distant and inaccessible.

Second, they not only describe the purpose of the modern humanities as the recovery of this human essence but also presume its historical necessity, as though the humanities were a particular form of Hegel's "cunning of reason" or Kant's "hidden plan of nature."

Third, they presume that as it erodes confessional religions and moral traditions, a uniquely Western modernity creates the very needs the humanities emerge to satisfy.

Fourth, they presume that the modern humanities did or, under the right conditions, could satisfy those distinctly transcendent needs previously met by religious and moral traditions. As reconceptualized by Niethammer and others, the humanities transformed canons of sacred texts into cultural canons, adopted and adapted reading practices, established new forms of socialization, and institutionalized these practices and objects within the temple of Western liberal culture—the modern university. *In essence, the development of the modern humanities both depended on and played a crucial part in the rise of the modern research university.* This relationship is central to our account.

Finally, as described by Niethammer, Dilthey, and Marquand, the modern humanities are an epiphenomenon of a modernity in which they have fixed functions. Chief among these functions is "the historical transferal of faith" and moral power away from established forms of religion, especially Western forms of Christianity, to the canons, ideals, practices, and institutions that emerge to legitimate the modern humanities' compensatory claims.[80]

Just over thirty years after Niethammer made his case for the compensatory role of the modern humanities, however, the very premise of his functional, ideologically committed conception of the modern humanities seemed in doubt. Their sacred power appeared already to have eroded. The teacher and educational reformer Friedrich Diesterweg called the behavior of "the humanities professors" of the 1830s "a scandal," characterized by "scuffles, malicious attacks, spiteful remarks, effeminate passion for gossip, deceitful backbiting, constant factiousness and us-against-them mentality, and just plain hubris."[81] In particular, Diesterweg bemoaned the proclivity of modern philologists and philosophers to engage in acrimonious debates over competing "ways of reading and interpreting" a text or to get into defensive arguments over Kantian or Hegelian systems instead of studying and celebrating what is simply human. The force of Diesterweg's portrayal of the German humanities professoriate derives from a contrast with what he presumed to have once been. Who could legitimately teach the humanities, since scholars had ceased to embody them? The modern university had deformed those moral exemplars of humane virtue into self-seeking specialists trafficking in the "lifeless details" of pedantry. Humanities professors no longer believed in the power of the sacred objects they had been called to tend and teach. They had lost faith in the historical task of the humanities to maintain the human.

By the end of the nineteenth century, intellectuals and scholars in the United States would claim that German ideas about knowledge, research, and universities had infected American higher education with a desire for specialized and technical expertise. As Diesterweg and his contemporaries demonstrate, however, nostalgia-laden declensional critiques of a modern, disciplinary knowledge had been a key element of the German discourse around higher education since the 1830s.

That the modern humanities have been in permanent crisis, then, stands to reason. They have repeatedly failed to do what has been promised of them. More contemporary debates (i.e., dating from about 1980) about the state of the humanities, their relation to society, their moral and pedagogical value, their institutional shape, and other points of contention, when considered in light of these nineteenth-century German debates, don't seem so novel. Indeed, their main motifs have proven remarkably persistent.

CRISIS AGAIN

In 1929 Eduard Spranger, a conservative nationalist who was, at the time, Germany's leading scholar of neo-humanism, gave a lecture on the "crisis of the humanities." Speaking in Berlin to the German Academy of Sciences, he situated the crisis historically. As both a cause and an effect, it was connected, he said, to a larger cultural crisis that stretched back over centuries in which the "positivist" ideals and methods of the natural sciences had infiltrated the humanities.[82] Recently, however, things had reached a breaking point. Scholarship and science were now thought to be, in a way, meaningless.

In Spranger's view, one shared by many others, the German sociologist Max Weber bore much of the blame for this loss of meaning. Ten years earlier, Weber had published *Scholarship as Vocation*, a book based on a speech he delivered in Munich in 1917 that had provoked an immediate outcry. Many intellectuals and scholars objected to what they considered the main claim of that now famous lecture: that disciplinary knowledge is tightly limited in the kinds of questions it is equipped to help answer, and that, to the extent possible, it should be conducted value free, without moral presuppositions.[83] Neither Spranger nor most any other German interested in such questions would have objected to placing such restrictions on the natural sciences. In the Germany of the 1920s, the persona of the natural or physical scientist largely remained that of the second half of the nineteenth century: an individual committed to a brute mechanistic understanding of nature and the pursuit of the invariant structures of the natural world so as to project future conditions. Concerned only with what was or what rationally could be, this scientist had little interest in what *should* be. Thus, he had nothing to say about how one *ought* to live and believed as a matter of principle that he should refrain from projecting his necessarily human *values* onto the natural world.

What Spranger and many of his younger contemporaries rejected, however, was the extension to the humanities of Weber's scholarly norms, which, in their understanding, were the same as those of the natural sciences. Pushing against the position they attributed to Weber, they insisted that worldviews and value claims were the very "roots of the humanities."[84] What scientists dismissed as prejudices and biases scholars in the humanities embraced as meaningful and orienting values. In taking this stance, Spranger nonetheless worried that having reasserted their humanism in the face of Weber's asceticism, the humanities now seemed doomed to a "Babylonian" conflict of values and worldviews.

Like many other German intellectuals and scholars, Spranger saw two paths out of what Weber himself had called the "polytheism of values." One led to a "new" humanities. Favored by younger participants in the debate, this path ultimately led to abandonment of the epistemic and ethical ideals that had oriented the German research university for a century: the pursuit of the unity, integration, and consilience of knowledge to be achieved through the practices of university-based scholarship. Universities would be replaced by "Weltanschauung academies"—institutions of higher education defined by an explicit and comprehensive worldview and distinct moral framework. These institutions would usher in an era in which the conflict among values and traditions would play out neither within individual institutions nor across and among disciplines but through conflict-prone encounters between and among institutions defined by their distinct Weltanschauungen.

Spranger preferred the second of the two paths, which he called "scholarship squared." By this, he meant knowledge that—owing to a redoubled commitment to discipline, self-critique, shared purpose, and truth—would ultimately bring about a historical resolution of the conflict of values, worldviews, and cultures. The author of countless hagiographic essays and books on Germany's neo-humanist heroes such as Wilhelm von Humboldt, Spranger considered the humanities wholly continuous with the tradition of disciplinary, university-based scholarship. Central to this tradition was the belief that disciplinary scholarship was the most developed form of human reason and was capable of reconciling conflicting worldviews and ultimately realizing the unity of reason in history. The humanities themselves would solve the crisis of culture and with it the long-standing crisis of the humanities. Weber had tried to deprive the humanities of their world-historical mission. Spranger reasserted it. For him, the humanities had a historical and metaphysically infused task: to save people from an untenable condition, "the eternal discontent of the unresolved dialectic."[85]

In the penultimate chapter of *Permanent Crisis*, "Max Weber, Scholarship, and Modern Asceticism," we reckon at length with the debate unleashed by the publication of Weber's *Scholarship as Vocation* in 1919. The chapters preceding that discussion focus on the period between Niethammer's 1808 polemic on humanism and the lecture by Weber that formed the basis for his book. Over the course of the long nineteenth century, the modern research university arose across Germany and created the conditions for the modern humanities to be institutionalized as something approximating the self-understanding of the academic humanities today. Amid growing pressures and related social, institutional, and intellectual transformations, the humanities took on the constellation of expectations that continues to define them and to produce the crisis discourse that has, in a kind of feedback loop, helped shape those expectations. It is emblematic of this circular thinking that the persistence of a diagnosis of crisis has long been read as a sign of the humanities' durability.

At the core of the conceptualization of the humanities as university-based forms of disciplinary knowledge is a deep ambivalence about values, notions of the good, and morality itself. The gap between what the humanities promise and what they do most readily in the context of institutions of higher learning should be plain to see. Yet it hasn't received the attention it deserves. Although the observation that the humanities are perennially in crisis is now a standard feature of discussions about American higher education, much of the discourse about the humanities tends to obscure important forces that have created and widened this gap. It diverts attention from persistent contradictions and problems by sounding familiar rallying cries: The humanities are in crisis because modern society has lost sight of what really matters in life; the humanities are in crisis because universities are managed like corporations; the humanities are in crisis because humanities professors subscribe to theories that encourage hostility toward or suspicion of art and literature, and so on.[86] When people reckon with ongoing crises—and more specifically, ongoing crises that threaten them in basic ways—they often look for one dramatic, all-encompassing cause: the Great Recession, our xenophobia-tinged STEM obsession, neoliberalism, the coronavirus. Identifying a situation as a crisis can foreclose the possibility that it came about not because of an unexpected, sudden event but because of chronic, even structural conditions.

Assertions of their inherent goodness are often made to add urgency to declamations that the humanities are in crisis. Both self-consciously conservative and progressive versions of this assertion have promoted a crisis consensus that encourages people to defend the modern humanities with nostalgia while obscuring what ought to be restored and why. The unceasing reiteration of the imperiled virtue of the modern humanities has made for exhausted self-justification and institutional inflexibility. The humanities matter; they certainly matter to us. But how well served are they by "the humanities," whose modern meaning was born of crisis and is freighted with defensiveness, overpromising, and other concomitants of crisis talk? If this question sounds blithe, we hope that by the end of this book we will have answered it in a serious way.

The six chapters that follow this introduction focus on nineteenth-century German figures and institutions. Given that, it might seem presumptuous or simply provincial of us to refer to *Permanent Crisis* as a book about the self-understanding of "the humanities." Myriad knowledge practices that contemporary scholars would probably identify as part of "the humanities" do not fit within the historical and geographical framework of this book. Scholarly traditions devoted to preserving, interpreting, and transmitting all that is written, for example—what some might call textual or philological practices—flourished not only across early modern Europe but throughout the world.[87] The history of the book and reading in Africa long predates the spread of education under European colonialism.[88] Textual practices and knowledge thrived in the Indo-Persian world of the seventeenth and eighteenth centuries and long before.[89] In short, any study concerned in particular with the history of textual practices and literary knowledge should not be limited to European ideals, much less nineteenth-century German models.[90] Neither should such a study presume that the conflicts and contradictions of nineteenth-century German scholars and educated elites can be transposed onto different places and times without significant misunderstandings. Yet this is just what some scholars have done in the name of the "truly globalized university" when suggesting that disputes among nineteenth-century German scholars—"the struggle between historicists and humanists, *Wissenschaft* and *Bildung*, scholarship and life"—exemplify something universal in a tradition of knowledge and learning they presume to be global and continuous.[91]

Nonetheless, the modern humanities emerged from these more proximate conflicts and contradictions, which lent them the sense of crisis that would come to define them. In order to understand the formative attempts to define the purpose and practices of the modern humanities, it is necessary to understand these relatively recent and distinct conditions from which they developed. Germany, of course, was not the only site of such conflicts, and at times we turn our attention to France and England in the nineteenth century—to figures like Auguste Comte and John Stuart Mill. But nineteenth-century Germany was where and when the "crisis" system of the modern humanities first took shape. It was there and then that wide-ranging and multifarious scholarly traditions and forms of learning were first crafted into a relatively stable system and set into a structure of epistemic and ethical norms rooted in a new institution: the modern research university. It was then that the humanities were modernized.

In our final chapter, "Crisis, Democracy, and the Humanities in America," we shift our focus to the United States and follow administrators and scholars as, starting around 1870, they adopted and adapted the German ideal of the research university for their own purposes. Among other things, we rewrite one of the master narratives of American higher education. According to this account, German academic culture helped modernize humanist scholarship in the United States by providing models for the systematic study that began to supplant connoisseurship at American colleges and universities in the late nineteenth century. This isn't wrong. Thousands of American scholars *did* spend time at German universities during the nineteenth century, including most of the people who led the transformation of American higher education, such as Henry Tappan, Andrew Dickson White, and Daniel Coit Gilman, all of whom tried to foster the culture of German disciplinary scholarship, or *Wissenschaft*, as they helped to create America's first research universities. Yet it wasn't until the twentieth century—with its world wars, economic upheavals, and technological transformations—that the humanities in the United States developed their modern sense of purpose, their modern self-understanding as "the humanities." When they did, they were profoundly influenced by a different strain in German academic culture: not so much an outright rejection of the research ideal as a movement to transcend it. Culture was in crisis because there was too much technology, too much *Wissenschaft*, and the mission of "the humanities" was to be the "new *Wissenschaft*" that might redeem it. The United States, too, saw the modern "humanities" given birth by the spirit of crisis.

## CHAPTER ONE

# The Modern University and the Dream of Intellectual Unity

In the fall of 1903, the Harvard psychologist Hugo Münsterberg issued a programmatic statement about the unity of knowledge. The occasion was the upcoming St. Louis Congress of the Arts and Sciences, which would bring together European and American academics in an event marking the centenary of the Louisiana Purchase. Asked to be one of the conference planners, Münsterberg threw himself into the role. He was German—William James had lured him to Harvard—and he helped ensure the participation of such luminaries as fellow German social scientists Ferdinand Tönnies and Max Weber. Münsterberg hoped to make the event in St. Louis a point of convergence not just for eminence but also for what he portrayed as an intellectual movement arising from the "growing feeling of over-specialization in the sciences today."[1] Writing in the *Atlantic Monthly*, Münsterberg enjoined all those scholars participating in the conference to "strive toward a unity of thought . . . instead of heaping up once more . . . scattered specialistic researches." "Such disconnection," he conjectured, wouldn't go over well "with the American nation," with its "instinctive desire for organization and unity in work." Münsterberg thought the Midwest would be the perfect place to begin a concerted pursuit of intellectual unity in America.

But several American scholars spoke out against his plan, objecting not so much to the goal of unity as to how he construed it, which they saw as constraining rather than liberating. They had a point: Münsterberg had developed a narrative in which the flawed unity designs of nineteenth-century materialists—flawed, in his view, because they reduced life to passive, inert mechanism—had given way to the dualism of the natural sciences and the modern humanities. A new "idealism" was now, in turn, overcoming this dualism, and would, he thought, preserve differences between values and physical facts while allowing for unity by means of unspecified common philosophical principles. The result would be an ordering of the academic world in which "every theoretical and practical science would find its exact place."

John Dewey complained that Münsterberg's proposal ran counter to "the live-and-let-live character" of contemporary "science," enshrining as the ultimate authority "a particular methodology emanating from a particular school of metaphysics." William James criticized Münsterberg's "resolute will to *have a system* of absolute principles and categories." Such a system might, paradoxically, lead to silos of knowledge rather than consilience, James warned.[2]

Another reason for the wariness may have been that in late nineteenth-century America, the ideal of the unity of knowledge had been vigorously invoked in attempts to preserve the broadly Protestant basis of the traditional American college. Institutions such as Princeton, Yale, and William and Mary designed their curricula and structured student life around the notion that scientific and theological knowledge were mutually enhancing and that moral philosophy could synthesize them in a grand unity.[3] Münsterberg's attempt to link institutional design and aspirations to unity, however, came out of a different tradition of unity thinking, one that rose to prominence in Germany in the age of idealist philosophy and played a central part in discussions of higher education in general and the humanities in particular, contributing vitally, and in ways that may seem surprising, to a persistent sense of crisis in the humanities. Indeed, in order to understand how that sense of crisis developed in nineteenth-century Germany, we must examine how unity thinking became so important there— important enough for Münsterberg to have staked his career on bringing it to the United States.

## ON THE USES OF AN IDEA

To be sure, the dream of the unity of knowledge isn't an exclusively German phenomenon. It stretches back at least as far as the pre-Socratic Greek philosopher Thales of Miletus and the emergence of the first monotheistic religions, and it has found purchase in a variety of places and times. Peter Galison and Lorraine Daston have made the case that the ideal of unity found a special resonance in nineteenth-century Germany. This, according to Galison, was where the ideal began its career as a "regulative part of scientific theorizing." Although German idealist philosophers created the necessary foundation in the first half of the nineteenth century, it was only with "the so-called 'Professors' Revolution' of 1848," Galison maintains, that the unity-of-knowledge principle became a frequently invoked tenet across the sciences.[4]

For German natural scientists of the nineteenth century such as Hermann Helmholtz, Emil Du Bois-Reymond, and Rudolf Virchow, all of whom wanted to see the German territories unified under a modern constitution, there was a political resonance to the epistemology of science and an epistemological resonance to the politics of nation building. When the push for unity in 1848 failed, they found compensatory purpose and satisfaction in continuing to advance the cause of scientific unity.

Similarly, Daston maintains that German intellectuals and scholars of the late nineteenth century embraced the unity ideal most forcefully. That context was "the place and period during which the contradiction between the ever finer division of labor in the sciences and the striving toward the unification of the sciences was felt with unprecedented intensity."[5] In explaining how this special situation took shape, Daston, too, underscores the importance of both German idealism and the question of German political unification.[6] As scholarship became more fragmented in the late 1800s and as the quest for the unity of knowledge seemed, accordingly, to grow more quixotic, scholars with liberal commitments, such as the historian Theodor Mommsen, expressed a sense of disappointment most sharply. Disillusioned with political unification under Bismarck, they had found solace in the pursuit of intellectual unity, and now even that wasn't turning out as they had hoped.

Certainly, in discussions of German versions of the unity-of-knowledge dream, idealist philosophy has loomed large. When they spoke of the ideal, Friedrich Schleiermacher, J. G. Fichte, Wilhelm von Humboldt, and Friedrich Schelling may not have meant the same thing, but all four thinkers—and others as well—relied heavily on the notion of an ultimate unity of knowledge. It figures prominently, for example, in their writings on university reform, which is what concerns us here. They invoked the unity of knowledge as a regulative ideal in making the case that the modern university should be a *free* community of scholars and students pulling together in the pursuit of liberal learning and pure scholarship with philosophy at the center of the undertaking.

Lecturing in 1808 Schelling claimed that "philosophy, which apprehends the whole of the human and touches upon all aspects of his nature, is even better suited [than mathematics] to free the mind from the limitations of a one-sided education and raise it into the realm of the universal and absolute." Expanding on the connection between intellectual unity and human freedom—again, a key element in German idealism—he went on to say that "knowledge of the organic whole of all sciences must therefore precede a particular education focused on a single specialty. Whoever devotes himself to a particular science . . . must know how he should relate this particular science to himself so as to think not as a slave but as a free man, in the spirit of the whole."[7]

Despite the salience such rhetoric enjoyed, the "unification enthusiasm" of Schelling and other reformers has received little sustained attention. The entry for "The Unity of Science" in the *Stanford Encyclopedia of Philosophy* discusses some of the thinking that underlay the reformers' passion, namely, Kant's conception of knowledge as "a whole of cognition ordered according to principles."[8] The entry says little, however, about the unity ideal in later idealism. Nor do any of the works in its lengthy bibliography focus on the importance of the ideal there. Perhaps the mantra-like character of unity claims such as Schelling's has discouraged fine-grained analysis of the type that Karl Lamprecht's specific plans for achieving interdisciplinary unity have attracted.[9] In short, scholars have tended to speak about the rise of the unity-of-knowledge ideal around 1800 in broad terms even when their subject is the discourse of university reform in which the ideal played such a vital part.

This is indeed the case in two of the most important works on the formation of the modern university produced in the last fifty years—R. Steven Turner's "The Prussian Universities and the Research Imperative, 1806–1848," and Thomas Albert Howard's *Protestant Theology and the Making of the Modern University*. Turner addresses the unity-of-knowledge ideal at length, but the point of his observations isn't to explore why the university reformers were so profoundly invested in it. Turner's goal, rather, is to distinguish one notion of unity—the synthesizing notion of the idealists—from another—the analytic notion of the philologists and historians who helped initiate a kind of empirical turn in the 1830s.[10] The analytic conception, Turner says, was articulated best by the philologist August Boeckh, who extolled the individual scholar capable of recognizing "in the depths of his limited object the idea of the whole in microcosm."[11] For his part, Howard repeatedly remarks on how Schelling and Schleiermacher appealed to the principle of the unity of knowledge in their discussions of university reform, but his observations in this regard are mostly summaries and paraphrases. Like Turner, Howard doesn't fully consider the intellectual, political, and social purposes served by the unity-of-knowledge ideal.[12]

Yet the unity ideal invites political interpretations, and not just because of the connection Galison, Daston, and others have stressed. If a synchronous relationship between scientific unity and political unification could be posited, could there not also be a similar relationship between intellectual totality and totalitarianism? After the Second World War, a number of writers pointed to such a link. In *Minima moralia* (1951), his "reflections" from a life damaged by fascism, Theodor Adorno claimed that "the whole is false," thereby inverting Hegel's dictum "the true is the whole."[13] Writing with Max Horkheimer, Adorno had gone at least as far in *Dialectic of Enlightenment* (1947). There Horkheimer and Adorno identified a causal relation between the Nazi hatred of "foreign elements" and hostility to difference on the part of philosophical systems that operate according to the logic of conceptual understanding.[14] Elaborating this thought in *Minima moralia*, Adorno condemns Friedrich Schiller for wanting to derive social reality from just "one principle" and speaks darkly of the mindset that characterizes such a desire: "In the innermost chambers of humanism, as its actual soul, an anger rages in its imprisonment; as a fascist, it turns the whole world into a prison."[15]

Writing less epigrammatically, the historian of science Anne Harrington has traced the lines of "holism in German culture from Wilhelm II to Hitler." Her goal isn't to show that German holism necessarily culminated in the Nazi variant of it, but neither does she portray that variant as unwarranted. Nazism is a part of German holism, which Harrington follows back to Goethe's "vision of wholeness"—a "science of life" in which "the products of nature and art [were] treated one as the other, aesthetic and teleological judgment mutually illuminating each other."[16] The association is of course suggestive.

Although she emphasizes the diversity of holism in Germany, Harrington views German holism more generally as a hostile response to what were taken to be Newton's atomizing, mechanistic theories. The writings of late nineteenth-century German university professors offer a treasure trove of general support for this perspective. "Almost everybody [in the academic community] by 1900 complained of the decline of the unity of science and scholarship," Charles McClelland has observed.[17] More specifically, many intellectuals and scholars associated threats to the unity-of-knowledge dream not only with increasing specialization, as Mommsen and other liberal scholars did, but also with what they regarded as the nightmarish aspects of modernity: the growing domination of technology in nearly all areas of life, democratization, social fragmentation, materialism, rootless individualism, and so on. They mixed an epistemological lament with conservative social theory. Intellectual culture—and society along with it—was succumbing to centrifugal forces, which remained ominously abstract but for their devastating effects.

For decades, educated elites repeatedly argued that what was needed was a recommitment to the whole for which the unity-of-knowledge ideal provided the best model. Devotion to intellectual unity became a symbol signifying an allegiance to "true learning" and much more: the deeply held spiritual values that distinguished German *Kultur*, despite its present condition, from the mere "civilization" of the West. In 1914 German academics and intellectuals celebrated the outbreak of war in just these terms. The philosopher Alois Riehl, for example, wrote, "The belief in the reality of the intellectual and spiritual world, in the life of the whole which transcends the existence of the individual, this belief, which awoke in all of us during the early days of August, must never more die out."[18]

Political and social conservatives weren't alone in worrying about the modern German university. Its capture by capital and an ever-expanding state bureaucracy and the splintering of their research structure—trends accelerated by the tumult of the Weimar Republic—threatened cultural coherence and social stability. And philosophers, philologists, and historians weren't the only ones to appeal to the unity ideal. Well into the twentieth century, German natural and physical scientists (as we will see in later chapters) regularly invoked it as well, often when in roles of institutional leadership, as an orienting and definitive ideal for all German scholars and universities.

The links between the discourse of unities and wholes and reactionary dispositions, however, are clear enough to have led to forms of what Michael André Bernstein calls "backshadowing." This, as its name suggests, is foreshadowing in reverse.[19] When discussing how figures like Humboldt understood and used the unity-of-knowledge ideal, prominent intellectuals and scholars projected backward the use of neo-humanist tropes in the reactionary discourse that flourished around 1900, making the early neo-humanists sound like fretful late nineteenth-century mandarins. Some of Humboldt's most influential writings on university reform weren't discovered until the 1890s, and it was not until the early 1900s that the myth of Humboldt as the founder of modern higher education was constructed by men like Adolf von Harnack and Eduard Spranger, both of whom were quite selective in their exaltations. The centenary celebrations for the University of Berlin around 1910 provided an international platform for the creative reimagining of German neo-humanism.

Having been established in the early twentieth century, this reinvented neo-humanist tradition became the prism through which later scholars understood nineteenth-century concepts and institutions now primarily associated with Humboldt. Anthony La Vopa, for instance, has claimed that Humboldt conceived of his proposal to "unify all branches of knowledge" as the "unitary antidote" to the "modern" ill of "specialization."[20] In his account of Humboldt's reform efforts in *The Postmodern Condition* (1979),

Jean-Francois Lyotard focuses on what he takes to be Humboldt's most important suggestion—that philosophy "must *restore* unity to learning" (emphasis added).[21]

The unity-of-knowledge ideal elevated the pedant to a priest and the student to a scholar by endowing learning with a systematic, almost holy end: the promise of coherence and a higher calling. Not only would those engaged in pure learning hover above mundane vocational study; they would be doing so in the service of a grand objective that required systematic thought yet had a sacred, Romantic resonance. In addition, the unity-of-knowledge ideal played an important role in the struggle to overturn the well-established hierarchy of the faculties in universities, which situated arts and sciences below the professional faculties. What Turner calls the synthesizing version of the unity ideal claimed a privileged place for philosophy in the university. As Kant stressed in *The Conflict of the Faculties* (1798), an essential text for neo-humanist reformers of higher education, philosophical thinking could be brought to bear on any area of knowledge; thus, it allowed for meaningful exchange among different fields. No mere preparatory discipline, philosophy, as the idealists conceived of it, was, in Frederick Beiser's phrase, the "foundation of all knowledge."[22] When practiced well (or "critically"), philosophy could sustain meaningful thought and communication across university fields; it could unify a notoriously hierarchical and, for many, archaic, guild-like institution.[23] More, too, than a regulative ideal for the organization of the university, the notion of the unity of knowledge had direct implications for the practice of scholarship. Scholars from across the university used the ideal to define their once diffuse domains of scholarly interest as distinct and valuable disciplines.[24]

Fittingly, the unity-of-knowledge ideal also brought together some ideas and values that both antimodern and progressive discourses appropriated, such as the veneration of community. In part, the ideal's conceptual and semantic flexibility gave it widespread traction and became a core component of the modern research university. But if the unity-of-knowledge ideal was an epistemological value, an organizational principle, a piece of ideology, and a Romantic trope, it was also something more. Or rather, being all those, the unity-of-knowledge ideal early on became a rhetorical flashpoint: a privileged vehicle for articulating crucial anxieties, fears, and hopes. Indeed, in marshaling the unity ideal, neo-humanist educational reformers of the early 1800s express a motif central to *Permanent Crisis*: the idea that the processes of democratization, secularization, and bureaucratic rationalization make liberal education possible even as they imperil it. This, we believe, is what accounts for the extraordinary force of the unity-of-knowledge ideal and why, even after idealist philosophical systems lost much of their influence, the discourse surrounding the ideal remained crucial to the debate about the well-being of universities in the context of distinctly Western modernity.

THE CAREERIST SCHOLAR VERSUS

THE PHILOSOPHICAL MIND

If Max Weber delivered the requiem for the ideal of the unity of knowledge in the 1917 lecture that became the book *Scholarship as Vocation*, then Friedrich Schiller announced the advent of the ideal in 1789 with his inaugural lecture at the University of Jena, "What Is Universal History and Why Study It?" When he accepted a faculty position at Jena, Schiller probably had few illusions about university life there. He had visited Jena two years earlier and written to a friend that the students, almost a fifth of the city's population, smoked in the streets, brawled in the pubs, and emptied their chamber pots out of their windows and onto unsuspecting pedestrians. "The students delight in terrorizing honest citizens," he wrote.[25]

But in his inaugural lecture, Schiller used the study of history to consider a different threat facing the university: an instrumental and utilitarian relationship to education and knowledge among students — and faculty. In so doing, he helped standardize some of the idioms that would characterize German debates about university reform and intellectual vocation for the next century and more.

Addressing a crowd of more than four hundred students and faculty, Schiller began by describing the wrong and right attitudes toward the study of universal history, a prominent topic among late eighteenth-century German intellectuals, who, like their Scottish contemporaries, sought meaning and reason in history, not just singular events. To grasp the unity of the past and understand its relationship to a meaningful future required not only what Kant had called an "idea" of a universal history but also a hopeful and expectant disposition.[26] The wrong disposition, said Schiller, is that of the "careerist scholar" (*Brotgelehrte*). The careerist, evidently a pervasive figure at German universities, cares about getting the maximum reward, in terms of money or prestige, from the smallest investment of time and energy. Uninspired and therefore uninspiring, lazy but also competitive, he seeks to protect his expertise by insulating it from other fields and from new knowledge and by impugning whatever might force him to expand or revise his learning. "There is thus no more implacable enemy, no more small-minded bureaucrat, no one more willing to excommunicate their foes" than a careerist scholar.[27] To label someone a careerist scholar was to render an intellectual and a moral judgment against him as not only a bad scholar but also a bad social actor, an impediment to the communal striving after the whole of knowledge.[28]

But the careerist scholar is also a tragic figure. "It is an unfortunate man," Schiller claims, "who works with the noblest of all tools—science and art—yet wants and achieves nothing greater than the day laborer with the most common tools! Who roams the kingdom of the most perfect freedom bearing with him the soul of a slave!"[29] This, of course, raises the question, How is it that the careerist scholar comes by his low soul? Like all too many people, he puts crude and immediate gain over the higher reward. His doing so is particularly sad, since the higher reward in his case is the highest reward, namely, "the most perfect freedom." But the general phenomenon is clearly widespread. Not everyone can be like Schiller, who forsook economic security and risked incarceration to pursue his calling of artistic creation and open-ended study.

Though he doesn't rule out the possibility that his lecture might convert the careerist scholar to his own higher account of the scholarly life, Schiller seems more concerned about the "young man of genius" who begins to act like a careerist scholar, someone who

> lets himself be talked into gathering knowledge with a wretched fixation on his future profession. His professional scholarly field will soon disgust him as a piecemeal patchwork; desires will awaken within him that he cannot satisfy; his genius will rebel against his destiny. . . . He will see no purpose in his work, and yet he will not be able to bear the absence of that purpose. The arduous labors and insignificance of his professional activities will crush him, because he cannot oppose to them the cheerful spirits that accompany only keen insight and the prospect of completion. He will feel cut off, torn away from the context of things, because he has failed to connect his efforts to the great totality of the world.[30]

How is it that the young man of genius "lets himself be talked into" vocationalism, that "wretched fixation on his future profession," in the first place? At this point, what might have come to mind among Schiller's listeners was the campaign for utilitarian education that had recently led to the founding of professional academies for mining, medicine, and other fields, as well as the popularity at German universities of "cameral studies," basically professional training for aspiring bureaucrats.[31]

Although Schiller moves on from the anatomy of the careerist scholar, the second part of his lecture might have prompted his audience to consider further why a young man of genius would opt for isolation over "completion," meaning, and "intellectual community." For in this section, Schiller offers big-picture ideas that suggest what might be motivating the gifted careerist. With news of revolutionary activity in Paris creating much excitement among Jena intellectuals, Schiller laid out nothing less than a vision of historical progress. He describes how the supplanting of the rule of superstition and ignorance by a rational order has created peace and security (where there had been endless war), tamed the environment, led to the promulgation of "wise laws," and brought about an ever-greater measure of "truth, ethical development, and freedom." Humans had "fled from the blind compulsion of accident and poverty to the gentler rule of contracts, and given up the freedom of the beast of prey to salvage the nobler freedom of humanity."[32]

Unlike Rousseau, who had portrayed humans in their precivilized state as superior to their descendants, Schiller characterized early humans as creatures at the mercy of their own fears and hatreds who in many cases "had barely raised their language from animal sounds into a system of comprehensible signs." Even the classical world looks bad in comparison with the present: "The shadow of a Roman emperor, persisting on this side of the Apennines, does infinitely more good now than the terrifying original did in ancient Rome, for it holds a useful state system together through concord, while the earlier one crushed the most active human powers into a slavish homogeneity."[33] According to Schiller, human reason, indeed, reinvents institutions built in less rational times: "It is true that some barbaric remnants of previous ages have made their way into ours as well—the products of chance and violence, which should not be perpetuated in the age of reason. But what shape has human reason conferred upon even this barbaric legacy of antiquity and the Middle Ages! How harmless, or even useful, reason has often made what it has not yet dared do away with!"[34]

Anticipating the accounts of a modern society he would offer in *On the Aesthetic Education of Humankind* (1794) and *On Naïve and Sentimental Poetry* (1795), Schiller suggests in the inaugural lecture that this historical process of rationalization, however salutary, has fragmenting effects. He also implies that the world of "bourgeois advantages" produced by rationalization is one where self-interest largely reigns. Indeed, culture itself is a function of the desire for status. One critic has even written that in the inaugural lecture Schiller conceives of culture as "nothing other than the drive for distinction."[35] In certain areas, our "wise laws" push back against the inequality to which this drive leads. In others, self-interest itself helps ensure the smooth functioning of those laws—for example, treaties that aim at keeping world powers from going to war. Yet self-interest and the drive for distinction also compromise our use of the "nobler freedom" of thought that rationalization has allowed for (by clearing away superstition and liberating so many of us from the constant struggle with necessity). "Narrow judgments stemming from self-interest" foreshorten our understanding of world history, with the result that we see ourselves merely as "individuals" rather than as parts of a meaningful whole: "the species."[36]

Here, then, Schiller offers an implicit explanation for why even those young men of genius fated for nobler freedom allow themselves to be talked into going the way of the careerist scholar, who chases "praise from newspapers" and "honorary professorships" more than truth—and often at its expense. In gesturing toward such a dynamic, Schiller could have been thinking about the University of Göttingen, at the time the most prestigious university in the German territories and the prime example of academic mercantilism. Founded in 1737 under the direction of Karl Friedrich Hieronymus Münchhausen, it was explicitly established to make money for the state, which is why some of the university's own faculty referred to it as "a big commercial enterprise." It is also why satirists—much as some do in the United States today—had fun with the idea that higher education had become a service set up to attract paying customers (especially wealthy young Englishmen looking for a continental adventure) whom it brazenly catered to in its course offerings.[37]

But while Göttingen was known for its emphasis on cameral studies, it was also famous for its strength in the liberal arts, and a much higher percentage of students enrolled in the arts and philosophy faculty than at other German universities. Münchhausen had decided that hiring star academics in the liberal arts and sciences would attract wealthy students from out of state, who had to pay higher tuition than their local counterparts. Not only that, Münchhausen designed a university that encouraged his famous employees to burnish their reputations further and thus increase their appeal in the eyes of young aristocrats looking for a fashionably well-rounded education. (This was a courtly trend that existed alongside the Enlightenment preference for utilitarian schooling.) In 1789 the University of Göttingen library held thirty thousand volumes, far more than its competitors. And Göttingen's many luminaries—for example, the philologist Christian Heyne and the biblical scholar Johann Michaelis—had more freedom to study and write as they chose than humanists elsewhere. The theology faculty's power to censor the faculty of arts and philosophy—a fact of life at German universities at the time—was greatly reduced at Göttingen.

Many Göttingen scholars used their freedom to good effect. Yet Münchhausen's rationalizing of a ("barbaric") medieval institution, which involved steering it away from the old guild ethos, didn't facilitate intellectual exploration alone. Göttingen's emphasis on scholarly productivity and reputation—and the financial rewards the university offered for these things—

encouraged some faculty members to protect their turf and engage in the recycling of research and other forms of résumé padding. When Friedrich Gedike visited Göttingen in 1789, having been sent by the Prussian king to identify the best practices of "foreign universities," he was generally impressed. He was also taken aback by the faculty's unwillingness to speak candidly about the university. Preserving its reputation as an institution where faculty could grow financially comfortable, Gedike conjectured, was more important to them than open exchange. Thus, "it is more difficult here than elsewhere to elicit from the professors reliable accounts of all those things one would wish to know about."[38]

The alternative to this kind of careerist attitude is, according to Schiller, the outlook of the "philosophical mind," who makes the most of the dawning freedom of thought in academia. Such a mind does this by committing to the ideal of the unity of knowledge, for pursuing knowledge as a totality means subordinating one's immediate interests and any kind of practical concern to a larger good. It means trying to serve a community much more than trying to distinguish oneself: "The careerist scholar divides, the philosophical mind unites. [The latter] has learned early on that in the intellectual realm, as in the material world, everything is interrelated. . . . Nobly impatient, he cannot rest until all his ideas have been integrated into a harmonious whole."[39]

For all its purity, this intellectual striving has a utilitarian aspect. It equips those who engage in it with a broad perspective that proves useful in making all kinds of practical decisions. Invoking what would become axiomatic among neo-humanist and liberal educational reformers, Schiller suggests that those with philosophical minds will thrive not only as scholars but as professionals generally. Viewing things from the "midpoint" and treating them as parts of a whole creates meaning. Schiller pities the careerist scholar for isolating himself and occupying himself with fragments, which makes his work feel "purposeless." However, in the world Schiller describes, the problem of meaning is of much greater scope. Although Schiller acknowledges that he and his audience are Christians, he also stresses that Christianity is an object of historical study whose institutions and development cry out for an analysis not constrained by Christian commitments. This situation is thrilling in that it creates space for the kind of open-ended inquiry Schiller prizes as the highest ethical and intellectual good. But such freedom also has a certain menace—even for scholarship. Absent an ordering framework such as that putatively provided by Christianity, things can seem random, including the cultural objects that humanists study. They lack the meaning and purpose that accompany the sense of being part of a larger whole.

The unity-of-knowledge ideal is salvific with respect to this problem of seeming chaos and randomness as well. We are edging toward the kind of significance Karl Marx would ascribe to scholarship about fifty years later in his most pointed statement on secularization: once people have "shed" religion, "scholarship becomes their unity."[40] Why study universal history in 1789? Schiller's concluding answer is that doing so imbues "phenomena" with "purposefulness."

> The more often, and the more successfully, he [of the philosophical mind] repeats his attempts to link the past with the present, the more inclined he will be to take what [the philosophical mind] sees as the interplay of cause and effect and link the two in a relation of means and end. One phenomenon after another starts to free itself from blind approximation, from lawless freedom, and take its proper place within a coherent totality.[41]

Since one can see the totality of history only from an omniscient perspective, the coherent whole with which humans operate is necessarily a product of the finite human mind—an informed, meaning-bearing fiction that, as Schiller puts it, "exists in the ideas" of the philosophical mind. Scholarship appears to be the process of revising one's sense of the whole and testing it against alternative notions with the criteria for the test not entirely reducible to logic and systematic thought. "The view that wins the day," writes Schiller, "will be the one that offers more satisfaction to the intellect and more contentment to the heart." There is an affective dimension to the unity-of-knowledge ideal.[42]

Schiller's lectures in Jena, it would turn out, didn't offer students enough of either intellectual satisfaction or heartfelt contentment. Having run up against the very sort of proprietary attitude he had criticized in his inaugural speech, Schiller was forced to move from historical to philosophical topics in his teaching. Since philosophical instruction at Jena was so thoroughly dominated by Karl Reinhold, one of the first self-identified Kantians and a popular professor whose lectures often attracted hundreds of students, Schiller had little chance of success there. What chance he had was narrowed further by the fact that he didn't have a gift for lecturing in philosophy. In 1793 he decided that the few lecture fees he collected didn't repay the effort he put into preparing his courses, and he abandoned his academic adventure early. But he stayed in Jena, which had become a vibrant center of philosophical exploration, and the ideal of the unity of knowledge would remain part of local conversations about university reform.

## THE SCHOLAR'S VOCATION

Theodore Ziolkowski has argued that the unity-of-knowledge ideal "was brought home with a vengeance" in Jena by "the compelling moral presence who took the lectern in 1794 and developed an entire philosophical system based on what Schiller called, in passing, that 'midpoint' from which the philosophical mind surveys and unifies its field of knowledge."[43] That "moral presence" was Johann Gottlieb Fichte, whose 1794 inaugural lecture series, "On the Vocation of the Scholar," was every bit the sensation "What Is Universal History and Why Study It?" had been.[44] At least in theory, students welcomed the prospect of university reform and moral uplift. But it wasn't only the students who were cheering. Schiller was in the audience and was enthused. Having encouraged friends to read Fichte's lectures, he cited them in *On the Aesthetic Education of Humankind*.

Fichte made explicit what Schiller had only suggested—that the ideal of the unity of knowledge was not simply a metaphysical, historical, or philosophical project; it was an institutional one. More specifically, it was a university one, and the university-formed scholar had a particular claim to it.[45] Fichte referred to his lectures as "Morals for Scholars,"[46] and in a printed announcement he alerted students to what they could expect:

> All our inquiries must aim at humankind's supreme goal, which is the improvement of the species to which we belong, and students of the sciences must, as it were, constitute that center from which humanity in the highest sense of the word radiates. . . . It becomes increasingly necessary to bear the following questions seriously in mind: what is the scholar's vocation? What is his place in the scheme of things? What relation do scholars have to each other and to other men in general, especially various classes of men?[47]

Fichte repeatedly returned to the question of the scholar's "vocation" in subsequent years, refining his formulation and integrating it into his (also developing) philosophical system. He eventually tied his claims about vocation to sharp criticisms of the lack of intellectual coherence at German universities, where "nothing is learned as a whole, only these isolated scraps."[48] He made this remark in his 1807 "plan" for an "institution of higher learning to be established in Berlin," which he composed—and submitted to a royal adviser—just as prospects for educational reform in Prussia were dramatically improving. Commentators like to point out that Fichte's attempt to seize the historical moment has an uncompromising character. Fichte wanted, for example, to jettison the professional faculties, so as to give the greatest possible emphasis to the teaching of idealist philosophy. Yet much of his proposal deals with what today might be considered issues of access and inclusion. Having grown up poor, Fichte was able to study into adult-hood only because a wealthy patron had recognized his talent and stepped in to support him. He wanted any new institution of higher learning in Berlin to be accessible, indeed, hospitable, to students who lacked means but possessed the requisite aptitude and tenacity.[49]

These ideas weren't unique to Fichte. As disparaging as he and many of his contemporaries were toward utilitarian higher education and as forbiddingly high as they set the bar for university study (it's difficult to generate cultural prestige without exclusion), their notion of *Bildung* drew on the burgeoning democratic and liberal spirit of the times. Its moral power drew, in part, on the ascendant ideal of the basic worth and dignity of every human being, a notion central to Kant and those schooled in his system and based on the presumption of the universality of reason. Although the normative claims of this ideal were never realized, it mattered that *Bildung* was, potentially, for everyone. These ideals about freedom had important implications for the project, spearheaded by Karl von Stein, of working toward greater popular participation in government in the German territories. "The notion that education should not merely train people for the civil service or the professions but form people as culturally versatile self-governing citizens," as one scholar recently put it, "was developed at the beginning of the nineteenth century by Wilhelm von Humboldt . . . and given the name of *Bildung*."[50]

Fichte, in his way, advocated democratizing education or at least increasing access to it, contending that any future university in Berlin should, where necessary, provide students with food, since hunger is inimical to good study. He was also concerned about how the social diversity of the student body would affect the collective striving after knowledge "learned as whole." Community and communication were central to that project, and Fichte framed questions of access, diversity, and inclusion in terms of the unity-of-knowledge ideal. If students reflected its ethos in their relations with one another and "merge[d] together into a spiritual and intellectual whole, forming a single organic student body," the university would become both democratized and unified.[51] Fichte's interest in a more accessible university, however, should not be mistaken for an egalitarian social project. Like most of his German idealist contemporaries, he focused on *potential* and made few, if any, claims about political egalitarianism. He envisioned the community of university scholars as a distinct social class that would oversee the historical development of society as a whole. Whereas Schiller's universal historians narrated the progress of humanity, Fichte's scholars actively advanced it.

The unity ideal was thus the answer to the potentially disquieting effects of democratization, a process that the architects of the proposed university in Berlin simultaneously embraced and were wary of as something that could undermine the ethos of their ideal community. When Fichte delivered his inaugural lectures in Jena in 1794, however, the debate about establishing an institution of higher education in Berlin had not yet begun. To be sure, Fichte drew on his reflections on scholarship and vocation from the 1790s in the "plan" he sent to Karl van Beyme, an adviser to the Prussian king who would later play a role in the founding of the University of Berlin. Still, invocations of the unity ideal after 1807—Schleiermacher's, Humboldt's, and Fichte's—belong to a different moment, when grand philosophical claims regularly mixed with mundane questions about how to build an institution.

Like Schiller, Fichte didn't have a long career at the University of Jena. But whereas Schiller eventually lost interest in teaching as students lost interest in him, Fichte was eventually driven out of Jena. While students enthused over Fichte's high-minded rhetoric about the historic and social importance of the scholar's vocation, they were much less taken by the young professor's pointed criticism of their secret societies and bawdy entertainments, and eventually and rather violently they turned against him. He was forced to resign his position in 1799 after being accused of atheism. Though his successor, Friedrich Schelling, was known for his religiosity, it's unlikely that Fichte's fate at the University of Jena left Schelling with the impression that all was well with German higher education.

A philosophical *wunderkind*, Schelling, still in his midtwenties, arrived in Jena soon after Fichte left and in the middle of his most productive period. Having published his *Ideas for a Philosophy of Nature* in 1797, he was close to finishing another highly original and influential work, the *System of Transcendental Idealism* (1800). In both works Schelling attempted to go beyond the existing ways of dealing with the question of whether the distinction between the subjective and the objective was itself subjective or objective. Fichte had famously come down on what his contemporaries took to be the subjective side, arguing that the "I" posits the distinction between itself and the "Not-I." Schelling, a self-proclaimed "Spinozist," maintained that the distinction is neither subjective nor objective but rather something that relates to an underlying unity that humans can sense only through "vital intellectual intuition."[52]

Schelling was close to the Romantic circle in Jena. In 1803 he married August Wilhelm Schlegel's ex-wife, Caroline, an important Romantic thinker in her own right. Like Schlegel's brother Friedrich, Schelling thought that "modern skepticism," as Terry Pinkard puts it, and reflection, or what Schelling himself called "reflective philosophy," distract us from a pre-reflective unity.[53] This he described as "the absolute," in which "the ideal" and "the real" are "one." Reflection imposes artificial order and divisions on the world. Rational reflection creates, for the subject, the problem that the subject then tries to solve. Schelling was a thoroughly post-Kantian thinker in this regard. He accepted the basic Kantian claim that knowledge of the world was a product of both empirical intuitions (sense data) and categories of understanding inherent in human rationality—that the rational subject could know the world but only through his own rational efforts. But Schelling bristled at the consequences of a universe without inherent meaning or, at least, a meaning seemingly inaccessible to humans. Like many of his post-Kantian contemporaries, he was dissatisfied with the prospect of a world in which meaning was merely projected onto it by humans.

Nowhere did Schelling appeal more intensely to the ideal of the unity of knowledge as a source of reenchantment than in his "Lectures on the Method of Academic Study," presented at the University of Jena in 1802 and published in 1803. "For it is self-evident that, if this original knowledge is the infinite conforming to the finite in ideal terms, action is likewise how the finite conforms to the infinite. Each of these expresses the same absolute unity of original knowledge, either in the idea or in being-in-itself."[54] Similar passages abound. Schelling presented his students with a way of thinking that he claimed would enable them to understand the finite as bearing features of the infinite and to see their thought and action as conveying something of the "absolute unity of original knowledge." Transcendental idealism, he promised them, could help them overcome the alienation from the underlying unity that reflective philosophy had done much to bring about. Schelling makes explicit the point toward which Schiller only gestured.

Elsewhere, Schelling, like Fichte, picks up on Schiller's notion of the midpoint, using that very term: "The more a scholar conceives of his particular area of study as an end in itself, even treating it as the center of all knowledge, the midpoint of an all-encompassing totality that reflects the whole universe, the more he will strive to express ideas and universals in that area of study."[55] As Schiller asserted in his inaugural lecture, if scholarship is practiced in relation to the unity-of-knowledge ideal, then it acquires a meaning and purpose that both take it beyond itself, toward total knowledge, and ground it in an actual scholarly community. By foreswearing any instrumental relationship to his particular field of study and seeing it (and presumably his work too) as an "end in itself," every scholar can potentially justify and legitimate his particular field and concerns as a midpoint of all knowledge. On this account, academic specialization is not a problem to be overcome but an essential and beneficial feature of any modern knowledge undertaking.

Although Schelling's discussion of such ideals elsewhere can tend toward detailed arguments about seemingly abstract concepts, in these lectures he accomplishes similar philosophical goals by thinking in explicitly institutional terms—that is, in terms of the university and its organization of scholars and scholarship. His question is straightforward: how can a new university be organized around the unity-of-knowledge ideal? Schelling delivered the addresses that make up "Lectures on the Method of Academic Study" not long after the publication of *The Conflict of Faculties* (1798), in which Kant asserted that the philosophical faculty—the faculty of arts and sciences—is the freest and thus highest of the university's faculties with regard to intellectual rank if not institutional position. While Kant didn't call for a formal restructuring of the university hierarchy, he advocated the redistribution of authority, prestige, and power within the institution. With the possible exception of Göttingen and to a lesser extent Halle, in 1798 German universities were widely considered intellectual wastelands blighted by the turpitude of their students and the pedantry of their professors. In 1792, perhaps the most notable work in favor of abolishing universities appeared—Johann Heinrich Campe's *General Revision of the Entire Educational System*. Three years later, Berlin's highly regarded Wednesday Society discussed the topic, giving serious consideration to Campe's way of thinking.[56] The situation in German universities remained desperate until the founding of the University of Berlin in 1810. Indeed, half the universities in the German territories dissolved in the years immediately following the Napoleonic conquests, some being too small and fragile to withstand the tumult while others were in areas occupied by the French. Yet the conversation about university reform intensified around 1800 as Kant's text resonated and the Prussian government showed some encouraging signs of interest.[57] Schelling, perhaps more than Schiller, had reason to think structural change could be in the offing, which may explain his more direct approach to the actual structural problems besetting German universities.

Schelling laments that the university, as currently constituted, simply turns students loose into the "chaos" of its course offerings, leaving them to negotiate a welter of different disciplines and approaches without any meaningful orientation. Students with any sense for "the whole" feel as though they have been "launched upon a vast ocean without compass or guiding star."[58] The "better minds" respond by trying to study everything, but, overwhelmed by the task, they inevitably do so in a "random, disorganized way" and fail to "penetrate to the core" of anything.[59] Eventually, they see how "fruitless their efforts have been" and leave demoralized.

Meanwhile, the lesser lights seek refuge in whatever path they consider likely to lead to professional success. The intellectual capacity they primarily cultivate is their ability to assimilate information. In this context the unity-of-knowledge ideal functions not only as an agent of reenchantment—understood here as a Romantic poeticizing of the world in the face of countervailing forces, what the philosophically inclined poet Novalis termed *potentiation*[60]—but also of rationalization. Heeding its imperative—that is, beginning with philosophy, which "apprehends the whole"—will create order and coherence where there had been disarray and put an end to a shameful waste of human resources.[61] The circumstances obtaining as a consequence make starting in this way especially important. If "modern skepticism" alienates us from the underlying unity of subject and object—real and ideal—modernity, Schelling suggests, is also bringing things together with unprecedented speed. "The demand" for knowledge of the "living relationships among the forms of knowledge" has "never been more urgent than in our present age." A "new, more universal organ for perception, one for almost all objects, is taking shape."[62] Like Schiller and Fichte, Schelling thinks that the processes of modernity unify even as they fragment.

Schelling also identifies distinctly modern challenges to curricular coherence in higher education. He argues that nostalgia for a coherent but now lost world of Greek and Roman antiquity, for example, had encouraged a form of historical scholarship that treats "knowledge of the past" as "knowledge itself," or an end in itself. Such a disposition to knowledge prioritized "erudition" as a guiding ideal for German scholars in the seventeenth and much of the eighteenth century. Intellectuals and scholars formed in these traditions prized comprehensiveness and the organized display of what was known, especially in relationship to how knowledge had taken form in printed texts. The persistence of these epistemic ideals and practices, Schelling suggests, has hampered the development of universities. "Initially, the enormous quantity of what had to be learned, simply in order to process what there was to know, was what made people split up knowledge into so many different branches, and thereby unravel the living, organic structure of the whole into the tiniest possible strands."[63] In yet another example of the pernicious paradox of modernity, the same conditions that enable the progress and advancement of knowledge also undermine it. In the case of erudition, the invention and continued improvement of print technologies enabled the broader distribution of what people had learned and then passed on over time; these technological advancements eventually led to the proliferation of print, then to the surfeit of print. In order to manage the growth of printed objects and interact with the knowledge transmitted over time, scholars devised ever more complex schemes and systems to organize print. Eventually, they began to mistake these organizational techniques ("different branches") for actual knowledge. The experience of eighteenth-century intellectuals and scholars exemplifies how, paradoxically, modern processes pull against what Schelling presumes to be the modern age's more fundamental, more progressive spirit. Ultimately, however, he thinks that modernity can also repair these relations between center and periphery (whole and part) by making them more manifest. And that, essentially, is the purpose of the university—to form knowing subjects better equipped for striving after the unity of knowledge, that is, "knowledge itself."

Schelling contrasts his ideal of the university with bourgeois society and what he considers its ethos of instrumentalism: "as long as bourgeois society continues to pursue empirical ends to the detriment of the absolute," it will have a superficial identity that contrasts with the "absolute purpose" of the university.[64] Furthermore, "in order to achieve its aims," the state simultaneously constrains and separates its subjects. It relies on "distinctions" that arise from "the suppression of the range of personalities and the direction of their powers in various, very different directions to make them better instruments of the state."[65] The university should be no stranger to distinctions; Schelling envisions an aristocracy composed of talented and devoted students regardless of their social class. (This, in effect, was Fichte's democratization of education—an intellectual elite formed not on the basis of class but on intellectual and moral capacity. The neo-humanists wanted an intellectual meritocracy and showed some awareness of the material and social challenges such an ideal faced.) The university forms people (i.e., young men) by uniting them around a "single" purpose—the pursuit of scholarship. Such an education "produces rational thinking," which, in turn, allows for "a lasting formation of the self, the worldview that leads directly to self-identity and thus a genuinely blessed life."[66] Challenging bourgeois society, the modern state, and established universities to improve themselves, Schelling presents a stark choice: they can either persist with their lesser form of rationalization, the way of fragmentation and superficiality, or take the university, which is for the few, as a "model organization," fostering unity and perhaps even committing themselves to the higher modern rationality that proceeds from a universal perspective and makes for a fullness of existence. This shift would have clear advantages for individuals—who doesn't want such fullness? Its appeal for the state is more difficult to discern. Schelling, to be sure, was speaking in a lecture hall context he regarded as a site for forming students and advancing knowledge, not proposing particular, concrete reforms. The reform proposals of Schleiermacher and Humboldt certainly aren't short on philosophical arguments and normative ideals, but they address questions of institutional design in an entirely different way. Despite their differences, each of the idealist philosopher-reformers conceives of the university as a distinct whole, but all of them ground that *universitas* not in confessional religion or the state but in a self-sustaining community of scholars and students formed by shared practices and virtues. This is the neo-humanist ideal of the unity of knowledge.

## THE UNIVERSITY AS ORGANIZING INSTITUTION

On October 14, 1806, Napoleon led the French army into battle against Prussian troops. The confrontation took place in Jena, and it exposed the Prussian army, long a source of pride, as backward and inept by comparison, as did the even larger-scale destruction of the army at Auerstedt the same day. Within a month, the Kingdom of Prussia was under the complete control of the French Empire. Prussians didn't confine their subsequent self-reckoning to the fitness of their military, however. While Hegel, Schelling's successor in Jena, famously declared that with the modern state casting aside all barriers to its extension, history had reached its end, others were focused on the more immediate issue of how to reform and renew the Prussian state.

In the decades before 1806, several reform efforts had been undertaken, one culminating in the promulgation of the mildly modernizing General Prussian Legal Code of 1794. Prussia's crushing defeat by Napoleon proved a greater impetus for reform. Within a year, Friedrich Wilhelm III had appointed the reform-minded Karl von Stein as his chief minister. Although Napoleon removed Stein from office in 1809 after French agents intercepted a letter in which he expressed hope for Prussia's imminent liberation, Stein accomplished much in his brief tenure: pushing through the abolition of serfdom, instituting general conscription, and, not least, setting into motion the overhaul of Prussia's system of education. Stein not only created a new government agency for the latter purpose, the Section for Religion and Public Education, he also recruited Wilhelm von Humboldt, who had been leading a comfortable life as a diplomat in Rome, to lead it.

One of Humboldt's immediate tasks was to figure out how to address the demise of Prussia's most prestigious institution of higher learning, the University of Halle, which, like several other universities, had been closed in the wake of the Napoleonic conquest. In 1807 Friedrich Wilhelm III had signaled his support for establishing a new institution in Berlin. The Prussian capital, which had lived in the shadow of Paris for decades, had no local university, but it was home to an array of smaller institutions and important collections, including the Prussian Academy of Sciences, anatomical theaters, natural history collections, and medical and veterinary clinics. This infrastructure of disparate and loosely related intellectual and scientific resources made Berlin an ideal site for a new institution of higher learning, especially of the sort intended to organize and unify knowledge.[67]

Fichte wasn't the only German intellectual to recognize that this was a unique opportunity to reform higher education. The theologian and philosopher Friedrich Schleiermacher, who lost his job when Halle closed, heard from his Halle colleague Friedrich Wolf that one of the king's advisers was soliciting design ideas for an institution of higher learning in Berlin. (That it would be called a university was far from certain given the fact that for many German intellectuals around 1800, *university* connoted a medieval, guild-like institution.) Schleiermacher decided to join the conversation even if no one asked him to. In 1808 he drafted a blueprint for a university in Berlin, which he published as "Occasional Thoughts on German Universities." In it Schleiermacher combined a clarifying and compelling articulation of neo-humanist ideals about education and knowledge with a detailed, frank analysis of the challenges of institutionalizing these ideals.

Schleiermacher begins teasingly, reflecting on the nonsystematic, merely "occasional" or popular character of his text. He contrasts his proposal with the idealist educational theories propounded by his contemporaries, especially with respect to that central epistemic ideal, the unity of knowledge. "The spirit of the systematic as the highest principle, the immediate unity of all knowledge," he writes, "cannot be presented as existing all by itself in pure transcendental philosophy, like a ghost, as some have unfortunately tried to do, thereby conjuring up phantoms and unearthly beings."[68] When Schleiermacher drafted his proposal, he was especially known for his translations of Plato and his *On Religion: Speeches to Its Cultured Despisers*, both of which demonstrate a philosophical and theological sensibility more dialogic and pluralistic than "transcendental" or even systematic.[69] Schleiermacher, who preached most Sundays, sought different social forms for intellectual work and thinking, what he and his onetime roommate Friedrich Schlegel referred to as "sym-philosophy." For Schleiermacher even more than for Schiller, Fichte, and Schelling, knowledge required sociability; it was a communal activity. He not only found the abstractness of Fichte's idealism off-putting but also rejected what many of his idealist contemporaries sought—a single, foundational philosophical viewpoint.

At the same time, Schleiermacher consistently invoked the unity-of-knowledge ideal but in a different and more nuanced manner than Schiller, Fichte, and Schelling.[70] "In the area of knowledge," he writes, "everything is so interdependent and so interconnected that we might as well say: the more something is presented in isolation, the more incomprehensible and confused it will seem."[71]

Despite Schleiermacher's real differences with how Schiller, Schelling, and Fichte understand the unity-of-knowledge ideal, his use echoes theirs in at least one important way. Each of them uses the ideal to make a claim that functions descriptively as well as normatively: modernization both enables and threatens the neo-humanist project of education. By appealing to the ideal, Schiller and colleagues implicitly describe the present as fragmented, disjointed, and incoherent, but they also argue that the present ought to be made whole again. This normative unity, they suggest, should function at various but related levels: historically, ethically or morally, epistemically, and institutionally. Historically, the unity ideal entails the progressive self-realization of reason in time. Schiller's universal history provides a model for a meaningful unfolding of history. Ethically or morally, the unity ideal entails a deep and sustained relationship between knowledge and life. It orients and sustains the integration of an individual's various identities and commitments. Epistemically, the unity ideal orients the endless process of relating facts, evidence, and arguments across fields and specializations. Finally, Schiller, Schelling, and Fichte give the unity ideal institutional shape not in the church, state, or even local communities but in the university, which, for neo-humanists, embodies the unity of morality, truth, religion, and social belonging.

Writing to his fiancée on Christmas Day 1808, when the manuscript of "Occasional Thoughts on German Universities" was with the printer, Schleiermacher expressed a desire to integrate his major activities—scholarly, domestic, ecclesiastical—then complained that "it is only in this most recent time when men divide and separate everything that such a joining of interests is rare."[72] Yet he does not simply lament or resist the fact of intellectual and social differentiation. Schleiermacher identifies positive elements amid the differentiating, even fragmenting effects of modernity: the gradual dissolution of established social hierarchies, the proliferation of new forms of socialization, the untethering of knowledge from monolithic theological and state control, the profusion of possible identities, and the emergence of different kinds of knowledge and different ways of knowing.

Intellectual specialization in particular enables individuals to attend more carefully to a broader range of objects and different aspects of the world, the ideas and activities of different people, and the development of distinct practices to sustain it.[73]

Modernity, furthermore, moves in other directions as well. Like Schelling, Schleiermacher sees unifying tendencies alongside fragmenting ones in the present age. Large "powerful states" have united entire linguistic territories, a process that, according to Schleiermacher, is good for the unity of knowledge, since the scholarship that "arises in one language forms . . . a unified whole," and scholarly communication, crucial for the production of knowledge, is easier within a unified territory. However, Schleiermacher has no illusions about what drives these consolidating states. Increasingly unbound from tradition and religion, they are, as in Schiller's lecture, motivated by self-interest in its cruder form: the desire for wealth and power. This leads them to prioritize knowledge that advances the pursuit of those things, especially "knowledge that can be measured" and "concrete discoveries." States in the age of academic mercantilism often try to use universities for their own "immediate purposes," and academics are sometimes "co-opted" into putting "political considerations" ahead of scholarly ones. By contrast, the impulse for pure knowledge that is "primarily concerned with the unity of knowledge and the common form of all knowledge" stems, Schleiermacher emphasizes, from "free inclinations, out of an inner urge."[74]

Making a normative argument about their proper function, Schleiermacher contends that universities should serve as an ethical counterweight to the state, an assertion that is advanced in most neo-humanist writings on higher education. For Schleiermacher, striving after knowledge is necessarily a communal effort—"the first law of any attempt at knowledge must be: communication."[75] Such striving is not, primarily at least, a recovery of some lost metaphysical or theological unity, but its effective creation in the present. The instrumental mindset—a "money-grubbing" mentality, to use Schleiermacher's term—goes along with a proprietary attitude toward knowledge. To relate to knowledge in this way is to deny what Schleiermacher considers its essentially social character. Like Schiller's philosophical mind, Schleiermacher's true scholar is selfless and generous and only too happy to see others surpass his efforts.

Such a scholar would also make an effective and, thus, good bureaucrat. Schleiermacher formulates this point in a number of ways, perhaps most strongly as a warning: If the Prussian state is to coerce universities into focusing "only on directly practical matters," it will rob itself of "the most essential advantages that the sciences and scholarship provide." "Less and less," he writes, "will the state be able to conceive of and carry out great things, or to uncover, with sharp insights, the roots and interconnectedness of all its mistakes."[76] But would the prospect of a continual supply of capable and responsible government officials prove sufficient to induce the state reliably to sponsor neo-humanist education and such an education's primary internal purpose: the unification of ethical formation with systematic scholarship, that is, *Bildung* with *Wissenschaft*? In contrast to Schiller and Schelling, Schleiermacher attempts to reconcile what the state and university owe each other and articulates their duties and responsibilities in this regard. He insists that universities need "protection" and material support from the state to be able to carry out their educational and intellectual mission even if states are disinclined to recognize the value of that mission or are tempted to interfere with it in order to satisfy their own immediate needs. Not only do they co-opt professors' scholarship; states frequently assume that attempting to control the flow of knowledge with foreign states serves their own domestic interests by ensuring that the benefits of intellectual progress will remain within fixed political borders. Such a protectionist attitude runs counter, of course, to the notion that knowledge is a social good that flourishes best when not unduly constrained by the boundaries that signify states' political interests.[77]

Yet Schleiermacher maintains an outlook of wary optimism. He claims that German states relish the prestige attached to nonvocational higher education.[78] Speaking of neo-humanist institutions of higher learning as "universities in the German sense" was, indeed, a way of enhancing their prestige. Whereas Fichte had explicitly framed scholarship as a source of national renewal in his *Addresses to the German Nation* (1807), Schleiermacher operated more by way of suggestion. France had recently reformed its system of higher education, converting it into a series of specialized schools. German universities would express and further elevate the higher German spirit by devoting themselves to a much grander goal: "the totality of knowledge."[79]

Such knowledge, Schleiermacher also intimates, has taken on greater practical importance for the state. Ever the conciliator in "Occasional Thoughts," he argues that even as university professors stand up for their independence from the state, something the better ones will intuitively do, they should welcome the bureaucratic oversight of the state with respect to procedures such as hiring and ceding control in areas where vestiges of guild practices remain, such as inherited professorships and the persistence of the family university (*Familienuniversität*), in which faculty positions were passed on like any other form of aristocratic inheritance.[80] But Schleiermacher, writing at a dramatic moment of bureaucratic expansion and reform, suggests that the most important challenge facing universities is the need to convince modern states of the practical and social benefits of education and learning oriented toward knowledge of the whole. First, modern states have to be compelled to understand that "good governance . . . requires true knowledge." Second, modern states—and the general public—must also be made to understand that universities are the institutions that can best create and cultivate knowledge. They do this by forming men who are capable of pursuing the kind of knowledge of the whole they need in order to be citizens and statesmen with real perspective:

> To awaken the idea of systematic knowledge, of science, in the noble youth . . . so that it becomes second nature for him to view everything from the perspective of systematic inquiry, see individual things not in isolation but rather in their intellectual interconnection and place them in a larger context, always with reference to the unity of all knowledge . . . this is the task of the university.[81]

As a theorist of hermeneutics and more specifically of the relationship of parts to wholes within language systems and texts, among groups of texts, and between texts and their intellectual contexts, Schleiermacher had a profound investment in actually working out his ideas about the interconnectedness of knowledge.[82] Add to this his desire to distinguish his thinking about the unity of knowledge from Fichte's and Schelling's views and a partial explanation for the frequency with which he invokes the unity ideal in "Occasional Thoughts on German Universities" emerges. By emphasizing different aspects of the unity-of-knowledge ideal in different contexts, Schleiermacher impresses on his readers that for him, there are different tenets and goals animating the distinct yet deeply related historical, ethical, epistemic, and institutional forms of unity. These include presenting "the totality of knowledge in such a way that the principles and blueprint of all knowledge are brought to light," "confirming the insight into the nature and connectedness of all knowledge," developing original ideas about how language systems make for a unity of knowledge, and creating an environment of academic freedom. If all knowledge is interconnected, then interfering with the pursuit of knowledge in any one area means interfering with it in every area.[83]

## THE STATE'S INTEREST IN SCHOLARSHIP

There is another reason why Schleiermacher repeatedly returns to the unity of knowledge: He wants to make it clear that it is *the* organizing principle of the university he is imagining. For Schleiermacher, the unity ideal must ground the institutional structure and pedagogical practice of any distinctly *modern* university. *Wissenschaft* stands in for a self-sustaining intellectual practice with its own internal goods, virtues, and ideals, and thus sustains the authority and legitimacy of a disciplined, specialized, university-based form of knowledge. During the nineteenth century, Schleiermacher's was the most influential neo-humanist vision of university reform. It was only in the early twentieth century that Wilhelm von Humboldt's vision, discovered by a biographer in 1896, supplanted it.

Indignant about being merely a section head and not a minister, tired of having to manage difficult personalities, and eager to get back to a life in which he had time for his own scholarship, Humboldt resigned from his formal role in leading educational reform in June 1810, after only sixteen months in office. On his way out, he appointed Schleiermacher chair of the commission tasked with drafting the statutes of the University of Berlin. Humboldt and Schleiermacher differed, to be sure, on key aspects of university reform. Perhaps most notably, Schleiermacher was less adamant about the importance of producing new knowledge at the university. Though he clearly wanted professors to be engaged scholars, he recommended that they focus primarily on teaching during the first parts of their careers. Once they had turned fifty and could no longer relate to young students, they should move to academies and devote themselves to research.

By contrast, Humboldt famously stressed that a chief aim of the university is to "join objective knowledge with the process of forming the subject."[84] Professional academies, in Humboldt's writings, seem barely necessary, since universities are at least as productive in the realm of research—and probably more so (because, he believed, being around young minds helps professors think creatively). On most of the basic issues, however, Schleiermacher and Humboldt agreed. Indeed, many scholars think Humboldt has received too much credit for designing the modern research university and Schleiermacher too little.[85] With his gift for resonant formulations—for example, "solitude and freedom"—Humboldt is the one whom university presidents around the world now routinely cite. However, if his main statement on how the University of Berlin should be organized hadn't been found just in time for figures like Adolf von Harnack to carry out celebratory myth building around the hundredth anniversary of the university's founding, we might today be talking about the "Schleiermacher Model," perhaps even about Schleiermacher University in Berlin.[86] "Occasional Thoughts on German Universities" certainly had a profound influence on Humboldt. In 1808 however, Humboldt had long been concerned with such paradoxes as how inaction on the part of the state can be a kind of action as well as with the state's proper role in human development. Questions about how closely Humboldt's plans for the university resembled Schleiermacher's and how much Schleiermacher's influenced Humboldt's remain just that, questions—though questions worthy of sustained attention. For us, what matters is that both Humboldt and Schleiermacher appropriated the unity-of-knowledge ideal.

In Humboldt's memoranda describing the proposed university, the unity-of-knowledge ideal functioned as an epistemic and ethical norm. According to its normative purpose, the university should combine the creation and transmission of objective knowledge with the formation of the subjects of knowledge, the scholars and students of the university; serve as a (nationalistic) vehicle for establishing the legitimacy of neo-humanist education as well as for bolstering its prestige and ethical value; and, finally, act as an institutional go-between mediating the interests of a community of scholars and the interests of a modern state.

For Humboldt, too, the modern state is an engine that runs on self-interest. To be sure, its rationalizing tendencies can help the university in crucial ways. Nonetheless, Humboldt believes that academics require state oversight on important matters in which territorialism, defensiveness, and patronage lead to bad decisions—especially with respect to hiring. Yet the state also wants "character and action" from universities, not "talking."[87] What the state must realize, contends Humboldt, is that acquiring precisely the knowledge that "comes from within and can be cultivated within" rather than merely "collecting facts" is what "transforms character" (and thus forms the most capable citizens).

Humboldt further argues that whenever the state "meddles" in the production of knowledge or the training of students, it fosters "one-sidedness" and acts as an "impediment" to the appreciation of knowledge "in itself and as a whole"—that is, to the very perspective needed for effective state action. That the state creates the external structure of the university and provides financial support sets up a situation of permanent tension, in which something purportedly "higher"—*Wissenschaft* or scholarship as a comprehensive form of life or the ideal of a pure knowledge—is always pulled down toward a "more base material reality."[88] Humboldt nevertheless seems hopeful about the prospects for the founding and flourishing of a Prussian university in which students and professors can come together "for the sake of knowledge," that is, "knowledge as a whole." He based this hope in part on the idea that this *pulling down* did not sully an otherwise pristine knowledge; rather, it was its realization in human-shaped and intended forms. This tension was not something that should be resolved or overcome; it ought to remain permanent. The modern university was a medium through which competing purposes and ends could be productively organized.

In his memorandum to Friedrich Wilhelm III, Humboldt writes that Prussia's defeat and political fracturing have revealed the unifying power of the highest intellectual culture among Germans. The "German tendencies" that best embody this culture are nothing other than the unifying ones at the center of the new university's design: everything is derived from "first principles," everything is "developed toward an ideal," and "the principle and the ideal" are "connected in a single idea." Not only is the unity-of-knowledge ideal of great practical value to the state, the "single idea"—and thus the new university—also allows for a sense of cultural cohesion and mission at a time when the state desperately sought one.[89] Defeat and fragmentation have created the enabling conditions for a salutary unity that, as Lyotard noted, keeps the disparate activities and aims of the university from pulling away from one another.

The final strophe of the cantata Clemens von Brentano wrote for the dedication of the University of Berlin begins with these lines:

This royal house belongs
To the totality, universality, unity
General validity
Of scholarly wisdom,
To academic freedom!

These lines appeared in the *Berlin Evening News* on October 15, 1810, their publication intended to coincide with a dedication ceremony planned for that day. As another newspaper reported five days later, however, the ceremony never took place: "Our university was not, as had been previously promised, dedicated on October 15th . . . because there was not enough time to take care of the necessary arrangements."[90] The house of scholarship, freedom, and unity lacked chairs, finished lecture halls, and professors. Yet the notion of the unity of knowledge remained an epistemic and ethical ideal, gradually, haltingly, and variously institutionalized in German universities throughout the nineteenth century. Just as important to this ideal as the "totality, universality, unity" (*Ganzheit, Allheit, Einheit*) celebrated in Brentano's cantata were differentiation, distinction, and specialization. These were constitutive features of modern research universities. They were not foisted on previously whole and integrated institutions. There was no unity without differentiation—no *Einheit* without *Vielheit*.

The unity-of-knowledge ideal would also be used to sustain a vision of the ideal scholar, a scholarly persona who embodied a distinct way of life. With his description of the "philosophical mind," Schiller outlined the scholarly persona's basic features and characteristics and, just as importantly, defined what it was not with his description of the "careerist scholar." Over the course of the nineteenth century, the "careerist scholar" remained the antipersona, the anti-ideal that would prove just as vital to sustaining a vision of authoritative knowledge. The force of its negative normativity was almost as pervasive and powerful as the positive persona of the *Wissenschaftler*. Nietzsche's "last men," defined by the hedonism of constrained hopes and a utilitarian relationship to knowledge, were updated versions of Schiller's careerist scholar, both serving to highlight the goods but also the poverty of modernity and its rationalizing effects. The ideal of the unity of knowledge, then, remained a salient feature of nineteenth-century German institutions. It crystalized how the unsalutary effects of the definitive practices of the modern research university are not simply accidental. Rather, these effects inhere in the practices themselves. In the case of *Wissenschaft* and the ideal of the unity of knowledge, specialization would, in certain ways, deform scholars, students, and universities in general. The epistemic and ethical dangers and limits of specialization, for example, belonged to the very modern forms of knowledge advocated by the neo-humanists. The most fruitful debates, then, would concern themselves with trying to clarify these inherent dangers and limits and seek to constrain their possible damage.

As we trace the emergence of the modern humanities throughout the chapters that follow, the relationship between unity and specialization is a crucial point, one often lost, both in nineteenth-century Germany and today, amid apologies for the humanities based on the assumption that specialization undid some presupposed prior unity and value of *the humanities*. It is a refrain that courses through the laments of the melancholy mandarins from 1830s German intellectuals to twenty-first-century American English professors. But the modern humanities were not a casualty of the modern university and specialization—they were a product of them. The humanities never recovered, reconciled, or reconstituted some unity of knowledge undone by specialization. As a moral and rhetorical project, however, the humanities succeeded in obscuring the distinctions and divisions introduced by the modern university: they did this by holding out the false hope of a unified knowledge.

## CHAPTER TWO

# The Lament of the Melancholy Mandarins

In 1832, more than three decades before Matthew Arnold gushed over Prussian universities in what we would today call a best practices report, the French philosopher Victor Cousin produced a similar work, also effusive in its admiration, for the French government.[1] Though not as well-known as Arnold's account, Cousin's was quickly translated into German and English, and in France, Britain, and the United States it became a source of inspiration among educational reformers. Drawing on Cousin's depiction, Henry Tappan, the first president of the University of Michigan, later argued for the creation of Prussian-style universities in the United States, where until the final decades of the nineteenth century instruction at most colleges was organized around a fixed curriculum and designed to form good Protestant gentlemen. Compared with the largely unregulated lives led by students in Prussian universities, the lives of American college students could feel stifling. Tappan wrote,

> In no part of the world has university education been so enlarged and made so liberal and thorough . . . [as in] The Educational System of Germany, and particularly of Prussia. . . . Thorough in all its parts, consistent with itself, and vigorously sustained, it furnishes every department of life with educated men, and keeps up at the universities themselves, in every branch of knowledge, a supply of erudite and elegant scholars and authors for the benefit and glory of their country, and the good of mankind.[2]

Unsurprisingly, Cousin's report was warmly received in Prussia. For many commentators, however, the status it conferred wasn't enough to lift the mood of doubt about the Prussian system's quality and prospects.[3] That Prussia's institutions of higher learning were more dynamic than their counterparts elsewhere was certainly a point of pride in some circles. Yet with its reactionary currents and leadership, the restoration order established in the German territories after Napoleon's defeat in 1814 prompted frustration and, eventually, ennui among the cultural elite. The poet Heinrich Heine characterized this moment as "nothing but owls, censorship edicts, prison stench, novels of resignation, changing of the prison guard, bigotry, and imbecility."[4]

For all his skewering of the present, Heine had little patience with nostalgia for the past, yet it was with an air of melancholy that he marked 1832, the year of Goethe's death, as the end of Germany's "art period." Comparing intellectual life in restoration Berlin to what she had experienced there around 1800 with classicism, Romanticism, and the German and German-Jewish enlightenments vibrant and interacting, the salon hostess Rahel Varnhagen wrote to a friend in lugubrious terms: "It has all vanished, all of it: the whole constellation of beauty, grace, coquetry, warmth, emotion, wit, elegance, cordiality, the drive to develop ideas, real sincerity, free social exchange, and articulate play."[5]

Now Varnhagen herself was gone, having died in 1833. Friedrich Schlegel, one of the architects of German Romanticism, passed away in 1829, Hegel in 1831. When the philosopher Friedrich Schleiermacher died in 1834, an ardent eulogist stressed that he had been a "man of his time," not the present one.[6] Wilhelm von Humboldt died in 1835; like Schleiermacher, he was a much-admired scholar with obvious ties to Romanticism and neo-humanism, and he was of course a creative bureaucrat who helped transform Prussia's entire system of education. It isn't difficult to imagine why at this moment some Prussian artists, intellectuals, and scholars regarded previous decades with envy. Viewed in relation to recent American cultural history, the 1830s were to nineteenth-century Prussia what the 1980s were to the United States: a period of retrenchment when the cultural, political, and sexual revolutions of the preceding decades seemed dangerous, exciting, and transformative.

Not coincidentally, both decades produced landmark books about the decline of the modern university. In America the 1980s had Allan Bloom's *The Closing of the American Mind* (1987), probably the all-time best-selling contribution to the genre. In Prussia the 1830s had Adolph Diesterweg's *The Rot at German Universities* (1836), which may well have originated the genre. These are classic humanists' accounts of higher education in trouble in which the university's deviation from the liberal mission articulated by Schleiermacher and Humboldt is considered both a cause and a "symptom," as Diesterweg put it, of a larger malaise.[7] In what remains a feature of the genre as well as a central element of the permanent crisis of the humanities, Bloom and Diesterweg use the modern university as a propitious site for sweeping criticisms. Their goal was to show that something was generally and deeply wrong with their respective contemporary cultures. They could have chosen worse strategies than trying to show that culture was failing to thrive even in an institution purported to be committed to its exploration and transmission.

Since achievements pointing to high academic quality can always be disregarded or reframed as signs of decay, it doesn't matter whether the universities in question sit dominantly atop the world rankings, as US schools did in the 1980s, or enjoy the prestige Prussian universities had in the 1830s. Elite status allows for dramatic gestures of critique in a way that lesser reputations don't. If even the iconic nonvocational institutions recognized to make up the top stratum of the higher-education pyramid are being overrun by the values of the outside world, and if those values are aggressively out of sync with open-ended reflection, what chance does the life of the mind have? How better to stress the urgency of the present than by claiming that the age's brightest youth are being corrupted by the very institutions charged with forming them into virtuous, capable, and responsible adults? Bloom subtitled his book *How Higher Education Has Failed Democracy and Impoverished the Souls of Today's Students.* He called the university's shortcomings "an intellectual crisis of the greatest magnitude, which constitutes the crisis of civilization."[8] A hundred and fifty years earlier, Diesterweg used much the same language, casting Prussia's crisis of higher education as one of "civilization's life or death issues."[9]

This isn't to suggest that either author chose to write about the university for merely tactical reasons. Although each worked at the edges of specialized disciplinary communities, both were enmeshed in the academic culture of humanist knowledge. Diesterweg, whom we will focus on here, studied history, philology, and philosophy in Heidelberg before earning a doctorate in history in 1811. He then taught at an experimental, reform-minded secondary school in Frankfurt and later audited philosophy lectures at the University of Berlin—his primary point of reference in *The Rot at German Universities.*[10] He spent much of his adult life writing about education and training teachers.[11] In the preface to *The Rot at German Universities,* he writes that he loves "education and *Bildung* above all else."[12]

In order to understand how and why an entire literature concerning the modern university's decline emerged and to put early instances of the genre into meaningful conversation with more recent ones, generalizations about the zeitgeist in the 1830s and 1980s can be only a starting point. Diesterweg's specific grievances, many of which resonated widely and can be seen in works by nineteenth-century German scholars as different as Friedrich Nietzsche and the historian Theodor Mommsen, are also important. So, too, is recognition that Diesterweg's sense of crisis was a function of new expectations for the university. Or, rather, it was a function of tensions operating both *within* a powerful new set of ideals and *between* those ideals and the institutional circumstances they helped to form in the face of various external pressures.

In Diesterweg's day, Prussian universities maintained their own detention centers, where students found guilty of violating codes of conduct could be held for weeks at a time. The staff tasked with overseeing the cells were expected to speak Latin. Less than 1 percent of Prussia's population of seventeen- to twenty-four-year-olds enrolled at postsecondary schools, most all of this cohort being male and white. The myriad institutional changes that have transformed postsecondary education, from enrollment trends to architectural and design changes, certainly affected the meaning and use of the educational ideals that had shaped Diesterweg's idea of a university. These ideals have been adopted and adapted to fit different contexts and evolving self-perceptions, epistemologies, politics, and methodological commitments. They have also been deployed to advance institutional agendas made possible by expansion. Yet even while accounting for such appropriation and reinvention across space and time, core aspects of these ideals have not only persisted, they have remained remarkably consistent since the early nineteenth century.[13] To a large extent, they have also crossed disciplinary and political divides.[14]

Consider how Bloom, a pessimistic elitist, compares to progressive scholars like Christopher Newfield and Wendy Brown, who write about the plight of US public higher education in ways he would have considered wrongheaded. For Bloom, liberal higher education—that is, liberal education in the sense of study that isn't subordinated to practical or technical considerations but that centrally involves the open-ended pursuit of truth—requires certain forms of exclusion. Accordingly, the democratization of higher education, in the sense of expanding access to it, poses a threat to its survival. This is decidedly not how Newfield and Brown see it. While access is a crucial issue (which we address at length in a later chapter), for the moment we want to stress the near consensus concerning basic educational aims. Newfield and Brown have insisted that state universities should have a greater share of public resources in order to make affordable a version of liberal education not that different from the one for which Bloom thought he was writing a requiem.[15] Disagreements about the canon, curricular inclusiveness, and the place of politics and values in the classroom certainly matter, but they shouldn't be allowed to obscure all that is held in common.

Like Geoffrey Galt Harpham, a former director of the National Humanities Center, Brown and Newfield promote *Bildung*, a term Newfield has adopted, as has Harpham .[16] Harpham seeks to cut through what he describes as the "defensive, moralizing, banalized discourse that has for many years been associated with the humanities and liberal education."[17] For Harpham, it's the *way* we talk about the humanities and liberal education — the discourse, not its objects (particular books, canons, works of art)—that needs to be reworked. Indeed, Harpham doesn't simply employ *Bildung* as a handy rubric. He presents his own notion of humanities education as descending directly from Humboldt's idea of not only training people for the civil service but forming them in a "more holistic way as culturally versatile and self-governing citizens."[18]

Distinguished intellectuals and scholars in the United States and Britain have issued similar calls to reformulate how we talk about the humanities, but not necessarily to reconceive of the humanities themselves. Among them are Danielle Allen, Martha Nussbaum, Helen Small, Stefan Collini, and Andrew Delbanco.[19] Small concludes her trenchant analysis of the defenses and related values of the humanities by calling for new formulations of the humanities' significance, not for new conceptions of what they could be or do in higher education, much less whether the humanities as an institutional form of knowledge remain compelling and meaningful.[20] If there are academic humanists who want to overhaul the humanities — Cathy Davidson, an English professor who considers herself a disrupter from within, surely counts as one—at least for the time being, they are outliers. One could argue, moreover, that with her various proposals for curricular reform, Davidson is proposing to blaze a trail to a well-known goal: independent mindedness and productive character development through open-ended, largely humanistic, supradisciplinary study.[21]

Certain key ideals and objectives, such as forming "self-governing citizens," are not the only things to have endured. Some of the most important pressures that have threatened to undermine those ideals and objectives have also persisted. In fact some of the pressures are effects of ongoing processes of modernization—such as the push for bureaucratic rationalization—that allowed for the institutionalization of those ideals in the first place. In basic ways, then, the dynamic that drove Diesterweg's sense of crisis is similar to the one at work today. As a result, the literature of university decline—especially the prominent strand we're concerned with here, a genre we call the lament of the melancholy mandarins—has a number of recurring features, not only particular themes and complaints but also tenacious contradictions and paradoxes that reveal much about the critics who write it but also about the permanent crisis of the humanities. So how did this dynamic of permanent tension take shape?[22] The answer begins with an earlier crisis in higher education (which we began to examine in the previous chapter) and a different critical discourse about the university, which dates to the late eighteenth century and which Diesterweg invoked nostalgically as early as 1836.

## NEO-HUMANISM REVISITED

We saw in chapter 1 that distrust of universities ran high in eighteenth-century Europe. They were often seen as sclerotic environments where traditional privileges encouraged indolence and thus stasis. Adam Smith complained that Oxford and Cambridge professors had reached the point where most had "given up even the pretense of teaching."[23] Those institutions had become, he added, "sanctuaries in which exploded systems and obsolete prejudices found shelter and protection after they had been hunted out of every other corner of the world."[24]

The situation was especially fraught in the German territories in part because a culture of rowdiness had earned German universities a reputation for turning nice young men into hellions or worse. With an air of resignation rather than surprise, a Prussian bureaucrat reported about his visit to the University of Göttingen in 1789: "during the few days I spent here, a group of several drunk students first attacked a young woman in the street, then followed her into her own house and mistreated her so horribly that her life was in danger."[25] The Prussian Legal Code of 1794 included extensive provisions for student misconduct (debts, dueling, etc.). When the reform-minded minister Karl von Stein was confronted with the idea of founding a university in Berlin, he responded skeptically, saying, "But think of all the illegitimate children who would be born there every year."[26] Such circumstances made for good literary material; academic satire was one of the most popular genres of the era, with even Frederick the Great penning a contribution: the comedy *L'école du monde* (1742). Universities faced more existential threats than literary satire, however. Technical institutes in mining, veterinary medicine, and various other fields proliferated as an Enlightenment favorite. Finishing academies sprung up to serve German aristocrats who wanted to emulate the French model of courtly culture. Founded mostly at the end of the seventeenth and the beginning of the eighteenth century, scientific academies and societies functioned as centers of knowledge discovery and transmission. Learned and influential commentators consequently began to ask, Do we even need universities?[27]

By the end of the eighteenth century, this protracted sense of crisis led to a fundamental reimagining of higher education. Although there was no manifesto advancing a series of agreed-on principles, a set of ideas and ideals emerged that will be familiar to anyone who has read today's rationales for a college-level general education program. Writing in 1807 the philosopher J. G. Fichte claimed that in their present form, German universities couldn't justify their existence. They would have to transmute themselves into institutions where, through open-ended study, young men from all social classes could learn to think systematically but also boldly and independently, becoming "artists of learning." Doing so would mean fostering capacities that would serve them well on whatever career path they took while making them fuller people. The education imparted by universities should be a "free and infinitely adaptable possession, a tool we can readily apply to life."[28]

The theorists of university reform tapped into multiple cultural debates, ranging from anxieties about modern egoism—as Friedrich Schiller described it—and information overload to the Kantian ethos of unconstrained critique and the self-legitimation needs of a rising professional class. They were doing so, moreover, at a time of upheaval and opportunity. With Prussia's armies crushed by Napoleon, half its territory gone, and its finances in ruins, King Friedrich Wilhelm III nevertheless signaled his approval for the project of founding a university in Berlin. In 1807 he told a delegation of professors, "We must replace with intellectual powers what we have lost through physical ones." It was a remarkable avowal of support, but it wasn't a blank check. The philosopher Friedrich Schleiermacher and the scholar-statesman Wilhelm von Humboldt were keenly aware of the state's affinity for what Schleiermacher called "knowledge that can be measured" and that has "immediate effects."[29] While taking that into account, they made the case that open-ended research and instruction not tethered to the state's immediate aims would enhance Prussia's prestige and serve its economic and political interests in a way that the "un-German" focus on vocational training recently adopted by French universities could not. Impractical education would have a more profound and lasting practicality.

Both pragmatic and idealistic, this approach to reform created significant design challenges, which Schleiermacher and Humboldt nonetheless embraced. By emphasizing the "occasional"—or really functional—character of his university writings, Schleiermacher encourages readers to view them as performative illustrations of his claims about the benefits of systematic thought for bureaucratic problem solving. He mobilizes the hermeneutic principles his scholarship came to be known for, which centered on how part-whole relationships order our understanding, to answer such questions as how the old four-faculties structure could actually complement liberal reform.

Schleiermacher's friend Humboldt also drew on his scholarly work in his proposals for university reform. Humboldt admired classical Greece for what he saw as its ability to harmoniously combine competing cultural tendencies.[30] Like Schleiermacher's, his blueprint for the university emphasizes potentially productive relationships between objectives and activities that don't seem to go together very well, such as selfless collective striving and status building; teaching and research; autonomy and oversight; free self-development and disciplined formation; the boundless pursuit of knowledge and intellectual unity; the preservation of tradition and the embrace of the new.[31] In this model, as in Kant's essay on the "Conflict of the Faculties," the university's special dynamism derives from internal permanent tensions.[32]

Appointed by Friedrich Wilhelm as the first head of Prussia's Section for Public Education and Religion, the agency created in 1808 to oversee educational reform on all levels, Humboldt avoids talk of moral purpose and educational ideals in his formal reform proposal of May 1809. He simply indicates that the new university would be like other Prussian institutions of higher learning, only better, because it would be able to take advantage of the existing scholarly and scientific infrastructure in Berlin. As part of his plan to reform the entire system of education, from primary schools to universities, Humboldt presented the king with an enhanced version of existent Prussian universities. Meanwhile, in a government known for its thrift yet nonetheless broke, he fended off attempts from rivals to interfere. Humboldt also had to consult with as well as recruit academics, a group he regarded as worse than a wandering troupe of actors.[33]

## LIBERAL ARTS IN ILLIBERAL PRUSSIA

The University of Berlin's founding moment in October 1810 was in fact long on anticlimax, as scholars tired of the myth of Humboldt's great triumph like to point out. There were still tenants living in the building the king had given to the university—the stately Prince Heinrich Palais on Unter den Linden. More significantly, for the purposes of this book, the university's original mission statement, written after Humboldt resigned in the summer of 1810 and not actually adopted until 1817, reads a bit like the one the Republican governor of Wisconsin Scott Walker (served 2011–2019) had hoped to install in place of language known, since 1912 when Charles McCarthy introduced the term, as the Wisconsin Idea. Walker wanted to delete the lines "search for truth" and "improve the human condition" from a law defining the purpose of the University of Wisconsin and add the phrase "meet the state's workforce needs." Similarly, the purpose named in the University of Berlin's first statutes is to prepare qualified students "to enter the higher offices of state and church service."[34]

Humboldt understood that building a university according to his high-minded ideals would be difficult. He acknowledged that ultimately "the best one can do is hire capable men and let the university take shape."[35] Beyond securing funding, the most important task was to establish an ethos of systematic, open-ended thought through scholarly, pedagogical, and administrative practice. Despite numerous setbacks, Humboldt had recruited prominent figures dedicated to doing just that, such as Friedrich August Wolf, Carl Savigny, Fichte, and Schleiermacher.

Just as vital to the development of the University of Berlin, however, was a protracted effort by members of the faculty and the Prussian bureaucracy to articulate the new university's institutional ideals and objectives long after its founding. When classes began in the fall of 1810, scholars and students acknowledged many of the reformers' ideals, but they didn't necessarily agree on what those ideals actually meant, how they related to one another, or why they ought to orient the university. It wasn't until the philosophy faculty finally completed and adopted its own statues in 1838 that the initial reform ideals were fully articulated and publicly endorsed. According to the statues, all students would receive a "general education in systematic thinking,"[36] which would "serve as the basis" for more specialized education in a particular area. There would be no essential difference between general and more specialized education: in fact, individual lectures would serve both functions as once. Faculty members also committed themselves to offering only one kind of instruction, liberal instruction, so that, as the statutes directed, "external practical considerations will not compromise pure scholarly interest."[37]

By the time the philosophy faculty approved that formulation, the University of Berlin had overtaken Göttingen as the preferred destination for foreign students in the German territories. As illustrious as Göttingen—an exception to university dysfunction in the eighteenth century—still was, Berlin had a more developed system of research institutes and more rigorous standards for both regular appointments and the awarding of doctorates, which professors invoked in faculty meetings with a palpable air of superiority.[38] By the 1830s, two decades after its founding, the University of Berlin had become a research university—albeit one without much research equipment—with a clear commitment to liberal education.[39]

Part of what was at stake in the institutionalization of the reform ideals was status. Even when framed as enabling a paradoxical practicality, the claim to freedom from practical considerations was—and to some extent remains—a claim to a privileged and protected social position, one set apart from the exigencies of the day. This claim has also been a liability for universities and not only because it invites charges of elitism and snobbery, no matter how progressive the packaging. Critics of noninstrumental (or useless, as they might say) education have also attacked it as a threat to religious and traditional values *and* for failing to promote modernization effectively, sometimes leveling both accusations at once.

This was certainly the case in the Prussia of the 1820s and 1830s, which was in some ways an improbable setting for the emergence of an institutional commitment to liberal learning and research.[40] The prison stench Heinrich Heine evoked had a profound effect on university life because conservatives in Friedrich Wilhelm's circle considered universities the most dangerous incubators of political subversion.[41] Relentless in their alarmism, they largely succeeded in convincing the king that institutions of higher learning oriented to utilitarian purposes, such as training civil servants, would be less likely to undermine political stability and challenge established religious belief, which they thought were mutually dependent. Less liberally oriented universities might also play a direct role in solving other problems that threatened the social order. For instance, food production was lagging badly behind population growth. How would all the vaunted "speculation and critique" at Prussian universities, one royal adviser derisively inquired, help feed people?[42]

Karl von Altenstein, Prussia's minister of culture from 1817 to 1840 and a champion of the reform ideals, had to maneuver constantly to protect liberal education. Having witnessed Prussian universities lose their exemption from censorship in 1819, he fought a number of battles head-on, but he also devised administrative solutions, such as his "general plan" for higher education in Prussia. He wanted to make the University of Berlin Prussia's flagship institution and organize it around liberal education and pure research. He imagined the smaller regional universities as mixing liberal *Bildung* with professional training. Despite what the statutes of its philosophical faculty set forth, however, even in that least professional division, the University of Berlin ultimately combined those two things—the liberal and the practical. Perhaps in response to the demand for more immediately useful knowledge, Altenstein hired a number of natural and physical scientists who pursued what today would be called applied research in addition to their more properly scholarly or noninstrumental research. One taught courses at technical schools on the side and edited a periodical called the *Journal for the Advancement of Industry*. Another stressed the importance of taking students on factory visits. Both worked as professors at the University of Berlin in the 1830s.

Perhaps the most significant challenge to the presumed divide between liberal and practical (or technical) education, at least for members of the philosophy faculty, came with the Reform Edict of 1834, which, among other things, professionalized the faculty by declaring its members responsible for preparing and then examining students who wanted to teach in *Gymnasien*. Such rationalizing reforms—codifying curricular goals, establishing uniform requirements, designing exam protocols—increased the role of universities and their faculties in credentialing and legitimizing teachers and other civil servants. Resistance to that professionalizing tendency didn't necessarily realign university instruction with the ideals of liberal general education that the statutes of the philosophical faculty at the University of Berlin had codified. Berlin's philology seminar had been preparing prospective *Gymnasium* teachers for state exams since its founding in 1812. The exams became appreciably more rigorous after the Reform Edict of 1834. By then, Altenstein had felt obliged to reprimand the renowned Berlin philologist August Boeckh for neglecting his teacher training responsibilities in his celebrated philology seminar. Intent on forming philologists who could wield specialized research techniques, Boeckh had apparently failed to comment on his students' basic command of Latin, a professional liability for any student hoping to secure a position at a *Gymnasium*, since the exams required students to write essays and conduct oral interviews in the language of classical Rome.[43]

Unsurprisingly, then, some critics complained that philology seminars focused unduly on method and technical problems, reducing bigger questions about how ancient Greek and Roman literature could teach one how to live to personal afterthoughts. Pure research, it appeared, had become its own form of narrow vocationalism. Max Müller, a scholar of Hindu and comparative religion who had studied philology at the University of Berlin around this time, later recalled, "What Latin vowels could or could not form elision in Horace or Ovid was a subject that cost me much labor, and yet left very small results as far as I was personally concerned. One clever conjecture . . . was rewarded" with the highest praise, "but a paper on Aeschylus and his view of a divine government of the world received nothing but nodding approval."[44] Under such circumstances, how would students and their teachers attain the "inner knowledge" that, for Humboldt, "transforms character"?[45]

Some philologists defiantly claimed that technical training in philological methods was fully consonant with *Bildung* as Humboldt had conceived of it. Boeckh insisted that "no problem is too small for philology," arguing that scholars could find the macrocosm in the microcosm and connect learning to life.[46] Specialized philological work could seem, however, not only micrological but also "mechanical," an aspirational notion for the acclaimed scholar Karl Lachmann, who sometimes suggested that he wanted to eliminate any trace of subjective contemplation from the process of reconstructing ancient texts.[47] "We both can and must," wrote Lachmann, "edit without interpreting."[48]

In the 1830s the cultural standing and epistemic authority of philology and history continued to increase thanks in part to acts of disciplinary self-assertion like Leopold von Ranke's famous distinction between historical and philosophical knowledge and Boeckh's regular lectures on philology's exemplary role as a modern discipline.[49] These were among the first systematic attempts to model modern academic disciplines, articulating and organizing discipline-specific methods, traditions, and practices for new generations of young scholars. These efforts helped establish the authority, legitimacy, and prestige of philology and history but did little to articulate, much less to establish, such authority and prestige for these disciplines as a set of related forms of knowledge or parts of a collective project, what only decades later and under different circumstances would be called *die Geistes-wissenschaften* ("the humanities").

Although the neo-humanist university reformers offered neither a unified concept of systematic thought nor a common and fully coherent account of their most basic ideals, they did identify philosophy as the university's unifying agent. They thought philosophy enabled communication across disciplines and sustained the collective striving they prized as an ethical good and source of meaning. Lecturing in 1802, Friedrich Schelling had asserted that philosophy makes possible "knowledge of the organic whole of all sciences."[50] Echoing Schelling years later, Schleiermacher proposed that every professor, regardless of faculty or discipline, not only be capable of lecturing but also be permitted to lecture in the philosophy faculty. These regular appeals to philosophy, however, didn't entail a commitment to a particular system or even a shared set of arguments—Kant's so-called critical system or Fichte's idealism. When the neo-humanist reformers invoked the university's need for philosophy, they sought to induce a particular desire and prompt a distinct disposition, both of which were best expressed by the ideal of the unity of knowledge, as discussed in the previous chapter.

## THE COST OF SPECIALIZATION

By the mid-1830s, however, philosophy had begun to lose its privileged position in the scholarly imagination. Physiologists such as Hermann Helmholtz and Emil Du Bois-Reymond would soon claim that natural scientists would be the ones finally to unify the sciences and disciplines. Their "unification enthusiasm" was as consequential as the one more commonly associated with idealist philosophers like Schelling.[51] In Helmholtz's view, moreover, theoretically informed empiricism could attain the highest levels of disciplinary knowledge and scholarship; it could also serve as the basis of moral education or *Bildung* or self-formation. Yet it wasn't until the second half of the nineteenth century, when industry lobbyists began pressuring the German state to support research with immediate technological applications, that the natural sciences became funding magnets. Helmholtz, for example, received 1.5 million marks for a physics institute in the 1870s. But looking back in 1893 on the restoration period as rector of the University of Berlin, Rudolf Virchow identified 1827 as *the* moment of transition from the "era of philosophy" to that of the natural sciences.[52]

Wilhelm von Humboldt probably would have agreed that a profound shift had occurred, although he would not have shared Virchow's apparent triumphalism. In 1831 he said that regardless of their individual disciplinary affiliation, members of the Prussian Academy of Sciences had until recently considered themselves parts of one body with common aims. Now, he lamented, the Academy had effectively split into two groups, with members of the historical and philological section on the one side and members of the natural sciences section on the other, each group treating the other "as an adversary."[53] This atmosphere of fragmentation did not just permeate conflicts between disciplines; it developed within certain individual disciplines as well. This was especially the case in philology, where scholars equipped with critical methodologies and techniques to identify errors and corruptions in old editions of ancient texts and establish genealogies used their tools on (or against) one other to establish the disciplinary excellence of their own scholarship. Even a scholar as widely admired as Boeckh—who served as the rector of the University of Berlin five times—had to contend with the charge of dilettantism. Things got bad enough that an annual conference of philologists to foster collegiality was instituted in 1838.

Yet Altenstein committed to philosophy. He believed it could discipline the disciplines and as well as students' youthful fantasies and nationalist fervor into rational and devoted service to the state. He admired Hegel most of all and continued to advance the philosopher's cause even after his death, appointing one of his most conservative students, a so-called Right Hegelian, to his vacant chair in 1835.[54] The appointment led to charges of favoritism as well as to the perception that speculative philosophy would maintain its canonical status at Prussian universities even after Hegel's death. Altenstein thought otherwise. In 1837 he wrote to the king to request that civil service examinees be required to have a thorough "allgemeine Bildung," or liberal education, with a strong philosophical component. He supported his position by rephrasing a series of now standard neo-humanist claims: a "high level of liberal education" on the part of civil servants would enable different sectors of the government bureaucracy to understand their interconnectedness and function as "a whole." Furthermore, Prussian bureaucrats would command more "respect" from society generally if they had had a liberal education rather than a merely professional one. Yet Altenstein also acknowledged how unpopular philosophy had become. Tenacious as always, but now sounding rather forlorn, he reasoned that if people were going to criticize philosophy as a "blight," they should at least know something about it.[55]

A few years later the philosopher Henrich Steffens, an important figure in the conversation about university reform around 1810, evoked the 1820s and 1830s as a time of dying intellectual dreams. In a memoir composed in the early 1840s, he wrote that the previous decades had seen the "disappearance" of the "inner unity of all scholarship, which was my animating principle and played a decisive part during the founding of the University of Berlin."[56] Altenstein's successor as minister of culture, Joseph von Eichhorn, also claimed that German universities had declined, victims of the lecture's stultifying pedagogy. Eichhorn was much more conservative and committed to the state than Altenstein, but he sought to ensure what he called in 1844 the "double vocation" of universities "to foster" scholarly knowledge and "to prepare" young men to serve both the state and the church.[57] Working with King Friedrich Wilhelm IV, he thought the best way to do so was to assert further state control over the university.

It was in this context that Eichhorn lured the veteran system builder Schelling to the University of Berlin in the hope that his natural philosophy would have a moderating influence on students and, given his turn to religion late in life, inject a measure of piety into the academic environment. Eichhorn wasn't the only one with outsized expectations. Crowds of more than four hundred turned out for Schelling's first lectures in 1841, among them Friedrich Engels, but his listeners soon lost interest. Within two years, his audiences numbered in the lower double digits.

There was irony in Eichhorn's attempt to recover something of the high-minded neo-humanist reform ideals: Schelling's hiring was a symptom of an emerging star system that contributed to the sense of the fragmentation and loss of purpose constantly lamented by critics such as Steffens. During Altenstein's long tenure the importance of a professor's disciplinary standing—won through national renown achieved through print—rose while that of his collegiate standing, achieved through dedicated service to an individual institution, decreased. Prolific researchers thought to be inept at teaching or administrative work were promoted over their colleagues' objections.[58] With professorial mobility less restricted than in the previous century, producing research through publication, not changing lives in the classroom, became the surest path to a lucrative offer from a rival university.[59] Although Schelling was known for the abstract, mystical character of his writings—Heine called him "Confucius"—he proved adept at this financial game. In 1841 he negotiated a contract that made him the highest-paid professor at the University of Berlin; indeed, not until 1910 would any professor at the university land a more lucrative one. Schelling's contract also allowed him to keep his position at the University of Munich.

The academic job market evolved in tandem with the culture of disciplinary specialization. With the formalization of the right to lecture in 1816, young scholars hoping to qualify as private docents or adjunct lecturers were required to prove their mastery over a highly focused domain. Henceforth, the right to lecture was granted only to specialized scholars. The road to attaining even the precarious, unsalaried position of private docent had become much longer and more difficult, but it culminated in a credential that accorded status and marked whoever had it as a highly trained professional—trained, that is, to do one thing: be an academic.[60] Such an investment of time and effort made other lines of work unattractive. Our contemporary system of reliance on adjunct professors and precarious labor has its roots in these earlier forms of exploitation. Private docents and adjunct lecturers merged as a specialized, committed, flexible, and inexpensive labor force as adjunct teaching positions increased much faster than professorships. Between 1810 and 1835, student enrollment at the University of Berlin went from 262 to nearly 1,800. The ratio of nonregular faculty to regular faculty changed from 1 to 1 to about 3 to 1, with private docents and lecturers constituting the fastest-growing group, especially in the faculty of arts and sciences. By 1855 the number of lecturers in that faculty had increased fivefold since 1810 while the number of regular professors hadn't quite doubled: The latter figure stood at only 24.[61]

Private docents and lecturers received no regular salaries, only lecture fees, but the full professors took the highest-enrolling and therefore most remunerative courses for themselves. Demanding a more equitable distribution of power, the junior faculty at the University of Berlin revolted in 1848.[62] In the meantime, lecturers, many of them living on the edge of destitution, had strong incentives to use their teaching to advance their research by choosing specialized topics. Mixing a managerialist insistence on measurable results with liberal thinking, Altenstein rewarded work that was quite literally presentable—his was a no book, no promotion system—but he also valued academic self-regulation.[63] If younger scholars were to move up the ranks, their work had to impress experts, which generally entailed remaining within a disciplinary paradigm. Furthermore, the climate of political distrust only encouraged scholarship of a technical nature among desperate job seekers.

Student life was also out of step with the ethical and intellectual designs of the reformers. Published in 1835, the popular novel *Felix Schnabel's University Years* uses the revered phrase "scholarly education" (*wissenschaftliche Ausildung*) to satirize days spent drinking large quantities of beer and not studying interspersed with days spent drinking massive amounts of coffee and trying to memorize information for state exams.[64] A tight job market for university graduates had encouraged a culture of studying for the test, and that, the novel suggests, is what a "scholarly education" mostly consists of. The year before *Felix Schnabel* appeared, Prussia's Abitur Edict had mandated that admission to a university would require students to go through the secondary schools (*Gymnasien*) Humboldt had designed to promote *Bildung*, which were supposed to ennoble young scholars and pave the way for further ennoblement at the university. For observers like Adolph Diesterweg, who had studied with Schleiermacher and directed a teacher training seminar in Berlin, something had gone wrong. In 1835 the faculty of law at the University of Berlin, perhaps the most professional of the faculties, had almost twice as many students as the philosophy (or arts and sciences) faculty. University students seemed interested in learning only for the sake of gaining career advantages.

## DIESTERWEG AND THE LITERATURE OF DECLINE

Diesterweg's book *The Rot at German Universities*, which appeared in 1836, registers all the anxieties and conflicts that we have been discussing. Invoking his idol Schleiermacher, Diesterweg vigorously juxtaposes his reading of neo-humanist educational ideas to what he considers the research and teaching practices dominating Prussian academia in the 1830s. The purpose of a university education, he writes, is twofold. First, the university should cultivate in students "genuine systematic and critical thinking" (*ächte Wissenchaftlichkeit*), whose most basic feature is the "capacity to think for oneself."[65] Second, the university should form students pedagogically, that is, develop their character. Diesterweg sometimes combines the two under the now familiar notion of *wissenschaftliche Bildung*, a phrase one might translate, accurately if not elegantly, as "liberal education with an emphasis on scholarly thinking."[66] Today, in 1836, Diesterweg maintains, universities do neither. He attributes this failure in part to external circumstances beyond the university's control. The "reigning spirit of the most recent past," which he sees as marked by superficiality, "manifests itself" in the university's problems.[67] Nevertheless, professors are largely to blame for the lamentable state of higher education, which, he notes, directly contributes to the stagnation of contemporary society. More than anyone else, professors are in a position to break the cycle of mutually reinforcing sociocultural and educational decline, but they refuse to do so.

How exactly are professors failing to halt cultural decline? Diesterweg points to the culture of specialized research and universities' habit of hiring almost exclusively on the basis of research productivity. Because teaching and research require different capacities, the system saddles universities with men like Hegel, whom Diesterweg calls "one of the worst teachers in history."[68] Between university philosophers spinning incomprehensible abstractions and the philologists and historians who treat all students like future members of their profession, assailing them with "barren facts" and technical training that feels like "manual labor," German universities actively discourage free, independent thinking. No wonder, he reckons, so many students spend their days drinking instead of attending lectures and eventually repudiate the life of the mind.

Diesterweg wants every student to engage actively with big ideas and questions, to develop independently a sense of the unity of knowledge, guided by expert teachers who speak and think in clear terms. Hence, he argues that the lecture system should be abandoned in favor of "dialogic" education. Doing so, he contends, would push students closer to the true end of knowledge, but he also acknowledges that the recent increases in university enrollments would complicate a complete transition from lectures to seminars. Liberal education derives much of its moral authority from its democratic aspirations and virtues but is difficult to scale up. (Even Bloom, in his elitist way, tried to ground his case for liberal education in a good-for-democracy argument.) Pushing against Schleiermacher's ideal of research for its own sake in order to salvage his own notion of *Bildung* as moral transformation, Diesterweg argues that students and teachers interested in a real, transformative education should reflect on how their pursuit of knowledge intensifies their intellectual powers and experience of life.[69] (There's a reason many scholars have preferred his writings about education to Nietzsche's.[70])

Many obstacles stood in the way of the reforms Diesterweg demanded in *The Rot at German Universities*. For Diesterweg, the late 1830s were not only a time of general cultural malaise; they were also a time inhospitable to the ideas that simultaneously foster intellectual independence and character formation in the classroom. Lessing's and Kant's thought, which enjoyed such importance during "the good old days," as Diesterweg puts it without irony, had been pushed to the margins in a time that routinely mistook signs of specialized expertise, such as opacity, for depth of knowledge and intellectual creativity. Even the culture of student debauchery that raged during that earlier time somehow seems less appalling than its counterpart in the 1830s. The reason, Diesterweg conjectures, is that professors don't devote their energy and time to teaching and developing the character of their students because professors know that only research will advance them professionally. He writes that many professors aren't bothered by the sight of students sleeping in class or carving messages into their seats. This is what the student experience of "academic freedom" has come to: freedom from all authority, guidance, and formation. Universities are no longer sacred communities held together through shared sources of authority and common purposes. They have become modern institutions in which individuals pursue their own purposes largely unaware of and so uninterested in the desires of others, much less those of a community.[71]

To be sure, some professors do care about teaching, but only, contends Diesterweg, as a means of drawing bigger lecture fees. For professors, students are "just numbers." Instructors give students what they want, not what they need, in order to attract the maximum head count, even if that means "flattering today's idols." By asking little while freely offering praise, professors position themselves to serve on exam committees, for which they receive additional fees. Even before grades, what amounted to grade inflation was a serious blight in Diesterweg's telling.[72]

Furthermore, the new mobility of professors has made institutional loyalty and collegiality obsolete. The very people who are supposed to display the ennobling effects of studying ancient literature move restlessly from position to position, chasing ever-higher salaries while neglecting to form meaningful personal connections with students and colleagues. Should it surprise anyone, Diesterweg repeatedly asks, when students decide what and how to study based on material concerns?[73] They are doing what they see their teachers do.

Diesterweg's book doesn't only feature a whole constellation of complaints that we find in more contemporary accounts of the university's decline; it also shares certain failures with its descendants. Some are obvious: pervasive exaggeration, a critique of cultural superficiality that is itself often superficial, a near total reliance on anecdotal evidence, and a general humorlessness. Other problems are more subtle. One is the unacknowledged tension between promoting the capacities necessary for "rational" and "critical thinking" and calling for the kind of "faith and piety" toward the material of the humanities assumed to permit transformative experiences in the seminar room. Diesterweg enjoins professors to model independent critical thinking for students; he also exhorts them to become "priests of ideas."[74] We want to consider a related but different tension, contradiction even, that characterizes Diesterweg's book as well as the work of several contemporary chroniclers of liberal education in crisis: despite a professed commitment to it, there is a confused attitude toward academic freedom.

## ACADEMIC FREEDOM AND THE MANDARINS' DILEMMA

For Diesterweg, liberal education relies on academic freedom. At the core of liberal education is open-ended exploration, especially of big ideas.[75] For students to realize their own *Bildung* in the neo-humanist sense, the university classroom must be a radically free space regardless of whether the learning and teaching taking place in it constitute or are grounded in original research.[76] Yet even if creating new knowledge isn't a professor's or an institution's primary goal, wherever students and teachers act, writes Diesterweg, as "free inquiring scholars," there will always exist the possibility of new knowledge.[77] Liberal education relies on the freedom of scholars and students to transform old knowledge and to create new knowledge, to engage in a form of inquiry whose end point and ultimate conclusions they do not know. Liberal education relies, then, on an appeal to those people and institutions empowered to grant and sustain such unencumbered inquiry.

Significantly, neither Schleiermacher nor Humboldt, among the first to underscore the unending and open-ended nature of research, appealed to the corporate privilege of scholars in making the case for academic freedom to the Prussian state. Neither claimed that scholars had a right or a legitimate claim to academic freedom strictly because they were members of a legally recognized corporate body. In making their cases for academic freedom, they appealed, rather, directly to the interests of that agent they considered most capable of safeguarding such freedom: the state. They argued that the state would more probably get the knowledge that it wanted and that society needed if the state didn't interfere with the creation of scientific and scholarly knowledge.[78] With this frankly pragmatic conception of what justifies academic freedom — recognizing and acknowledging who has the political and social power to guarantee the type of scholarly inquiry they valued — they sought to secure for scholars an institutional space in which modern disciplinary knowledge could be practiced with an open horizon in which conventional wisdom and fixed opinion would inevitably be upset. They conceived of academic freedom in terms similar to those of Richard Hofstadter and Walter Metzger, who in 1955 wrote about the "searching function" of academic freedom.[79] In short, the modern notion of academic freedom referred most properly to an unbounded pursuit or search for knowledge and found its justification in an appeal to the interests of those agencies considered most capable of protecting it.

Humboldt's commitment to academic freedom compelled him to link research with liberal instruction—the endless pursuit of knowledge with teaching—in the modern university. Uniting them, he thought, bolstered the latter's claims on freedom. Indeed, it's this notion of academic freedom that found its way into the Prussian constitution of 1850, which plainly states, "Disciplinary scholarship and its findings are free." It is also the notion that Diesterweg, who was pushed out of his position in 1848 because of his liberal views, himself presumed. Where he defines academic freedom, he speaks of the imperative "not to limit" scholarship and the importance of freely conveying its results. In addition, he repeatedly associates the freedom of liberal education with the searching function ideal, writing, for example, that the goal of liberal education is "to be become free through searching for truth."[80] Open-ended intellectual searching—discussion, reading, and thinking, whose conclusions and purposes even only unfold over time—liberates faculty and students alike for self-development in this model in a way nothing else seems to.

We discuss mid- and late nineteenth-century mandarin writings on the university in subsequent chapters. Let us now jump forward to the second decade of the twenty-first century, where we can observe much the same tension we found in Diesterweg's account persisting in mandarin literature of liberal education's decline. In 2014, William Deresiewicz won acclaim and a large readership for his book *Excellent Sheep*. An essay adapted from it in the *New Republic* quickly became the most online viewed piece in that magazine's history. Deresiewicz argues that in the era of neoliberalism, our best universities are chasing prestige and wealth as never before. Thus, they pour resources into eye-catching campus amenities with no educational significance and, at the expense of the liberal arts, build up the professional programs that appeal to their students, who are themselves creatures of the neoliberal era, one in which the only value that matters is market value, though to their credit many universities seem to be struggling with that.

Similarly, most professors, in Deresiewicz's view, focus on specialized research, which is the means to higher standing within their disciplines and the path to success as academic entrepreneurs. In this they are abetted by their employers, because the prestige of universities remains largely a function of research productivity (and research dollars generated). What has gotten lost is the kind of education that fosters intellectual independence and character development—the very things, in short, that might lead today's students to demand such an education. Like many other critics, Deresiewicz compares the plight of the humanities and "real education" in the present with the situation in the 1960s, which he presents as a golden age of rising enrollments and genuine curiosity. Yet he fails to mention the publication and success of books in the 1960s such as J. H. Plumb's *The Crisis of the Humanities* and Daniel Bell's report on the crisis of the general education system at Columbia University. Among Columbia's problems, according to Bell, was a crushing lack of engagement on the part of vocationally oriented students.[81]

If *Excellent Sheep* struck a chord, it also had its skeptics. One of the more prominent was the Harvard psychologist Steven Pinker. Without invoking the German sociologist directly, Pinker identified himself with a purportedly Weberian tradition of understanding how university study should work, a tradition whose key text has long been *Scholarship as Vocation* (1919). Drawing on a series of prior reflections on academic freedom, Weber tried to realign neo-humanist educational ideals amid social disarray at a time when the unity of teaching and research seemed to be coming undone. He argued that professors should teach students how to think systematically about the material they present in the classroom and should train more advanced students in specialized methods. Other things, like the soul building Deresiewicz advocated, exceed the capacities and responsibilities of the university. Pinker asked, What does it even mean "to build a self or become a soul"?[82] What would qualify professors to help with that?

Deresiewicz parried that liberal education should indeed have a strong character-formation component, and shame on Pinker for thinking otherwise. Liberal higher education should entail "moral education," as he put it. And moral education will only flourish far away from the Pinkers of academia.[83] Deresiewicz's message is clear: the research imperative is bad for transformative liberal education at the undergraduate level, or, again, for "real education." In his book he maintains that the "foundational compromise" of US higher education—"housing a liberal arts college at a research university," linking the creation of new knowledge to teaching—has "proved untenable."[84] He made the point a little more obliquely but just as emphatically in his exchange with Pinker.

Like Diesterweg, however, Deresiewicz hesitated at a crucial moment, implicitly aligning himself with the same Weberian outlook that had been marshaled against him. Weber himself had wanted universities only to promote scholarly values and virtues, those necessary for a culture of research, such as openness, "intellectual honesty," independence, and attention to detail. The flip side of his position is that those same values would be difficult to cultivate without freedom. This is what Weber meant when, in an essay on threats to academic freedom, he wrote of how such "a castration of the freedom and impartiality of university education . . . can crush the development of students' own distinct character."[85] The key point is that when Deresie-wicz named the values that universities should cultivate in their students, he enumerated the same scholarly ones Weber had singled out, maintaining that moral education "develops students' abilities to make autonomous choices—to determine [their] own beliefs, independent of parents, peers, and society."[86] Standing in a Munich lecture hall almost exactly one hundred years earlier, Weber had told the university instructors in attendance that "our aim must be to enable the student to discover the vantage point from which he can judge the matter in light of his own ultimate ideals."[87]

Deresiewicz presented himself as attempting to recover a tradition of American moral education that predates and clashes with research culture. As an advocate of open-ended liberal study that fosters the development of character, of general liberal education, however, he fell into the same contradictions as Diesterweg. Both argue that liberal education is at odds with the research imperative, and yet both in effect acknowledge that the very possibility of liberal education requires the ideals and norms that constitute the modern research university and, in particular, the research imperative and the intellectual freedom to which it lays claim. As Edward Said suggests in a late essay, thinking about academic freedom is "different in each society," and certainly academic freedom had meanings in restoration Prussia that it doesn't in the United States today.[88] Yet a central notion of it has persisted across cultural divides—Joan Scott's fairly recent definition sounds a lot like Diesterweg's: "academic freedom protects those whose thinking challenges orthodoxy."[89] Attempting to inculcate comprehensive and ultimate moral commitments and to stipulate how students ought to lead their lives clashes with the searching ideal on which academic freedom in the modern research university relies. Deresiewicz's case for college fits not so much with the classical American college tradition of moral education as with the one in which his Weberian antagonists stand. After all, with their fixed curricula and focus on student discipline, classical American colleges sought to form Christian gentlemen committed to a broadly Protestant morality, character, and dogma, not independent thinkers committed to scholarly ideas and the creation of new knowledge.

Imported to the United States by figures such as Henry Tappan and established through a complex, ongoing process of reappropriation, educational ideals developed in Germany around 1800 have helped bring about astonishing things, like libraries with seven million volumes rising out of cornfields in the Midwest. In the late nineteenth century, Tappan's University of Michigan became, as Clark Kerr put it, "a German-style university," while Harvard transformed itself into "a land grant type of institution, without the land."[90]

Yet in both the United States and Germany, the project of modern liberal education at the postsecondary level proceeded under intense pressures. At the beginning of the twentieth century, as William Rainey Harper was shaping the University of Chicago into an institution devoted to research but also to professional and undergraduate education and being a good community partner, his counterpart at the University of Illinois was doing otherwise. Andrew Draper, a university president without a college education, inveighed against liberal learning and research as "cultivated aimlessness" that led away from the "virile life" and was bad for society.[91] In taking this position, he could count on political support, much to the dismay of some humanities scholars, both real and fictional. Having modeled the school in her novel *The Professor's House* on the University of Illinois of Draper's day, Willa Cather has her narrator sigh, "The state legislature and the board of regents seemed determined to make a trade school of the university."[92]

The pushback against the complex system that has enabled liberal education to survive hasn't only come from those who want higher education to be oriented toward professional or vocational study. Humanities scholars, too, have called for the end of this system of competing yet mutually dependent ideals that has been at the heart of liberal higher education in the United States (even more than in Germany). In effect, both Diesterweg and Deresiewicz's narratives of decline conclude with a call that the pursuit of research be decoupled from the shaping of students' souls or teaching.

As the response to Deresiewicz's book suggests, the lament articulated in *Excellent Sheep* still resonates. Even in the era of neoliberalism, the character-building ideal of *Bildung* has significant bipartisan middlebrow support. Deresiewicz sees himself as a progressive antielitist, but he invokes Bloom, with whom he shares a number of basic views, as an ally.[93] Thus, books that decry the culture of specialized research in the name of a classical *Bildung* and moral education can win a broad audience, particularly if they can present the crisis of *Bildung* in higher education as a symptom of a larger cultural crisis that a return to *Bildung* might help to solve.

Melancholy mandarins, as we have observed, often position themselves outside the academic mainstream: Diesterweg, Bloom, and Deresiewicz certainly do. Yet calls to recommit to a value-centered, moral education have also come from the ultimate insiders of American higher education. After having expressed her concern that democracy around the world was breaking down, former Harvard president Drew Gilpin Faust warned colleagues, students, and their parents at a 2016 commencement ceremony that "with the rise of the research university in the late nineteenth and early twentieth century, moral and ethical purposes came to be seen as at odds with the scientific thinking transforming higher education. But in today's

world I believe it is dangerous for universities not to embrace their responsibilities to service and values as well as to reason and discovery."[94]

## IN PRAISE OF PERMANENT TENSIONS

Moral education and scholarly sensibilities did, in fact, clash at US universities during the period of institutional remaking Faust refers to. Nonetheless, it's striking to read a distinguished historian of that era brushing aside
the complicated, backbreaking, yet fairly successful attempt by institutions
such as her own to combine "moral purpose" and "reason and discovery,"
teaching and unbounded inquiry. As much as he was committed to the endless pursuit of knowledge, William Rainey Harper drew on Fichte's talk of the
university's secular holiness in the service of an ethical mission, invoking
for higher education the role of "Messiah of democracy."[95] He may have
worked himself to an early death trying to calibrate the University of Chicago's commitment to the ideals of research and moral education. Andrew
Dickson White, Cornell University's founding president, campaigned aggressively against what he asserted was religion's war on science, acquiring many enemies along the way. Yet he never understood this struggle on
behalf of research to mean that universities didn't have a responsibility to
"service and values" as well as moral education. White wanted to make the
modern university a place where "the most highly prized instruction may
be afforded to all—regardless of color or sex," which, of course, won him yet
more enemies.[96] He claimed that American universities could achieve both
liberal and practical ends but only if they could overcome what had always
held them back: the sectarian college system. Confessional and sectarian
religious institutions and traditions, White argued, had prevented American universities from becoming "nurseries of the love of learning and the
love of freedom [like the] great universities of Germany."[97] The emergent
research university nurtured ideals, loves, and values of its own.

Recognizing this fact renders the absolute distinctions—drawn by melancholy mandarins such as Diesterweg and Deresiewicz—between research
and liberal learning or moral education a false one. Universities shouldn't
try to deliver ready-made worldviews or inculcate in students ultimate moral
values. This constraint, however, does not mean, as we show in detail in
chapter 6, that universities are descriptively or normatively amoral and ethically neutral institutions. To the contrary, rightly understood, the modern research university is distinguished by particular ideals, practices, and values,
and its purpose is the advancement of scholarship and the education of students according to scholarly norms. Put differently, the moral purpose of the

research university is to inculcate a distinctive character, to form students into mature, independent, self-reflective subjects with the capacity to think clearly and understand their own ultimate values. These are not ultimate ends or values, and yet they are ends and values nonetheless.

The failure to recognize the ways in which the modern research university tied epistemological claims to ethical ones and knowledge to character helps account for another key feature of the melancholy mandarins' lament. In contrast to White's antipathy toward the historical relationship between sectarian religion and American higher education, the melancholy mandarins have always maintained a more ambivalent relationship to religion. From Diesterweg to Nietzsche and Deresiewicz, the melancholy mandarins have worried that a "real" liberal education cannot be sustained without the common social bonds, moral resources, and practices that religious traditions have historically provided to (and denied) particular groups. Diesterweg criticized the state's use of public schools as a mechanism for religious indoctrination under the famously pious Friedrich Wilhelm IV—this stance cost Diesterweg his position as the director of a teacher training institute in 1847. Nevertheless, he concludes his reckoning with the modern university with the question of whether or not "religion [is] . . . an indispensable, necessary means for achieving *Bildung*." Given the wanton lifestyles of students, the lack of coherent curricula, and the indifference of entrepreneurial professors toward moral education, should religion, in some ecumenical form of Christianity, "return to universities . . . as lectures, church services, and classes"?[98] Could religion in such form ground university curricula and moral education? These are clearly pressing questions for Diesterweg—and open ones, too; he doesn't try to answer them.

In the nearly two centuries since the publication of *The Rot at German Universities*, melancholy mandarins have consistently returned to these same questions, routinely pointing to "religious" colleges and universities as the last bastions of coherent curricula and moral education and wondering whether any purportedly secular attempts at unity and coherence simply draw parasitically on religious traditions. If some advocates of *Bildung*—Deresiewicz, the professor of American studies Andrew Delbanco[99]—have remained ambivalent about the necessary relationship between universities and religions, however, another group of contemporary critics has not. Working through a framework mostly borrowed from Alasdair MacIntyre, the historian Brad Gregory, for example, has recently described the university as the "secular . . . domain of Weberian facts, not values—except contradictorily, for the one hegemonic and supreme value that no judgments about competing truth claims pertaining to values or morality should or can be made." Knowledge in the "Western world," Gregory writes, is characterized by its "separateness and separability both from the uses to which it is put, and from the personal lives, particular beliefs, social practices, and specific commitments of those who create and transmit it." Knowledge is thus distinct from morality—from questions about how one ought to live, and why. "Research and education across the entire domain of knowledge is separable from and independent of the rest of human life."[100] Gregory can dismiss such specialization, fragmentation, atomism, and plurality because he seems to at least intimate the truth of a mostly implicit Catholic Thomism.

One doesn't have to share Gregory's implicit confessional commitments (or any solutions he suggests follow from them) to sympathize with elements of his appraisal. In fact, different commitments have led to similar diagnoses of the condition of the modern university and the prospects for intellectual vocation. The literary scholar Thomas Pfau eloquently explains how this can be so:

> For the past two decades or so, the majority of those working in the humanities and the interpretive social sciences have witnessed the value of focused and sustained learning and the integrity of fields be progressively diluted and frittered away by an increasingly separate class of professional administrators. The prevailing impression is one of administrative hubris and a top-down, micro-managerial approach intent on fitting academic research on the Procrustean bed of donor-driven funding models and neo-utilitarian criteria of "relevance." Is it not, then, at least plausible that one should want to inquire into the deep genealogy that has caused higher education to be redefined as a corporate endeavor, and knowledge as some amorphous "experience" pragmatically peddled in the academic marketplace? . . . Is Gregory not right to worry "how the *kinds* of knowledge thereby gained in different disciplines might fit together, or whether the disciplines' respective, contrary claims and incompatible assumptions might be resolved"? . . . Do we not ignore at our own peril Augustine's distinction between the intrinsically normative intellectual virtue of *studiositas* and a strictly procedural, agnostic quest for new information (*curiositas*)?[101]

Although we would challenge much of Gregory's history and reject most of the conclusions he draws from it, we agree with Pfau when he enjoins us to take positions like Gregory's seriously, to try to understand the deep roots and durability of Gregory's sense of lack. The crises of the university (and especially the humanities) aren't spontaneous events; they are consistent features of the modern university and the kinds of knowledge it produces. More specifically, despite all the persistent features of the melancholy mandarins' lament and the historical insight they can provide, one important point has largely been lost—an awareness of the limits of universities. Although Diesterweg devotes most of his repining to an account of the civilizational ruin embodied in universities, he qualifies his complaint. The education of the young and maintenance and development of the broader culture aren't the responsibility of professors and universities; they are the responsibility of the "entire culture" and the "life" that all people lead. "No educational institution, no lecture, no method can replace whatever is missing in these institutions, social relationships, in life, in the mind and spirit."[102] In a way, Diesterweg was right. The danger that modern universities have faced over the subsequent decades and centuries isn't simply the gap between ideals and reality, specialization, bureaucratic expansion, or fragmentation; the peril lies, rather, in the explosion of expectations and the overpromising done on their behalf.

Nowhere did the explosion of overpromising and inflated expectations become more definitive and onerous than in what came to be called, in the nineteenth and early twentieth centuries, the humanities. It was in this period that the humanities came to stand in for liberal education as such, a stance the melancholy mandarins have never tired of reasserting. "Teaching and the humanities," Deresiewicz declares, are the "meat, the middle, of a liberal arts experience." They constitute college and everything that college has come to evoke.[103] This was not always the case. Similarly exclusive claims were rarely made on behalf of earlier humanistic forms of knowledge such as the *studia humanitatis*. In the following chapters, we consider how the modern humanities took shape as the conceptual and institutional domain for much of the overpromising of universities and the locus for questions about how to live, ideals, and values. The humanities came to stand in for the contradictions and tensions that, as we have traced in this chapter, characterized nineteenth-century liberal education or *allgemeine Bildung*: tensions between method, research, and ways of knowing on the one hand and ethos, teaching, and questions of how to live on the other. The scholars who helped establish "the humanities" as a distinct institutional domain within the modern university and identified themselves with it gradually claimed (and sometimes gained) a monopoly over these questions and concerns, especially as other scholars (natural and physical scientists in particular) began to regard such questions as outside their own domains (witness Pinker). Yet the academics who did so much to make the humanities

possible within universities also inherited all of the contradictions and confusions that beset Diesterweg in the 1830s. We can see this most clearly in
understanding how the thinking about crisis and decline among German
intellectuals and scholars shaped the actual practice of scholarship in the
decades that followed.

## CHAPTER THREE

# Philology and Modernity

In January 1869 Friedrich Nietzsche was offered a professorship in classical philology at the University of Basel. Just twenty-four and lacking a completed dissertation, Nietzsche was thrilled.[1] Upon learning the news, he sang melodies from his favorite opera, *Tannhäuser*. The position had, to be sure, what some scholars might have considered a drawback. In addition to teaching eight hours a week at the university, Nietzsche would be required to give another six hours of Greek language instruction at a local *Gymnasium* (known in Basel as the *Pädagogium*). Nietzsche told Friedrich Ritschl, his dissertation supervisor at the University of Leipzig and one of Germany's leading philologists, that that would be fine. Ritschl enthusiastically passed the message on to the selection committee along with his imprimatur, and the appointment was made.

Since Ritschl was, as he put it, "willing to stake" his "whole reputation on the hire turning out to be a success," he must have been confident, when Nietzsche set off for Basel, that he had just helped launch another brilliant academic career.[2] But not long after assuming his professorship, Nietzsche began to show signs of disillusionment with the kind of work—studies of Diogenes Laërtius, contributions to an Aeschylus lexicon, analyses of Roman and Greek meter—that had prompted his mentor to tout him as the most precocious student he had ever encountered. It was at this time that he pledged to "publicly expose" the whole Prussian system of education.[3] He soon made good on his promise in a five-part lecture series at Basel's city museum in the winter of 1872 titled *On the Future of Our Educational Institutions*. Speaking before appreciative crowds numbering nearly three hundred, Nietzsche took aim at the three principal components of Prussia's celebrated pedagogical system: the *Realschule*, the *Gymnasium*, and the university.[4]

Nietzsche's lectures didn't portend a clean break. He continued to profess admiration for Ritschl, and for years he wrote his adviser to express his desire to return to the kind of philological study at which he had excelled as a student. In developing his ideas about history, human perception, and moral psychology, moreover, Nietzsche would draw on an array of academic works in philosophy, philology, and the natural sciences. But he had become, and would remain, deeply suspicious of modern scholarly knowledge—of *Wissenschaft*.

As for the ancient world, Nietzsche's love of antiquity was lifelong, and he kept trying to make sense of the paradoxes and problems of modernity by engaging with ancient Greek literature. If his earliest publications lack the rhetorical brilliance and exhortatory mode of address of his later works, both sets of writings, as James Porter has shown, often take up the relationship between antiquity and modernity.[5] Receiving less attention have been the continuities in Nietzsche's specific claims about the role of scholarly knowledge in that relationship. By the time he delivered *On the Future of Our Educational Institutions*, Nietzsche had already come to regard modern education and academic knowledge as both crucial symptoms and drivers of processes—above all, secularization, rationalization, and democratization—that cut off modern Europeans from the resources of antiquity. As he exclaims in the lectures, "philologists perish and are reduced to dust due to the Greeks—we can live with that loss. But for antiquity itself to shatter due to the philologists!"[6] There is, however, a crucial twist in the lectures, which Nietzsche conveys more through intimations than explicit arguments. Secularization, rationalization, and democratization, he suggests, also create the very institutional and social conditions that make possible the kind of humanistic *Bildung* and *Wissenschaft*—education and knowledge—that he thinks late nineteenth-century Germans so desperately need.[7]

In the previous chapter we outlined how early nineteenth-century debates about the purposes of the university revolved around competing ideals of liberal education and the relationship between the pursuit of new knowledge conceived of as research and moral education. In this chapter, we trace how these debates developed, in the later nineteenth century, into a related conflict involving two competing notions of the "humanities" (*Humantitäts-bildung*), as Nietzsche sometimes called them. On the one hand there was a broadly humanistic tradition associated with "classical education" and general liberal education: Nietzsche champions an idiosyncratic version of this notion in the Basel lectures. On the other hand there were the modern humanities as a set of previously distinct, highly specialized academic disciplines. Advocates and practitioners of both forms of the humanities understood themselves to be operating in the tradition of neo-humanist ideals; both aspired to provide moral education (*Bildung*) and scholarly knowledge

(*Wissenschaft*). However, each form of the humanities represented a different account of what pursuing those things entailed, what goods they might afford, and how best to engage with what both presumed to be their proper objects of study—the cultural products that provide insight into human beings. Nietzsche's paradoxical relationship with classical philology—his simultaneous embrace and disdain of the discipline—reveals the fault line that emerged in the last third of the nineteenth century between these two forms of the humanities and foreshadows the triumph of the modern humanities over the humanistic forms of knowledge that preceded them.

## THE AMBIVALENT PRODIGY

Nietzsche's lectures on education weren't a farewell to academia, an ur-example of what is now known as "quit lit." He retained his professorship for another seven years, and during that time he took his teaching responsibilities seriously, even formally proposing improvements to the Greek curriculum at the *Gymnasium* where he taught.[8] With *On the Future of Our Educational Institutions*, he joined a reform-minded but increasingly contentious public debate about the German education system rather than opt out. Besides ones that were familiar, he brought commitments and concerns to the discussion that were unorthodox, some of which well predated his Basel appointment.

As pleased as Nietzsche was to be entering the ranks of professional philologists, he had expressed doubts about the field—and his place in it—in the years leading up to his hiring. This was due in no small part to the influence of Arthur Schopenhauer, whose writings Nietzsche first encountered in 1865, and whose originality, stylistic vitality, and aristocratic model of cultural production had made an immediate impression. By the autumn of 1867 Nietzsche was outlining an essay—which he would never complete—on Democritus and the "history of literary studies in antiquity and modernity," the aim of which was to impress "a number of bitter truths" on philologists.[9] The first of these, writes Rüdiger Safranski, a Nietzsche biographer, was that "all enlightening thoughts" come only from a few "great geniuses," "who most assuredly did not pursue philological and historical studies."[10] Nietzsche didn't yet count himself among their number. But he certainly felt inspired by Schopenhauer, and he wondered whether a career in the academic discipline in which he was distinguishing himself would stifle the creative impulses he sensed welling within him.

As Safranski has put it, drawing on Nietzsche's own words, even as a student Nietzsche "began to see himself as a philosophical writer who had moved beyond the confines of philology to a state of 'drifting' into 'the unknown,' with the restless hope of at some point finding a goal at which to rest."[11] Hence, Nietzsche's remark from 1865: "How easy it is to be guided by men like Ritschl, to get pulled away onto the very paths that might be most alien to one's nature."[12]

In short, Nietzsche was ambivalent. Writing to friends and family as a student in Bonn and Leipzig, he had sometimes evoked the brilliance of his professors with breathless enthusiasm, and he engaged intensely with a number of academic works. Yet the writings that really captivated him, such as Friedrich Lange's *History of Materialism* (1866), tended to encourage the epistemological skepticism Schopenhauer had helped to awaken.[13] Lange not only affirmed his affection for Schopenhauer, Nietzsche wrote to a friend in 1866, but modeled how "the most rigorous, critical point of view" could lead not only to tearing down beliefs but also building up and creating new ones.[14] Lange also convinced Nietzsche early on, as Tamsin Shaw has noted, that people had a psychological need for beliefs that could be shared and that constituted a "coherent view of the world."[15] Although a strictly rational form of knowledge might provide the basis for such a shared worldview, only the more philosophically inclined were likely to find it compelling; most other people would long for more. Philosophy, Nietzsche wrote in the winter of 1872–1873, "cannot create a culture"; it could only prepare, sustain, or temper it.[16] Throughout his career, Nietzsche would follow Lange in trying to understand not only how beliefs and ideas erode but also how they become authoritative, legitimate, and effective.[17] By the late 1860s he had begun to distinguish the analysis of concepts and the pursuit of truth from the creation and formulation of ideals and values. "Who," Nietzsche asked, quoting Lange, "wants to refute one of Beethoven's claims, and who wants to find an error in Raphael's Madonna? Art is free, in the realm of concepts, too."[18]

During his time as Ritschl's student, Nietzsche brooded over the idea of doing philology in such a different, dithyrambic key. In July 1868 he confided to Ritschl's wife, "Maybe I will find a philological subject that can be treated musically, and then I will babble like an infant and heap up images like a barbarian who has fallen asleep in front of an antique of Venus, and I will still be in the right despite the 'flourishing haste' of the exposition."[19] A few months later, Nietzsche met Richard Wagner, a fellow admirer of Schopenhauer, and a man he regarded as the rare "living illustration" of what the word "genius" meant. It would be hard to overstate Wagner's importance for Nietzsche over the better part of the next decade, namely, the 1870s. Propelled by an element of personal infatuation—he would write rapturously in his correspondence about evenings spent at the Wagners' home in Tribschen—Nietzsche soon came to see Wagner more or less as Wagner saw himself: as a force for cultural rebirth in a society degraded by a host of "modern" phenomena, such as the press.

Nietzsche's Wagnerian transformation had a profound effect on the young philology professor's relationship to scholarship and the university. Not long after moving to Basel, Nietzsche considered giving up his professorship and embarking on a lecture tour to promote the Wagnerian cause, a project he actually carried out in most of his work until the publication of *Human, All Too Human* (1878). In the second public lecture he delivered in Basel, "Socrates and Tragedy" (1870), which lays out the basic argument of *The Birth of Tragedy* (1872), Nietzsche certainly carried out this cultural renewal agenda. Developing a theory that upset his fellow philologists but resonated in Wagner's circle, Nietzsche claimed that Greek tragedy began to "decompose" when, as a result of the advent of "Socratism," language gained the upper hand over music. In the draft of the lecture Nietzsche gave the Wagners, he went so far as to conclude with the line, "This Socratism is the Jewish press of today; need I say more?"[20] Wagner had just been much criticized over the reissuing, in 1869, of "Jewishness in Music," his anti-Jewish essay of 1850, and while the Wagners appreciated Nietzsche's loyalty, the advice from Tribschen was to avoid "stir[ring] up the hornets' nest" again.[21] Nietzsche complied, but when he ended the lecture with intimations of a coming rebirth of tragedy, even though Wagner wasn't named, the audience probably knew whom the speaker had in mind as Europe's prospective cultural savior. With Schopenhauer and Wagner as his lodestars, Nietzsche grew more ardent in the belief that he should himself be working toward something like a revolution in culture.

In a December 1870 letter to his friend Erwin Rohde, Nietzsche writes of his dream of creating an "untimely" alternative to the existing educational system. This alternative would draw inspiration from Schopenhauer's contempt for the dullness of the university lecture hall and follow Wagner's institution-building efforts in Bayreuth, where he had had a theater constructed for the staging of his work. Nietzsche's epistolary cri de coeur exceeds in intensity and sweep even the most abject mandarin lament discussed in the previous chapter:

> Let us slog on in this university existence for a few more years; let us take it as an edifying sadness that must be tolerated earnestly and with astonishment. This should be, among other things, a period of learning for teaching for which it is my task to train myself—only I have set my sights somewhat higher.

For, in the long run, I also realize what Schopenhauer's doctrine of university wisdom is all about. An utterly radical institution for *truth* is not *possible* here. More specifically, nothing truly revolutionary can proceed from here.

Later, we can become real teachers by hoisting ourselves with all possible means from out of the atmosphere of these times and by becoming not just wiser but, above all, better human beings. Here, too, I feel the need to be true. And that is another reason why I cannot tolerate this academic air much longer.

Thus, one day we will cast off this yoke—for *me*, that is certain. And then we will found a new Greek academy. . . . From your Tribschen visit you will know of *Wagner's* Bayreuth plan. I have been considering whether we, *for our part*, should not likewise break with philology as it has been practiced and with its *views on education*. I am readying a big *adhortatio* for all who have not yet been completely suffocated and swallowed up by the present moment. How lamentable it is, though, that I must write to you about this and that we have not yet *discussed* every idea together! And because you do not know the whole apparatus, my plan may seem to you like an eccentric whim. But it is not *that*; it is an urgent *need*.[22]

Perhaps few of Nietzsche's contemporaries harbored fantasies of founding a new Greek academy, but the general criticisms and hopes he took up in articulating his "urgent *need*" were on many minds around 1870. After all, Nietzsche was talking about a problem that, as shown in chapter 2, Adolf Diesterweg had already articulated for a broad audience in the 1830s and that loomed ever larger as scholarly specialization proceeded. In the most general terms, it was the problem of the (perceived) widening gap between moral education (*Bildung*) and scholarly knowledge (*Wissenschaft*). The research university no longer formed "better human beings" but instead did no more than impart knowledge. Within the context of Nietzsche's letter to Rohde, "radical" truth, so unattainable under present institutional conditions, would be truth that promoted *Bildung* and enhanced life, the standard by which knowledge should be assessed, not just per Nietzsche but according to Diesterweg as well. But whereas Diesterweg hoped that the core neo-humanist educational ideals could eventually be effectively institutionalized in the modern university, Nietzsche, as a young professor working in an institution that had changed dramatically since the 1830s, had his doubts. So would quite a few of the German scholars who read his work and shared his concerns, including Max Weber.

## EDUCATION AND UNIFICATION

Nietzsche arrived in Basel less than two years before the Prussian victory over Napoleon III in the Franco-Prussian War and the founding of the German *Kaiserreich*, or Second Empire, with Prussia as its dominant state. He was a keen and engaged observer of the cultural conflict that, thanks mainly to Otto von Bismarck's machinations, emerged in the wake of the war: the *Kulturkampf*, a decades-long conflict between the Catholic Church and a Protestant-dominated German state. Bismarck's battle to secularize the Second Empire, waged through bureaucratic chicanery, was in Nietzsche's view a mere skirmish in the struggle to define Germany's religious and cultural future. Writing to a friend in 1870 anticipating Prussian victory, Nietzsche warned that "we must be philosophers enough to remain sober in the universal ecstasy, so that the thief does not come and steal or diminish something that, for me, all the greatest military deeds, even all national uprisings, cannot compare to. For the coming period of culture, fighters will be needed. We must save ourselves for this."[23] For Nietzsche, the sectarian hostilities between Catholic Church and state roiling the new German empire were to be seen against the backdrop of an even more fateful battle for culture, and the outcome was far from certain. Nietzsche, like Wagner, questioned whether political unity would easily translate into cultural and spiritual greatness. Indeed, while recuperating from the dysentery and diphtheria he had contracted as a military medic, Nietzsche told his friend Carl von Gersdorff that he regarded Prussia "as a highly dangerous power for culture."[24] The modern state, he worried, sought not only to subordinate confessional challengers to its power but also to co-opt and instrumentalize all cultural resources in order to make itself "humanity's highest end."[25]

Unlike many of his scholarly contemporaries, however, such as the natural scientists Hermann Helmholtz and Emil Du Bois-Reymond or the historians Theodor Mommsen and Heinrich Treitschke, Nietzsche was also skeptical of the more liberal hope that education and modern, expert knowledge would unify Germans. The intellectual authority and integrity of the institutions that perhaps could have effected such a unification—elite educational institutes such as the *Gymnasien* and the universities—were being appropriated by state ministers and bureaucrats for political purposes. Inspired by Wagner, Nietzsche considered liberal rationalism a modern form of hedonism, mere pleasure seeking that distracts from higher purposes and that ultimately cannot satisfy the deepest human desires.

He also worried that alliances between scholarship and the state of the kind that liberal academics like Du Bois-Reymond proclaimed in the wake of the Franco-Prussian War would be bad for scholarship and thus ultimately bad for German society as well.[26] In his lectures on education, Nietzsche argued that the modern German state sees true moral education or *Bildung* as a threat, which is why it encourages the weakening of both *Bildung* and *Wissenschaft* through liberal pedagogical techniques that train *Gymnasium* students to make critical judgments about texts they should instead be learning to venerate. Democratization (or at least the German version of it) and disenchantment reinforce each other in *On the Future of Our Educational Institutions*.

With heightened anxieties about the state of culture and the shifting educational landscape in a newly unified empire, Germany's intellectual and political elites engaged in an intense and sweeping debate about schools.[27] That Nietzsche charged headlong into this debate stands to reason. He believed in the primacy of culture over other fields of human activity; indeed, education had been his life, aside from two brief, physically calamitous stints in the military.

Furthermore, Basel, a city with a strong tradition of the kind of classical education Nietzsche saw as having been pushed aside in Germany, was a propitious place for him to deliver his message about cultural decline. Jacob Burckhardt praised its inhabitants as "citizens in the fullest sense of the word," thereby invoking for Basel the status of a city of the Italian quattrocento.[28] For Burckhardt, Renaissance Florence represented not the recovery of classical ideals of harmony and unity but rather a prelude to nineteenth-century European cities in which "an energetically meritocratic world of atomized individuals competed with one another without regard for traditional religious, social and moral constraints."[29] In such an agonistic and highly individualistic world, a small group of elite personalities could reinvent a culture. In the second of his *Untimely Meditations*, Nietzsche directly invokes Burckhardt's study of the Italian Renaissance, asking whether it might take "no more than one hundred productive, active people, raised in a new spirit, to eliminate the false culture so fashionable in Germany at present." Isn't it encouraging, he asks, to see that the "culture of the Renaissance raised itself up on the shoulders of such a group of one hundred men?"[30]

Many participants in the debate about education offered proposals specifying how much instruction students should have per week in Latin, mathematics, and so on. By contrast, Nietzsche emphasizes that he was not interested in giving audiences "tables and new hourly course plans for the *Gymnasium* and the *Realschule*."[31] Yet throughout *On the Future of Our Educational Institutions*, he advances widely shared positions. Some of the voices that resonate in the lectures belong to people whose cultural politics were otherwise very different from his. Of these voices, some entered the schools debate a little later than he did, after government measures like the creation of the category *Realgymnasien* (which seemed to flaunt the mingling of classical and vocational education) and the pedagogical saber rattling of Wilhelm II ("I want soldiers, not students!") had further stirred things up.

One such voice belonged to nationalist historian Heinrich von Treitschke, a towering figure in the academic establishment for most of the Second Empire, and thus a person writing from an institutional position very different from Nietzsche's. Known as "the Apostle of Prussia," Treitschke had succeeded Leopold von Ranke as the most prominent professor of history in Germany and as the leading advocate of a distinctly political (or nationalist) vision of the writing of history. In marked contrast to Nietzsche, Treitschke believed that only the modern (German) state could realize the promise of personal freedom, and between 1874 and 1896 he regularly made the case in his lecture course titled simply "Politics," which was attended by hundreds of Germany's future elite.

A charismatic lecturer who didn't simply read aloud from his works, Treitschke eventually included among his large and diverse following the African American civil rights advocate and founding figure of sociology W. E. B. DuBois. Treitschke longed for the political goods of the modern state—individual freedom and national unity—which he thought could only be achieved through the "mass movements" of modern political parties. Yet he also worried that this development would inevitably lead to the "dangers of democracy."[32] In *The Future of the German Gymnasium* (1883), Treitschke gives an anxious account of his country's cultural demise and pleads for the *Gymnasium* as an institution of crucial importance for German national identity. Distressed about government attempts to open the educational system to students without an *Abitur* from a classical *Gymnasium* and to broaden the *Gymnasium* curriculum to include modern languages, more mathematics, and more natural and physical science, Treitschke wonders, "Who will maintain the aristocracy of our learned *Bildung* and preserve the education of our youth from leveling . . . [and prevent] the decline of our culture?"[33]

Treitschke didn't simply warn of the diminution of a national spirit. "The greatest danger that threatens the culture of modern man," he also writes, is that he must read amid "the never-ending distraction of our inner life, in the excess of mental impressions and information of all kinds that assails us daily, stripping our minds from nature."[34] Invoking Socrates's worries about the invention of writing in the *Phaedrus*, Treitschke claims that the "danger" of "pseudoknowledge and pseudothinking" has risen immeasurably since the advent of the printing press and the proliferation of newspapers and periodicals.[35]

Treitschke wrote in an era of major changes for German-language journalism. The great liberal dailies published in German, among them two of the continent's best newspapers, the *Berliner Tageblatt* and the *Neue Freie Presse*, were founded between 1854 and 1872. For an observer like Treitschke, the increase in quality had the paradoxical effect of making matters worse. The better journalism became, the more easily its offerings of "pseudoknowledge" could be confused with their genuine counterparts. Moreover, thanks to new modes of financing and new mechanisms of production and distribution (the rotary press dates to 1846), the newspaper industry of the late nineteenth century grew to be just that: a modern industry, with thicker, more frequent editions. The increase in quantity was endlessly fretted over. "Modern man," Treitschke laments, reads "on average ten times more than he can mentally manage." These reading habits result, he believed, in a character formed by ephemeral impressions and incapable of recognizing, much less embracing, anything of lasting value and meaning.[36]

Journalism figures prominently in Nietzsche's Basel lectures on education. Cast as his recollection of a forest dialogue among an irascible old philosopher who has much in common with Arthur Schopenhauer, the philosopher's younger companion (Nietzsche himself as a student), and a fellow university student, the lectures often read like an experiment in creative nonfiction, abounding with elaborate descriptions of the sylvan scenery, for example. Although the old philosopher, who has a contrarian streak, often rejects the assertions of others, one set of claims he readily endorses is this diatribe against journalism, uttered by his younger companion:

> In practice, the daily newspaper takes the place of education, and anyone, even a scholar, who still lays claim to culture or education typically relies on this sticky layer of mediation grouting the gaps between every form of life, every social position, every art, every science, every field—a layer as reliable and sturdy as the paper it's printed on tries to be. . . . Think how useless even the most laborious work is for a teacher who wants to lead even one student back to the infinitely distant and hard-to-grasp Hellenic world, the true homeland of our culture, when this same student an hour later will reach for a newspaper.[37]

Here and elsewhere, the lectures resemble the observations of today's more anxious technology critics, who worry that that our compulsive checking of

Facebook feeds, Twitter notifications, and email alerts leave us hyperstimulated and underfocused. The younger companion claims to have tracked the deeper roots of his day's crisis of attention to the well-formed dispositions that Germans bring with them when they come to rely on their new media. To put it in more contemporary terms, our iPhones haven't made us distracted—we already were. Those who design and sell new technologies (digital or print) take advantage of the ways in which people have already been formed by an array of cultural technologies and techniques. Similarly, the younger companion maintains that journalism hasn't so much transformed nineteenth-century Germans as exploited the social and cultural "gaps" left in the wake of a modernity characterized by the simultaneous— even mutually reinforcing—expansion and contraction of knowledge. Newspapers and periodicals (or iPhones and laptops) subsume older media (Greek dramas or Christian Bibles, for instance) and become the "sticky layer of mediation" holding societies together.

One of the paradoxes of Nietzsche's lectures is the suggestion that the triumph of journalistic superficiality owes much to an unlikely source: the academic specialist. As his young stand-in in the forest dialogue says, "In Germany, where they know how to drape such painful facts in a glorious cloak of ideas, they even admire this narrow specialization among our scholars and view their straying ever farther from true education as a moral phenomenon: 'loyalty to particulars' or 'sticking to one's last' is celebrated above all else."[38] Concerned only with cultivating the "narrowest" expertise, German academics have ceded broader questions and concerns to writers and thinkers outside the university. The younger companion declares that "in every general question of a serious nature, and especially the deepest philosophical problems, the academic or scholar as such no longer has anything at all to say, while a sticky, adhesive layer that has worked its way between all academic disciplines—journalism—finds its calling precisely here, and carries it out according to its nature: as day-labor, as its name suggests."[39] Thus, as the lectures put it, specialization helps bring about a situation in which "people have democratized the rights of genius," and the journalist has "taken the place of the genius."[40] Despite sharing this view, and for all his crotchetiness, the old philosopher isn't as pessimistic about the prospects for real education. Neither was Nietzsche early in his career. In the introduction to the lectures, he claims that unlike the current "culture of lies," real (i.e., aristocratic) education has "nature" on its side:

> Permit me merely to predict the future out of the entrails of the present, like a Roman haruspice, which in this case involves neither more nor

less than predicting the eventual victory of an educational tendency that already exists, even if at the moment it is neither popular, nor respected, nor widely prevalent. But it will triumph, I say with supreme confidence, because it has the greatest and mightiest ally of all: *Nature*.[41]

## THE DEBATE OVER THE EVOLUTION OF THE SCHOOLS

By the second half of the nineteenth century, the German education system was widely considered the best in the world. German elementary schools educated a greater percentage of the population than their British and French counterparts. The *Gymnasium*, the secondary school that prepared young Germans for university study, was known for its rigorous instruction, especially in classical languages. German universities were celebrated for their culture of academic freedom, for their devotion to the ideal of research, and for the fruits of that devotion: innovations across the disciplines, from cutting-edge chemistry labs to philological studies and editions still used today. Foreign students flocked to Germany. In 1879 nearly six hundred Americans studied at German universities, a total far greater than the number of students at most large American universities, the transformation of which into research institutions had only just begun. American students came to Germany not only to master domains of knowledge but also, as the philosopher Johann Gottlieb Fichte had put it, to learn how to learn.

Yet for a number of reasons, throughout the *Kaiserreich* there was much hand-wringing over the entire educational system, as was shown in the previous chapter. Most of the worries in Nietzsche's day weren't new; they had become more intense and widespread as certain tendencies, like academic specialization, had grown more prominent and as major social changes had occurred. These changes included an expanding government bureaucracy whose workforce increased fourfold from 1873 to 1910 (from about a half million to about two million); the acceleration of Germany's economic boom in the years after unification (and the bust that soon followed); the increasing importance of "technology transfer" to economic competitiveness; and the cultural pressures that attended Germany's arrival as a world power. These are just a few of the developments that gave urgency to the debate about education. The central question was, How could Germany's elite secondary schools be reformed to serve an advanced industrial society? Yet many of the participants rejected the very premise of the debate. For them the problem was that in their rush to make education relevant and modern, reformers were discarding the primary feature that had made Germany's schools and universities the object of international envy: their unapologetic exclusivity.[42]

In Nietzsche's time, only about 3 percent of German schoolchildren, many of them from families with means or with high social standing achieved through education (i.e., the *Bildungsbürgertum*), went on to attend a *Gymnasium*. But amid calls to make education more practical, things did in fact change. In 1859 the Prussian Ministry of Culture issued new rules that responded to calls for reform by dividing *Realschulen*—secondary schools with an ostensibly more practical or modern orientation—into two categories: a "first order" that required Latin as well as a modern language such as English or French, and a "second order" that required only modern languages. Whereas the *lateinlose* (Latin-less) schools in the second order trained students for professional careers for which a university education was considered unnecessary, those in the "first order" prepared students for the university. It wasn't until 1870, however, that students with an *Abitur*, the diploma traditionally awarded only to graduates of the classical *Gymnasium*, from a *Realschule* of the "first order" were declared automatically eligible for admission to a university. Just before Nietzsche delivered his lectures on education, then, Prussia had begun to combine certain elements of vocational and classical education and to deny the classical *Gymnasium* its monopoly as the sole entryway to Prussian universities—precisely what men like Nietzsche and Treitschke didn't want. Between 1890 and 1914 the number of *Realschulen* surged from 138 to 180 in Prussia while the number of *Gymnasien* edged up by only thirteen, to 367. After Germans could attend a university with an *Abitur* from some of the higher *Realschulen*, total enrollment at German universities increased dramatically, from just over thirteen thousand in the late 1860s to about thirty thousand by the mid-1880s.[43] The growth was such that the government went from encouraging the expansion of enrollment to worrying about whether there was "an overproduction of the educated," as Prussia's minister of culture put it in 1882.

Writing to a friend in 1885, Wilhelm II complained about the "scalpel of the fanatical philologists" teaching at the *Gymnasien* under which every sentence of antiquity was "halved and quartered until the skeleton was found."[44] A diverse group of observers shared this concern, even some who didn't share the Kaiser's practical orientation in matters of pedagogy.[45] "Fifty years ago," one critic remarked in 1890, "there was a common basis, a shared and holy ideal among *Gymnasium* students. Today, this basis has been destroyed, and one searches for new ideals. . . . Homer and Sophocles, Xenophon and Plato were regarded as an earthly Bible."[46] As he inveighed against democratization, vocationalization, the venality of a status-obsessed professoriate, and an assortment of further ills that were, in his view, blighting the educational landscape, Nietzsche, too, evoked the neo-humanist past with longing.

## A THEORY OF EDUCATIONAL IMPERATIVES

In the introduction to the Basel lectures, Nietzsche sets forth as his "thesis" the idea that "our educational institutions, built originally upon entirely different foundations, are presently dominated by two tendencies, seemingly opposed but actually equally ruinous in practice and ultimately converging in their effects. One is the drive to *expand education* as much as possible; the other is the drive to *diminish and weaken it*."[47] He doesn't yet identify where these drives originate, merely remarking that the latter tendency robs education of its independence by pushing it into the service of the state. In the lectures themselves, the situation turns out to be even more paradoxical. When the old philosopher condemns the ideal of broadly educating "the folk" as both the blueprint for a "saturnalia of barbarism" and a threat to "the natural hierarchy in the realm of the intellect," he could be attacking either progressive or capitalist educational aims.[48] Both, Nietzsche's characters suggest, are responsible for a "ruinous" expansion—and weakening—of the system. Progressive educational goals not only included expanding access to humanistic education but also using humanistic education as a way of liberating the "free personality" of the individual. Such thinking has resulted in a pedagogy concerned mostly with helping young people simply express themselves. Instead of learning reverence and seriousness—which is what they should be doing as semiformed adolescents, according to the lectures—*Gymnasium* students become habituated to putting forth ill-informed, unripe judgments about the most sacred matters. For Nietzsche, this is what cultural journalists do. Thus, from the *Gymnasium* on, students bear what the old philosopher calls "the repulsive mark of our aesthetic journalism."[49]

But it's the system and principles of advanced capitalism managed by technocrats—then known in Germany as political economists—that pose an even greater threat to real education. Or at least that is what the younger companion thinks: "I felt I could tell where the call for the greatest possible expansion and spread of education was coming from most loudly and clearly. Expansion is one of the favorite political-economic dogmas of the day."[50] Large swaths of the population, he argues, have bought into this dogma—and the notion of happiness in which it comes packaged—with catastrophic results for the educational system: "What the moral code operative here demands is . . . a *rapid* education, so that you can start earning money quickly, and at the same time a thorough enough education so that you can earn *large amounts* of money. Culture is tolerated only insofar as it serves the cause of earning money, but that much culture is also demanded."[51] The tendency most responsible for pushing education toward expansion—German capitalism—is thus *simultaneously* the one most responsible for pushing education toward a utilitarian narrowing. Capitalism pressures *Gymnasien* and universities to increase access and enroll more students while also pressuring them to focus on economic utility. Such a system ultimately produces, as Nietzsche would put it more than a decade later, the "last men."

One important strand of the schools debate concerned educational access for women and girls, and although from an early age Nietzsche had counted among his conversation partners women whom he respected as serious intellectuals, demands for inclusion from any large group unsettled him. If the problem with education was in part waning exclusivity, then making half the population potential university students would, in this view, only accelerate its decline.

Before 1800 German states had few schools for girls that provided any sort of formal education beyond the elementary level. Between 1800 and 1870, however, state support for women's education increased markedly. By 1872 the newly established German Empire could boast 165 municipal or state-sponsored higher schools for girls. But these paled in comparison to their counterparts for boys in terms of quality, rigor, and orientation. The schools for girls ended at age fifteen or sixteen compared to eighteen or nineteen for those for boys. Latin, Greek, mathematics, and science were not included in curricula for girls; instead, the higher schools for girls focused on sewing, drawing, and dancing.

In 1872 a group of 164 teachers, almost all male, gathered in Weimar to discuss possible reforms of the higher schools for girls. The teachers rejected the curriculum of the traditional humanist *Gymnasium* and endorsed instead a more "realist" version that included modern languages but no science and little math. Although the group embraced the exalted language of *Bildung*, the purpose of such an education for women was sharply distinguished from that of an education designed for men. Women needed to be educated and cultivated to ensure, as the conference's final report put it, that the "German husband would not be bored."[52]

In the 1860s some women began to attend university lectures as auditors, and at least two foreign women, both Russian, earned doctorates in 1874 at the University of Göttingen. But by 1880 almost all German universities had cracked down on the mostly informal arrangements that allowed women to audit, and in 1886 Prussia issued a decree reiterating the ban on female students. Unsurprisingly, the demands for inclusion continued, growing in force. In the 1880s various advocacy groups, old and new, such as the Women's Welfare Association, the German Women's Association, and the Women's Reform Association, began submitting petitions to both state and national legislatures.[53]

Women weren't permitted to matriculate at most German universities until 1908, but by then other pushes for inclusion had changed the makeup of the student population appreciably. Starting in the 1860s the propertied middle class had begun to show a keener interest in seeing its children, whether male or female, burnish their families' material success with the status afforded by high academic credentials. Another motivation for broader inclusion came from private and state interests hoping to make commercial use of university training and new knowledge in the natural sciences. As Germany's dye and pharmaceuticals industries developed into lynchpins of the economy in the second half of the nineteenth century, for example, they increasingly sought out closer relationships with universities and university-trained scientists. In addition, with the founding of the Second Empire and the full legal enfranchisement of Jews in Germany, the percentage of Jewish university students increased sharply. By 1885 Jews made up slightly more than 1 percent of Prussia's population but nearly 10 percent of its university students. The number of foreign students at German universities also rose dramatically after 1871. Of the 223 female auditors at Prussian universities in 1896, fifty-three were American. (Nearly thirty were German Jews.) The slow process that gradually increased access to German universities wouldn't have escaped Nietzsche's attention in 1872.

## CRISES OF THE HUMANITIES AND HUMANIST KNOWLEDGE

As the debate about the future of education rumbled on toward the twentieth century, universities were changing in other ways as well. Not only were there more students but also they were studying different things. The disciplines that had historically anchored the lower faculty (the philosophy or arts faculty, which traditionally included all fields of study except law, medicine, and theology) were ceding their dominance to the natural sciences and mathematics. Between 1841 and 1881, the percentage of students enrolled in philosophy faculties to study philosophy, philology, and history declined from 86.4 percent to 63.9 percent. Enrollment in mathematics and the natural sciences, in contrast, increased from 13.6 percent to 37.1 percent. Similarly, between 1868 and 1881 the segment of students enrolled in philosophy faculties to study history, philology, and philosophy dropped from 60.0 percent to 53.5 percent, whereas enrollments in mathematics and the natural sciences moved the other way, going from 20.6 percent to 32.4 percent.[54]

In the context of such shifts, Nietzsche made a series of claims that will sound familiar to anyone who follows debates about the fate of the humanities and the purpose of higher education in the twenty-first century. As hedonistic-utilitarian conceptions of education increased and enrollments declined, he feared, (neo)humanistic study would soon be eclipsed. Once this happened, Germany's youth and the generations to come—already lost in the tumult of "secularization" and the "ebbing" of religion and a true sense of the sacred—would be left spiritually impoverished.[55]

In contrast to the charts and tables that filled the reform tracts of the day, detailing how many hours of Greek or science *Gymnasium* students should take, Nietzsche offered polemics with both conventional and idiosyncratic features, chiliastic-sounding appeals to a "purified German spirit" as the greatest and also most "mysterious" hope for change, and a series of ideas for redressing the situation. Make language instruction productively rigorous; teach students to be "physically repulsed" by examples of Germany's "pseudoculture"; use the classic German authors—for example, Goethe and Schiller—to help students develop the "sense of form" needed to appreciate ancient models; recruit inspiring teachers; admit *Gymnasium* and university students more selectively, so that those with insufficient academic talent are put on the useful path of vocational training; provide support for gifted students without means.[56] The *Gymnasium* and university should be both meritocratic and aristocratic—no genius left behind! Although Nietzsche hazarded suggestions for improvement as expressed in his lecture series, especially through the old philosopher and his young companion, he grasped better than many of his contemporaries—and better than many of ours—how difficult any real reform would be.

Some of today's most earnest defenders of the humanities—Mark Edmundson and Andrew Delbanco, for example—have made a kind of credo of the claim that undergraduates can and often do emerge from the humanities classroom transformed. Delbanco, for example, claims that this tends to happen when students are guided effectively through the process of "fighting out within and among themselves contending ideas of the meaningful life" with great works prompting and enriching their discussions.[57] Nietzsche also thought that university students were capable of engaging with this kind of challenging and potentially transformative material. Indeed, he has the old philosopher effuse over the "the honest German drive for knowledge" that resides—and, for the most part, remains locked—within the German people. Like many authors critical of the "sorry state of academic ethics" and humanistic education, from Diesterweg in the 1830s to William Deresiewicz in 2015, Delbanco considers a contemporary cultural obsession with money the key factor in these troubles, writing of "the contagion of money."[58] But for Nietzsche the challenge of activating students' drive for "true" learning was even more formidable:

> The feeling for classical Hellenic culture is so rare, resulting as it does from a combination of the most strenuous educational struggle and artistic gifts, that only a brutal misunderstanding enables the *Gymnasium* to claim to awaken it. And awaken it in people of what age? Young enough that they are still yanked blindly around by the gaudiest fashions and inclinations of the day, when they have not the slightest sense in themselves that this feeling for the Hellenic, *if* it ever is awakened, must immediately turn aggressive and express itself in a constant battle against the supposed culture of the present. For the *Gymnasium* student of today, the Hellenes as such are dead.[59]

The best hope for overcoming the malaise of modernity, Nietzsche believed, was an embrace of radically foreign and ancient cultures. But such an encounter required the very shift of values that a genuine connection with antiquity promised to bring about. If true education were thus necessary for true education, to paraphrase a line in Nietzsche's preface, where could education begin?

Evoking this situation, which in some ways strongly resembles the cycle of cultural and educational malaise Diesterweg outlined in his book about universities in decline, the old philosopher intones, "Helpless barbarian, slave of the present day, lying in the chains of the passing moment and hungering—always, eternally hungering!" How could teachers hope to revive a pedagogical ideal and its values when the culture on which they depended was, in effect, "dead"? What happens, that is, when there are no longer educational institutions dedicated to providing what Nietzsche called a "humanities education" (*Humanitätsbildung*)?[60]

When the younger companion, who has resigned his position as a teacher, despairs over what he takes to be the futility of imparting ancient Greek culture to students who will soon "reach for a newspaper," the old philosopher encourages him to have faith. The philosopher's attempt to offer reasons to be hopeful only deepens the erstwhile teacher's doubt. The old one asserts that a change for the better will happen, but the mechanisms of that change—for example, "the renewal of the true German spirit"— and how they might be activated remain unclear. The same can be said of the more concrete vehicles for progress the old philosopher identifies, such as German classicism. He insists that properly studying Schiller and Goethe will help *Gymnasium* students acquire access to the culture of ancient Greece, but he also admits that present-day students can't even read the German classics, much less the Greek classics. The present is so far gone that "the narrowest, most limited points of view," those of modern disciplinary scholarship, "are in some sense correct, because no one is capable of reaching, or even identifying, the place from which all these points of view are in the wrong."[61] With "emotion in his voice," the young companion responds, "No one?" Thereupon both he and the old philosopher fall silent, and the third lecture in *On the Future of Our Educational Institutions* comes to a dolorous end.

Through this and similar exchanges between the philosopher and his companion, Nietzsche evokes what he elsewhere describes as the "restlessness of secularization." As he writes in "Schopenhauer as Educator" (1874), a follow-up of sorts to the Basel lectures, "the rivers of religion recede" as "scholarship and the sciences, without any moderation and pursued blindly, splinter and undermine all established belief."[62] In contrast to the Kantians, Hegelians (left and right), and Marxists, who in their philosophical histories of secularization happily anticipated the historical realization of reason, Nietzsche wasn't sanguine about reason's progressive promises.[63] For him, secularization—or "making worldly" as the German term *Verweltlichung* Nietzsche uses might be more literally translated—didn't necessarily entail the advent of a common and shared exchange of reasons and rational justifications. Rather, it brought, quite simply, incoherence, an "excessive lust for knowledge, an unsatisfying joy in discovery . . . a frivolous deification of the present or numb renunciation of it, everything *sub specie saeculi*."[64] For Nietzsche, this was precisely the problem of the modern humanities: could they remain disciplinary forms of knowledge and simultaneously function as cultural practices that require faith and reverence from those who profess them?

## NIETZSCHE AND HUMBOLDT

In *On the Future of Our Educational Institutions*, Nietzsche's main response to the fundamental questions of *Bildung* and *Wissenschaft* is a radical if vague vision of a pedagogy of the future. The radical nature of his conceptualization hasn't always been acknowledged. Indeed, commentators have repeatedly claimed that Nietzsche's lectures on education essentially hark back to Wilhelm von Humboldt's "neo-humanism."[65] The claim has some merit: like Humboldt, Nietzsche placed the formation of the individual through the free cultivation of the highest faculties at the center of the educational process. Thus, it is possible to argue that Nietzsche's model of education draws on the democratic ethos of neo-humanism. Nietzsche's concerns about the intrusion of state interests into the university also resemble Humboldt's worries about the relationship between university and state. Like Humboldt, moreover, Nietzsche vigorously advocated a certain kind of inclusiveness. Having himself been officially designated an "impecunious student," he was concerned that talented, economically disadvantaged would-be matriculants were being left out. (Even when adjusted for inflation, the cost of being a German university student rose throughout the nineteenth century, and public support available to students without private means was far from ample.) Without such inclusiveness, Nietzsche repeatedly intimates in the Basel lectures, the educational system won't be able to promote intellectual excellence effectively.

At times, then, Nietzsche does identity with the tradition of neo-humanism (and its inclusive spirit). The lectures explicitly invoke the ideal of "classical education" (*klassische Bildung*), a phrase with Humboldtian resonances. Furthermore, several of the statements about the Greek model in *On the Future of Our Educational Institutions* read like attempts to channel the spirit of German classicism, something that many of Nietzsche's contemporaries sought to do in addressing the schools question. The old philosopher lyrically (if floridly) asserts that German students must have "these teachers, our classic German writers, to sweep us away with them under the wingbeats of their ancient quest—to the land of their deepest longings, Greece."[66]

Despite these similarities, however, the ancient Greece that Nietzsche upholds as a model for modern Germans differs profoundly from the one revered by German classicism and neo-humanists. Humboldt, for example, praised such aspects of Greek culture as the harmonious balance of different characteristics, symmetry, and simplicity.[67] The old philosopher doesn't look to the study of Greece to facilitate a process of development— or *Bildung*—whereby Germans would take on those qualities. Whereas J. J. Winckelmann (1717–1768) had admiringly identified grace and quiet greatness as core principles of ancient Greek culture and first articulated the ideals of German classicism, Nietzsche had recently celebrated the Greeks' "brutality" and "animal appetite for destruction."[68] As the old philosopher says, "A true purification and renewal of the *Gymnasium* can proceed only from a deep and violent purification and renewal of the German spirit."[69]

Neither Humboldt nor any of his contemporaries celebrated "violent purification" in their writings on education reform and *Bildung*. They also would not have welcomed the emphasis Nietzsche's old philosopher lays on the curtailment of freedom: "All education begins with the very opposite of what everyone so highly esteems nowadays as 'academic freedom.'" Humboldt thought that both schools and students needed academic freedom and that anyone, or at least any man, had the potential to achieve *Bildung*, to develop a "free autonomous personality" and unfold to "full humanity." Inspired in part by democratic thinking about the self, Humboldt's classicism was a liberal one.

Yet Nietzsche's distance from neo-humanism should not be exaggerated. For all his emphasis on freedom, Humboldt also saw *Bildung* as involving "restriction," a key term in his writings, and subordination, too.[70] He is said to have admired the soaring yet severe address Fichte gave upon becoming rector of the University of Berlin in 1811. Fichte called for the strict disciplining of students in the service of higher freedom. Thus, in the Basel lectures when Nietzsche mocks a pedagogy that encourages the "free personality" to hold forth (prematurely) on the classics, he targets not so much neo-humanism itself as what he takes to be its late nineteenth-century corruption. With their more aggressive rhetoric of subordination, the lectures don't break with neo-humanism; they radicalize certain elements of it.

What agitates the old philosopher most is that "every student is treated as being capable of literature, as someone *allowed* to have opinions about the most serious people and things," when "any true education will strive with all its might precisely to *suppress* this ridiculous claim to independence of judgment on the part of the young person, and to impose strict obedience to the scepter of the genius."[71]

The old philosopher's contemptuous description of German *Gymnasium* students anticipates Nietzsche's similarly disdainful description of "the last man" in *Thus Spoke Zarathustra*, written between 1883 and 1885:

The earth has become small, and on it hops the last man, who makes everything small. His race is as ineradicable as the flea-beetle; the last man lives longest.

"We have invented happiness," say the last men, and they blink. They have left the regions where it was hard to live, for one needs warmth. One still loves one's neighbor and rubs against him, for one needs warmth.

Becoming sick and harboring suspicion are sinful to them: one proceeds carefully. A fool, whoever still stumbles over stones or human beings! A little poison now and then: that makes for agreeable dreams. And much poison in the end, for an agreeable death.

One still works, for work is a form of entertainment. But one is careful lest the entertainment be too harrowing. One no longer becomes poor or rich: both require too much exertion. Who still wants to rule? Who obey? Both require too much exertion.

No shepherd and one herd! Everybody wants the same, everybody is the same: whoever feels differently goes into a madhouse.

"Formerly all the world was mad," say the most refined, and they blink.

One is clever and knows everything that has ever happened: so there is no end of derision. One still quarrels, but one is soon reconciled—else it might spoil the digestion.

One has one's little pleasure for the day and one's little pleasure for the night: but one has a regard for health.

"We have invented happiness," say the last men, and they blink.[72]

Each of Nietzsche's variations on the melancholy mandarin's lament relies less on the propositional truth value of a particular claim than on the rhetorical force that, as Tamsin Shaw explains, Nietzsche intends to derive "from the fact that we [readers] recognize in ourselves the 'last man' and yet at the same time find such a being contemptible."[73] Nietzsche's description of the contemptible students and teachers in the Basel lectures, the "last men" in *Zarathustra*, or the haughty onlookers in the *Gay Science* (1882) presupposes a counterideal—a healthier way of living. Nietzsche hopes to stoke a desire for alternate forms of moral authority. Although his characterization of the contemptible figures remains fairly consistent throughout his work, that of the counterideal and the new forms of moral authority is less so. But *that* humans require such a holistic ideal and a comprehensive orienting moral authority, Nietzsche never seems to have doubted. The question remains, however, as to where such forms of authority might come from and how they might compel faithful commitment. For Nietzsche the severe critic of Christianity, secularization is a problem because it has alienated contemporary humans from forms of moral and spiritual greatness and the ways of living that could sustain them—above all, from those of the ancient Greeks.

Seeing everywhere a ruinous orientation toward comfort and an unwillingness to suffer or endure the suffering of others for the sake of better forms of life, Nietzsche put his faith in exceptions, and from an early age he regarded the ultimate purpose of education as the fostering of such individuals' success. "My religion, if I can call it that," Nietzsche would write in 1875, "lies in the work for the creation of genius."[74] This assertion resonates with a central claim in the Basel lectures. Culture, according to the old philosopher, is created and transmitted by genius, which is developed through "all-consuming" training and the utmost seriousness, as the Greeks and Romans knew. Education should therefore have as its end the promotion of genius; where genius isn't nurtured, it will fail to flourish—to the detriment of a community or nation. At times, *On the Future of Our Educational Institutions* frames genius in conventional terms, as the agency through which real works of art are produced: this is what Kant had claimed.[75] Nietzsche certainly had in mind Wagner, who may have attended the second Basel lecture. The younger companion frames the genius as the kind of cultural savior Wagner hoped to become—"the redeemer from the present moment." The lectures as a whole propose that genius should have the kind of significance for national identity that Wagner claimed for himself and his art.

The old philosopher posits that genius is of supercultural provenance; it has a "metaphysical origin." Yet, paradoxically, an individual genius can also take on and exemplify the true nature of a collective that has strayed from itself:

> For a genius to appear, to emerge from a people; to reflect as it were the whole image of a people and its particular strengths in its full array of colors; to reveal this people's highest purpose in the symbolic essence of an individual, and in that individual's eternal work, thus linking his people to the eternal and freeing it from the ever-changing sphere of the momentary—all of this the genius can do only if he has been ripened and nourished in the motherly lap of his people's culture.[76]

The old philosopher doesn't seem to care that only a small fraction of students possesses such genius. One genius, he contends, can have a transformative effect on those around him. The lectures conclude with the philosopher making just that point by conjuring a genius placed in an orchestra made up of the kind of boorish mediocrities whom, he suggests, nineteenth-century Germany has excelled at producing:

> But finally, your imagination soaring, put a genius—a real genius—in the midst of this mass. Right away something unbelievable happens. It is as if this genius has entered by an instantaneous transmigration of soul into all of these savages, and now only a single inspired eye looks out of them all. . . . Now when you observe the orchestra in its sublime storms or heartfelt laments . . . then you too will feel what a pre-established harmony between leader and followers is like, and how, in the hierarchy of spirits, everything strives to create such structure. You can guess from my simile, though, what I see as true educational institutions, and why I do not in the least grant the university that status.[77]

Lacking the right kind of discipline and with ever more students, instead of a favorable environment for genius, Prussia's schools provide a "reveling in anarchy and chaos; in short, the literary traits of our journalism and, no less, of our scholars."[78] Thus, the lectures describe a vicious cycle in which Germany's schools themselves engender the conditions of their demise.

Yet the malaise in German culture and education was ultimately a symptom of a much deeper problem, of a culture struggling to find meaningful, sustainable forms of life in modernity—that is, after the death of God. The twilight of the gods and idols didn't spell the end of religion. Humans would always employ these meaning-bearing techniques and habits. Nietzsche's concern was, rather, with the kinds of practices that would take hold once Christian practices had dissipated, with whether they would promote cultural health and strength.

Nietzsche was particularly concerned with how the state had insinuated itself into all other forms of authority, co-opting the internal ends and goods of other communities, institutions, and practices to its own narrower interests.[79] The state's self-serving, utterly hypocritical "construction of the sacred," he wrote, had corrupted Christianity: "Because it has been used in a hundred different ways to drive the mills of state power, Christianity has gradually become sick to its marrow, dissimulated and false. It has degenerated into an oppositional relation to its original goal."[80] In the Basel lectures, Nietzsche worries that the state will usurp the cultural and moral authority of educational institutions, the *Gymnasien* and universities, and also intellectual life in general. But what particular forms of life and values would Nietzsche consider healthy? What counterideals and alternative values would be better than those orienting the contemptible lives of the "last men"?

In the Basel lectures and in other texts on antiquity written around the same time, such as *Homer's Contest* and *The Birth of Tragedy*, Nietzsche poses the same question: what forms of life can sustain a culture other than or parallel to those of Christianity?[81] For Nietzsche, Christianity represented unhealthy and distinctly modern ways of being in the world, practices that cultivated shame, guilt, pessimism, and a longing for a different world. New, healthier forms of life were needed.

Modern culture, in Nietzsche's view, found one of its most salient and sickly expressions in the new Reich, which he thought was characterized by a false individuality that was fostered and intensively reinforced by the education and media machines. It was a commodified personhood that amounted to impotent assertions of preferences and opinions that were in reality merely the products of larger cultural forces and institutions. What were needed were ethical resources that could help modern Germans not just resist but even overcome these manifestations of the newly constituted German state.

Ancient Greece, Nietzsche believed, provided such ethical resources. In one of the deepest tragedies of modernity, however, scholars had stopped helping people gain access to those resources in a way that would be advantageous to culture and life. As modern functionaries, scholars instead desiccated antiquity. Indeed, in *On the Future of Our Educational Institutions*, the old philosopher denigrates contemporary philology as yet another example of cultural decline:

> Gradually, a profound exploration of the same eternal problems has come to be replaced by a historical, in fact a philological, pondering and questioning: What did this or that philosopher think or not think, and is this or that text rightly ascribed to him or not, and even: is this or that reading of a classical text preferable to the other? Nowadays the students in our university philosophy seminars are encouraged to ponder emasculated philosophical considerations such as these, whereas I myself have long since been accustomed to see such scholarship as a branch of philology, and to judge its practitioners according to whether or not they are good philologists. As a result, of course, *philosophy itself* is banished from the university altogether.[82]

A few years after he gave the lectures on education, Nietzsche penned a series of notes for a work he provisionally titled "We Philologists." Here he extends the critique of his discipline that began to find its mature expression in the lectures. Nietzsche still identified with his discipline (it's *we* philologists, after all); he just deplored what had become of it.

True scholarship, Nietzsche writes in 1875, has been "falsified through the incapacity of the majority" of scholars with their "false standards."[83] There once was a genuine *Wissenschaft*, a scholarly culture to be admired. But its downfall is now epitomized by the collapse of a branch of knowledge in which "99 out of 100 philologists . . . shouldn't be philologists."[84] Most had entered philology as a profession and treated it as another instance of modern labor, taking on piecemeal tasks assigned by senior scholars in specialized forms of intellectual industry. They blindly labored under the delusion that industriousness and attention to detail would allow them to reassemble antiquity anew and whole. This modern type, "academic man" (*der wissenschaftliche Mensch*), "is a real paradox."[85] As the catastrophe of modernity unfolds around him, "academic man" fusses over textual details.

## INDUSTRIAL PHILOLOGY

In lamenting how philology had become a factory-style operation, Nietzsche probably had in mind, among others, the historian Theodor Mommsen, who referred to his own work as "the heavy industry of scholarship." With the publication of his *Roman History* (1854–1856), the basis for the decision to award him the Nobel Prize for literature in 1903, Mommsen became a major figure in and beyond German academia. Mark Twain once noted the excitement tram conductors displayed upon recognizing Mommsen on the streets of Berlin. But he never actually finished his history of Rome, devoting much of his prodigious energy instead to organizing massive data collection projects, the nineteenth century's equivalent of today's so-called digital humanities. These projects' scale rivaled that of scholarship in the natural sciences and impressed government funding agencies, which amply supported Mommsen's data gathering. By the end of the nineteenth century, his Corpus Inscriptionum Latinarum (CIL), in which he aimed to collect all Latin inscriptions from the territory of the former Roman Empire, had brought him research funding equivalent to US$2.5 million in today's dollars. Monumental scholarship on the classical world had representational value for the Prussian and, later, German states. Mommsen wrote that Friedrich Althoff, a minister who championed the historian's work, believed that there was a "deep internal bond between scholarship and the state," one that was to no small extent responsible for "Prussia's greatness and Germany's position in the world."[86] It helped that Mommsen served as the permanent secretary of the Prussian Academy of Sciences, the most important state funding agency, from 1873 to 1895.

Unabashed in his top-down management style ("one leads, many labor," he wrote), Mommsen presided over hundreds of scholars who together operated as collecting armies that performed narrow, mostly mechanical functions, creating a model that was emulated widely, and not only in the humanities.[87] His organizational practices inspired the German astronomer Arthur Auwer, for example, who successfully proposed a project to systematically collect and compare all fixed-star observations between 1750 and 1900, the *Thesaurus positionum stellarum affixarum*.[88] Yet for all his devotion to tightly managing scholars — "workers," as he called them — and having them give themselves over to individual technical tasks, Mommsen himself worried about specialization.

Like so many nineteenth-century German scholars, Mommsen mourned the passing of the ideal of the unity of all knowledge. Without the sense of purpose it afforded, scholars were like "journeymen serving no masters," he wrote.[89] Scholarly asceticism was one way of making sense of the new conditions of industrial scholarship. "We are neither complaining nor laying blame," he continued. "Flowers necessarily wither as the fruit forms. And the best of us now find that we have become specialists."[90] Some evidence suggests that Mommsen saw scale or bigness as means of sustaining neo-humanist ideals amid the culture of specialization he did so much to advance.

Since Mommsen's big humanities projects were housed in the Prussian Academy of Sciences, that is, outside the university, one of their effects was to contribute to the decoupling of teaching and research, the unity of which had been so important to Humboldt. Yet Mommsen claimed that these projects made the academy a new kind of model community. Whether consciously or not, he invoked the language of neo-humanism to portray the academy as a place where, in contrast to the university, "equal personalities" came together, without "rank and estate" being taken into account, to pursue their intellectual work.[91] Even with its factory-style mode of production, in a certain crucial respect the academy resembled the university of *Bildung* imagined by the neo-humanist educational reforms more than "the university of full professors" and precariously employed adjuncts of the late nineteenth century did.

But Mommsen's contemporaries did not endorse his attempts to reinvent the neo-humanist tradition. (Nor have later commentators.) Speaking of Mommsen, the philosopher Wilhelm Dilthey wrote in 1895, "It is hard to imagine how anyone could write about the age of early Christianity without any religious feeling." For Dilthey, this meant without any sense of identification.[92] The scholars in Basel whom young Nietzsche admired most generally loathed Mommsen, considering him a disenchanter of the classical world and the arch-Prussianizer of the humanities. In 1851 Mommsen had lambasted one of those scholars, the philologist Johann Bachofen, for failing to distinguish between what could "actually" be known about the language, customs, religion, and legal institutions of ancient Rome and the literary tradition's "later chatter of scholars and poets about the fatuous legends."[93]

In response Bachofen wrote that "Rome and the Romans are not Mommsen's real concern. The heart of the book [*History of Rome*] is . . . the apotheosis [in and through Rome] of the boundless radicalism of the new Prussia."[94] Like Bachofen, Jacob Burckhardt, the other Basel scholar Nietzsche fervently admired, had been educated by neo-humanists in Berlin, and he shared Bachofen's concerns. Burckhardt questioned whether for all their capaciousness, Mommsen's projects left room to contemplate the fruits of antiquity. Summing up the impressions of Mommsen's critics, Lionel Gossman has observed that Mommsen and his Prussian colleagues "stripped [antiquity] of its glory, of everything that made it unique and different from the present, greater and more richly human" and "remodeled to conform to the gray fragmentariness of contemporary Berlin."[95]

Whether or not these impressions are ultimately accurate, their implication is clear. Mommsen was largely uninterested in how classical culture might help late nineteenth-century Germans learn about themselves and how they should live. Mommsen was concerned with authenticity: inscriptions were physical objects, to be tested according to standardized mechanical processes. Collectors and editors of epigraphs had struggled for centuries with forgeries or inscriptions of uncertain provenance. In order to separate the "fakes" from the "authentic" inscriptions, Mommsen designed a system that advanced epigraphy into a specialized and highly technical science and drew on modern critical methods of philology.[96] For him, the goal of historical scholarship at the end of the nineteenth century was to produce a resource for future scholars, that is, scholars who might one day interpret classical culture. In the meantime, scholars must restrict themselves to constructing an archive for the future.

Celebrating "our industriousness" as the distinguishing feature of German knowledge production, Mommsen treated the scholars laboring on the CIL accordingly, driving his bookish and barely remunerated workers not to let up as they tracked down inscriptions all over the Roman world. Never mind such things as the extreme July heat in North Africa. The correspondence of these workers makes clear what sort of pressure he put them under. A typical line, from a note written in 1865, reads, "Mommsen's most recent letter impressed on me that I need to spend every moment on the CIL."[97] In his lectures, Nietzsche speaks bitterly of a factory-style system of philology in which "every squandered minute would be punished."

## CRISIS MANAGEMENT IN A NIETZSCHEAN KEY

While Mommsen was busy organizing information, Nietzsche was excoriating his fellow scholars for losing sight of philology's real task. Ultimately, he argued, the purpose of philology was not to advance knowledge or accumulate, in Mommsen's words, an "archive of the past."[98] Rather, it was to cultivate stronger, healthier human beings on the model, however idealized, of the ancient Greeks. The real philologist isn't a detached observer but rather a lover of antiquity, someone who seeks to transform himself through a passionate encounter with a distant culture. Every worthwhile field of study, Nietzsche wrote, should be kept in check by a "hygienics of life"—practices by which whatever one learned could be integrated into the culture of the here and now.[99]

Professional philologists disassemble antiquity and its exemplary cul-

ture "reason by reason," Nietzsche wrote, while believing they would do
the world a great service by recovering antiquity "as it actually was."[100] Yet
with their endless historicizing and critical microscopy, they hasten the irrelevance of the classical world. For true philology, Nietzsche believed—
echoing Goethe, Schiller, and Friedrich Schlegel—ancient Greece was a
culture of genius that inspired awe and self-transformation.[101] It had the
potential to liberate moderns from their habits and assumptions. But philology had succumbed to professionalization and its parsimony of the
spirit. The narrowing of the discipline turned philologists and classical
scholars like Mommsen into the clearest examples of the perils of modern
academic knowledge. Their inveterate and reductive historicism had sun-
dered them and their students from the help that Greek antiquity could
give moderns and weakened a visceral respect for a healthier culture. Their
modern knowledge got in their way and thus in the way of modern culture's
rebirth as well.

What Nietzsche called "the objective-castrated philologist" is another
form of the "last man" type—the cultured liberal philistine, the pathetic
figure of modern man. He is another modern subject of knowledge whose
education has taught him to "sit lazily and inactively to the side" even as he
sees himself as a model of assiduity. Scholarship has rendered him "impotent," incapable of creating a new culture that could sustain better forms of
life.[102] The university and its secondary institution, the *Gymnasium*, force
students to ask how might they sacrifice themselves to disciplinary scholarship and find themselves (and their careers) in its practices and values. But
for Nietzsche, that was the wrong question; again, they should be forced to
ask, what is the value of *Wissenschaft* for us today? Is it a healthy, animating activity? Or, like the *Gymnasium* as depicted in the Basel lectures, does
it promote a culture that is "bloated" like an "unhealthy body"? Academic
knowledge, Nietzsche proposes in the "We Philologists" notes, should ultimately be concerned with the problems of the present; the value of antiquity
lies in how its study can shed light on our now. For Nietzsche, these were not
primarily epistemological challenges—he never asserted that there were no
facts about antiquity. Rather, the challenges were ethical and existential.
Here, at least, he even allowed that philology in itself wasn't bad. "Against
the discipline of philology," he wrote, "there is nothing to say. The problem
is that philologists are also the educators."[103]

In his notes for "We Philologists," Nietzsche compares the decline of philology to that of religion:

> It's all over for religions that believe in gods, providence, rational world
> orders, miracles, and sacraments, just as it is for certain kinds of holy

living, and for asceticism, because we can easily explain all these things as effects of a damaged brain or illness. There is no doubt that the opposition of a pure, disembodied soul and a body has nearly been eliminated. For now, sickness, disaster, and misfortune are explained by scientific assumptions and conclusions. Who still believes in the immortality of the soul?[104]

Philologists were thus the forerunners of the townspeople who mocked the madman who ran around the marketplace crying out, "I'm looking for God! I'm looking for God!," only to realize that "we have killed him—you and I!" Like the townspeople, whose haughty laughter betrayed their inability to fully grasp the consequences of the death of God, philologists had no idea what their destruction of antiquity had done. Suffering from that most modern of diseases, skepticism, they had somehow managed to transform it into a scholarly virtue.[105]

Nietzsche considered the decline of philology into a skeptical practice just another sign of what had become of *Wissenschaft*. What was once a culture dedicated to the unity of knowledge and life had degenerated into a form of "Socratism." Yet Nietzsche continued to insist that philology is still needed to help modern humans develop their own forms of life in the post-Christian world to come. "Disciplinary scholarship," he writes, requires a "doctrine of health," a higher form of oversight, a form of "surveillance." The "drive to knowledge" alone would be just as unhealthy as the "hatred of knowledge."[106]

After invoking for himself the status of a "child of older eras, especially the Greek one," Nietzsche writes in *Untimely Meditations*: "This much I believe I am permitted to say about myself on account of my position as a classical philologist. I wouldn't know what the point of classical philology would be in our time if it weren't as follows: to work upon our time in an untimely manner, which means working against our time and thus upon our time, and it is to be hoped, in doing so, for the benefit of future times."[107] The ultimate purpose of philology and the study of antiquity is thus to gain a better understanding of one's epoch and to develop cultural practices for living a better life. In this sense, Nietzsche's vision of philology is unabashedly presentist. It shares the same ends as all forms of education, history, and science—crafting individual and collective life in a modernity that Nietzsche diagnosed as bad for one's health. There is no institution you should respect more "than your own soul," he writes in "We Philologists."[108]

The historical problem of how to pursue knowledge of the past *and* put it in the service of life is the paradox that would structure Nietzsche's entire oeuvre, starting with *The Birth of Tragedy*. Nietzsche's notes for "We Philologists" conclude not with another discussion of this paradox but with a demonstration of its possibilities. For philologists to become truly creative, they must pose a basic question: how had Greek and Roman antiquity come to be the basis for modern, elite German education? "That there are scholars who devote themselves exclusively to researching Greek and Roman antiquity" wrote Nietzsche, most every educated (nineteenth-century) German would accept as fair, even praiseworthy.[109] But why did these same specialized scholars, of whom he was one, teach Germany's future elite in *Gymnasien*? And why were the ancient cultures of Greece and Rome the models for modern Germany? In short, suggests Nietzsche, the reason is prejudice.

Nietzsche considered "classical antiquity" a double projection.[110] First, the Roman Alexandrians invented a distinctly *Greek* antiquity; second, centuries of Europeans, and especially nineteenth-century Germans, invented both Greek and Roman "antiquity" as a part of modern philology. In part Nietzsche's critique is driven by his own preference for a Greek culture that he argued preceded the rationalization embodied in Socrates. As he argued in *The Contest of Homer* and *The Birth of Tragedy*, later Roman notions of classical Greece obscured this earlier and, for Nietzsche, better culture. Just as the Alexandrians created their own ideal Greek culture, the moderns created their own Greek-Roman antiquity, but they did so in the name of *the human*.

The problem of philology's prejudice, however, was not simply one of anachronism; more and better history would neither diminish the prejudice nor improve German *Gymnasien*. The problem was the assumption underlying Germany's entire educational system—the continuity, moral salience, and universality of *the human*. As a corrective, Nietzsche proposed to distinguish between *das Menschliche* (that which is human) and *das Humane*.[111] Whereas the Latinate "the human" (*das Humane*) referred to a free-floating abstraction, the vernacular *das Menschliche* referred to concrete forms of human life. The "human" does not refer to universal human solidarity, a sense of community or identity, or compassion but to the projection of vague desires and ideals onto a past in order to legitimate interests and concerns in the present. The classical human was an invented tradition, not a universal insight.

Nietzsche's argument was not simply historical; it was also moral. *The human*—and the litany of collocations that had only relatively recently emerged around it, such as *humanity, humane, humanistic*, and *humanism*—gives a moral sheen to abstractions and vagaries that can all too easily veil the more particular, concrete, and lived distinctions shaping actual lives. Yet as Nietzsche understood, *the human* had come to be used as a moral reason whose mere invocation, without evidence or argument, was used to make sense of the world and compel action within it.

By the end of the nineteenth century, as we show in subsequent chapters, *the human* had also come to be used as the foundational concept and figure for an invented tradition: the modern humanities, as though the *human* had sustained a common form of inquiry and knowledge that stretched over millennia from the ancient Greeks and Romans to late nineteenth-century Germans. It is in this sense that the problem of historicism and the human intersect to form one of the paradoxes of the modern humanities: how to pursue knowledge and put it to the service of life. This historical paradox is an analogue to the challenge of naturalism: how does knowledge about the world, "an effect of the nervous system," as Nietzsche called it, gain normative force? What does it mean to "translate humanity back into nature"?[112] How, in other words, does knowledge about *the human* gain normative force and shape how people live?

Although *On the Future of Our Educational Institutions* doesn't raise that question directly, it helped turn historicism into a problem by highlighting the gap between ethical promise and pedagogical experience that defined debates about the fate of humanistic knowledge around 1900. Indeed, the Basel lectures stress the importance of creatively reimagining antique models of learning in a present whose pedagogical failures are causes and effects of just the modern ills Nietzsche would spend the rest of his life diagnosing. In order for antiquity to serve as a vital resource in the modern world, modern philologists had to overcome the very thing they loved. The capacity to extricate oneself from this paradox was, as Nietzsche understood it, genius, something he considered inimical to the modern humanities and incompatible with the research university.

CHAPTER FOUR

# The Mandarins of the Lab

It was a physiologist, not a philologist, who introduced the humanities to the Germans of the mid-nineteenth century: "Time and again, reality has revealed itself much more purely, and in a much richer way, to the science that is true to its laws; the greatest efforts of mystical fantasy and metaphysical speculation pale by comparison."[1] Thus reads the epigraph of Wilhelm Dilthey's *Introduction to the Humanities*. Published in 1883, just a decade after the founding of the German Empire and amid the debates about education, industrial scholarship, and knowledge discussed in the previous chapter, Dilthey's two-volume tome gave formative expression to an emerging understanding of what we term the *modern humanities*. A philosopher with an abiding interest in physiology and psychology, Dilthey compared his ambitions to those of the seventeenth-century English philosopher and statesman Francis Bacon, who had sought to renew the sciences of nature by outlining a "sure," inductive method and destroying the idols blocking "men's minds."[2]

Dilthey drew his epigraph from an address the physiologist Hermann Helmholtz had delivered as rector of the University of Berlin in 1878, "The Facts of Perception." Although Dilthey had studied in Berlin under the philologist August Boeckh and joined the Berlin faculty in 1882, he was not in Helmholtz's audience that day. But it did not matter: many of Helmholtz's words had wings, as the Germans say. Helmholtz enjoyed prestige among his fellow physiologists and physicists as well as renown in Germany and beyond as a leading "spokesman of science."[3] By 1871, when he became chair of physiology at the University of Berlin, two collections of his essays and lectures had already been published, addressed not only to his fellow natural scientists but to scholars across the disciplines and Germany's educated elite. A few years later, his highly successful translation helped introduce the more popular writings of one of Victorian England's most influential scientists, the physicist John Tyndall, to German readers.[4]

Helmholtz exemplified a new scholarly persona: a natural scientist who not only conducted specialized research but also, like his colleagues Emil Du Bois-Reymond and Rudolf Virchow, asserted and defended the ascendant legitimacy of the natural sciences, arguing for their cultural and epistemic authority both within and beyond the university. As leading figures of an exclusive group of prominent, university-based "scientific opinion leaders," Helmholtz and his colleagues didn't seek to democratize natural science or make it a common knowledge as much as shift the basis of the authority and legitimacy of Germany's elite from a literary education to a natural scientific one.[5] "An increasingly lively longing for instruction in the natural sciences is stirring among educated circles," wrote Helmholtz in 1874. "And I don't think it can be dismissed as . . . a meaningless and fruitless curiosity. I consider it an entirely legitimate spiritual need deeply related to the forces driving our contemporary processes of spiritual development."[6]

Yet in discussing the natural sciences in "The Facts of Perception," Helmholtz spoke as much about their limits as their potential to meet any "spiritual need." It was the prospect of limits between and among sciences and scholarly disciplines—and the possibilities for different forms of knowledge those limits implied—that Dilthey found compelling in the great physiologist. The occasion for "The Facts of Perception," delivered in the university's auditorium to Helmholtz's faculty colleagues, was threefold: to commemorate the birthday of King Friedrich Wilhelm III (r. 1797–1840), to memorialize the king's decision in 1807 to fund a university in the midst of the French occupation, and to salute the University of Berlin's first two decades (1810–1830) as an epoch of poets and philosophers. The setting and the occasion, while fitting for self-congratulation, Helmholtz evidently felt also called for a warning. Only eight years after Germans had fought to unify themselves, the rector told his colleagues, the nation had lost sight of the "eternal ambitions of humanity," ambitions once nourished by the university and its sustaining project: *Wissenschaft* or university-based disciplinary knowledge. The problem Germany's leading university now faced, he continued, was how it could overcome the widespread "cynical contempt for all of humanity's ideal goods."[7]

Although philosophers such as Johann Gottlieb Fichte and Friedrich Schleiermacher had helped found the university and make it famous, now, more than seventy years later, natural scientists were best equipped, Helmholtz said, to defend these "ideal goods" and guide the university through the modern age. Helmholtz described this new scholarly persona, the natural scientist, as an "astute thinker with an uninhibited feeling for truth" and a desire for "facts of experience."[8] These virtues were promoted by the "sure grounds" of the natural sciences, which constrained any tendencies to exceed what could be posited on the basis of facts. Helmholtz knew that his talk of epistemic limits and constraints might strike his faculty colleagues as unduly "modest" when compared to the "high-flying plans" of the pantheon of German philosophers, which played to their longings for "absolute knowledge," in Hegel's phrase.[9] Although he hesitated to offer his Berlin colleagues metaphysical insight, he did offer them a moral imperative: each should conduct himself as a "mortal . . . with a clear eye for truth and reality."[10] The ideal natural scientist, the person they should aspire to become, cultivated an almost abstemious attention to "law-like regularity" and "fidelity to truth."[11] These were new virtues for a new epoch in which the natural scientist was to be the moral exemplar.

Like many of his contemporaries, Dilthey shared Helmholtz's unwavering commitment to what both considered a uniquely modern form of knowledge: *Wissenschaft*, or disciplinary, university-based scholarship. Most importantly, Dilthey and Helmholtz believed that disciplinary knowledge in this sense had liberated humans from theological dogma and metaphysical fantasies even as both scholars remained dubious of some of its more idealist origins.[12]

For Dilthey in particular, however, there was still something missing. In their relentless pursuit of causal explanations, natural scientists had set aside such things as ideals, meaning, and values, bracketing out a distinctly human and (human and moral) moral way of being in the world along with them. As a response to this perceived lacuna, intellectuals and scholars such as Dilthey heralded the modern humanities not simply as a set of specialized scholarly disciplines but, he wrote, as "humanity itself."[13] The modern humanities, the disciplinary forms of knowledge first institutionalized in late nineteenth- and early twentieth-century universities in Germany and then in the United States, and the narratives that would define and legitimate them, were devised to compensate for the historical, conceptual, and moral lack many late nineteenth-century German elites and intellectuals experienced with the ascendance of the natural sciences.

As scholars such as Dilthey and Helmholtz debated the authority, legitimacy, and limits of academic knowledge, German universities were undergoing deep and, for many, disruptive changes. There was, as discussed in chapter 2, rapid expansion of the student population. During the half century from 1820 to 1870, it had held steady around thirteen thousand. Then, in only four decades, total enrollments at German universities more than quadrupled, state expenditures for research activities increased even more steeply, entrance requirements were changed, women were admitted, and many of the tools and technologies used in specialized research were transformed. In 1910, a century after the founding of the University of Berlin, the

German research university as envisioned by Wilhelm von Humboldt and his contemporaries had changed radically notwithstanding the rhetoric of continuity resounding in the speeches given at centenary celebrations.

Another key element in this transformation was the attempt by an array of intellectuals and scholars to consolidate and institutionalize a range of previously distinct disciplines and fields as a generally coherent endeavor under the banner of the *Geisteswissenschaften*, or what we translate as "the modern humanities."[14] The story of the *Geisteswissenschaften* as narrated by their advocates from Dilthey's day to ours has consistently been one of crisis and decline in which capitalism, industrialization, technology, and the sciences eroded the humanities' cultural legitimacy and epistemic authority. What was true for German mandarins—the historian Fritz Ringer's term for mostly reactionary humanist scholars who decried the liberal state and their loss of cultural prestige and power around 1900—has remained so for both politically conservative and progressive supporters of the humanities, however different their points of emphasis, epistemological tenets, and strategies of justification.[15] For nearly a century and a half, claims about a "crisis of the humanities" have constituted a genre with remarkably consistent features: anxiety about modern agents of decay, the loss of authority and legitimacy, and invocations of "the human" in the face of forces that dehumanize and alienate humans from themselves, one another, and the world. These claims typically lead to the same, rather paradoxical conclusion: modernity destroys the humanities, but only the humanities can redeem modernity, a circular story of salvation in which overcoming the crisis of modernity is the mission of the humanities. Without a sense of crisis, the humanities would have neither purpose nor direction.

There is a further paradox. Although they typically suggest otherwise, these accounts of decline inadvertently demonstrate that the humanities did not precede the maelstrom of modernity but emerged from within it. Echoing the tradition of framing we examined in chapters 1–3, the central narratives of the modern humanities show that the humanities were themselves an effect of the same forces that elicited dismay and foreboding among their defenders. Again, Dilthey will prove historiographically, rhetorically, philosophically, and ethically exemplary in all this. His efforts to define and defend the modern humanities as a distinct form of knowledge were based largely on an assertion that they could fulfill a crucial social function: spiritual compensation for the stultifying and enervating effects of the modern cultural and social crisis. In the final three decades of the nineteenth century, one of the most prominent manifestations of these putative depredations was natural science. With his epigraph for *Introduction to the Humanities*, Dilthey explicitly registered how the natural sciences shaped the kind of knowledge the humanities were purported to provide. For Dilthey, the distinct character of the humanities derived from the scientific ordering and disenchantment of the world, which both threatened the humanities and made them modern. Crisis was their fate—and their justification.

Dilthey, Helmholtz, and all those debating the limits and possibilities of knowledge lived in what Rudolf Virchow called "the age of the natural sciences."[16] A nineteenth-century German physician, Virchow helped establish pathology as a discipline and was, like Helmholtz, a prominent popularizer of natural science. Speaking in 1893 to his faculty colleagues at the University of Berlin as their newly elected rector, Virchow identified Alexander von Humboldt's address at the inaugural meeting of the Congress of German Natural Scientists and Physicians in 1827 as the dawn of this new age, the moment when Germany began to mature from being the land of poets and philosophers to being the land of physiologists and physicists.[17]

As we saw in chapter 1, however, the disdain for metaphysical systems did not extinguish the desire for the unity of all knowledge; it lingered in scholars such as Virchow, Helmholtz, and their fellow pioneering physiologist Emil Du Bois-Reymond. Indeed, this desire informed their hopes as well as their ambivalence about the rapid rise of natural science.[18] While celebrating the "age of the natural sciences," Virchow acknowledged that questions concerning the "essence of the human mind" remained unanswered. He also warned that natural scientists' inability to answer such questions would leave open the "door for mysticism" and irrational movements such as antisemitism.[19] Du Bois-Reymond had delivered an epoch-defining speech on the limits of natural science in 1872. For him, as for Virchow and Helmholtz, adherence to the boundaries of natural science was a core virtue of the truly modern and liberal scholar. These three mandarins of the lab who helped popularize and legitimate natural science in late nineteenth-century Germany understood that insisting on the epistemic limits of the natural sciences would have cultural and ethical consequences both good and bad. Indeed, even as they feared a return of the myths of metaphysics and theology, they ultimately helped, however unknowingly, to create the narrative and self-understanding of the modern humanities.

Intellectuals and academic humanists who feared their impending irrelevance or diminution—for example, Dilthey—paid close attention to the attempts of natural scientists to identify the boundaries of knowledge. Over time they embraced the "door" the natural scientists had left ajar as an acknowledgment of the insufficiency of modern scientific knowledge as well as an invitation to redress that lack. For most German intellectuals and scholars around 1900, this "door" led not back to metaphysical fantasies or theological premises but to a possible fulfillment of the perceived social and moral needs of the age of the natural sciences, an age that, as Nietzsche put it, the tumult of "secularization" and the "ebbing" of religion had left spiritually impoverished.[20] What lay beyond that "door" and how something as ill defined and prospective as the modern humanities might satisfy such needs, however, remained unclear. In order to have any legitimate claim on cultural and epistemic authority, the humanities had to be *wissenschaftlich*: they had to embody the virtues and practices of specialized, disciplinary, university-based knowledge. Yet they could not be scholarly in the way the big, data-driven philology projects discussed in the previous chapter were. They had to be *more* different from the natural sciences. What were needed, as the philosopher Heinrich Rickert put it in 1890, were the "nicht naturwissenschaftlichen" disciplines—the not-natural-scientific disciplines.[21]

## THE RISE OF PHYSIOLOGY AND MÜLLER'S MANDARINS

Around 1850 one discipline in particular epitomized the burgeoning success and stature of the natural sciences in Germany: physiology. And more than anyone, Emil Du Bois-Reymond, Hermann Helmholtz, and Rudolf Virchow came to embody its authority and legitimacy. Each had studied under Johannes Müller (1801–1858), whose encyclopedic *Elements of Physiology* (1838) helped train the first generations of German physiologists. Müller's appointment in 1833 as chair of anatomy and physiology on the University of Berlin medical faculty came at the beginning of a shift of the center of the experimental life sciences from Paris, Oxford, and Cambridge to Berlin, and, just two years after Hegel's death, marked a changing intellectual and scholarly landscape in the Prussian capital itself.[22] Soon after arriving in Berlin, Müller transformed the university's anatomical theater and museum into "evil-smelling," poorly outfitted labs. He worked tirelessly, lecturing on physiology and human anatomy, leading dissection labs thirteen hours per week, overseeing Berlin's Anatomical Institute and Anatomical Museum, administering exams to candidates from all of Prussia's universities, and somehow finding time for his own research and writing.[23] According to Müller, the ideal physiologist combined careful observation of natural forms and objects with more philosophically informed theorizing about their possible relationships.[24]

It was in the pungent and packed halls of the Anatomical Museum and Anatomical Institute that Du Bois-Reymond, Helmholtz, and Virchow encountered the figure who for decades modeled the virtues, ideals, and limitations of natural science. Regardless of the criticisms they eventually leveled at their teacher once they established themselves as physiologists, they considered Müller a figure to both emulate and surpass. In post-Hegelian, postidealist Berlin, *their* Müller embraced empirical observation, stressed the importance of tools and technological aids (especially the microscope), insisted on the value of experimentation, sought physical laws to explain life, and was committed to method.[25] By requiring his students to use microscopes, Müller tied research into the processes of life to instruments and technology.[26] He also helped his students become professional natural scientists by securing their access to tools and specimen collections, helping publish their research, recommending them for academic (and related) jobs, and even, in the case of Helmholtz, helping secure a release from military service.[27]

As their own research and careers developed, however, Müller's best students sought to distinguish themselves from their teacher. Du Bois-Reymond, for instance, derided Müller's "inadequate theoretical education," "vitalistic reveries," and insufficiently "mathematical conception" of natural science;[28] Virchow criticized his insistence on treating pathological growths as "given, completed things" instead of "developing" tissues;[29] Helmholtz, more gently perhaps, commented that his devotion to morphological and anatomical techniques made him less receptive to methods derived from chemistry and physics.[30]

Du Bois-Reymond, Helmholtz, and Virchow considered Müller not simply a scholar or *Wissenschaftler* but more precisely a natural scientist, or *Naturforscher*. Each in his own way continued to rely on Müller as the exemplar of what a natural scientist ought to become. Helmholtz, for example, wrote, "There was one man in particular who inspired and oriented our work in the right direction: *Johannes Müller*, the physiologist. In his theoretical views, he still favored vitalist hypotheses, but in the most consequential points he was a natural scientist, steady and unwavering. He considered all theories only hypotheses, which had to be tested against the facts and about which solely facts could decide."[31] Central to this shared conception of natural science as practiced, theorized, and eventually popularized by Müller and his students was the conviction that natural science was, most centrally, a set of individual and collective exercises and practices through which people were formed according to distinct epistemic ideals and virtues. As Helmholtz, Du Bois-Reymond, and Virchow came to practice and promote it, physiology didn't just produce knowledge about animal electricity, sensory perception, or human disease. It developed human capacities of mind, body, and moral character. Physiology was a form of natural scientific *Bildung*, or moral formation.

Du Bois-Reymond, Helmholtz, and Virchow sought to develop the natural sciences—especially physiology and, for Virchow, pathology—both within and without the community of scientists. As highly esteemed researchers, they pursued and related to their particular fields as modern, university-based disciplines with their own internal goods (new knowledge, disciplinary coherence, scholarly community). They also understood natural science to be a collective endeavor. Not only did these three natural scientists theorize mental, nervous, and perceptual processes; prepare and conduct experiments to test those theories; and collect and analyze data to advance and revise them, but they also participated in numerous scientific societies and associations and, crucially, edited, read, and wrote for the specialized scientific periodicals that proliferated during the nineteenth century. Du Bois-Reymond and Helmholtz were key members of the Berlin Physical Society. Virchow founded the *Archive for Pathological Anatomy and Physiology and for Clinical Medicine* in 1847, which he and his coeditor intended as a "carefully edited" periodical devoted to cultivating the "natural scientific point of view." All of these activities were part of what Helmholtz described as the collective "organization of knowledge," which he considered the responsibility of every modern scholar.[32]

Outside the scientific community, in both academia and society in general, Du Bois-Reymond, Helmholtz, and Virchow promoted natural science as a public good both as members of cultural and scientific societies devoted to similar causes and as independent speakers and writers. As highly visible members of a cultured class of elites, they helped popularize and legitimate the promises of natural science: insight into the natural world, technological innovation, social progress, and *Bildung*. In 1849 Virchow cofounded another journal, a weekly titled *The Medical Reform*, which sought to publicize the social progress made possible by physicians as a way of establishing their "scientific" expertise and thus legitimating their cultural authority.[33] Du Bois-Reymond, Helmholtz, and Virchow addressed fellow cultured elites in public lectures, professionals at national congresses and meetings, and faculty across the disciplines at traditional university celebrations. Many of their speeches were occasions of collective memory and institutional ritual, such as the addresses each delivered as rector of the University of Berlin, a position all three held at different times between 1869 and 1893.

Many of these more popular, official speeches were quickly published in journals and essay collections, buttressed by footnotes and bibliographic detail. Despite their often incantatory tone and liberal use of pieties on the greatness of German culture, the speeches were skillfully crafted, as the electrical engineer Werner Siemens, founder of the industrial behemoth that still bears his name, put it, to extirpate "superstition," ensure limitless technological progress, and advance industry.[34] They also encouraged listeners and readers to conceive of natural science and the *Naturforscher* as capable of providing what "humanism required": "sustaining the health, well-being, and morality of the human race."[35] Even as they held out the prospect of immediate practical benefits for society, they tried to make the natural sciences a central element of liberal education and *Bildung*.

As cultural elites arguing for a humanistic *Bildung* and liberal education, even if they were to be based in the natural sciences, Helmholtz, Du Bois-Reymond, and Virchow were also mandarins. But they were of a different sort than those Fritz Ringer described in his study of the reactionary humanists circa 1900.[36] Ringer adapted the mandarin concept from Max Weber, who had used the term in his writings on the sociology of world religions to describe a distinct cultural class from which centuries of Chinese civil servants had been recruited.[37] Although the rank of any individual Chinese mandarin was determined by the number of tests he had passed, the broader class was distinguished by its literary education, or what Weber called its *Bildung*. For the Chinese mandarins, *Bildung* was knowledge obtained "through writing." Their authority and legitimacy derived from their knowledge of and capacity to interact with texts.

In applying the mandarin concept to nineteenth-century Germany, Ringer used it to describe an entire class of elites set apart by "differences in cultivation." Its members, among them civil servants and state bureaucrats, enjoyed privileges and prestige that were a function not only of their technical knowledge and skills but also of, in Ringer's words, the "general education" they had received, particularly in the classical *Gymnasium*.[38] Thus, along with knowledge, the German education system produced the social bonds and distinctions that enabled the formation of the mandarin class.

The cultural authority of the mandarins Ringer and Weber described derived from literary *Bildung* as manifested particularly in philology and philosophy. In contrast, Virchow, Du Bois-Reymond, and Helmholtz, mandarins of the lab, owed their cultural authority and legitimacy to their status as natural scientists. What made them mandarins, not simply natural scientists, was, ultimately, the neo-humanist conception of research as constituting a form of *Bildung*.[39] Each in his own way, the mandarins of the lab adopted an essentially neo-humanist notion of culture as first articulated by Kant and Schiller and then elaborated by Fichte, Humboldt, and Schleiermacher. Culture, wrote Kant in 1788, is the "cultivation of a rational being's capacity to set its own ends through freedom." "Arts and sciences," he continued, prepared humans for the "authority" of reason and the elevation of the "powers of the mind."[40] For the mandarins of the lab, natural science had become, as Du Bois-Reymond would write in 1877, the "absolute organ of culture" and, thus, the central agent of moral transformation.[41]

As they strove to legitimate the modern natural sciences as sources of cultural authority and moral transformation, the mandarins of the lab also sought to balance what they recognized as the largely utilitarian ethos of natural science with the epistemic ideals of *Bildung* and *Wissenschaft* as epitomized by philology, philosophy, and history—the unity of knowledge, the commitment to goods internal to the practice of science, and the ethical potential of knowledge practices.[42] They attempted to reconcile these tensions not only by, in Helmholtz's words, celebrating the "multiplication of human powers through machines," such as steam engines, steel cannons, and weaving machines, but also by interpreting these developments as harbingers or even agents of a new humanism. The natural sciences were the form of liberal education and study for the modern age that would not only improve the material conditions of society but also contribute to the "improvement of political organization and the moral development of individuals."[43]

Yet as they established themselves within and outside the university, the mandarins of the lab began to express an ambivalence about the ascendant and, for some of their contemporaries, absolute authority of the very culture they had helped craft and had come to represent. On one side, they resisted the unbridled optimism of their more ideologically minded materialist contemporaries such as Jacob Moleschott, Carl Vogt, and Ludwig Büchner, who in the aftermath of the failed 1848 revolution looked to natural science to usher in political and social progress. On the other side, they defended natural science against increasingly strident and organized criticism from intellectuals and scholars in search of non–natural scientific forms of knowledge and meaning—that is, epistemic and ethical resources not based exclusively on observation and experimentation. In so doing, the mandarins of the lab presented natural science as itself an ethical resource that should be considered an "ally" of other, non–natural scientific forms of knowledge.[44] This implied, of course, that these other disciplines provided something the natural sciences could not. With their claims to having a privileged relation to modern *Bildung*, the mandarins encroached on the traditional territory of philology, philosophy, and history, compounding the sense of marginalization in those fields. Hence Dilthey's defiant invocation of Helmholtz on the comparative weakness of the humanities at the beginning of *Introduction to the Humanities*. But again they left the door open a crack.

HELMHOLTZ ON THE RELATIONSHIP OF THE
HUMANITIES AND THE NATURAL SCIENCES

As industry, technology, and the natural sciences began to flourish in the 1840s and after the failed revolution of 1848, many German intellectuals and scholars sought a coherent and countervailing form of knowledge. Although some turned to particular disciplines—Johann Gustav Droysen to history, August Boeckh to philology—there was an another effort, initially disorganized and inchoate, to offer a compelling account of the capacity of a collective set of disciplines to counter the impending "absolute rule" of the natural sciences.[45] Well into the second half of the nineteenth century, Hegel's philosophical system, despite increasing resistance among young scholars identifying themselves as natural scientists, continued to shape these efforts.[46] Between 1831, the year of Hegel's death, and 1860, there are only "scattered" instances of the appearance of *Geisteswissenschaft* and even fewer instances of its plural form, *Geisteswissenschaften*.[47] When the term does appear, it is primarily in texts written as encyclopedic or pedagogical introductions to university studies and based on some variation of a Hegelian schema of knowledge.[48] The authors of these Hegel-inspired schemas considered philosophy and *Wissenschaft* to be "synonymous" and, when rightly practiced, defined by a common purpose: "to secure" the principles and relationships of all other forms of knowledge or sciences.[49] Even as Hegel's influence waned and various forms of empiricism, naturalism, and materialism gained influence across Germany, the *Geisteswissenschaften*, like the natural sciences, were considered lower "levels" of reason's historical development.[50] Lamenting the continued inability of scholars who studied the past to establish history as a coherent and distinct discipline, Droysen wrote in 1843 that "*Geisteswissenschaften* continued to vacillate wildly."[51] They had no continuity, no clear boundaries, no coherent theory, and no particular method of their own.

In 1854 Andreas Ludwig Kym, a philosophy professor in Zurich who had studied in Berlin, introduced a narrative that would frame university-based knowledge in German-speaking lands for the remainder of the century: "The world cleaves itself into two halves. Nature forms one, and history or mind [*Geist*] forms the other. When humans concern themselves with nature, the natural sciences develop. When humans concern themselves with history or with the mind, the humanities [*Geisteswissenschaften*] develop. Each of these halves then further divides itself."[52] Each half then develops into the object of a form of knowledge particular to it. Humans come to know nature through the natural sciences; they come to know history and mind through the humanities. Underlying this basic division of knowledge is this "well-established fundamental insight into the difference between matter and mind."[53] The division between the natural sciences and the humanities was not simply epistemic, a matter of different methods and objects of inquiry; it was also ethical. Kym called scholars who studied nature by means of natural science "realists" and those who studied history and mind "idealists."[54] Scholars in either group understand themselves and what they do because they are formed into a distinct "Weltanschauung— a realist or materialist one or an idealist or spiritual one." Neither ontological nor logically given, these two categories were embedded in time and even, as Kym claimed, exemplified by distinct personae: the physiologist and the theologian.

> Whereas the physiologist with his Weltanschauung devalues mind while empowering mechanical force, the theologian wants mind and freedom. He does not tolerate attempts to explain religion and morality merely from the movements of brain fibers, just as the logician would never concede that a thought is nothing more than a secretion of the brain. And were a physiologist to muster the courage to claim something like this, then he would also have to prove which complex of movements of brain fibers give us religion and which produce the virtues.[55]

In this conceptualization the humanities have no legitimacy of their own, a claim that Kym emphasizes by identifying a theologian as their exemplary practitioner; instead, they are defined by what they oppose—an ontological materialism Kym ascribes to the natural sciences. Although Kym initially suggested that it was the task of philosophy to unify these distinct Weltanschauungen, he ultimately concluded that they could be reconciled only by an immanent teleology that only the theologian's theistic commitments could guarantee.[56]

By tying categories of knowledge to particular Weltanschauungen, Kym expressed a common desire among many intellectuals and scholars for something more than an additional category of reason to counter the ascendance of the natural sciences. His more historical and cultural account of the natural science–humanities dyad portended a possible path out of the tumult of midcentury battles over which disciplines would assume cultural authority and legitimacy. "One would have to be blind," wrote the law professor Johannes Kuntze in 1856, not to see that

> philosophical speculation has completed the cycle of scholastic systems, and now German philosophy languidly gnaws on the remains of

inherited glory. . . . Natural science has proliferated with such a force and pomp that the pressure of its sheer mass seems ready to burst or, at the very least, completely transform the entire structure of knowledge. One senses that after such deeds and cataclysms of the human spirit, knowledge will surely, as it were, organize itself anew—until now the schisms, isolations, and boundaries have always grown sharper. . . . The world of knowledge has given birth to a hundred worlds, and each one has its own king. It is, perhaps, a rule of many, an interregnum, but one must wonder how a unified empire of knowledge can be recovered. Faith and knowledge, or more accurately, faith and research, stand opposite one another as though armed for the decisive battle. Natural science and the humanities have emerged as enemies. And in this confrontation two titanic elements explode one upon the other—materialism and idealism, a monolithic empiricism and a protean teleology.[57]

## HELMHOLTZ ON THE WARRING
## FACTIONS OF KNOWLEDGE

In 1862, as efforts to articulate a countervailing knowledge were gaining traction and more than two decades before Dilthey published his own systematic account, a scholar who understood himself to be neither a philologist nor a philosopher but a physiologist and natural scientist offered one of the most coherent and clarifying accounts of the warring factions of knowledge. That scholar was Hermann Helmholtz. In his inaugural lecture as prorector of the University of Heidelberg, Helmholtz used the term *Geisteswissenschaften* to discuss the purpose of the university and the responsibility of scholars. Addressing his faculty colleagues as both a "philosopher of science" (in David Cahan's words) and an elected university administrator, he said he felt compelled to address the assertion, now common both inside and outside the university, that the natural sciences had "gone off on [their] own, isolated path" and were tearing the "*universitas litterarum*" apart.[58] Instead of defending the natural sciences, however, he blamed the antagonism on the continued influence of Hegel and quickly sought to consider what still unified the university. He focused on facts, emphasizing their ubiquity and the urgent need for scholars across the university to analyze, organize, and interpret them. The proliferation of objects—material things, observations, and measurements that could be collected, organized, and then marshaled as evidence—had increased as the forms and techniques of empirical observation had improved.[59] Whether in the form of epigraphic fragments from ancient monuments, scattered notes in an archive, newly collected plant specimens, or precision measurements from laboratory experiments, the sheer stuff of scholarship had begun to make scholars "dizzy." To think that Johannes Kepler—the seventeenth-century scholar known in 1861 and today as an astronomer—held faculty positions at the same university in Grasz in both mathematics and "morals" "makes us laugh," Helmholtz said. After Hegel (who had made scholars dizzy in a different way), and amid the evidentiary overproduction of empirical practices, how would any of them, the new Heidelberg prorector asked his colleagues, "be able to see the whole [and connect] the threads of the whole and find his way?"[60]

In one sense, Helmholtz's answer, delivered as counsel and conclusion, was clear: regardless of discipline or field, to practice modern and thus specialized scholarship was to do so empirically, to use inductive methods. Exactly how a particular scholar practiced this basic commitment to empirically based inquiry, Helmholtz continued, was what distinguished him as either a natural scientist or a scholar of the humanities, that is, a member of the *Geisteswissenschaften*. Among the humanities Helmholtz included the study of religion, law, language, art, and history, and he noted that each of these subjects had a "psychological basis." They were also connected, as he wrote elsewhere, by the philological and historical sciences, which he termed "helping sciences." Whereas natural scientists used "logical" induction to arrive at universal rules and laws, scholars in the humanities employed "artistic induction" to make judgments. The modern humanities scholar, such as a philologist, ultimately relied on his "psychological sense of tact" to "feel out" how discrete facts fit together.[61] Over the following decades, despite Helmholtz's revisions of his own account, this initial methodological distinction remained a common, if vague, sketch of the production of knowledge at German universities. It resonated with scholars and intellectuals for whom the university had become the central cultural institution, because, like Kym's largely unknown account, it distinguished between two opposing and easily identifiable personae, each standing in for a particular culture of knowledge: the intuitive, interpretive humanist versus the evidence-based, law-seeking, logical natural scientist.

As Helmholtz pointed out, both natural scientists and modern humanities scholars performed "intellectual work,"[62] and like any skilled activity, it had to be perfected through repeated exercises. It was in this sense that the natural sciences and the humanities were related but distinct. Although they shared a general commitment to empirically based methods and ideals, each had its own culture of epistemic and ethical formation. Using very broad strokes, Helmholtz delineated the boundaries between them, cursorily evoking their particular methods, notions of evidence, and practices. The natural sciences and the modern humanities, as he put it, culti-vated different "mental activities" and moral characters.[63]

These two cultures of knowledge were not of equal value, however. In a Prussian-dominated academic culture that for decades had upheld classi-cal philology as the exemplary scholarly discipline and primary resource for *Bildung*, not just for scholars but for all cultural elites, Helmholtz ar-gued that the natural sciences provided a superior education. With the pos-sible exception of grammar, he claimed, humanities disciplines did not typically yield "strict, universally valid laws." It was precisely the pursuit of laws allowing for "no exception," however, that would ultimately enable scholars to conquer nature.[64] To commit oneself to such an uncompromis-ing quest required distinct ethical techniques and virtues. The true natural scientist, Helmholtz said, relied on "the steely work of self-consciousness" to develop the capacity to focus exclusively on causal connections "undis-turbed" by personal "hopes and desires." The ideal natural scientist was, for Helmholtz, a kind of man as machine, built to serve as a technical instru-ment for an entire culture.[65]

Over the course of their careers, Du Bois-Reymond, Helmholtz, and Vir-chow repeatedly argued that natural science was not merely "useful" but— as Virchow wrote in 1893, drawing on Humboldtian and neo-humanist tropes—the "free development of an honest and beautiful personality whole unto itself."[66] Virchow, the pathologist and physician, translated the philological neo-humanism of the early nineteenth century into a medical and natural scientific one. Natural science developed both the individual and society by providing not only technological advances that sustained the body but also disciplined practices, ideals, and virtues that formed human minds and desires. "Classical texts" had long provided the primary material for developing "moral and aesthetic feeling" and intellectual capacities, but now, wrote Helmholtz in 1874, "we must point out that this important mo-ment . . . in the history of education has passed." "In the future" the natural sciences would have to play a central role; the "health of the further devel-opment of the nation depended on it."[67]

To think like a natural scientist was to think and act as if nature could be accounted for with lawlike regularity. It was, as Weber said in 1917, to "count on" the regular functioning of the streetcar and sun alike and to orient your behavior accordingly, taking as a given that no "mystical, incal-culable powers" would impede you as you went about your day.[68] Whereas those habituated into the natural sciences developed a capacity to unify individual observations and experiences into universal laws, scholars who practiced the modern humanities, claimed Helmholtz, faced almost "insurmountable difficulties" when they attempted to attain such lawlike knowledge, and so they tarried with the particular.[69] The natural scientist did not simply have faith in the lawlike regularity of nature; he had what Du Bois-Reymond called a "drive for causality" to lift observed phenomena up into a law, which he could then expand as a hypothesis to other, as yet uninvestigated phenomena.[70] In this way, as Virchow explained, the natural scientist used every observation, law, and hypothesis as a "lever" for the unceasing work of research.[71]

A commitment to precise measurement buttressed the natural scientist's respect for facts and cultivated trust in the orienting epistemic ideal of natural science—the lawlike regularity of nature. The very act of attempting to measure physiological or nervous functions forced a natural scientist, in Helmholtz's words, to "proceed very slowly," focusing on one point at a time.[72] Helmholtz directly contrasted the mathematical rigor and precision of the ideal natural scientist to the "laxity" of the philologically educated *Gymnasium* student, who merely memorized the "long lists" of exceptions that professional philologists had conveniently collected. In declaring generalizable knowledge for themselves, limiting other disciplines (e.g., philology, history, religion) to the study of particulars, and professing their unmatched commitment to rigor, the mandarins of the lab also claimed the mantle of wholeness, unity, and universality in a university and intellectual elite culture that remained committed to such ideals.

Just months before his death in 1894, Helmholtz observed that the natural sciences more effectively realized the ends of "humanity" than any "moral sermonizing" aimed at consoling or exhorting individuals.[73] Furthermore, these ends had a "much deeper moral significance" than mere utility. The virtues and goods cultivated by the natural sciences enabled humans to join together to realize the "universal purposes of humanity, purposes that could not be limited to any one individual, not even one nation or continent, but necessarily [transformed] the work of the individual into work for the purposes of humanity." Helmholtz claimed that natural science could reshape, even redeem, a "cultural elite," those "classes capable of judgment," traditionally educated in the "literary studies" of the classical *Gymnasium*, enabling them to better "lead our states, educate our children, maintain moral order, and preserve the treasures of knowledge and wisdom of previous generations."[74] The mandarins of the lab adopted and adapted both the language and the key ideals and values of neo-humanist *Bildung*.[75] They did so not only as a means of securing greater support for their chosen fields but also, as we shall see, because they believed that the natural sciences could civilize and cultivate individuals and society.

## WHAT EXACTLY WAS THE HUMANISM
## OF THE NATURAL SCIENCES?

The humanism of the natural sciences, as articulated primarily by Helm-holtz and Du Bois-Reymond, differed in significant ways, of course, from the neo-humanist traditions that managed to be at once canonical and em-battled throughout the nineteenth century. It is nevertheless important to make these fundamental distinctions explicit, especially given the common conflation, both then and now, of *the humanities* and *humanism*.

First, the humanism espoused by the mandarins of the lab was enmeshed with instruments, tools, technology, and media to a degree that other disci-plines such as philosophy and philology rarely were.[76] (Indeed, many of the mandarins' contemporaries thought physiology and other natural sciences portended an encroaching antihumanism.) The precision measurements needed to study animal electricity, for example, required new instruments and tools, which compelled natural scientists such as Du Bois-Reymond to work closely with local Berlin mechanics and technicians. Between 1841 and 1848, Du Bois-Reymond collaborated with the mechanic Johann Georg Halske, who in 1847 joined with Werner Siemens to found the Siemens and Halske Telegraph Construction Company, for the purpose of designing a galvanometer sensitive enough to detect electrical current in the nerves of frogs.[77] Describing their work together years later, Du Bois-Reymond wrote, "Our need for advice and help with all things mechanical drove us into [Ber-lin's] workshops, where at the sides of talented artisans we learned all sorts of useful ways to grip and hold tools. They also familiarized us with the structure of these tools and instruments down to the very last screw, as though we were dealing with the anatomy of animals."[78] Working with this equipment and in these workshops in pursuit of what Du Bois-Reymond called "an image of the animal machine" blurred the absolute boundaries between human, animal, and machine on both the practical and theoretical levels. As Du Bois-Reymond noted, machines became bodies, and bodies became machines.[79]

Second, and relatedly, the mandarins of the lab practiced their human-ism in different spaces than did scholars typically associated with such ideals—not around the seminar tables of the philologists, physicists, or mathematicians but in the emerging "laboratories" of Berlin's natural scien-tists. These "laboratories" were rarely dedicated spaces outfitted with all the required equipment, tools, and supplies; for instance, as students and young scholars, Helmholtz and Du Bois-Reymond experimented in their small apartments, crowded hallways, and closets—wherever they could find space to construct their apparatuses.[80] The natural scientist, as Virchow explained, had "to be in contact with real things," and this eventually required "big institutions" that could sustain, house, and pay for the spaces that made such contact possible.[81] Müller's students helped establish the laboratory as a necessary, if initially ideal, space for experimentation, instruction, and the cultivation of the natural scientific persona. Before 1850, functioning laboratories where, as Helmholtz recalled, "a student himself could actually interact" with things he was reading about in his books and hearing about in his lectures, were extremely rare in Prussia.[82] Speaking at the inauguration of the Physiological Institute in Berlin in 1877, for the establishment of which he had petitioned the Ministry of Education for over two decades, Du Bois-Reymond described the historical development of his discipline and its pedagogical distinctiveness not as a series of discoveries and theories but as what physiologists had actually done. He described in detail the instruments they crafted, the machines they used, the experimental apparatuses they designed, the chemicals they bought—all the ways they had learned "to grip" the phenomena of life.[83] Implicitly comparing his new "Palace of Science" with the conditions he had faced as an aspiring natural scientist, he described how he had been forced to conduct experiments in his own private apartment, where "the frogs and the rabbits got him into trouble with his neighbors."[84] He also noted how the laboratory was much more than a place to experiment; it was also a space where all the tools, media, and supplies for doing physiology could be collected and organized. To experiment was to observe and think with instruments, graphs, apparatuses, and one's own body, and to do so in a controlled setting where one learned how to observe and act like a natural scientist. The "Laboratorium" transformed people.[85]

Third, the humanism of the mandarins of the lab prioritized numeracy and quantification over literacy. Müller's students did so in part out of a common antipathy toward natural philosophy, especially the vitalism they considered its defining feature. Scholars beholden to natural philosophy, including his own teacher, Du Bois-Reymond argued in 1894, "unashamedly" relied on the unsubstantiated existence of living forces to account for any organic function they otherwise could not explain.[86] Du Bois-Reymond and Helmholtz devoted most of their early experimental work to constructing an alternate model according to which the functions of living organisms could be explained by observing, measuring, and theorizing about their internal causal mechanisms. They studied muscle contractions, visual perception, auditory perception—a range of mental, nervous, and perceptual processes previously deemed too momentary to perceive and, thus, not amenable to efforts to break them down into discrete units, measure them, and understand them through quantitative reasoning. In so doing the two scientists acknowledged that the unaided human senses were incapable of directly perceiving many organic processes and phenomena, including those that occurred in human beings. With the assistance of what Helmholtz called "artificial methods" and mediating machines, technologies, and methods, however, these once unknowable processes could be observed, measured, and better understood. Du Bois-Reymond used his galvanometer to quantify life processes and, thus, to account for them in strictly material and mechanistic terms. Physical-mathematical methods and their related tools helped, as Du Bois-Reymond wrote, to create a "mathematical image" of the causal relationships of natural phenomena.[87]

The attempt to quantify life, especially mental life, would have wide-ranging effects on notions of the human, not the least of which was to rekindle older debates about mind-body dualisms in new terms by asking what could and could not be observed in the human psyche. The emphasis on quantification concerned not only what could be tested and discovered but also the disciplining of potential natural scientists and the extirpation of unwanted ideas and concepts, such as the notion of a vital life force. Wherever these methods become "second nature," wrote Du Bois-Reymond, "those despised weeds of certain physiological explanations which retard the flourishing of science will have little soil in which to grow."[88] These debates about what could and could not be measured and accounted for by quantitative reasoning further defined the fault lines between the two cultures of disciplinary, university-based knowledge.

Fourth, the humanism of the mandarins of the lab upended the established rank and role of science over technology (of *episteme* over *techne*, theory over practical action).[89] Although they argued for what their critics dismissed as an impure form of knowledge, the mandarins of the lab espoused a commitment to many of the same ideals and virtues typically associated with the unity-of-knowledge ideal and disciplines such as philology and philosophy. They suggested that these same ideals and virtues were bound up with and even occasioned by mere machines and mastery of the techniques, skills, and knowledge necessary to use them well. Physiologists relied on technology and tools to gain insight into living bodies, life, and, most arrestingly, humans.[90] Natural scientists could direct the merely instrumental uses of technical knowledge, mathematical calculation, and even the natural sciences themselves toward higher ends; they could transform them, as the chemist Justus Liebig put it in 1840, into "the media of intellectual formation and the research of nature."[91]

The natural sciences provided humans with more than just another "lever" for a factory or the know-how to produce a new machine; they were central elements of a distinctly modern "intellectual culture" whose ultimate end was "truth."[92] In one of his early attempts to fuse technical knowledge and skill (*Technik*) and empirical investigation with the ideals of neo-humanist scholarship, Du Bois-Reymond and five other young natural scientists founded the Berlin Physical Society in 1845. Scholars without university appointments, they wanted to distinguish themselves as a coherent social group opposed to the continued influence of vitalist ideas and devoted to studying the mechanical processes that underlay all natural phenomena. After only two years the society had sixty-one members, including not only young natural and physical scientists with doctoral degrees but also six army lieutenants (most likely from the Prussian military's artillery and engineering school and its war school) and six master mechanics.[93] Bound by their antipathy to Müller's vestigial ideas about vital life forces, they met fortnightly in the home of Gustav Heinrich Magnus, a professor of physics and technology at the University of Berlin. In his elegant house in the Kupfergraben district, Magnus had created a private laboratory that far surpassed anything the university could offer. (He had acquired much of the equipment, however, with a 500-thaler-a-year budget that Karl von Altenstein, Prussia's minister of culture from 1817 to 1840 and an educational reformer, had been providing since 1833.) Although they welcomed mechanics and technicians and developed deep relationships with Berlin's emerging industries, the core members of the society saw themselves as scholars and natural scientists whose ultimate goal was "to draw the technical world into the University."[94]

Finally, the mandarins of the lab claimed that a humanism based on natural science was more liberating—in the sense of being more reliable in its cultivation of individual autonomy—than the established neo-humanism attached to philology and the study of Greek and Roman antiquity. Those formed into the rigors and precision of the natural sciences developed an "absolute reliability of thought," Helmholtz wrote, that in turn enabled them to rely on their own mental capacities and to recognize no other authority but "their own intellect."[95] By contrast, students trained only in philology, Helmholtz noted disparagingly, tended to make judgments about disputed questions by appealing to their teachers, who themselves had probably turned to recognized "authorities" for their own putatively authoritative judgments. Philology encouraged epistemic vices such as "sluggishness and tentativeness."[96] Similarly, Virchow associated the metaphysical assumptions of natural philosophy with the deference of its practitioners to "forms of autocratic authority" (both political and cultural), whereas he associated the commitment to empirical observation and precise measurement of the experimental natural sciences with the "sovereignty" of the human.[97]

As envisioned by the mandarins of the lab, a natural science that had been both tempered and ennobled could transform a preliberal self—enslaved to external authorities, limited by the finitude of human perception, isolated by selfish interests, and incapable of desiring, much less discerning, the universal—into a modern, scientifically enlightened member of humanity. At the least, it would enable an elite, liberal vanguard unified by a (reimagined) humanism and propelled by a modern scientific rationality to improve society. In his 1862 prorector's address and in public speeches over the following three decades, Helmholtz consistently argued that the goods of the natural sciences, both epistemic and ethical, were not just for specialized scholars or universities—they were for the German public, the nation, and ultimately humanity. Helmholtz, as well as Du Bois-Reymond and Virchow, intervened in the heated debates about secondary and higher-education reform that caused so much consternation in Prussia and, later, a unified Germany.[98] Each of them rarely deviated from his public message: the natural sciences had become the primary source of epistemic authority, the model of *Wissenschaft*, so they should also become the primary model and source of *Bildung* in *Gymnasien* and universities.

## THE LIMITS OF THE NATURAL SCIENCES' HUMANISM

Just as they celebrated the power of inductive method, mathematical analysis, and a focus on universal laws to keep metaphysical ideas at bay, so, too, did the mandarins of the lab embrace the power of moral and social rules and laws to discipline individuals and societies. What distinguished "educated from less educated nations," wrote Helmholtz, was a superior legal structure and the "moral discipline of the individual."[99] For the mandarins of the lab, as we saw above, natural science had a key role to play in disciplining and educating a cultural elite committed to a broadly liberal humanism—the cultivation of individual freedom and rational self-governance and the preservation of rights and the material progress of the state and society through scientific and technological knowledge.[100] In essence, modern humans—subject to the unprecedented effects of industrialization, technological change, political upheaval, and the erosion of theological and aristocratic authority—needed experts to help constrain the all-too-human propensity to submit to theological dogma and metaphysical delusion. They needed help understanding their place within the lawlike order of the natural world. They needed natural scientists. The mandarins of the lab adopted Kant's liberal vision of guardians responsible for maintaining a healthy public reason, and they adapted it to the "age of the natural sciences."[101]

Yet natural scientists also needed boundaries in order to delimit their own claims to authority. They needed them in order to keep out competing claims, not only from traditional and institutional authorities, such as confessional religions and the state, but also from more established forms of knowledge, such as philology and philosophy. Helmholtz's prorectoral address in Heidelberg did just that. "If the advantage of natural and physical sciences is that they have greater perfection in form," he told his colleagues, "the advantage of the humanities is that they deal with a richer material that lies closer to the interests and feelings of humans, namely, the human mind itself in all its various drives and activities."[102] For Helmholtz, the natural sciences, especially those characterized by mathematical rigor, were more consistently and fully "disciplined" (*wissenschaftlich*) than those fields of study he identifies as humanities. That is because, he suggests, the former were more fully developed than the latter. Although he claims that he does not intend to "devalue" the humanities, he suggests that whereas the natural sciences formulate rigorous laws, the humanities merely "shed light on," "apprise," or "deliver news." Whatever knowledge humanities disciplines might create, in Helmholtz's account, such knowledge cannot as easily be generalized into "rules and laws."[103] For Helmholtz and the other mandarins of the lab, the need to expand from particular to general should be the orienting epistemic ideal. Whatever epistemological "richness" might accrue to the humanities, then, ultimately rests on the empirical forms of knowledge most fully developed in the natural and physical sciences. When Helmholtz described the "relationship" between the natural sciences and the humanities, he did not use the neo-humanist trope "unity of knowledge." He wrote instead about the "link" that connected the "work" of scholars across the university. The unity of the modern, disciplinary sciences resulted not from a prior metaphysical reality, a divinely created cosmos, or even a community dedicated to knowledge itself and the cultivation of an ideal intellectual but from "the power of the human intellect over the earth."[104]

Just as the knowledge they created differed, so, too, according to Helmholtz, did the way in which scholars in the natural sciences and scholars in the humanities realize the common goal of ensuring the dominion of human reason. It is this distinction—more than any particular difference in method, object, or epistemology—that would become central to the modern humanities. Scholars in the humanities, wrote Helmholtz, worked "directly" to expand this human dominion by making the "content of mental life richer and more interesting, separating the pure from the impure." Scholars in the natural sciences, in contrast, worked "indirectly," seeking to liberate "humankind from the law-like, external forces of the material world that intrude upon it."[105] Helmholtz claimed to consider the task of the humanities the "higher" one but also the more difficult. Though the humanities provided psychic succor, consolation, and compelling fodder for the development of "richer" individual mental lives, the natural sciences sought ultimately to free humankind from the indiscriminate force and burdens of natural necessity. On Helmholtz's account, the goods of the humanities accrued primarily to individuals, those of the natural sciences to all of humankind.

By dividing modern, disciplinary knowledge into the natural sciences and the humanities, Helmholtz raised as many epistemological and methodological questions as he answered. He also clarified two definitive features of the emergent research university: (1) different disciplines produced kinds of knowledge that were not only distinct but of disparate value, both within and outside the university; and (2) the organizing divide among these different kinds of knowledge ran along a single fault line between those scholars focused on (a mechanical) nature and those focused on a (more complex) human mind and its products.[106] Ostensibly, such a division split the intellectual labor and responsibility between two cultures of knowledge. The natural sciences could not assuage the psychic anxieties they helped stoke. Such a concession, however, left little room for legitimate forms of knowledge not modeled on the natural sciences. The primary purposes left for non–natural scientific knowledge were individual moral consolation and psychic succor.

Helmholtz had not simply identified a schism in the order of university-based knowledge; he had made a sharp delineation between knowledge and values, truth and moral life. He identified the modern humanities with concern for entities—religion, the state, law, art, language—that satisfy "certain psychic needs," and the natural sciences with the liberation of humankind and the possibility of progress.[107] Though the natural sciences possessed an unrivaled capacity to deliver technical goods, power, and freedom, the modern humanities could do things the natural sciences could not. Even Helmholtz hesitated to grant the natural sciences unconstrained capacities, holding some in reserve for the humanities that were derived at least partly from his belief that materialism was best understood as a formal or methodological commitment, not a statement about the way the world actually is, much less a coherent and self-sustaining worldview. He remained committed, that is, to the irreducibility of human thought to matter and, therefore, prevailing passive mechanist models.[108]

## DU BOIS-REYMOND ON THE LIMITS OF
## KNOWLEDGE AND THE HISTORY OF SCIENCE

The mandarins hardly spoke with one voice in taking up the inadequacies of the natural sciences. Rudolf Virchow, perhaps the most triumphalist of the Helmholtz–Du Bois-Reymond–Virchow troika, confidently expressed the idea that the natural sciences were an unparalleled resource for advancing a common "humanism."[109] New techniques for measuring physical processes would position humans to go further than ever toward meeting the humanistic challenge of the Delphic oracle "Know thyself!" Du Bois-Reymond shared much of Virchow's optimism but nevertheless struck a somewhat different tone in texts such as his famous lecture "On the limits of natural scientific knowledge," delivered in Leipzig in 1872.[110] More than Virchow, perhaps even more than Helmholtz, Du Bois-Reymond devoted himself to public advocacy on behalf of the natural sciences. By end of the 1870s, he had largely stopped publishing new research and devoted himself to defending the "ideals of science through ritual and repetition," whether in the addresses he republished as essays in the *Deutsche Rundschau* and *Popular Science Monthly* or the regular addresses he gave in the lecture hall of his Physiological Institute, which he described as "a theater."[111] In his Leipzig lecture (and the printed versions that quickly followed), Du Bois-Reymond amplified Helmholtz's ambivalence about the ascendant authority of the natural sciences. He also established a rhetorical frame and the conceptual terms that would structure the debate about the order of knowledge for decades. Du Bois-Reymond reproved his colleagues in the natural sciences for succumbing to metaphysical temptations and exhorted them to recognize and live in accord with their ignorance.

But Du Bois-Reymond didn't just echo previous calls for constraint; he spelled out, just as Bismarck was drawing Germany's political borders, two absolute limits to what natural scientists could legitimately claim to know: There was and would remain, he argued, an unbridgeable gap between knowledge based on the "mechanics of atoms" and the essence of matter (and force) as well as between knowledge and human consciousness. Du Bois-Reymond's lecture landed like an "unexpected explosion" from the center of the natural and physical sciences, namely, the chair of physiology at the University of Berlin.[112] Quickly published, it sold out in two weeks. Two additional printings followed within a year.

Du Bois-Reymond told his audience—mainly university professors—that the limits he posited on the knowledge that could be acquired by natural scientists meant that some of the most persistent questions in the history of knowledge would go unanswered, such as the centuries-old "contradiction" between a "mechanical Weltanschauung" and "freedom of the will."[113] Like Helmholtz and Virchow, however, Du Bois-Reymond suggested that these epistemic limits rendered the natural scientist "Herr und Meister" of a domain where his power to "analyze and synthesize" remained virtually untapped. The mature, exemplary natural scientist understood that realizing such power required him to "humbly comport himself to his not-knowing." Echoing the Kantian ethos of embracing the productive possibilities of limits, Du Bois-Reymond tied constraint, discipline, and limits to liberation. These virtues would enable scholars to practice a natural science "unperturbed" by metaphysical and theological "dogmas" tied to "old philosophical ideas that would die."[114]

Du Bois-Reymond argued that such limits would also focus natural scientists' attention on that which set them apart: pursuit of the lawlike regularities of the natural world. Du Bois-Reymond concluded his lecture thus: "Confronted with the puzzle [of matter and force], the natural scientist has long grown accustomed to declaring his *ignoramus* with a masculine renunciation."[115] As cofounder of a gymnastics club, the Berliner Turngemeinde, Du Bois-Reymond extolled the exertion and occasional pain a well-trained gymnast endured.[116] Like gymnastics, scientific experimentation required abstention, self-denial, and discipline, moral virtues that helped form the ideal (masculine) body and the mind. With respect to the problem of consciousness, the ideal natural scientist "must once and for all" commit himself to a related but more final declaration—*ignorabimus*—and cultivate an abstemious relationship with truth.

Within the limits of force and matter and human consciousness, Du Bois-Reymond laid out two problems facing any attempt to transform natural science into a coherent, self-sustaining worldview. First, by clearly limiting what natural scientists could know (not just what they currently did know), he implied that Virchow's "door" would remain ajar. Second, the limitations to what could be known about consciousness and subjectivity undermined what many nineteenth-century intellectuals and scholars had understood as physiology's ultimate goal—to provide a comprehensive account of human consciousness and subjectivity based entirely on a passive, mechanistic model of nature. In other words, Helmholtz's ideal could not be realized. This limit entailed a strict boundary between subjective and objective domains, ensuring that natural science could never become a Weltanschauung and that psyche, mind, subjectivity, and the human would remain placeholders for that which could not be fully known.[117]

In 1877, five years after the publication of his lecture on the limits of natural science, Du Bois-Reymond elaborated on his concerns about the cultural consequences of natural science's rapid ascent by recasting in grand historical terms his arguments about the internal coherence and external, or cultural, goods of the natural sciences. In fewer than twenty printed pages, he recounted the progress of humanity and civilization over the millennia in terms of the gradual but ultimate triumph of science, an advance that not only granted humans control over the forces of nature but also developed their capacities to live and act in the world. Neither simply the "sum" of all knowledge about the natural world nor the mere application of such knowledge to the "overcoming and exploitation" of nature, natural science was, he wrote, nothing less than the "absolute organ of civilization."[118] The historical development of natural science gradually eliminated intellectually enslaving forms of "wonder"—"ghosts, spirits, lies, myths, speculation, prejudice, Eurocentrism, and superstition"—and replaced them with rational, predictable, and thus more manageable laws of nature.[119] Du Bois-Reymond described his history of science as the "actual" history of humankind because it revealed like no other history fully could the "collective work" of the "generations of researchers," which he regarded as the pinnacle of human culture and the possibility of the liberation of humankind.[120]

Induction, technical know-how, a desire to find causes, experimental technique, and quantitative reasoning formed the sure "ground" on which humans would finally be able to fix themselves amid the ungrounded speculation of metaphysics and theology. Natural science's transformation of human civilization was no contingent effect of history. "Destiny" and "fate," Du Bois-Reymond maintained, had guaranteed it. Natural science was *the* force of historical reason; natural scientists were its agents.[121]

Du Bois-Reymond's historical naturalism rested on an apparent paradox. The origins of modern natural science were theological, having emerged, he claimed, from Christian dogma and practice. According to his own account, religious monism first introduced the concept of a universal, singular truth. The polytheism of the ancient Greeks and Romans prevented them from developing what he termed a "drive for causality."[122] Before the emergence of this drive to discover the underlying cause of things, ancient Greeks and Romans, he claims, related to truth as though it were merely a plaything. It was not until Jesus Christ declared that he came into the world to "testify" to "the truth" that *the truth* became an object of serious pursuit. The Christians' "awesome seriousness" about an absolute truth, "the ground of all things," prepared humankind for "modern research," and Christian dogma and practice "compensated natural science for the asceticism for which it was also responsible."[123] Over the centuries, natural science cultivated this "drive for causality" that lifted human civilization out of an unscientific—mythical, theological, and metaphysical—past and delivered it into a future of technical and material progress.

By locating the origins of natural science in the incarnation of Christ and Christian theology and practice, Du Bois-Reymond not only affirmed but also amplified the suggestion he had made in his 1872 Leipzig lecture that the epistemic limits of natural science were also in some sense moral limits. If a phenomenon could not (potentially, at least) be explained according to the methods and premises of natural science, then in effect it didn't exist in the natural world. Anything thought to exceed these limits was not in any legitimate sense knowledge. This essentially removed uniquely moral questions from the domain of knowledge and truth and framed them in terms of therapeutic effect, personal capacity, and affect. It is significant that Du Bois-Reymond felt compelled to provide a genealogy of natural science's most basic values and claimed to have found them in a drive that had existed for millennia. By tracing its development so far back in time and to theological origins, he suggested that modern natural science was inevitable, even natural. This account helps explain the ambivalence that attended the otherwise enthusiastic defenses the mandarins of the lab marshaled for natural science: the uncertainty about whether it could serve as a source of moral authority and legitimacy by providing compelling norms and values and whether it could even justify itself with any but the most utilitarian ends.

Yet Du Bois-Reymond went beyond ambivalence. Although the natural sciences represented the highest and noblest "strivings of the human mind," he wrote, they also developed some of its basest, most utilitarian instincts. He grouped these together in what would become a German catchphrase for decades: the "Americanization" of culture. This modern malady, he explained, reduced all goods to their immediate and economic utility and turned "technology" into an idol. If the natural sciences were the only source of mental training and sole model of intellectual activity, then the human "disposition [would become] narrow, dry, hard, and bereft of the muses and graces." If practiced in isolation, the natural sciences would break "the habit of mind" that had enabled an entire culture "to orient itself within the realm of the quantitatively indeterminate."[124] The irony was that the modern natural sciences had liberated Germans from the manacles of metaphysics and theology only to deliver them into a mundane existence bereft of great works of human imagination and creativity. If Goethe were alive today, Du Bois-Reymond told his audience, he would not be able to write *Lenz*, *Werther*, or *Faust*.

Like many late nineteenth-century German cultural critics, Du Bois-Reymond lamented a decline of great literature and art and the simultaneous spread of utility thinking. Like Nietzsche, who eagerly awaited the arrival of creative genius, he did so not because these poems, paintings, and other creative works provided new knowledge but because of the common life he assumed they sustained. These were not mere cultural objects to be consumed. They contained the aesthetic and moral ideals of an elite cultured class. Like his fellow mandarins of the lab, Du Bois-Reymond recognized the limits of a natural scientific *Bildung*, especially the incapacity of this particular form of *Bildung* to meet certain cultural, moral, social, and, more fundamentally, human needs. Even if natural scientists eventually were able to reduce all natural phenomena to simple mechanical forces and demonstrate, as Helmholtz wrote, that this "reduction" was the only one permitted by natural phenomena, such an "objective truth" would still be only an idea of human reason, not sure metaphysical knowledge about the inherent character of nature.[125] However successful its defenders and promoters proved to be, natural science was not an epistemic solvent that purified nineteenth-century cultures of all metaphysical and theological desires. By framing debates about competing notions of evidence and method in terms of cultural authority and legitimacy, the mandarins of the lab helped shape a broader debate about what could be known and how. They thus helped clear a path for a different resource that could provide shared moral and political ideals if little in the way of knowledge.[126] Addressing this purported lacuna would become the self-appointed task of intellectuals and scholars seeking to define the modern humanities.

Critics and scholars have often framed the shift from confidence in scholarly, expert knowledge to the embrace of cultural critique as a class-based and politically conservative, even reactionary project. The mandarins of the lab, however, did not share the political disposition of some of Ringer's more orthodox mandarins, who cultivated highbrow forms of cultural pessimism, hostility to industrialization, and fundamental doubts about liberal democracy.[127] In fact, Helmholtz, Du Bois-Reymond, and Virchow consistently argued for an alliance between the modern natural sciences and the liberal state, at least until the 1870s, when disappointment with the Reich tempered their confidence in liberalism, the state, and natural science's capacity to sustain both.

Although these shifts in the disposition of natural scientists were bound up with the debates about limits, they soon expanded to include worries that the very character of natural science—its progressive, propulsive modernism—threatened to undermine it. The steady accumulation of facts, relentless pace of discovery, and ephemerality of truths—what Virchow called the "half knowledge" of the natural scientist—changed the conditions of knowledge.[128] From across the disciplines, German intellectuals and scholars of the late nineteenth century wondered, as Lorraine Daston puts it, "what happened to the authority of scientific truths when they seem to have accelerated."[129] Some reacted to this question ambivalently, others elegia-cally. In any case, the mood of triumphal confidence and expectation, com-plicated from the start, became even more complex.

In 1877 Du Bois-Reymond argued that the best defense against the de-humanizing effects of an exclusively natural scientific *Bildung* was "more mathematics."[130] Inserting himself into the raging debate about educational reform, he asserted that the classical *Gymnasium* should devote at least as much time to training in quantitative thinking—what he called the "art of imagining relations among objects"—as it did to training in Greek and Latin.[131] A quantitative *Bildung*, not a philological one, could both ensure that Germans kept pace with the "modern intellect" and rescue them from Americanization.[132] "Conic sections not Greek texts," Du Bois-Reymond de-clared, would enable students to perceive the "unity of things" and reclaim German idealism for a new age—the unity of knowledge could be realized through new pedagogies and different forms of education.[133]

## THE FRAGMENTATION OF TRUTH

Du Bois-Reymond's *ignorabimus* declaration ignited debate well beyond the university. Within just a few years, it framed discussions about the fate of knowledge, higher education, and the crisis of the humanities that echoed well into the twentieth century. Yet as Du Bois-Reymond later acknowl-edged, his famous lecture on the limits of knowledge was not that original. Just a smattering of "erudition in older philosophical texts," he wrote in 1880, would correct the false impression that his own skepticism about the reach of human knowledge and awareness of the limits of materialism had contributed anything new.[134]

So why did the Leipzig lecture galvanize so many for so long? It was a matter of who delivered it, where, and why.[135] Perhaps with the exception of Helmholtz, Du Bois-Reymond was in 1872 the foremost embodiment of the cultural authority of the natural sciences. As the incumbent occupant of Müller's inaugural chair in physiology at Germany's most prestigious uni-versity, university rector, founder of multiple subfields of physiology, direc-tor of the Physiological Institute, and, beginning in 1876, secretary of the Academy of Sciences, Du Bois-Reymond was the public persona of the natu-ral sciences in all their institutional might. Furthermore, he delivered the *ignorabimus* declaration at the forty-fifth anniversary meeting of the Con-gress of German Natural Scientists and Physicians, a national federation founded in 1827 to represent and sustain the unity of knowledge in a politi-cally fractured Germany and amid the centrifugal forces of the disciplinary, specialized university. Du Bois-Reymond had laid down fixed boundaries, then, to an elite, highly educated community that had begun to understand itself in terms of natural science and its presumed capacity to promote unity in both culture and knowledge.

By the 1870s natural science had achieved a position that eclipsed university faculties and specialized periodicals. It had become a contested resource (as well as an instrument) in the competition for cultural authority and legitimacy, a cultural project propounded by polyvalent publics. Sustained in part by the expansion of new media and communication technologies as well as the proliferation of new kinds of social organizations, a sprawling network of voluntary societies, publications (including periodicals, book series, and newspapers), traveling lecture series, and festivals helped popularize the natural sciences among the German middle class.[136]

Parallel to these efforts to develop and sustain interest in the natural sciences among a broad and multifaceted public, university-based scholars addressed fellow academics as well as extra-university, cultured, and political elites in an effort to secure the legitimacy of natural science among both academic and nonacademic institutions. By continually arguing for the educational, cultural, political, moral, and social benefits of the natural sciences, scholars such as Du Bois-Reymond made the case for public and state support of specialized, research-oriented science. These advocates were not trying to bring the practice of natural science out of the elite confines of universities and into the hands of curious but untrained publics; they were trying to secure their own place in the central institutions of epistemic authority—universities.

Thus when Du Bois-Reymond castigated natural scientists for transgressing the limits of their knowledge in 1872, he leveled a critique from the center of natural science's authority and legitimacy that was directed at those with some capacity to affect its institutional situation. This would come to be seen as a distinct moment in the history of knowledge in Germany when the seemingly inexorable fervor for the natural sciences crested and, for some, began to move between ambivalence and resignation. When a fellow natural scientist of the stature of Du Bois-Reymond seemed to undercut many of the claims and assumptions of natural science's heyday, many prominent natural scientists reacted with shock or simply dismissiveness.[137]

Not all scholars shared Du Bois-Reymond's ambivalence about the potential of the natural sciences to propel not just technological or material progress but also cultural, moral, and political progress. Some continued to see in the natural sciences the possibility of an entirely new and unconstrained humanism. No individual scholar exhibited such confidence in natural science more than Virchow's onetime student and Darwin's "great German champion," the biologist Ernst Haeckel.[138] Years before he dismissed Du Bois-Reymond's *ignorabimus* declaration as a "pack of lies," Haeckel had claimed that the same "law of progress" underlying Darwin's theory of evolution could also be found at work "in the historical development of the human race." In all realms of human life—social, political, moral, and scientific—progress was a "natural law that no human force, neither the weapons of tyranny nor the curses of priests, will ever be able to suppress for long."[139] Du Bois-Reymond had rejected this very idea of scientific progress and development, wrote Haeckel, when he declared that the limits of human knowledge would remain "for eternity." In answer to Du Bois-Reymond's self-interested *ignorabimus*, issued from his secure mandarin enclave in the center of the "Reichshauptstadt Berlin," Haeckel concluded, *"Impavidi progrediamur!"* (Advance fearlessly!).[140]

And advance fearlessly Haeckel did. He spent much of his career developing his ideas into a naturalistic worldview based less on a strict mechanistic materialism than on a Goethe-inspired metaphysical monism. Haeckel believed that natural science had disproven the existence of a transcendent (nonmaterial) mind or spirit but also that nature was more than mere (passive mechanistic) matter. For him, mind and matter were modes of a single substance. His monism was a "vitalization of matter as much as a materialization of life."[141] Furthermore, by seeking to craft monism (or related forms of thoroughgoing naturalism or materialism) into a coherent Weltanschauung, Haeckel, perhaps more than any of its other nineteenth-century popularizers, attempted to demonstrate that natural science could do precisely what the mandarins of the lab had suggested it could not: provide a "systematic understanding of the world replete with cultural, moral, aesthetic, historical, and political dimensions."[142]

Seeking to demonstrate how such a Weltanschauung could work in practice, in 1877 Haeckel and three other scholars founded *Kosmos*, a journal, according to its lengthy subtitle, "for a unified Weltanschauung based on the doctrine of development, in conjunction with Charles Darwin and Ernst Haeckel, as well as a number of other excellent researchers in the area of Darwinism."[143] For years the natural sciences had been overshadowed by "the so-called humanistic sciences," wrote Haeckel and his coeditors in the inaugural issue, and had been forced to lead a "secret life away from the great masses."[144] "Under the banner of Darwin" a new "reformist school" had emerged to put "the human" where it belonged, not above nature as some timeless exception but "right in the middle," where a "unified Weltanschauung without contradictions" would finally become possible. For Haeckel and his coeditors, this new monist Weltanschauung would also finally realize the old neo-humanist dream of the unity of knowledge by bringing together all scholarly disciplines. But the natural sciences would set the conditions and terms of this unity. Those "sciences" that claimed a unique interest in "the human"—anthropology, psychology, history, ethics, economics, and the study of culture and language—they wrote, "will turn out to be no more than natural sciences."[145] Over the course of its nine-year life span, *Kosmos* published numerous articles that treated historical, literary, philosophical, and political topics from a manifestly natural scientific viewpoint, although one grounded in Haeckel's monism, with titles such as "Experimental Aesthetics," "Darwinism and the Talmud," "The Political Condition of Primitive Cultures," "Lyric as a Paleontological Weltanschauung," and "On the Morality of Ants."[146]

Whereas Haeckel and his allies thought that Du Bois-Reymond had woefully underestimated what natural scientists could know, others contended that Du Bois-Reymond had left no room for any other forms of knowledge. For instance, Eduard von Hartmann, a Berlin philosopher and the author of the well-received *Philosophy of the Unconscious* (1869), an account of a metaphysical absolute he claimed to have reached through an inductive method, praised much of Du Bois-Reymond's limit-setting agenda but argued that the practical effect of his attention-grabbing rhetoric was to have secured an epistemic monopoly for the natural sciences. The widely acknowledged epistemic humility of Du Bois-Reymond's limit-setting talk masked the unreflective hubris that the limits of natural scientific knowledge were "the limits of the human mind as such." The physiologist's absolute rejection of vitalism, for example, allowed for only one form of causality—an efficient causality that accorded with his mechanistic worldview. The totalizing character of the discourse about the limits of natural science amounted to an "inviolable dogma," a mark not of disciplinary, university-based knowledge but of "unsoundness of mind."[147]

Even some natural scientists agreed that Du Bois-Reymond had effectively fixed the limits not just of natural scientific knowledge but of knowledge as such. The Swiss botanist Karl Nägeli, known for his studies on cell formation and plant physiology, warned against making natural science the single paradigm of knowledge, arguing that "each natural scientific discipline finds justification essentially within itself."[148] The purpose of epistemic boundaries was to help police attempts to extend one form of knowledge beyond its proper domain. When a natural scientist starts "to philosophize" about "how and why," Nägeli wrote, he "ceases to be a natural scientist."[149]

Others, such as the historian Otto Lorenz, who spent most of his career at the University of Vienna, rejected Du Bois-Reymond's attempt to legitimate the authority of the natural sciences by writing its history. Lorenz asserted that by subordinating "humanistic studies" to the natural sciences, Du Bois-Reymond rendered them—despite his claims to the contrary— almost incidental to history and human being. The physiologist's lament about the absence of great art in the "technical-inductive age" revealed his support for the modern humanities as little more than "charity." On Du Bois-Reymond's account, Lorenz said, the humanities were sometimes consoling ornaments for polite society, moral props for a materialist age. If no more compelling case could be made for their "purpose" and "legitimacy," Lorenz warned, then there should be no illusions about the willingness of a "technical-inductive age" to indulge such costly and time-consuming entertainment.[150]

Underlying the more strictly epistemological concerns expressed in response to Du Bois-Reymond were questions about the cultural and institutional authority not only of natural science but of university-based, disciplinary, and specialized knowledge. For decades, the mandarins of the lab—all of whom by the 1870s propounded their defenses of natural science from Berlin, the center of German prestige—had worked hard to help establish the authority and legitimacy of the natural sciences within the research university. They sought more popular, nonexpert support only to the extent that it might result in better institutional conditions for natural science. They achieved this in large part, as we have seen, by offering a distinct account of their practices, purposes, methods, ideals, virtues, and history (and future). They also fought to distinguish natural science from possible competitors—for instance, the church or state, or philology and philosophy. This meant establishing and constantly policing disciplinary boundaries. The epistemology and ethics of disciplinary knowledge thus required a two-front battle, one internal and one external.

Internally, the mandarins of the lab argued for the continuity and coherence of the natural sciences in the face of the relentless production of new facts, new kinds of evidence, fresh research, and, quite simply, constant communication. Virchow, in particular, understood how the natural sciences disrupted established beliefs and traditional commitments both within and beyond the university. What many natural scientists celebrated as the liberating and demystifying power of empirical science, others experienced, he warned as early as 1860, as "destructive" and "revolutionary."[151] The natural sciences had not simply claimed the mantle of critique; the internal disciplinary structures that defined them—the way they created and legitimated knowledge—encouraged instability and constant change, undermining "the very existence of certain prejudices or beliefs." Anticipating anxieties about natural science's distinctly modernist character, Virchow frankly described how the unceasing flow of new data, methods, and knowledge left natural scientists, to say nothing of nonspecialists, with "fragments" of a whole they would never know.[152]

Externally, the mandarins of the lab argued for the coherence and continuity of the natural sciences with respect to the university as a whole and as a social institution whose authority and legitimacy were grounded in expertise and specialized knowledge. Virchow, for example, insisted that whatever the progressive, truth-seeking, and possibly "destructive" epistemic effects of their pace of knowledge creation, the natural sciences were ultimately a conservative and unifying cultural force, preserving as much as they disrupted. By assuming this role, the natural sciences had begun to assume a social function that historically had "fallen to the transcendent strivings of different churches."[153] The natural sciences might not have been able to solve the metaphysical conundrums of the mind-body problem, but, as Virchow eventually contended, they had by the 1870s at least come to sustain a particular form of belief. "There is, in fact, in science a certain realm of belief in which the individual no longer collects evidence of the truth of what has been passed down but allows himself to be instructed purely by way of the tradition."[154] For Virchow, natural scientific "belief" functioned similarly to "religious" belief in that it had become a shared cultural resource for how to live both individually and socially; it also had a "current of dogma."[155]

Such homogeneity required, as we have seen, a distinctly natural scientific *Bildung* and the exemplary figures capable of both modeling its practice and maintaining the integrity of its borders. As Virchow acknowledged in 1877, however, the cultural and institutional conditions of natural science had changed since the 1840s. Addressing the Association of German Natural Scientists and Physicians in Munich, Virchow said that natural scientists no longer needed to "demand" recognition and legitimacy; they had achieved that. "Now," in the late nineteenth century, the task of natural scientists was to fortify the "conservative side" of their domain: sure facts, a commitment to evidence and the value of experimentation, and an absolute rejection of "speculation" and "personal opinions." They also needed to adopt a new disposition: "moderation" and "resignation," or, in Du Bois-Reymond's formulation, "masculine renunciation."[156] In order for natural science to maintain its cultural authority and legitimacy, its practitioners would have to refrain from attempting to answer some of life's "most precious problems."[157]

Although in his 1877 Munich lecture Virchow echoed Du Bois-Reymond's denunciation of what he considered the unwarranted optimism of some natural scientists, his primary aim had been to rebut Haeckel, who just days before at the same conference had argued that his monistic evolutionary theory should form the basis for a "far-reaching reform" of the curriculum in German schools.[158] On at least one thing Virchow and his former student agreed: the pace of progress and discovery in the natural sciences was now "unfathomable."[159] Whereas Virchow regarded this inherent instability as grounds for stricter attention to disciplinary boundaries and adherence to epistemic limits, Haeckel used it to demonstrate just how "ignorant" Virchow was about the latest advances in morphology and related biological sciences. Instead of keeping up with these discoveries and theories, Virchow had become part of the "Berlin monopoly on knowledge."[160] Once he and the other leading natural scientists had reached Berlin and sat at the center of authority, with their chaired professorships and state-funded institutes, they had traded the pursuit of knowledge for the jealous protection of prestige; they had become mandarins.

Haeckel captured a key element of the late nineteenth-century contest over epistemic authority and legitimacy. In refusing to abide by the limits that the liberal mandarins of the lab insisted were necessary to maintain the standing of natural science, Haeckel showed how their arguments were concerned with adjudicating not only epistemological contests but ethical, institutional, and political ones as well. The debate about the limits of natural scientific knowledge was inextricable from the desire to maintain control over the claims of expertise as natural science became more accessible to nonelites outside the university. A crucial aspect of Haeckel's refusal was his insistence that the natural sciences and "the humanistic sciences" were not fundamentally different. So many of the errors and lack of understanding of evolutionary theory, he claimed, could be traced back to the epistemic ideals and virtues cultivated by the mandarins of the lab or, as Haeckel saw it, the reduction of natural science to "exact or simply experimental forms of evidence."[161] But this common demand, he wrote,

> derives from the widespread error that knowledge about nature must be exact. It is common to oppose such knowledge to all those sciences commonly collected under the term *the humanities*. But in fact, however, only a small part of natural science is exact, namely, that part that is based in mathematics, such as astronomy and higher-order mechanics, most of physics and chemistry, and a bit of physiology. . . . In the biological domains, the phenomena are too complex and variable simply to apply mathematical methods generally. . . . In these instances, what is needed instead of exact, mathematical-physical methods are historical-philosophical ones.[162]

As part of a new group of natural scientists who largely understood themselves in terms of their rejection of vitalism, Helmholtz had committed himself to a brute mechanist model of nature in which matter was inert and without agency. According to such a model, matter and mind were distinct, as were the ways of acquiring knowledge about them. Dividing the university into the natural sciences and the humanities, then, was not only a reasonable accommodation of the passive mechanist model of nature; it was also a way of institutionalizing it and enforcing its authority. When Haeckel touted various disciplines of biology as "historical natural sciences" and, thus, as the "unifying band" between the "exact" natural sciences and the "historical humanities," he threatened to undermine not just this regnant passive mechanist model of nature but an institution that over the course of the nineteenth century had come to be organized largely on its terms.[163] When Helmholtz invoked the ideal of the unity of the sciences, he did so in order to defend the relative autonomy and legitimacy of the university.

In 1877, after the initial Virchow-Haeckel exchange, Helmholtz reminded his colleagues in Berlin of their duty as university scholars: "You are in a position of responsibility. You must preserve the noble legacy [of the university] not only for your own nation but as a model for the widest circles of humanity."[164] Here, Helmholtz was not making a claim about the epistemological unity of the sciences, much less a metaphysical assertion about a single substance underlying them all. But Haeckel was. His rejection of the organization of the modern research university followed from his rejection of the passive mechanist model according to which it was organized. According to his metaphysical monism, "the historical and the mechanical," mind and matter, were inseparable.[165] Yet the modern German university had institutionalized these divisions by segregating the natural sciences and the modern humanities, disciplining scholars into ever more discrete domains within them and isolating certain questions about life from the appropriate ends of scholarship.

Although Haeckel continued to publish, he ultimately lost both the scholarly battle over mechanism (his more active, historical mechanism versus the more passive, immediate mechanism of his opponents) as well as the institutional one that bequeathed to the twentieth century the two-cultures model and the endless conflicts over boundaries, limits, and distinctions. One lasting consequence of Haeckel's defeat was, as Jessica Riskin writes, to further "quarantine" the natural and physical sciences from moral, historical, aesthetic, and political concerns.[166] With Haeckel's attempts to unify the sciences (again) largely contained, Germany's university-based scholars could continue to discipline themselves and knowledge. As we shall see, those who continued the search for a countervailing form of knowledge did so largely under the terms of the settlement Haeckel rejected and the mandarins of the lab continued to propound. In their eagerness to segregate moral, historical, and political questions from the sciences, however, the mandarins of the lab had, or so Virchow worried, left the door open to other, non–natural scientific ways of addressing these questions. Virchow probably considered Haeckel a case in point. His rebuke of Haeckel anticipated conceptions of the modern humanities for decades to come. Like Helmholtz in his 1862 Heidelberg speech, Virchow sought to relegate such needs and any possible answers to a strictly private and therapeutic domain. Natural science, he wrote in 1854 as he railed against midcentury supernaturalisms, "left it to the individual to explain the soul with a personal metaphysics or dogma."[167] The incompleteness of empirical knowledge allowed, even encouraged, the pursuit of supplementary explanations or ways of satisfying interests in life's "most precious questions."[168] Virchow considered it the task of well-educated elites to keep these personal pursuits, both their own and others', safely private. Questions about the soul, desires, and ultimate ends lacked the cultural, social, and political legitimacy of scientific knowledge.

By 1880, then, truth it seemed no longer had unified epistemic, moral, and religious or spiritual dimensions. It had been fragmented. As the critiques of Lorenz, Hartmann, and Nägeli suggest, many scholars and intellectuals reacted to the debate around the limits of natural science (as framed by the mandarins of the lab) as admissions of ambivalence about the legitimacy and authority of the natural sciences, especially their capacity to account fully for and cultivate the human. By insisting on the limits of natural science, Helmholtz, Du Bois-Reymond, and Virchow also kept open the possibility that something was missing in the "age of the natural sciences": a domain that seemed to many to lie just beyond the boundaries of natural science, in which value, meaning making, and moral agency, if not truth and knowledge, were not subordinate to the mechanical and quantitative ideals of the natural sciences. If natural scientists could no longer understand their purpose as seeking truth and making meaning, at least as other disciplines such as philosophy had previously conceived of those activities, then they would need ethical and moral supplements—or the modern humanities. It is not incidental that the German term *Geisteswissenschaften* only became widely established in the decade following Du Bois-Reymond's 1872 *ignorabimus* speech, long after Helmholtz's initial use of the term.[169]

Although the mandarins of the lab recognized the success of their effort to secure the authority and legitimacy of natural science both inside and outside the university, they also longed to ensure that authority and legitimacy for the future. This meant acknowledging not only the limits of natural science but also the lacunae its ascendance had left behind. What were, then, the terms of the settlement? Du Bois-Reymond acknowledged the need for the "not-natural-scientific disciplines," but he, like many of his contemporaries, insisted that whatever needs they might fill, such disciplines were not epistemic. They were broadly therapeutic, consoling, and cultural—but they were not knowledge.

In his 1882 rectoral address, Du Bois-Reymond mocked the attempt of Germany's most revered icon, Goethe, to play the natural scientist despite never fully committing himself to the "law of causality." Goethe's peculiar ideas—the ur-plant, metamorphosis, theories of light—amounted to nothing more than the "stillborn shenanigans of an autodidactic dilletante."[170] Like his own fictional Faust, Goethe had failed to grasp the wisdom of the *ignorabimus* declaration: to know that one cannot know and be satisfied with that knowledge. Goethe was a poet—the singer of satisfying songs, the creator of stimulating forms, the counselor of the human heart—not a scientist. Du Bois-Reymond and the other mandarins of the lab placed clear limits on what natural scientists could know; they nonetheless kept knowledge for themselves.

The story of the mandarins of the lab and their philologist, historian, and philosopher contemporaries counters the standard narrative of the two-cultures debate and the fate of the humanities in a modern age. Such a story is typically based on two premises. The first is that *the humanities* refers to a coherent tradition that stretches at least back to the *studia humanitatis* of the fourteenth and fifteenth centuries and, therefore, that the humanities preceded the natural and physical sciences. The second is that the humanities lost ground and meaning to the natural and physical sciences, that they fell victim to the alienating and fragmenting effects of modernity. On such accounts, the fate of the humanities could be understood as a subplot in a grand subtraction thesis of secularization.[171] Modernity gradually but inevitably came to slough off the humanities as another enchanted element of the past. Eventually the logic of modernity, so go certain stories of secularization, leads to the obsolescence of the humanities in the increasing power of the experimental sciences. We think this is all backwards.

The emergence of the modern humanities was a rearguard action by late nineteenth-century German intellectuals anxious to rescue what they feared was an endangered moral vision: the autonomous and morally capable human. With the weakening of traditional religious communities and political bonds, Germany's educated elite invoked the modern humanities, then imbued them with the potential to make meaning and provide the moral and social resources that had long been associated with religious communities and orthodoxies. The humanities were intended to fill a cultural and social need as articulated by late nineteenth-century Germany's cultural elite. Although people do not believe in the humanities, wrote Odo Marquand more recently, they "rely on them because . . . they simply have nothing left to rely on."[172] Yet the modern humanities were not, as Marquand further contends, an "unavoidable" historical response to the ascendance of the natural sciences or other historical processes. Their cultural and social functions were hard won. Scholars from across the philosophy faculty, including natural scientists, summoned disparate disciplines under one name—*Geisteswissenschaften*—in the hope of bringing into existence a cultural project: the moral consolation and unity of educated professionals. Their historical "progress" from out of *Wissenschaft*, the natural sciences, and, lastly, an array of disparate disciplines and into a fully developed and unified class of knowledge, Dilthey wrote in 1883, relied on the "need for a professional education of the elite classes."[173] This need existed because it was primarily these educated elites who seemed to suffer most from the specters of secularization, disenchantment, ennui, and all the other moral anxieties they associated with modernity. Everyone else was still struggling to survive with gods, religions, and metaphysics that persisted in a purportedly disenchanted age. As Weber would point out decades later, it was primarily the intellectuals who had begun to search for other consolations.

The chemist and rector of the University of Berlin, August Wilhelm von Hofmann, was one such intellectual. Testifying to the personal consolations of ancient Greek literature, he told his Berlin colleagues in 1881 that "reading Homer refreshes one's life. The civil servant's hoary face, in which time has etched the unmistakable trace of bureaucratic monotony, is transfigured when on occasion the sonorous hexameter of the *Iliad* unexpectedly rings in our ear. . . . What the Bible does for the masses, Homer does for the educated."[174] This was a therapeutic humanities for a bureaucratic and industrial age.

## CHAPTER FIVE

# The Consolation of the Modern Humanities

No one seized on the ambivalences and openings among the mandarins of the lab more determinedly than Wilhelm Dilthey. By the time *Introduction to the Humanities* was published, in 1883 (more than a decade after Du Bois-Reymond's Leipzig lecture), Dilthey had adopted Hermann Helmholtz's use of the plural form of *Geistewissenschaft—die Geisteswissenschaften*. In so doing, Dilthey distanced himself from the Hegelian insinuations that throughout the 1840s and 1850s had accompanied the use of *Geistewissenschaft*—a singular, human knowledge opposed to natural science yet, along with it, ready to be completed by philosophy. The *Geisteswissenschaften* were not a monolithic whole but rather a set of as yet unarticulated but related disciplines ranging from philosophy, philology, and politics to literature, theology, and political economy. In gathering these disciplines together and clarifying their relationship to one another, Dilthey thought he was doing for the modern humanities what Bacon had done for the natural sciences— outlining common methods, forms of evidence, and objects of study.

In the opening pages of the *Introduction to the Humanities*, Dilthey wrote that his effort to organize a range of academic disciplines had been driven by a desire to fulfill a social "need."[1] He compared contemporary German society to a "massive machine" maintained by the "services" of countless highly skilled people, and he included among them scholars of art, literature, history, politics, philosophy, and theology. Not a "consciously creative member of society," the scholar teaching and writing in any of these disciplines in a university worked in what was, more truly, a "factory," alienated from his "calling."[2] Indeed, alienation was what shaped modern social reality more broadly—not just political and economic institutions but also artistic, literary, and philosophical objects, self-understanding, historical consciousness, norms, values, knowledge. Between 1853, when Dilthey began his studies at the University of Berlin, and 1911, when he died as professor of philosophy there, Berlin transformed from a provincial city into a world-class metropolis. Its population increased nearly eightfold, from five hundred thousand to over four million; its highly compressed period of industrialization recast it as a place where "science, world industry and machines, and work," wrote Dilthey in 1887, had become the "sole basis of the social order."[3] From Berlin, Dilthey narrated the fast-paced and, for him, near-complete fragmentation of German society. Yet he also regarded the maelstrom of modernity as no sudden event. The social crisis and needs confronting late nineteenth-century Germans had developed over centuries, but so, too, he contended, had their historical solution: the modern humanities. Whereas Du Bois-Reymond had written a history of natural science in order to normalize its epistemic ideals, Dilthey had written a history of the modern humanities in order to legitimate theirs.

Ironically, however, as Dilthey made clear throughout the *Introduction*, the same forces that had alienated people from each other, their work, and the world had also given rise to the modern humanities. Dilthey conceived of the humanities as *modern* because like all sciences, (*Wissenschaften*), including the natural sciences, he reasoned, they relied on empirical evidence and methods to discover what physiologists such as Helmholtz and Du Bois-Reymond referred to as "lawfulness."[4]

## THE INCOMMENSURABILITY OF MENTAL LIFE

After completing his PhD and second dissertation at the University of Berlin, both on topics related to Schleiermacher's ethics, Dilthey accepted a faculty position in 1866 at the University of Basel, where he lectured on the history of philosophy, logic, and Schleiermacher and led seminars on philosophical method. While at Basel he also began to study some of the newer work in the natural sciences, eventually becoming "enthralled" by Johannes Müller and Hermann Helmholtz.[5] He even attended Wilhelm His's physiology lectures and studied dissection methods with him. In His, an embryologist, Dilthey would have encountered an advocate of an uncompromising model of nature as brute mechanism—the interplay of immediate causes. For His, the development of embryos was simply a function of "bits of matter pushing and pulling one another."[6] Such encounters, Dilthey noted in his diary, gave his thinking a "completely new impulse."[7] (He left Basel in 1868, a year before Nietzsche arrived.)

This new intellectual orientation toward the (post-Hegelian and antivitalist) natural sciences helped shape Dilthey's lifelong effort, as he described it in 1883, to eliminate metaphysics from all forms of modern knowledge. From Descartes and Spinoza to Schelling and Hegel, philosophers had heaped "hypothesis upon hypothesis" in a futile effort to build a "bridge" between the facts of consciousness and objective reality.[8] They only succeeded, however, in fomenting abstract disputes that distracted from life as lived. In contrast, scholars of the distinctly modern sciences, both the natural sciences and the humanities, created knowledge by "dissecting" experience.[9] For Dilthey, this was a historical fact. The "age of metaphysical rationales and justifications" had been superseded by the age of empirical knowledge, in which all forms of legitimate or "modern" knowledge were based in method, relied on empirical data, and strove toward communicable and, in a general sense, verifiable results.[10] Yet he struggled to reckon with what he acknowledged were the real epistemic, ethical, and social consequences of the dissolution of the (metaphysically grounded) unity of knowledge, however illusory it had been. The social "need" for a modern humanities arose out of the dual failures of metaphysics and the natural sciences to sustain a unified knowledge and, thus, as Dilthey understood it, to sustain resources for both individual and social "meaning," resources for making sense of one's life and the world as a whole.

Dilthey thought that the historical and conceptual failure of metaphysics had left in its place an "empire of given reality" that an array of sciences had divided among themselves, each claiming its own "piece."[11] Characterized by the borders and boundaries of emerging sciences, each staking its claim to coherence and legitimacy, this new arrangement of knowledge reflected not a divinely ordered cosmos or rational universe but rather the "social operation" of universities, academies, and other institutions of knowledge, each organized according to the division of labor Dilthey considered endemic to modern societies.

For Dilthey, Hermann Helmholtz represented, first of all, a postmetaphysical way of thinking, a Kantian-infused regulative disposition oriented toward thinking *as if*.[12] The physiologist, for example, considered the laws of causality, to use the Kantian language, transcendental, not transcendent. Although impossible to prove from the empirical investigation of nature, these laws had to be presupposed in practice. The new epistemic empire relied, as Helmholtz put it, on "trust" in scientific practices, the communities of science, and the institutions that sustained these communities' ideals and virtues: "Here the only advice that matters is: have faith and act!"[13] In order to liberate themselves from the dogmas of theology and the myths of metaphysics, modern intellectuals and scholars had to trust *modern* science. Second, Helmholtz remained committed to the idea of the university as an institutional form of unity, echoing Mommsen, Nietzsche, and the entire neo-humanist tradition.

Embracing the discourse of limits as laid out by the mandarins of the lab, Dilthey sought to establish a similar ground for trust in what the phi-

losopher Heinrich Rickert called the "not-natural-scientific disciplines"—
that is, the modern humanities.[14] In 1883 Dilthey framed the distinction
between the two classes of sciences in terms of the boundaries Du Bois-
Reymond had laid down. Quoting Du Bois-Reymond's formulation of the
second limit, the unity of consciousness, Dilthey wrote that human mental processes cannot be understood on the basis of their "material conditions."[15] From this borrowed premise, he sought not only to distinguish the
modern humanities from the natural sciences but to establish their coherence and social legitimacy. Yet Dilthey remained ambivalent even as he continued to argue for the distinctions between the two classes of knowledge
in the *Introduction to the Humanities* as well as in later revisions of many of
the concepts and arguments first laid out in that text. Indeed, he never fully
managed to clarify the basic distinctions he had drawn between natural
science and the modern humanities and why it was so important to make
them in the first place.[16]

The distinctions Dilthey drew between the natural sciences and the modern humanities in the *Introduction to the Humanities* were not, in the first
instance, methodological. Like Helmholtz, he argued that both the natural
sciences and the humanities were modern sciences and therefore relied on
empirical forms of evidence and methods. Just like biologists or chemists,
scholars of literature or religion collected and analyzed facts, generalized
through concepts, and adhered to similar epistemic ideals and virtues such
as rigor, precision, industriousness, attention to detail, and a commitment
to debate.

The distinctions were also not, on Dilthey's account at least, ontological.
He and those who followed in his wake strenuously sought to avoid any hint
of mind-body dualisms, which, he claimed, smacked of scholastic metaphysics and theology as well as the mind-matter dualisms Haeckel attributed to physiologists such as Helmholtz, Du Bois-Reymond, and Virchow.[17]
Dilthey did not base the differences between physiology and philology on
their objects of study. Both physiology and philological hermeneutics, for
example, were ultimately concerned with mental phenomena.

On what, then, did he ground the distinction between natural science
and the modern humanities? Ethical and political commitments. The distinction was ethical because Dilthey thought it concerned the possibility of
leading what he considered a free and good life. He based it on a prior commitment to the unique status of the human among other natural beings. He
embraced Du Bois-Reymond's second limit—the unity of human consciousness—and with it, the incapacity of modern natural science to account for
human consciousness and subjectivity, thus rejecting any claim that natural
science constituted a coherent and legitimate worldview. Dilthey wrote that

his "motivation" for distinguishing the natural sciences and the humanities reached "into the depth and totality of human self-consciousness."[18] Modern and, thus, for Dilthey, alienated society didn't simply need a new way of knowing the world; it needed a way of knowing that could assert the unity, maintain the integrity, and safeguard the autonomy of the human, which many nineteenth-century German intellectuals believed faced an unprecedented threat from the ascendance of a natural scientific model of passive mechanism.

Physiologists such as Du Bois-Reymond, whom Dilthey called "one of our first 'natural scientists [*Naturforscher*],'" had collected, analyzed, and interpreted material facts with great success, but they still could not explain what Dilthey called "mental facts."[19] These stood apart from the "mechanical order of nature" and were distinct from the natural facts, which natural scientists, with their inductive methods and tireless search for immediate causes, had successfully begun to explain.[20]

The coherence and function of the modern humanities, as Dilthey sketched them, relied on the "incommensurability" of material mechanisms (brute, passive, uniform, lifeless) and mental life (vital, active, particular, irreducible).[21] This incommensurability was the premise that made the basic distinction between the humanities and natural sciences possible. The borderland where the modern humanities emerged and became, as Dilthey wrote, "self-sufficient," lay at the far edge of the epistemic limits of the natural sciences.[22] The legitimacy of the humanities depended on the existence of a distinct account of the natural sciences, a passive mechanistic model of nature that quarantined natural science from questions of moral, political, and historical import. The need for a new and different form of knowledge arose because humans found themselves in a natural world that was "silent" and "alien."[23] It was this alienation that prompted the self-assertion that characterized the modern humanities. Over this "dead" nature, Dilthey wrote, the humanities "effuse a shimmer of life and inwardness."[24]

In short, then, Dilthey embraced a particular (though widely shared) model of nature, defined all natural sciences in terms of it, assembled an array of previously disparate disciplines and juxtaposed them to the natural sciences, called them *the humanities*, and, finally, asserted their epistemological and institutional monopoly over ethical and moral questions. By exaggerating the ambivalence and hesitation the mandarins of the lab expressed about the natural sciences, Dilthey identified a moral vacuum their ascendant authority had purportedly created and asserted the social need for a new form of knowledge to address it. In so doing, he also ascribed to each domain an underlying philosophical anthropology, one for which human being was simply part of the brute mechanism of nature, the other for which human being was an exception. In order to manage these different types of knowledge, he adopted a version of Kantian compatibilism—what he called a "double point of view" from which the human is both a unity of mental facts and a unity of bodily, material senses.[25]

Whereas Kant sought to unify the two points of view in various ways over the course of his career, Dilthey claimed that they could "never occur in the same act" of thinking and considered them the basis for the two "classes of sciences," the two domains in which natural science and the modern humanities take shape, acquire their purposes, and form their practitioners. They also provoke "antagonism" between scholars who find themselves in opposing domains.[26]

## THE MORAL PURPOSE AND HISTORICAL
## LEGITIMACY OF THE HUMANITIES

On Dilthey's telling, the ultimate purpose of the modern humanities is to provide an account of "the human" that limits the explanatory power of natural laws and ensures the sovereignty of humans over the natural world. In contrast to the natural scientist who is oriented by an ideal image of a brute mechanistic nature, the humanities scholar is oriented by an ideal image of a purposive, particular, and irreducible human being. The latter disposes scholars to conceive of human self-consciousness (and its products) as though it were more than merely natural. Dilthey ascribes more than a heuristic function to this ideal image and its role in defining the humanities, however. He suggests that it makes the humanities into an impregnable fortress whose ultimate function is to protect the inviolability of human autonomy: "Still unspoiled despite the continued investigations into the basis of mental life, the human finds in his own self-consciousness a sovereignty of the will, a responsibility over actions, a capacity to subordinate everything to thought and to resist everything within the bulwark of autonomy of his person, through which he separates himself from nature."[27] In cultivating this "sovereignty of the will" against the meaningless mechanisms of nature, the modern humanities make meaning possible, personal as well as historical, individual as well as social. Because humans can no longer rely on a divinely ordered cosmos or socially ensured hierarchies to provide shared and lasting meaning, they must rely on their own powers of assertion and meaning making. That is precisely what the modern humanities do, according to Dilthey. They enable humans to recognize that "the meaning of each individual existence is entirely singular and indissoluble to knowledge"[28] but also to understand individual existence in

relation to something that extends beyond it. Here and elsewhere throughout his career, Dilthey transferred Schleiermacher's textual hermeneutics,
with its emphasis on the relationship of part to whole, onto a moral and historical world of human action. Each individual existence "represents in its
own way, like a Leibnizian monad, the historical universal." The inscrutable
unity, coherence, and meaning of a particular human life was, for Dilthey,
a microcosm of a universal humanity and human historical-social reality.

With their insatiable search for lawlike regularities and "invariant structures," natural scientists, as Dilthey described them, could not but conceive
of humans, like all natural beings, as subject to universal laws. They could
not account for how humans gradually increased their "authority over the
earth" and "space through science and technology" because they focused
on the search for timeless patterns.[29] Dilthey considered this search for invariant structures and universal laws a necessary but insufficient task for
modern knowledge. He also longed for a form of knowledge that could situate particular, meaning-laden lives within a narrative of human development and liberation. In this regard, he ascribed to the modern humanities
the basic but morally burdensome task of accounting for historical instances of exemplary human action and, thus, ultimately defending human
agency and autonomy from the industrial, natural scientific, and technical
forces threatening to diminish it.

Although *Introduction to the Humanities* was one of the first extended
attempts to establish a distinct epistemology and method for the modern
humanities, Dilthey devoted the bulk of it to situating his more theoretical
reflections within a grand historical narrative, much as Du Bois-Reymond
had done for the natural sciences a few years earlier. But whereas Du Bois-
Reymond had sought to legitimize the natural sciences by stretching their
history back over millennia, Dilthey sought to legitimate the modern humanities by showing how they had developed out of the natural sciences
and thus shared with them a common origin—*Wissenschaft*. Conceptually,
the modern humanities relied on the empiricism first articulated by the
modern natural sciences. Historically, however, although they had developed from the natural sciences, they had eventually grown distinct from
and even superseded them.[30] Whereas Du Bois-Reymond's history culminated in a triumphant age of natural science, Dilthey's characterized the
age of natural science as one in which society had been convulsed by "social shocks" since the French Revolution.[31] He considered the modern humanities to be an effect of this historical tumult as well as the means of its
historical resolution.

Beginning with ancient Greece and culminating in nineteenth-century
Europe, particularly Germany, Dilthey traced how a range of knowledge

forms and practices, from astronomy and metaphysics to philosophy and psychology, arose out of historical necessity to satisfy intellectual, moral, and social needs. Smitten by the "scientific desire to build," French and English "positivists" such as Mill, Comte, and Spencer could not explain how different sciences related to one another because, wrote Dilthey, they could not give an account of the "origin" of development of these sciences.[32] Most importantly, they could not give an account of how or even whether these sciences formed particular human capacities over time. Echoing the positivists' "desire to build" and the aspirations of the mandarins of the lab for a distinctly natural scientific *Bildung* but rejecting the absence of development thinking he attributed to both the positivists and the natural scientists, Dilthey provided a historical argument for a distinctly humanities-based, conceptually coherent, and historically necessary set of disciplines that made "intellectual *Bildung*" possible.[33]

The history of the development of the modern humanities, in Dilthey's telling, was also a history of the liberation of the human from the myths of metaphysics, just as the history of the natural sciences was in Du Bois-Reymond's account. Realizing the promise of the humanities, however, required that readers understand and identify with how the humanities (in all their protoforms) had been lived and understood by those who had previously practiced them. It required, in other words, the very kinds of knowledge the humanities had made possible. Unlike Aristotle, Kant, or his own contemporaries such as Comte, Dilthey treated metaphysical arguments as "historical" and, thus, contingent "bodies of facts."[34] As such, he argued, metaphysical illusions, commitments, and systems could be overcome however habitual they had become. In order for "moderns" to realize such liberation, however, they had to "understand" how the "corrupting inheritance" of metaphysical myths persisted in the present, even if in different forms. The elimination of these myths and the possibility of a fully developed, modern humanities required a historical hermeneutics. First, the reader or incipient humanities scholar had "to immerse" himself in the "spirit" or experience of historical actors by engaging with their "tradition"—that is, the material forms and objects and "literature" from which their thinking and experiences had taken shape.[35] Second, the reader or scholar had to "live through" this mediated experience himself, relying on method to give rise to an experience in the present in order to understand the past. By offering this "tool" for understanding, Dilthey sought to transform "personal genius into a technique" that could constrain and discipline individual scholars and lend humanities knowledge a "certain level of universality."[36] Yet however *modern* the humanities became, noted Dilthey, they would always contain "something irrational, like life itself."[37]

Although he continued to elaborate his hermeneutic method until his death in 1911, Dilthey applied it to the "literature of the modern humanities" in the *Introduction to the Humanities* in order to recount the humanities' history and identify the "need"—the crisis that had brought them into existence, which he claimed could be traced back to a "problem" that arose in the Middle Ages.[38] What began as an antinomy of religious consciousness and metaphysics—the apparent contradiction between the idea of an omniscient and omnipotent God and the idea of human freedom, or the idea of an objective order of nature and the idea of freedom—developed over the centuries into the problem that now "constitutes the modern human."[39] When the "purposive order" of knowledge cleaves from the "totality of human nature," writes Dilthey, the human being loses his place in the metaphysical order and gradually develops the particular "trait" that marks his historical distinction—"a modern scientific consciousness." Dilthey considers this development significant because it introduces the differentiation of social systems of meaning—from art and religion to law and history—but also because it introduces the differentiation of human capacities. Not only must modern individuals manage multiple and often conflicting social systems and the particular identities associated with them; they must also develop capacities, habits, and skills—what Dilthey calls collectively "powers of the soul"—unique to each of them. It is as though, he writes, modern humans must learn to move each of their limbs independently and to use them with ever more exacting, precise, and differentiated effort.[40]

As Dilthey recounted their history, the modern humanities eventually freed themselves from the teleological accounts of *human* history and social reality rooted in theological and metaphysical ideas about the unity of "humanity." The "pace" of this separation, he wrote, was "slower" than in the natural sciences primarily because it took so long for the disciplines that would become the modern humanities to coalesce around a shared account of the historical-social world.[41] The natural sciences emerged first as a coherent form of knowledge because the scholars who initially articulated them organized them around a shared ideal image of nature as machine. Thus, these same scholars were better able to develop common methods, notions of evidence, and practices. Because scholars of art, history, society, philosophy, and literature shared no such premise, they pursued different kinds of knowledge largely independent of one another, each in a distinct "system of culture."

On Dilthey's telling, as the natural sciences gradually "eradicated" metaphysical "myths" and pushed aside theological principles, a similar pattern began to emerge across the various systems of culture: knowledge of individual relationships replaced metaphysical unity, causal concepts replaced natural purposes, laws replaced universal forms, imminent grounds replaced transcendent grounds, facts replaced myths and fables. In each instance, as natural science replaced metaphysical and theological frameworks with its own mechanistic framework, *nature* developed into a distinct reality and came to stand over and against the human and its own historical-social reality. In short, Dilthey used a historical narrative to project a nature-culture division back over centuries in order to legitimate as historical fact the existence of the same two-cultures division he had asserted in the opening pages of the *Introduction*. For Dilthey, this division was the permanent crisis that provided the modern humanities its legitimacy and authority.

## A NEW METAPHYSICS?

Similarly, the development of particular sciences (e.g., philology and history) dedicated to studying historical-social reality made systematic knowledge of this reality possible but also fragmented it. The development of historical "critique" by humanist scholars between the fourteenth and sixteenth centuries, for example, helped them better study textual materials passed down over time. But the more technical and empirical methods of philology, wrote Dilthey, also "destroyed the web of sagas, myths, and fables" spun by centuries of theocratic institutions whose authority rested on little more than assertions of divine will.[42] These same critical methods also destroyed any sense of a unified historical-social reality from which these very texts had been handed down via tradition and through which they could be understood. This was the conundrum of the modern humanities.

Just as the various natural sciences produced fragmented knowledge about nature before they coalesced around a shared model of nature as a brute mechanism, so, too, did sciences such as philology and history produce a fragmented knowledge of historical-social reality. The historical "problem" they inherited, then, was not only the possibility of human freedom but also that of a unified meaning and purpose not wholly defined by the brute mechanisms of the natural world and the moral limitations of the natural sciences. The "problem" of the modern humanities is that they have always been defined by what they are not—that is, the natural sciences—and by a compulsion or need for a wholeness not reducible to mere matter.

Despite their analytic methods and the fact that they have historically produced knowledge by "dismembering" what they seek to know, Dilthey wrote, the modern humanities enjoy a privileged position: they have been given the "human itself as a living whole."[43] In example after example, he recounted how scholars devised a "dead, rigid concept" of the human self or psyche in an attempt to describe human life but inevitably failed to account for the "total conditions of psychic life," ultimately reducing "mental life" to brute mechanism. It was the task of the modern humanities to counter such mechanization.[44]

In the concluding pages of the *Introduction to the Humanities*, Dilthey asked whether the modern humanities, even though they had "replaced a metaphysical investigation of the mental realm with an analytical one," had introduced a distinctly modern metaphysics in the name of *the human*.[45] Following publication of the *Introduction*, Dilthey spent much of the rest of his career attempting to establish psychology, in particular, as the "foundation" for the modern humanities, just as mathematics was for the natural sciences.[46] Dilthey most clearly conceptualized this effort in the mid-1890s when he distinguished between "descriptive" and "explanatory" psychologies. An explanatory psychology models itself on the methods and presuppositions, such as *causa aequat effectum*, of the natural sciences, and thus it seeks to "reconstruct the whole of mental life" from discrete units.[47] It relates to human mental life as though it were reducible to "a series of physiological processes."[48] A descriptive psychology, in contrast, begins with the "whole" of psychic life "given to . . . experience [*Erlebnis*]" and seeks to describe the relationship of its parts with respect to this given unity.[49] Dilthey associated explanatory psychology with the experimental methods and mechanist ideals of nature of Helmholtz and other natural scientists. He associated descriptive psychology with literary authors such as Rousseau, Goethe, Montaigne, and Shakespeare, whom he claimed provided full and coherent accounts not just of the processes of psychic lives but of their content.[50] "We hear endlessly how more psychology can be found in Lear, Hamlet, and Macbeth than in all psychology textbooks combined," Dilthey observed.[51] The task of the modern humanities, aided by such a descriptive psychology, then, is not just to explain human mental life and its products but to understand how and why humans act in the world and the general development of their "mental life." Such an understanding should account for the relationship of perceptions, drives, and dispositions as well as how these relate to a life lived in accord with and oriented by certain ends and values.[52] As he had already done in the *Introduction*, Dilthey distinguished the natural sciences and the humanities on the basis of the different forms of experience they support. With the former, "we explain nature"; with the latter, "we understand mental life."[53]

Conceding knowledge about the "external world" to the natural sciences, Dilthey claimed what remained as the domain of the modern humanities.

"The metaphysical [*das Meta-Physische*] of our life" as "personal experience, that is, as moral-religious truth," was the sure ground on which a new, non-natural scientific knowledge stood.[54] The religious "experience," which Dilthey defined as the "limit point" of all historical understanding, returned in his narrative to serve as the ground of a knowledge that exceeded the limits of natural science but also what can be known according to scholarly norms and logical consistency.[55] From the "depths of self-reflection emanates . . . the consciousness that the will cannot be determined by the natural order, whose laws do not correspond to its life, but rather only by something that the natural order leaves behind." It was this personal knowledge of the irreducibility of human consciousness and the autonomy of the human will that Dilthey thought would lead to knowledge of a "higher order with which our own life and death are enmeshed." Access to a meaningful, ordered reality proceeds neither through wonder at the infinite and well-ordered cosmos nor through adherence to inherited theological dogma but through a radically personal "gaze into the depths of one's own heart." This is why, notes Dilthey, an atheist may be better able "to live this metaphysics" than a confessing Christian whose idea of a transcendent God has become a "worthless husk" of its former self.[56]

For Dilthey, these lived experiences and the metaphysics of life were the borderlands of knowledge from which the modern humanities emerged, where the inscrutability of a life, both individually and universally, somehow guaranteed the meaning and worth of every human life. Dilthey understood life in this regard as the relationship of parts to a whole and claimed that every individual consciousness had immediate access to this inscrutable coherence. Furthermore, each individual human life stood in for a higher unity that was not simply particular to an individual but was a historical universal (e.g., a particular culture).[57] Modern sciences, both the natural sciences and the humanities, lacked the concepts and language to account for such personal or subjective knowledge of life, its wholeness and integrity. This was why Dilthey continued to assert that religious traditions provided important and meaningful concepts and language to describe the inherent integrity of human life even as their subjectivity and multiplicity conflict and run up against the limits of understanding.[58] What remained at the end of Dilthey's account of the modern humanities, then, was the assertion of a consciousness of the inscrutable unity of the human, both individually and universally. This was the condition for his primary legacy—the modern humanities. This new class of sciences, Dilthey argued, inherited the task of cultivating categories, concepts, and forms of scholarship that help humans better understand the ultimate coherence and meaningfulness of human life. These new sciences inherited the burden of connecting inner experiences to social and historical reality, of transforming a psychology of particular lives into a coherent set of sciences of human life generally.

With his spatial rhetoric—borders, limits, domains, independence— Dilthey connected the epistemological and historical distinctions between the humanities and the natural sciences to the university-based forms of knowledge with which he was already familiar as a late nineteenth-century German academic. Disciplines such as philology, literature, and religion found a home in one class, the modern humanities; chemistry, physics, and physiology found a home in another, the natural sciences. Per this perspective, what Dilthey called a "double point of view," the humanities were not so much a coherent epistemological project as they were a moral speech act. The question of their coherence and legitimacy concerned less what they *are* and more what they *do*, and what they do in a particular situation and what their audience deems them capable of doing.[59]

Like most German intellectuals of his day, Dilthey was working out the terms of a post-Hegelian settlement with the institutional and cultural ascendance of the natural sciences. It was clear that the natural sciences had won: political influence, capital investments from the state, larger university enrollments, and, most importantly, cultural authority were all accruing to the natural sciences. In the decades following the publication of the *Introduction to the Humanities*, the intellectuals and scholars who continued to pursue a countervailing form of knowledge against the natural sciences largely did so in terms of the settlement that Dilthey, following the mandarins of the lab, had laid out. In embracing the brute, passive mechanist model of nature, scholars may have quarantined the natural sciences from moral, philosophical, and political questions, but, however inadvertently, they had also acknowledged how persistent such questions remained and the inability of the university under its new disciplinary arrangement to address them. Before the mission of the humanities could be formulated in the terms we use today, the goods of the natural sciences had to be reduced to mere utility. Their relationship to their own metaphysical and theological past and the myths and presumptions of a divinely ordered universe had to be reshaped. This historical process, as narrated by both the mandarins of the lab and the scholars of "the not-natural-scientific disciplines," such as Wilhelm Dilthey, left a lacuna.

## THE DIVISION OF THE PHILOSOPHY
## FACULTY AND THE END OF AN IDEAL

Although Dilthey traced the origins of the permanent crisis of the humanities back over centuries, even millennia, more proximate causes could be found in the institutional conditions of early nineteenth-century German universities when the philosophy faculty, historically the arts faculty of the early modern university, became more autonomous and professionalized. Until then, the philosophy faculty of universities in Germanophone lands, like those across Europe, had embraced an array of fields from history, philology, rhetoric, and political economy to the early forms of biology, chemistry, and physics. These faculties also served a largely preparatory function for the higher, professional faculties of law, medicine, and theology, and the various fields and disciplines housed within them were what today might be termed service disciplines.

In the first half of the nineteenth century, two developments in particular began undoing this relative homogeneity and stability. With the founding of the University of Berlin in 1810, a disciplinary order of knowledge slowly began to take shape in universities across Prussia and other German-speaking lands. Universities began to privilege specialists who produced knowledge that fellow specialists deemed original and important, and they sought to reproduce these scholars and disciplinary knowledge by establishing specialized seminars in philology, theology, and soon thereafter mathematics and physics.[60] Just as crucial, however, were the educational reforms led by Prussia's minister of culture, Karl vom Stein zum Altenstein (see chap. 2). In 1834, as part of his long-term reform project, Altenstein introduced a compulsory *Gymnasium* curriculum and made the *Abitur*, the capstone exam for *Gymnasium* students, the sole entryway to university admission. This institutional change immediately elevated the prestige and importance of the philosophy faculty. Its members could now legitimately claim that preparing students for study in the traditionally "higher" faculties was not their job. They could, and did, focus on forming professional scholars in distinct disciplines—philologists, historians, physicists, and chemists.[61] Most importantly, the reforms of the 1830s in particular effectively made philosophy faculty members responsible for training highly specialized teachers for the *Gymnasium* and preparing them for state exams that required, among other subjects, deep knowledge of Greek, Latin, history, and literature. The philosophy faculty became a professional school, thereby gaining a new social importance and the brighter funding prospects that went with that.

The gradual introduction over the first half of the nineteenth century of the degree of "doctor of philosophy," an honor mostly denied denizens of the arts and sciences (or philosophy) faculties for centuries, further codified the elevated status and professionalization of the philosophy faculty.[62] Even as their position within the institution improved, professors in the philosophy faculty often sought to define the terms of their professionalization. In the 1830s professors at the University of Berlin insisted that philosophy faculties at all universities ought to devote themselves to instruction and scholarship unconcerned with "practical considerations."[63] It was not until it had largely become professionalized that Berlin's philosophy faculty first stipulated, in its statutes of 1838, that it offered only liberal education. This seemingly belated codification of an educational ideal crystalizes the tension that neo-humanist theories of higher education had, in effect, created by claiming that universities should pursue both pure knowledge and practical service to the state and society.[64]

It was in this context that the unity-of-knowledge ideal, first outlined as an institutional norm as *Wissenschaft* with the founding of the University of Berlin in 1810, began to take institutional and bureaucratic form. *Wissenschaft* embodied not just an institutional but also a broader cultural ideal of wholeness, coherence, and legitimate authority in a world in which "all that was solid melted into air, all that was holy was profaned." Writing in 1844, Karl Marx identified *Wissenschaft* as the "unity" through which the contradictions and illusions of metaphysics, morality, religions, and all other ideologies would be reconciled.[65] Around the same time, his fellow Left Hegelian Karl Ludwig Michelet went even further, writing that the "goal of history is the secularization [*Verweltlichung*] of Christendom," whose primary agent was the "holy flame of *Wissenschaft*, which will bring life-giving warmth to all nations and lift up the human race in the image of God in reality, which will be carried by the Germans, its true conservators."[66] And for Germany's highly educated elite, the philosophy faculty was *Wissenschaft*'s home.

The scholarly professionalization of the philosophy faculty, as well as its expansion in terms of enrollments and the differentiation and proliferation of disciplines, prompted philologists to complain as early as the 1820s about overspecialization and fragmentation and to worry about a rift between disciplinary, university-based knowledge, *Wissenschaft*, and "life."[67] By the 1860s these concerns had exploded into a debate that would drag on for decades over the alleged incoherence of the philosophy faculty. Some scholars, especially those who had begun to identify themselves as natural scientists, argued that the ideal of unity could be maintained only if the natural and physical sciences were split off from the broader philosophy faculty.

Internally, the fight to maintain an undivided philosophy faculty was in large part a fight to maintain a local unified corporate body as a check on the rapid growth of disciplinary communities that, eclipsing local communities, extended across Germany, Europe, and by the end of the century the world. Corporate university bodies were typically bound together by local traditions that included ceremonial events (rectoral addresses and founding ceremonies), hierarchies (of the various faculties, professorial rank, disciplines), and shared time and work settings, whereas the disciplinary communities cohered through more distributed forms of sociability, such as periodicals, annual meetings, letters, archives, methods, theories, and international organizations. Externally, the debate about the unity of the philosophy faculty stoked fears among professors and educated elites alike about the fate of the university's broader social function as a bulwark of trustworthy knowledge.

As shown in the previous chapter, many of the professors pushing to maintain the unity of the philosophy faculty did so even as they flourished within an institutional system that valued disciplinary knowledge above all else. Some of the most revered natural scientists of the nineteenth century—mandarins of the lab such as Hermann Helmholtz, A. W. von Hofmann, and Emil Du Bois-Reymond—praised the "common work of an undivided [philosophy] faculty" as the only "cure" for the "shriveling" of the scholarly vocation into mere specialization.[68] These scientists accepted specialization as a condition for the production of new scientific knowledge while simultaneously arguing, sometimes convolutedly, for institutional structures that sustained social and intellectual unity. Helmholtz's 1863 University of Heidelberg address, as we saw in the last chapter, proved paradigmatic in this regard. While he asserted the epistemic self-sufficiency and identity of the natural sciences as a group of heretofore unrelated disciplines, he also understood that the authority and legitimacy of the natural sciences depended on the continued authority and legitimacy of the university's distinct but institutionally unified cultures of scholarly knowledge.

The complex dynamic of debate explicated by Helmholtz persisted throughout the nineteenth century. Fritz Ringer famously divided German mandarin academics into two camps: "the orthodox," who were plainly reactionary, and the "modernists," who were critical observers of modernity without being cultural pessimists.[69] Yet examples of intellectuals and scholars who didn't fit into the analytic framework include representative insiders, not just quirky outliers. Friedrich Paulsen, perhaps *the* consummate insider in debates about German higher education circa 1900, was one. A professor of philosophy at the University of Berlin, Paulsen joined other eminent scholars in writing a celebratory exhibition catalog about German universities for the 1893 World's Fair, held in Chicago. As the preface to the volume read, the goal of the exhibition was to present to the world an image of German universities as "incubators" of modern knowledge completely devoted to modern science.[70]

In his own contribution to the catalog, Paulsen emphasized what he claimed was their defining virtue: their commitment to the "unity" of knowledge.[71] He described this norm as more institutional and social than metaphysical, emphasizing the sociability of knowledge, as J. G. Fichte and Friedrich Schleiermacher had done almost a century earlier and Helmholtz just decades before. The unity of knowledge consisted of the "social and scholarly interaction" of an "aristocracy . . . of mind," Paulsen wrote, echoing another neo-humanist visionary, Friedrich Schelling. "As the cleric once had," the German scholar, the student who had been formed and elevated to the highest ranks and inner circles of academic prestige and power, represented both the unity and the "intellectual leadership of the people."[72] Paulsen's language captured the esteem and authority that university-based scholars still presumed was their right at the turn of the century.

As crucial as this unity ideal had been to the historic success of German universities, its future, thought Paulsen, was bleak. Although, he wrote, the philosophy faculty had long bound together faculty and students from across the university and largely legitimated the university's cultural authority and relative autonomy, lectures in most disciplines, from philology and mathematics to history and the natural sciences, had taken on the character of "instruction in technical knowledge for specialists."[73] It should be no surprise, then, that students from other faculties, such as medicine and theology, no longer attended these lectures. Whereas many of his contemporaries, especially in philology and history, wished to reverse this change, Paulsen remarked matter-of-factly that "the division of labor cannot be undone." The very promise of modern knowledge depended on it, in fact. What was so deeply troublesome was also indispensable, more so than ever.

Like most critiques of university-based knowledge and specialization, Paulsen's was not only epistemological; it was also ethical. Unchecked, scholarly specialization deformed people through its disproportional development of human abilities, its impediment of healthy impulses, and its encouragement of insalubrious ones—above all, "one-sidedness."[74] Although writing ostensibly for an international audience, Paulsen directly addressed his fellow German scholars, enjoining them to remain true to their "calling" to be members of the university's community of teachers and scholars. The division of the philosophy faculty threatened the viability of this ethos and form of life. It imperiled the institution that had come to define the possibilities of intellectual vocation.

By 1900 Hofmann, Helmholtz, Paulsen, and countless other defenders of the traditional philosophy faculty had largely lost the battle for institutional unity. In 1863, one year after Helmholtz exhorted his Heidelberg colleagues to keep the humanities and natural sciences together, University of Tübingen professors voted to establish a natural science faculty. Hugo von Mahl, the first dean of the new Tübingen faculty, warned other universities that same year "not to remain behind the times."[75] Heidelberg voted to break up its philosophical faculty in 1890. The new university in Strasbourg opened in 1872 with two different faculties (philosophy and natural science), but faculty members of the universities in Breslau, Kiel, and Königsberg voted against such a division. When the University of Frankfurt was established in 1914, its faculty members voted against a unified philosophical faculty. The University of Berlin, the German institution of higher learning that identified most closely with neo-humanist ideals, also approved a split, although not until the 1930s.

## THE RETURN TO KANT AND REDRAWING THE BOUNDARIES OF KNOWLEDGE

The boundary drawing within the philosophy faculty only intensified after the publication of Dilthey's *Introduction to the Humanities* in 1883 as scholars across the university sought to cope with the changing conditions of knowledge. While attending the University of Berlin in the 1850s and early 1860s, Dilthey had begun to lay the philosophical groundwork for a knowledge that could counter the ascent of the natural sciences during a period when, as he described the intellectual atmosphere, "the emergent natural sciences" had prompted a complete reevaluation of what counted as trustworthy knowledge and how to organize it.[76] This period was marked by an often polemical and widely followed debate over scientific materialism.[77] Combined with the near collapse of Hegelian metaphysics and the ascent of the natural sciences, the materialism debate put philosophers, in particular, on the defensive. For philosophically inclined scholars such as Dilthey, the idealist metaphysics of the previous generations was no longer an option. Not only had natural science begun to undermine its legitimacy as university-based knowledge but also younger scholars found empiricism compelling because, as Dilthey put it, "you could actually do something with it."[78]

Yet many of these same scholars found the various scientific materialisms and philosophies of experience (e.g., those of Mill and Comte) unduly reductive, especially when used as methodological frameworks for studying human culture and activity. After his initial excitement upon reading Mill, Dilthey eventually concluded that Mill's method, for example, was doomed by its own "dogmatic rigidity."[79] For many German intellectuals and scholars, Dilthey included, a return to Kant offered a safe passage between the Scylla of metaphysical speculation and the Charybdis of absolute passive materialism. Just as importantly, a Kantian renewal would, they thought, return philosophy to its rightful place atop the hierarchy of disciplines by claiming for it the right to draw the new boundaries between the sciences. But the Kant that Dilthey and other German scholars sought to recover was not the metaphysician who had inspired the idealism of Schelling, Fichte, and Hegel; it was, rather, a chastened Kant whose arguments about the idealist sources of knowledge had always been constrained by a commitment to their empirical sources.[80] This return fit well with the broader shift in German philosophy in the second half of the nineteenth century away from building grand systems and toward policing epistemic boundaries and embracing more philologically inspired methods.[81]

The institutional character of this return to Kant is underscored by the widely acknowledged fact that it largely took shape in distinct schools associated with universities in Marburg and southwest Germany, especially in Strasbourg.[82] The Marburg school, led by Hermann Cohen and Paul Natorp, focused on questions of epistemology and method, especially as they related to the natural sciences, in an effort to further systematize Kant's so-called critical systems. The Southwestern or Baden school, associated with Wilhelm Windelband, Heinrich Rickert, and Emil Lask, sought to recover a more ambitious Kantian project concerned with questions of ethics, values, and history. Regardless of these differences, as a group the neo-Kantians thought that a newly disciplined and focused philosophy could adjudicate the most contentious disputes of the day, such as those about materialism, Darwinism, human consciousness, evolution, and the limits of the natural sciences. The neo-Kantians thus not only continued Dilthey's project, they also delimited what has ever since been widely understood as the proper object of study for the modern humanities—the products, expressions, creations, and objectifications of humans. The neo-Kantians developed entire epistemologies, methodologies, and ethics for studying what humans had created, from poems and novels to legal codes and religious traditions. Following Dilthey's lead, they introduced and systematized internal and external boundaries with the intention of establishing a distinct form of knowledge that was self-legitimating and not subordinate to natural science. In so doing they articulated the possibility of a distinct domain of knowledge and introduced an entire set of epistemic ideals, practices, and concepts that continue to shape the modern humanities.[83]

The Southwest school's call for an explicit return to Kant and attempts to outline a philosophy of value largely began with Windelband in Freiburg. A return to Kant would lead to a recovery of what he called, in 1882, philosophy's scientific, systematic "character," which he associated with Kant's "critical investigation" of the conditions, limits, and principles of knowledge. In suggesting such a distinction, Windelband sought to elevate philosophy to a science of sciences. Whereas individual sciences either "explained" causes, as in the case of empirical psychology, or "described" particular objects, as in the case of history or botany, philosophy scrutinized the conditions that made all other sciences possible.[84] The purpose of philosophy was to clarify the underlying principles and conditions that enabled particular sciences to make universal truth claims. In order for philosophy to fulfill its purpose, Windelband claimed (just as Dilthey had for the modern humanities in general), it needed a method.

By focusing on method instead of particular objects of investigation such as mind or nature, Windelband not only shifted the locus of distinction but also expanded the types of possible scholarly methods beyond those dominant in empirical disciplines. He identified two such methods: one genetic, the other critical. Whereas the former concerns the empirical validity of a given set of facts or even values (by explaining how values developed and came to be accepted as a matter of fact), the latter concerns the normative validity of values or those norms shared, as Windelband put it, by an "ideal of a normal human being."[85] The genetic method seeks to establish "factual validity" by identifying immediate causes; hence its legitimate claims to knowledge cover only a "certain ambit"—the individual or local conditions within which certain facts are the case or certain values are accepted. The critical method, in contrast, seeks to establish the normative validity of values—that is, not only *that* a value has as a matter of historical fact been accepted but rather that it *ought* to be accepted as universally and necessarily valid. In attempting to avoid both the metaphysical excesses of the German idealists and the specter of the various materialisms and naturalisms haunting post-Hegelian natural science, Windelband tried to carve out a distinct science of norms and values. By distinguishing between the factual and the normative, he, like Dilthey, hoped to cordon off an epistemic domain in which uniquely human forms of purposeful action and meaning making not only could be understood scientifically—systematically, open to empirical evidence, grounded in a method—but could also be distinguished and, thus, he thought, safeguarded from the brute mechanism of nature. The natural sciences, he contended, obscured just such a distinction.[86]

In 1883 Windelband moved to the University of Strasbourg, located in what was then a region of Alsace under German control. Although it traced its origins to a sixteenth-century humanist *Gymnasium*, the university was reconstituted in 1872 as a university of the new Reich in keeping with some of the reforms then sweeping German secondary and higher education. Significantly, the University of Strasbourg was founded not with the usual four faculties (philosophy, law, medicine, and theology) but with five. It was the first German university to be founded with a mathematics and natural sciences faculty that was separate from the traditional philosophy faculty.[87]

In 1872, a decade before Windelband arrived and as the university was being organized, Dilthey submitted an expert report to the Ministry of Culture recommending that the new configuration be adopted. After all, it wasn't the case that the philosophical faculty was a unified whole:

> A university is in fact divided into two halves, each one with its own internal organization. There is the mathematical-natural sciences division of the philosophical faculty, which functions as the foundation of the medical faculty and the technical sciences. And there is the historical-philosophical division of the philosophical faculty, which functions as the foundation of theology and law faculties and of pedagogical practice.[88]

What Dilthey did a decade later for *Wissenschaft* in his *Introduction to the Humanities* he did here for the University of Strasbourg, proposing that the university be divided into two distinct domains: *physis* and *psyche*, *res extensa* and *res cogitans*.[89]

On May 1, 1894, Windelband delivered his inaugural lecture as Strasbourg rector, a talk titled "History and the Natural Sciences" in which he rejected the Dilthey-inspired organization of the university he was now leading. "The splitting of the natural sciences and the humanities," though "common," he said, was "not a happy development." There was a gap between the theoretical organization of the "former faculty of arts" and the diversity of activities and ideas that had invigorated the particular sciences after the overexcitement of philosophical idealism earlier in the century.[90] Windelband promised his colleagues a Kantian philosophy that would organize all forms of knowledge and provide a "suggestion of the divine confluence of purpose" underlying them all.[91]

What Windelband actually did was sketch a new institutional order divided between the "natural scientific and historical disciplines." Echoing the premise of Helmholtz and Dilthey that all modern sciences were empirical and, thus, based on a commitment to empirical forms of evidence, Windelband said that both the biologist and the historian relied to some degree on "observable facts" and "experience" that had been "purified, critically shaped, and conceptually tested" by disciplinary, systematic knowledge. However, despite these commonalities, he continued, scholars on either side of this division ultimately ran up against an unbridgeable difference: not whether they valued empirical facts, but how.[92] Whereas the biologist sought the universal in the "form of natural law" (i.e., that which remained the same), the historian sought the particular "in historically determinate forms." Instead of the natural sciences and the modern humanities, Windelband argued for a different division, between the sciences of laws and the sciences of events, introducing, in doing so, his famous coinages "nomothetic" and "idiographic" to designate the former and the latter. Although Windelband described this division as fundamentally methodological and logical, it could also be understood as a distinction of "duration and scale."[93] Sciences in both domains are empirical forms of knowledge in a way idealist forms of knowledge are not, he said; both rely on empirically based notions of evidence, fact, and method. Relatedly, both concern objects in the world. The more meaningful distinction Windelband attempted to draw between the biologist and the historian, then, was one that highlighted different commitments to the scale and duration of their respective investigations. These prior commitments, while certainly related to method, concern not so much the logic of particular steps as more epistemic goals and intentions. Whereas the nomothetic sciences attribute more "scholarly value" and devote more attention to the universal, the same, and the invariant, the idiographic sciences attribute more "scholarly value" to and devote more attention to the particular, the contingent, and the distinct. Scholars practicing the former studied sameness; scholars practicing the latter studied difference. The demarcation between the two domains of scholarly investigation lies in a basic dispositional difference in how scholars relate to and understand the purpose of their inquiry, not in a given object of study or even a particular method. A scholar could study language, for example, by searching for the underlying, universal structures of an entire corpus or by attending to the distinctive form of a single poem. The "principle of division," wrote Windelband, was the "formal character of the goals of knowledge."[94]

The ways in which scholars encountered and ultimately evaluated empirical facts differed, then, not only methodologically but, more basically, ethically. They were shaped less by methodological or logical constraints and more by the character of (ideal) scholarly selves. And Windelband was clear about which scholarly persona he preferred. Those dedicated to the particularity of the "idiographic," he claimed, prefer living intuition to the dead abstraction of the nomothetic; they seek out the liveliness of humans rather than unchanging laws "lacking the earthy smell of sensuous qualities."[95] It is as though the natural and physical scientists work, ironically, in a world of abstractions and shadows, cut off from a pulsating, real life that can only be known in the particular.

Like Dilthey, Windelband related these distinctions in scholarly ethos to a more basic moral distinction between the two categories of sciences. Whereas the scholar disciplined according to the nomothetic ideals of the natural sciences regards the human being from the perspective of the lawlike regularity of a mechanistic image of nature, the scholar disciplined according to the idiographic ideals of the historical sciences encounters the "singular" worth of the "individual human life." Windelband traced the notion of the radical particularity of the human from the Christian Patristics, with their account of the "fall and redemption of the human species," to the emergence of the historical disciplines in nineteenth-century Germany. What connected them all, he wrote, was an unwavering commitment to the "innermost essence of personality" and a resistance to the universalizing abstractions that would threaten this essence and, thus, "individual freedom." For Windelband, there remains in all properly idiographic forms of knowledge "something inexpressible, indefinable." [96] It was in this, ineffable particularity, which exceeded all forms, facts, and theories, and about which thought could give "information," that Windelband claimed to find a "suggestion of the divine confluence of purpose." [97]

Over the course of his career, Windelband came to regard history as the general form of the modern humanities and, ultimately, in an essay published in 1910, recast his (Kantian) critical method as a historically based "philosophy of culture" that investigated the principles of the study of culture. [98] In adopting the term *philosophy of culture*, Windelband, as Frederick Beiser points out, was adopting and adapting the term *science of culture*, which his former student and later colleague in Heidelberg, Heinrich Rickert, had first used in 1898 to describe what he called "the not–natural scientific disciplines." [99] Rickert had attended Windelband's lectures in Strasbourg in the late 1880s but soon thereafter superseded his teacher with the publication of *The Object of Knowledge* in 1892, a landmark in neo-Kantian philosophy. Appointed in 1896 to a chair in Freiburg, where he served as Martin Heidegger's dissertation adviser and was briefly reunited with his former schoolmate Max Weber, Rickert relocated to Heidelberg in 1915. There he continued his efforts to expand Windelband's philosophy of value into a more robust philosophy of history and, more broadly, a philosophy of normativity. [100]

In 1898 Rickert and several of his philosophy faculty colleagues at the University of Freiburg met to discuss the possibility of organizing a scholarly society as a "counterpart" to the one natural scientists had established almost eighty years earlier, the Freiburg Society of Physical Scientists in Breisgau. At that first gathering of scholars from, as Rickert reported, "theology, jurisprudence, history, philology, political economy, and maybe also philosophy," the question of nomenclature arose. Whereas the biologists, chemists, geologists, and physiologists never doubted what bound them together as "men of the natural sciences," wrote Rickert, those gathered that day did not immediately know what "common activity" gave their group its coherence, though they presumed there was one. "True, we agreed on the term 'Society for the Science of Culture,' but the only reason why no one objected is that no one had something better to propose."[101] It was this continued "lack"—not just of a meaningful name but also of a shared concept of their common methods, interests, and tasks—that Rickert's colleagues invited him to address in the society's first lecture.

In that lecture, "Cultural Science and Natural Science," Rickert, like Dilthey and Windelband before him, began with a diagnosis of "how convoluted the problem of the organization of the sciences" had become.[102] The empirical sciences had fallen into two interest groups, with jurists, theologians, philologists, and historians in one camp and physicists, chemists, biologists, and geologists in the other. Yet whereas the "men of natural sciences" could readily give an account of themselves, the other group continued, despite the efforts of philosophers, to lack not only a common name for what they did but also, more importantly, a clear concept of their shared "interests, aims, and methods."[103] Part of this incapacity was a matter of historical priority. Like Dilthey, Rickert thought that the development of the natural sciences had long preceded anything that could be considered the humanities. Over the course of the nineteenth century, the natural sciences had ossified into a "natural scientific Weltanschauung" whose premises, methods, and practices rested on a metaphysical and methodological naturalism of which both its practitioners and the broader publics who confessed belief in it remained profoundly ignorant. Natural science had become "self-evident," and an entire German cultural elite now lived off the "interest" of its intellectual capital. This historical gap between known truth and felt truth, suggested Rickert, provided scholars such as those present at his lecture an opportunity. Drawn together by their opposition to the unrivaled (and, for many of them, increasingly illegitimate) authority of the natural sciences, they were all in search of "the not–natural scientific disciplines," disciplines that had the coherence and relative autonomy of the natural sciences without being the natural sciences.[104]

Like his former teacher Windelband, Rickert rejected Dilthey's term *Geisteswissenschaften* (literally, "sciences of mind"), which he thought evoked "the psyche" and thus was riddled with metaphysical presuppositions about "mental life."[105] Even if these metaphysically tinged presumptions were proven correct, Rickert considered them ultimately irrelevant to what "the not–natural scientific disciplines" needed most: "a doctrine of method." He thought that neither Dilthey nor Windelband had fully succeeded in this regard. Dilthey's repeated attempts to offer an alternative to natural scientific ways of knowing foundered on metaphysical dualisms, while Windelband's classification merely substituted Dilthey's metaphysical distinction (mind-nature) for another (particular-universal).[106] Rickert replaced his predecessors' paired oppositions—matter-mind, nature-mind, and nomothetic-idiographic—with another deeply Kantian dyad: nature-culture. He assiduously sought to define these domains in methodological terms. Scholars studied nature with natural scientific methods; they studied culture primarily with historical ones. Yet Rickert built on presuppositions about the qualities of the objects particular to each domain. Those who used natural scientific methods studied natural products, which grew "freely" from the earth, whereas those who used historical methods studied cultural products, which were yielded by purposeful human action. It was only to cultural products, objects produced by humans acting with intention, that "values" adhered.[107]

Despite his conceptual advances and terminological precision, Rickert largely accepted the same account of natural science Dilthey and Windelband had, which made his dismissal of natural science as an ossified cultural authority all the easier. Nature was brute mechanism: inert, regular, and predictable. It was simply a series of changes with no inherent value, good, or purpose. To study natural phenomena according to such a model, then, was to seek out lawlike patterns and regularities through concepts as well as numbers that shaped individual objects into smooth, homogenous forms that could be counted, compared, and, finally, generalized. The very practices that enabled scholars to posit such a passive, inert mechanism excluded as a methodological necessity the "particularity and individuality" of any given object.[108] Just as Dilthey and Windelband had done, Rickert saw the fault line of knowledge running through an interest in sameness and an interest in difference.

It was the concept of nature as inert mechanism and the history of science that was based on it that both legitimated Rickert's contention that there was a gap between what could be known to be true through natural scientific methods and practices and what was "felt to be true." Natural science, he asserted, could never fully exhaust the "inner diversity" of the real; it could never account for "particularities" of a given object.[109] There would always be a "suggestion," as Windelband had written in 1894, "of a divine coherence of ends" that exceeded human knowledge.[110] The knowledge that Rickert was outlining was, then, a moral necessity; it was needed to facilitate an encounter with a world not of predictable, passive mechanism but of agency, purpose, and value, a world full, deep, meaningful, and, indeed, closer to the creative and spontaneous mind of God: the world of human activity and culture.

It wasn't simply the neo-Kantians who bristled at what Rickert called the "obviousness" of natural science—the naturalness of naturalism.[111] Du

Bois-Reymond's exhortation to natural scientists to join his "*ignorabimus*" declaration with "manly renunciation" had proven exhausting and defeating for many.[112] Looking back in 1908 on the final decades of the nineteenth century, the physiologist Max Verworn described the "dour resignation" that had followed the "crippling" *ignorabimus* proclamation.[113] Du Bois-Reymond had taken note, revising, if not tempering, its tone. Speaking in the Academy of Sciences in 1876, he counseled his fellow "natural scientists" on how best to comport themselves within the limits he had laid down: instead of presuming to possess the truth, "strive" for it. The search itself was, after all, the "higher good."[114] In today's terms he was telling scientists to focus on the process of research rather than its results. Like the Roman emperor Severus issuing his final watchword to his soldiers as they fought in the north of England, Du Bois-Reymond exhorted his fellow natural scientists: "Let us work!"[115]

What Du Bois-Reymond was prescribing was asceticism, a life lived, as Rickert plaintively put it in 1898, in the shadows of "the real."[116] The self-discipline and abnegation required to become a natural scientist systematically suppressed "speculative ambitions," fantasies, even life itself, as Walther Rathenau wrote that same year, himself a trained physicist who would become one of Germany's leading industrialists and, eventually, foreign minister in the Weimar Republic.[117] Created and transmitted through experimentation, tools, and observations of a brute mechanistic world alien to lived human experience, the natural sciences produced knowledge that did not satisfy "our deepest drive for knowledge," the thirst that distinguished humans from other beings and served as "an absolute goal of existence."[118] Natural scientific knowledge was simply "uninteresting"; it had nothing to say about "human, moral, economic, social and national concerns . . . let alone the essence of matter and mind and the connections between them."[119] None of this, however, altered Rathenau's commitment to the natural sciences. As long as they continued to provide "mobility and comfort from the Pandora's box of technology," there was, he concluded, "no need for the modern humanities."

Like so many others around 1900, however, Rathenau could not rid himself of the thought that the dominance of the natural sciences might one day hollow out culture and human life:

> We need goals for our striving, convictions to go with all the knowledge
> we have collected. We need a living mind and new ideas. . . . Indeed, be-
> yond the knowledge in the natural sciences, there is a knowledge that
> is freer and richer, not in spite of being more personal but because of it.
> Thus, we wipe from our old tablets the rigid command of *ignorabimus*

and with a resolute hand, we write on the gates of the future: *Creabimus!* ["Let us create!"][120]

Ironically, the ascendance of the natural sciences had helped foment a crisis that made the modern humanities necessary or at least created the conditions that made such claims compelling.

Scientists, engineers, scholars, and intellectuals such as Rathenau himself cultivated, as Lorraine Daston has written, "an ambivalent modernism, enamored of the new while at the same time nostalgic for the old."[121] Beginning with the ambivalences and talk of limits among the mandarins of the lab and culminating in stark pronouncements like Rathenau's in the 1890s, many natural and physical scientists expressed in their more public writings "a sadness, yearning, and resignation" that was not just an epistemological stance but a social and ethical one as well. In a way, the natural sciences had become too successful for their own good. It was clear, as Werner Siemens wrote in 1886, that one law governed the "age of the natural sciences"—the law of "constant cultural acceleration." Deftly capturing the contradictions of the age, Siemens, an electrical engineer and industrialist, observed that scientific progress produced material goods but destroyed "ideal" ones; freed workers from the toil of the land but tethered them to factories; ended rule by birth but replaced it with the rule of capital.[122]

The constant pressure for natural scientists to deliver ever more practical benefits diminished science as a truth-seeking enterprise. How much significance should be assigned to a new scientific discovery when it would probably be disproven or substantially revised in short order? If scientific truths were purported to be "the sturdiest of all," writes Daston, what was the fate and value "of capital-T truth" when even those were revealed to be as ephemeral as anything else?[123] Pitted against the fleeting validity of (natural) scientific truths, the truths of the modern humanities, as described by Dilthey and those who followed in his wake, promised to be more lasting, more real, more human. The study of difference, the particular, the irreducible and ineffable, it turned out, brought one closer to the universal than the study of nature's lawlike regularity and sameness.

Energized by such thoughts, Rickert, as well as an increasing number of like-minded intellectuals and scholars, attempted to work through another "crisis of meaning": the "crisis of historicism." Although he developed the most perspicuous formulation of the modern humanities conundrum—affirming their reactionary self-conception as "the not–natural scientific disciplines"—he was also the first to recognize that focusing on the limits of natural science reduced all epistemic possibilities to the self-understanding and terms of the natural sciences—as Rickert put it, to ask too little of knowledge "as such."[124] To relate to the modern humanities as essentially "the not–natural scientific disciplines" was to conceive of all possible knowledge in terms of the concepts, ideals, history, practices, and virtues of nineteenth-century natural science.

For Rickert, even more dangerous than allowing the limits of natural science to determine the limits of all knowledge were the twin specters haunting historicism: nihilism and relativism. Historicism either provided high-minded scholarly cover for the contingent and arbitrary decision to choose one worldview over others or it precluded the possibility of living with a coherent and legitimate worldview. But Rickert continued to believe that a science of history and a related science of culture could be objective and thus that meaning could be derived from both. Otherwise, he feared, there would be only the blind, inert, meaningless mechanism of nature.

### FAITH AND THE SCHOLARLY LIFE

Like Dilthey, Windelband, and Rickert, Max Weber, another but decidedly different neo-Kantian, also sought to distinguish the natural sciences from other disciplines—such as economics, history, and philosophy—largely on the basis of his refusal to consider human action and subjectivity exclusively in terms of the brute mechanism he thought underlay most natural sciences. This effort was indeed Kantian, if loosely so. It was also very • much in line with the thinking of Dilthey and those who more immediately followed him in attempting to establish the theoretical groundwork for the modern humanities. From Dilthey to Weber, the scholars who sought something like "the not–natural scientific disciplines" simply accepted the model of nature (and thus the account of the natural sciences) as sketched by mid-nineteenth-century physiologists and physicists such as Helmholtz and Du Bois-Reymond. That model, as we saw in chapter 4, was largely an attempt to adapt the study of organic life to Kant's ideal image of nature as an inert, passive nature subject to universal and necessary laws. Weber rejected any positivist suggestion that facts could simply be collected without concepts (or theories or categories or other forms of rational thought) as well as any Comtean hierarchy of knowledge. In this sense he joined the efforts of many German scholars and intellectuals in a post-Hegelian theoretical landscape dominated by the natural sciences to come to terms with the institutional triumph of empirical forms of knowledge (from physiology and philology to biology and history) over metaphysical and theological ones and the deep dissatisfaction with the consequences that followed. His own thinking was profoundly shaped by the problems and scholars surveyed in the last three chapters.

Unlike Rickert, Dilthey, Nietzsche, and myriad other German scholars at the end of the nineteenth century, however, Weber rejected the discourse of crisis, in particular the anxiety and antagonism that characterized many of the decades-long efforts to separate completely the modern humanities from the natural sciences. Why?

Weber, as we shall see in the following chapter, committed himself to disciplinary scholarship, but he did not expect it to rescue humankind from the shipwreck of modernity. The goods of the humanities, like those of all modern sciences, were proximate, not ultimate. Rickert seems to have understood this about his colleague and friend. Just over a year after Weber's death in 1920, Rickert dedicated the third edition of *On the Limits of Forming Concepts in the Natural Sciences* to him. While German intellectual and university life had been overwhelmed in the first two decades of the twentieth century by Nietzsche's "romantic eccentricities and mushy aestheticism," Rickert wrote in the preface to that edition, Weber had "confessed his devotion" to disciplinary, university-based scholarship, that is, to *Wissenschaft*. Although Rickert acknowledged personally wanting more—namely, a comprehensive system of universal and necessary values—he claimed to have respected Weber's commitment to scholarship and the chastened disposition Weber thought followed from it. Rickert concluded his dedication by praising his friend's uncompromising devotion to disciplinary limits, clarity of thought, "restraint," and attention to the matter at hand. For all of his ascetic qualities, Weber the scholar modeled a form of life that was also expansive, teachable, and alive.[125]

But what did it mean to commit oneself to such a scholarly life when so many both inside and outside the university insisted that the present demanded more than discipline and restraint? Furthermore, how could Weber's religiously laden "confession" (*sich bekennen*) accurately describe his relationship to scholarship and academic knowledge given his purported commitment to concepts such as "value freedom" and "value neutrality"?

Rickert's conclusion to his 1898 lecture for his nonscience colleagues in Freiburg offers a possible answer by way of a contrast between ethical dispositions. There Rickert argued that like natural science, "nature" (logically speaking) was "nothing other than a theoretical cultural good." Like other such goods, such as art or law, "nature" was a product of human reason, and so it, too, was laden with values, which natural scientists had to take into account. The epistemic ideals, virtues, and values of natural science inhered not just in methods and notions of evidence but in its very model of nature.[126] In order to practice natural science and make knowledge claims about "nature," natural scientists thus had to presume the "absolute validity" of the value of nature as a "theoretical cultural good." They had to presume that "nature"—or rather the image of nature as subject to a law-like regularity (see chap. 4)—was universally and necessarily valid; otherwise, they would lack the epistemic ideals, norms, or values with which to orient their work.

There was, of course, a different way to view science and its possible goods, one, wrote Rickert, that presumed no such "absolute validity." To explain this alternative view, Rickert recounted a fable he adapted from Nietzsche. In some remote corner of the universe filled with countless flickering solar systems, there once was a star where, one day, clever little animals invented knowledge. It was the proudest minute in "world history." But it was just a minute. After a few breaths, the star collapsed and the clever little animals died. For Nietzsche, explains Rickert, this astral tale of animal knowledge illustrates "how abject, how shadowy and ephemeral, how lacking in purpose and arbitrary, the human intellect looks in nature." The realization that one's own or one's culture's highest values and concepts have no universal and necessary validity, that they, in fact, can simply collapse can be, to say the least, unsettling. Rickert noted, however, that on Nietzsche's telling, one might conclude, that "we" humans, like those astral animals, have been fortunate enough to have escaped the burden of recognizing how fragile our values are. This fate, noted Nietzsche, turned out to be especially beneficial for modern scholars because it enabled them to carry on with their careful, specialized work without asking why.[127]

For Rickert, Nietzsche's fable itself was consistent and, with respect to Nietzsche's interest in querying the value of truth for life, logical. But Rickert also found it troubling. For one thing, Nietzsche's fable completely undermined that which Rickert had sought to do in all of his own work: establish the universality and necessity of cultural science (and with it the study of values) as well as natural science. For another, the fable's own implicit view was necessarily the product of that long astral minute as well; its underlying, unstated commitment to the absolute priority of mere nature was itself a product of the human intellect it disavowed. In the end, then, thought Rickert, a view that tries to escape its own conditions of existence even as it charges the contemporary culture of the university with doing so was "a meaningless attempt of the modern scholar to jump over his own shadow."[128] Any attempt to escape one's own limited personal and cultural experience without the help of universal and necessary values was fated to fail. In Weber's case, then, concluded Rickert, a commitment to scholarship as a form of life required one to presuppose the absolute value of scholarship and be guided in one's daily activity by this presumption. The ultimate value of scholarship—why one ought to undertake it in the first place—could not be fully rationally ascertained, and yet it had to be presumed in practice. Despite Rickert's repeated attempts to systematize and secure their objectivity, values remained for him, as for Dilthey, resistant to being fully accounted for through empirical or even entirely rational methods. Values were part of what Rickert called an "irreal realm," an ahistorical realm in which values existed safe from the change and conflict that characterized the domains of history and natural science.[129] Although this realm existed independent of human intellection and physical reality, Rickert believed that it could be known. He devoted much of his life to the pursuit of such knowledge and to the development of a comprehensive, scientific system that he hoped would secure it. Like Kant, Dilthey, and Windelband before him, he believed that the conflict of values was apparent and would ultimately be reconciled through reason.

Weber did not share this faith. He believed in neither the existence of a transcendent realm of values nor in this ultimate reconciliation through history; he believed, instead, in the "eternal conflict" of values and the "irreconcilable" forms of life organized around them.[130] On the basis of this belief, he wanted to understand—historically, empirically, and philosophically—how these various forms of life and their associated forms of rational conduct developed and the kinds of people they formed. In 1917, three years before Rickert recounted Weber's "confession," Weber offered a more public one: a profession of his commitment to and faith in scholarship as his chosen vocation. It was also a highly personal one that revealed how the conflicts of the modern humanities had shaped his own life and laid bare the scope and significance of intellectual work for everyone living in a disenchanted age, not just self-christened intellectuals.

As we have seen in this chapter, the faith in the modern humanities shared by many of Weber's predecessors was driven by overpromising. This helps explain why Dilthey made crisis a constitutive feature of the humanities' self-justification, and thus why he made crisis into something the humanities needed even as he held out the promise that they would transform people's individual and common lives. He was not alone. His contemporaries, including Windelband and Rickert, helped establish not only what more than a century later seems like an intractable opposition between the natural sciences and the humanities (and human sciences more broadly) but also a canon of underlying distinctions: nomothetic and idiographic, universal and particular, nature as the realm of invariant laws and necessity and culture as the realm of freedom and spontaneity, facts and values, is and ought, universalism and constructivism, necessity and contingency, objective and subjective, quantitative and qualitative. These distinctions, in turn, came to organize a set of epistemic ideals, idioms, and values that would gradually be referred to not only as "the not–natural scientific disciplines" but as the humanities.

These nineteenth-century descriptions and distinctions were not simply the insights of epistemological acuity nor simply the fruits of pragmatic labor. They were as well an act of moral self-fashioning that was at once bold and defensive.[131] Bold because it claimed for the modern humanities the role of the only legitimate and capable resource of liberal and moral education. Defensive because this act was carried out in reaction to the rise and self-formulations of the natural sciences and because it grounded the mission of the humanities in terms of resistance to powerful forces hostile to the humanities and, thus, the human. In this way the modern humanities came to depend on crisis. Crisis defined their basic social function.

The thought experiments we have been discussing live on today in the presumption that something called *the humanities* can be both rigorously scholarly and uniquely positioned to study meaning making, value, and the subjective as well as uniquely capable of accounting for and even forming human action and intention, human agency, and purpose: the presumption, that is, that the modern humanities are distinct because they can be justified as both method and moral formation, or *Bildung*.[132] When other forms of inquiry or types of knowledge take on these concerns, they are often said to comport themselves "humanistically" (hence the more contemporary idea of the "humanistic" social sciences). As Helen Small notes, it is at these moments, paradoxically, that the humanities' claims to distinction are clearest: qualitative over quantitative reasoning; suspicion of methodology; celebration of interpretation and the related rejection of positivism; concern with the subject of knowledge, not just its object; valuation of the particular as well as the general.[133] But if, as we claimed in an earlier chapter, those who identify with the modern humanities have broadly accepted the self-understanding that emerged in nineteenth-century Germany, the issues of how it should be acted on and institutionalized have always generated debate. In presenting the modern humanities as both the systematic study of "mental facts" and a way of resolving individuals' and society's recurrent crises of meaning, Dilthey reenlivened—indeed, radicalized—a tension that began with the neo-humanists' insistence on the compatibility of *Wissenschaft* and *Bildung*. And as was the case in the early nineteenth century, institutional politics exacerbated the tension and shaped the definitive debates.

CHAPTER SIX

# Max Weber, Scholarship, and Modern Asceticism

In 1905 one of Wilhelm Dilthey's students, Eduard Spranger, offered "words of comfort" for fellow students overwhelmed by the "chaos" and "endless expanse" of modern knowledge: Your "need for totality" and, ultimately, the "primacy of life over scholarship," the twenty-three-year-old philosophy student wrote, will always lead you back to "the unending intellectual and spiritual work of literature and philosophy," where you will find the "unmediated, creative power of life itself" and attain your highest moral form.[1] Four years later, in a landmark biography of Wilhelm von Humboldt, Spranger, then teaching at the University of Berlin, was more specific, locating this "productive power" in German neo-humanism.

Few students shared Spranger's desire to unify life and modern knowledge through a return to the German neo-humanist tradition more than those associated with the Free Student Movement (FSM), a heterogeneous collection of student groups that first formed around 1900. Each of the groups sought to organize and represent "nonincorporated" students, those not affiliated with the traditional associations that dominated student life in German universities, especially the powerful *Burschenschaften*, aristocratic fraternities established during the Napoleonic occupation of the early nineteenth century as nationalistic—and thus subversive—student associations. As a counterweight to these groups, the student associations that constituted the FSM included not just typical German university students (male, Protestant, middle to upper class) but also those who were only then gaining access to universities: Jews, women, and students from working-class families.[2] These associations initially conceived of themselves as committed to unifying all students "regardless of political or religious beliefs" and fostering community where one largely didn't exist.[3] They organized literary clubs and lecture series, helped students find apartments and part-time jobs, and hosted athletic and social events. Such activities were especially important for the influx of lower-middle-class, female, and Jewish students, who were excluded from most established forms of student socialization.[4]

Within only a few years, however, the FSM expanded its platform and elevated its aims by adapting the idioms of nineteenth-century neo-humanism to a "modernist spirit."[5] In 1905, the same year that Spranger had offered his "words of comfort," the organizers of a planned FSM gathering in Weimar recruited a young philosophy student named Felix Behrend to develop these impulses into a coherent philosophical program. Drawing on the writings of Fichte, Humboldt, Schiller, and Schleiermacher, Behrend celebrated "the self-cultivation of individual personality," academic community, unity among students, the unity of knowledge, and academic freedom.[6] He also pitted these ideals against the reality of "careerist" and hyperspecialized education, depicting both kinds as pervasive in the natural sciences and the humanities.[7] After approving statutes along the neo-humanist lines Behrend had laid out, students at the Weimar event placed a wreath on Schiller's tomb, proclaiming that "we are filled with the joyful certainty that the spirit of idealism that you have awakened in us will live on for all time in Germany's youth."[8]

The students' worries about the future of higher education were not unfounded. After decades of enrollment growth, bureaucratic transformation, and continuous disciplinary reorganization and specialization, the intellectual and cultural order of disciplinary, university-based knowledge—the very order upheld by the neo-humanist ideals the FSM hoped to recover—had finally begun to topple. One of the most significant changes they were living through was loss of the privileged place accorded to ancient philology by Germany's cultural and intellectual elite both within and outside the university. Philologists had been complaining about hyperspecialization and its disenchanting effects on the study of Greek and Roman antiquity for more than half a century, of course. What was new was that enrollments in classical philology were declining even as those in other nonscience fields were increasing. By 1910 over a third of all students at the University of Berlin, for example, were studying in such fields.[9] By 1924 the number of students enrolled to study modern languages (German, English, or French) was six times more than the number enrolled to study ancient ones.[10] Once the paradigmatic discipline, classical philology was losing out not to the natural sciences but to emerging disciplines that included not only the study of national literatures and languages but also of music, art history, and religion.

The decline of student interest in Latin and Greek at the university level was motivated in part by system-wide educational reforms. On the secondary level, after 1898 students could gain university admission not just by studying at a classical humanist *Gymnasium* but, alternately, by studying at a *Realgymnasium* or *Oberrealschule*. The latter, more "modern" secondary schools required not only more math and natural science and less Greek and Latin but also more modern languages. With fewer hours of Greek and Latin in high school, students arrived at universities less prepared to study classical philology. Furthermore, the *Lehramtprüfung*, the civil service exam required of anyone wishing to teach in a secondary school, was revised to become more specialized. By 1898 the state required candidates to choose one of four areas of possible specialization—"modern languages" being one—each with its own protocols for required lectures and seminars.[11] By 1900 studying German or history provided a clear path to a profession. It was also during this period that the disparate disciplines that came to be known collectively as the modern humanities were gradually institutionalized. At the University of Berlin alone, between 1883 and 1916 twenty seminars and institutes in a range of such fields, particularly ones devoted largely to the study of modern cultures and languages, were established.[12]

Within decades of Dilthey's initial attempt to establish them as a bulwark against the natural sciences and the enervating effects of modernity, the modern humanities had won a secure place in the university, and they had done so in a fundamentally changed institution. With the pluralization of methods, ideals, and research aims, debates about method, technique, and disciplinary differences had become fixed features of the university even as they became fractal-like, endlessly repeating the same distinctions.[13] With the proliferation of institutes and seminars, the ethos, institutional organization, and forms of authority first introduced into the Prussian Academy with Theodor Mommsen's "big humanities" (see chap. 3) began to permeate universities, setting alongside the charismatic authority of the chaired, full professor that of the academic manager and scholarly organizer. By 1909, in fact, Max Weber had concluded that the "ascendance of the capitalist business model" had so transformed German higher education that the *universitas litterarum* (the ideal of the university as a corporation of scholars devoted to learning) had become a "fiction."[14] It was in this transformed system of higher education and under these conditions that the modern humanities gained their institutional form. Sustained by new fields, unprecedented financial investments, and exciting ideas, in many ways the modern humanities thrived. Yet the very forces and structures that allowed them to flourish also imperiled what the modern humanities promised: meaning, values, and, as Spranger and leaders of the FSM put it, life. Crisis had figured centrally in justifications for the modern humanities. Now it was also a condition of their institutional existence and hence their permanent crisis.

188 | CHAPTER SIX

## REINVENTING HUMBOLDT

The FSM's and Spranger's efforts to adapt early nineteenth-century neo-humanist ideals evoked precisely this fiction and a period imagined to have preceded the age of the natural sciences, a time when philology and philosophy dominated the university and stood in for the unity of knowledge and the continuity of a tradition of learning that stretched back to ancient Greece and Rome. This "fiction" summoned images of a different institution as well, one with smaller enrollments, engaged professors, and committed students. All of these efforts were also part of a much broader re-invention of a Humboldtian tradition.

In the late 1890s, while doing research for a biography of Wilhelm von Humboldt, the Berlin historian Bruno Gebhardt discovered in the archives of the Academy of Sciences a document dating from about 1809. Written by Humboldt himself, it was a fragmentary memorandum, which Gebhardt presented in his completed biography, *Wilhelm von Humboldt as Statesman*, as a founding text of the German research university and source of its enduring ideals and norms. Gebhardt thus helped inspire and legitimate broader attempts to recover and repurpose a purportedly Humboldtian ideal of the university—the "refuge of intellectual freedom," as he glossed it—for contemporary ends.[15] In addition to Felix Behrend's neo-humanist manifesto for the FSM, faculty members from across the political spectrum—from Spranger, a conservative nationalist, to the more liberal Karl Jaspers—advocated for the same principles that Behrend, channeling Humboldt, had formulated for the FSM platform.

Humboldt certainly had played a key part in establishing the University of Berlin, and given that institution's central role during the nineteenth century, many of the norms and ideals that guided German research universities in general. Humboldt's broad ideals, however, could be used to burnish different conceptions of how Germany's educational and research institutions should be organized.[16] In 1909 one of Humboldt's most ardent boosters at this time, the Berlin church historian and (with Theodor Mommsen) "big humanities" advocate Adolf Harnack, tried to convince Kaiser Wilhelm II to establish several research institutes completely independent of universities and largely devoted to making Germany more internationally competitive in the natural sciences.[17] Harnack was one of the first academics to master and understand how to use the bureaucracy of the modern research university. He told the Kaiser that his plan took advantage of Germany's higher-education system—its financial resources, infrastructure, vast network of highly trained civil servants—to realize possibilities Humboldt himself had imagined. The Kaiser believed him, and on October 11,

1910, as part of the centenary celebrations for the University of Berlin, he announced the founding of the Kaiser Wilhelm Society with Harnack as its inaugural president. Ironically, then, one of the most significant appropriations of the Humboldtian tradition served the ends not of a neo-humanist university as the FSM and many faculty members and intellectuals across Germany understood it but, as Harnack put it, those of the "heavy industry of scholarship . . . the mechanization of work [and an] overemphasis on collecting and processing materials as opposed to spiritually penetrating them."[18] As they sought to recover the Humboldtian tradition, German intellectuals and scholars were also reinventing it more decisively than ever. Frankly acknowledging this, Harnack invoked Humboldt even as he embraced a thoroughly transformed tradition.

In this sense the FSM sought to restore to health an (imagined) institution whose factory-like character had become obvious to critics and defenders alike. The FSM also drew much of its motivation and rhetorical power from precisely this gap between ideal and reality, a reinvented tradition and the contemporary world. Its leaders regularly mixed normative assertions about what the university should be with descriptive diagnoses of the university's current conditions.

## THE METAPHYSICS OF YOUTH

In its first two decades, the leaders of the FSM tried to maintain its close affiliation with the broader Germany youth movement, which encompassed groups with diverse political sensibilities, including the Wandervögel ("wandering birds"). Devoted to acquainting boys with nature and cultivating personal habits such as good hygiene, physical fitness, and abstinence, it was one of many youth groups united in the "struggle against everything false."[19] The leaders of the FSM also sought to expand access to the goods they claimed were internal to a neo-humanist education, and the way to do so, they argued, was for the FSM to maintain "strict neutrality" on any nonacademic topic and to abstain from any explicit "political activity."[20] In the years just before World War I, internal debates about the success of this stance began to overwhelm the movement, with one wing eventually denouncing its tepid liberalism and "pretension" to represent all students as politically naive and institutionally ineffective,[21] and another wing denouncing the "socialist" tendencies of those calling for more direct political action. In the middle was the largest group of students, anxious about turning universities into scenes of political and social combat. By 1913 the internal conflicts over the FSM's goals and tactics had spilled into the open. Hermann Kranold, a student-leader from Munich, argued that the movement's "fear of the word 'party'" undercut its aspirations to reform and proposed that the FSM split into two groups: a student organization committed to representing all students and an academic party committed to pursuing a "particular, content-filled program."[22]

Each of these tensions within the FSM—the reinvention of neo-humanism, the ambivalent relationship between politics and the university, the weighty expectations placed on the humanities—crystalized in the essays and speeches of an aspiring critic named Walter Benjamin, who gained national prominence in the FSM from 1912 to 1915 as a student-leader in Freiburg and Berlin. As was the case for many students who leaned left politically and advocated university reform, Benjamin's thinking owed much to Gustav Wyneken, a charismatic pedagogue and writer whom Benjamin himself affectionately referred to as the "Führer" of German youth.[23] Benjamin and the other young men and women attracted to Wyneken came predominantly from middle- and upper-middle-class families. According to Hilde Benjamin, the wife and biographer of Benjamin's brother Georg, the Benjamin brothers were part of an "intellectual elite" with a long list of grievances against how they were being raised and schooled—for example, their elders' "suppression" of any real intellectual desire, the "alignment" of educational institutions to the narrow interests of the state and military, and the "bourgeois morals" of middle-class German families, including their insincere invocations of neo-humanist educational ideals and the rhetoric of freedom that went with them.[24] Wyneken offered these young people an uncompromising, antiauthoritarian, and sweeping critique of Germany's key moral institutions—namely, its state-sponsored schools and universities—and also of the bourgeois parents who considered knowledge of art, literature, and philosophy—a liberal education—a necessary credential for membership in the German elite. Wyneken assured his acolytes that they possessed an "inner truthfulness" that made them the only agents of cultural renewal.[25] He also insisted that they not mistake institutional reform efforts or political action for their real purpose: to realize their destiny as the ultimate agents of history.[26]

In 1912 Benjamin began his studies at the University of Freiburg. Over the next three years, as he shuttled between Freiburg and Berlin and assumed various leadership roles in the local and national FSM, he published a series of essays on Germany's youth movements, the urgent need for educational reform, and what he termed "the metaphysics of youth." Echoing Wyneken, Benjamin asserted that Germany's students had a messianic mission not only to reform their universities but also to renew all of German society and, finally, humankind. With their "vibrating sense" for the power of pure mind, students would bring about "the new reality"[27]

In October 1913 Benjamin traveled to Breslau, where he gave a lecture arguing that the FSM had begun to split in two.[28] On the one side was the Breslau group, which distracted itself with "social engagement"—"a copy of public life" performed in local reform activities—and lacked the "inner, necessary connection with the spirit of the students' movement."[29] On the other was his own Freiburg group, which sought to reform life itself through a "new philosophical pedagogy" in which "youth and cultural values" clashed over readings, lectures, and discussion.[30] It was only by going in this latter direction, Benjamin believed, that the "youth" could achieve the historical task to which they had been called—realizing "*universitas*."[31]

On his way home Benjamin stopped near Kassel, in central Germany, to participate in the First Free German Youth Day. On October 11 and 12, 1913, over two thousand young people from across Germany gathered on Mount Meissner for what would quickly become remembered as a turning point for the FSM.[32] Organized by a broad range of youth and student reform groups, the event was part festival—including folk dancing, athletic competitions, and discussions of abstinence—and part cultural and political debate about the future of the FSM. Benjamin's own account of the event exemplified the Wynekians' increasing frustration. He lamented that "finding oneself," political "jargon," as well as hiking, dancing, and singing had distracted "2,000 young modern humans" from anything "intellectual." He was also deeply chagrined that "anti-Semitic taunts"—such as "Isaacsohn"—and militaristic chants of "Point your weapons!" repeatedly drowned out expressions of "common humanity."[33]

The following summer, having returned to study in Berlin and having been elected chair of the university's FSM group, Benjamin delivered two further lectures in which he laid out the core of the Wynekian critique of higher education as merely technical training. The only way to recover the authentic "productivity" of students, reconstitute the community of all scholars, and ultimately liberate the present, he wrote, was to cultivate a renewed "devotion to the unity of knowledge" and live it as a "protest against the vocational life."[34] Benjamin and his fellow Wynekians wanted not just to democratize university education but to reestablish the university as a domain unbeholden to economic and state demands.

Even after the bitter disappointments at Mount Meissner, Benjamin continued to insist that scholarship and the university could be renewed if they remained pure and free of explicit political conflicts, or what he described as "foreign bodies."[35] Bolstered by a Wynekian-inspired Hegelianism, according to which knowledge is fundamentally grounded in the processes intrinsic to the human mind, Benjamin believed that the mind's own activity, reflecting on itself and expressing itself, was the sole source of intellectual unity and authority. Unconstrained by economic, political, or social interests, such pure intellectual activity served the unity of knowledge.[36] Even after natural and physical scientists largely abandoned the ideal of the unity of knowledge, Benjamin and the Wynekians remained committed to a radically metaphysical version of it. In the tradition of nineteenth-century neo-Hegelians (but with a metaphysical account that many Left Hegelians would have rejected), they believed that all confessional and political conflicts, distinct ideas and forms of knowledge, and competing moral norms could be reconciled through a developmental process of intellectual and moral learning or *Bildung*. For them, *Bildung* was not only an individual process; it was a species-level process that proceeded over millennia. The most important domain of this developmental process—where the reconciling work of reason actually happened—was, as Benjamin wrote, in "the ideal goods, the expressions of the objective spirit, such as language and scholarship, law and morality, and art and religion"—the modern humanities.[37]

By opposing this domain—one example of what we have termed the modern humanities—to that of vocational and other technical or material interests, Benjamin and the Wynekians defined it negatively just as Dilthey had with the *Geisteswissenschaften*, Windelband had with the idiographic sciences, and Rickert had with the cultural sciences. But whereas Dilthey and those who followed him had identified the natural sciences as the primary countervailing force, Benjamin and the Wynekians assigned that role to ideologies, party politics, and factional interests. Through art, literature, and scholarship, they believed humans participated in a universal, rational historical process that transcended instances of particularity—aesthetic, religious, historical, legal, political—and allowed them to encounter "life" itself.

After Germany declared war on Russia in August 1914, the internal differences within the FSM rapidly intensified.[38] As the *Burschenschaften* aligned themselves with right-leaning, nationalist interests, the more left-leaning groups, including the Wynekians, sharpened their critique of the university and began to argue, as Immanuel Birnbaum, a student-leader in Munich, put it, that the FSM had to be turned into an "academic action party."[39] Prominent members of the FSM, including Hans Reichenbach and his brother Bernhard, moved further to the left, joining a group affiliated with *Der Aufbruch*, a journal that sought "to connect politics and philosophy."[40] Others would join the Spartacus League, a Marxist revolutionary movement founded in 1914. Benjamin soon began to express doubts about the metaphysics of Wyneken's "*objective* Geist," the historical calling of students, the promises of the humanities, and whether Wyneken's "theory" was commensurate with his "vision."[41] By October 1914, Benjamin had concluded that the university was a "swamp" that "poisoned" his attempts to embrace true knowledge, or *Geist*.[42] Although he continued his studies, writing a dissertation and then habilitation, Benjamin abandoned his earlier expectation that the university-based study of art, literature, and philosophy were the path to a transformed humanity.

## INTELLECTUAL WORK IN THE
## SHADOW OF THE UNIVERSITY

In the late summer of 1917 and in the midst of this tumultuous wartime debate about the purpose of the university, a group of students in Munich invited Max Weber to launch a lecture series on "intellectual work as vocation" with a talk on the work of the scholar.[43] The students were members of the Bavarian chapter of the Free Student Alliance (FSA), an organization of former FSM members led by Immanuel Birnbaum[44] and Karl Landauer, both of whom had been part of the broader group of students around Wyneken. They appear to have gotten the idea for the lecture series from an essay written by another Wynekian, Alexander Schwab, titled "On Vocation and Youth," which decried the contemporary use of "vocation" to distinguish productive and responsible employment from the distractions of "art, all scholarship unrelated to technology, and philosophy and religion."[45] The word *vocation* appealed to Birnbaum and Landauer because it suggested not only the labor performed in modern factories and universities but also a more comprehensive and integrated way of living; it was a way into the malaise of modern life but also, perhaps, a way out.[46]

That the students in Munich were drawn to Max Weber was understandable. Led mostly by Benjamin's Wynekian colleagues, the FSA championed the same neo-humanist ideals associated with the German research university—the pursuit of knowledge for its own sake, *Bildung*, academic freedom—at a time when those ideals appeared to be imperiled by disciplinary specialization, state intervention, the influence of industrial capitalism, and now the war. Writing over the years as a kind of insider-outsider—he had not held an academic job since his resignation as professor of economics at the University of Heidelberg around 1900—Weber had distinguished himself as an erudite and forceful defender of an ideal university that in some important ways aligned with the institution wished for by members of the FSA.

In 1908, for example, Weber had challenged the powerful minister in charge of higher education in Prussia, Friedrich Althoff, accusing him of violating the ideals of academic freedom and merit. The case in question concerned the appointment of the economist Ludwig Bernhard to a full professorship at the University of Berlin, Germany's largest and most prestigious institution of higher learning. The Ministry of Culture and Education, and in practice Althoff himself, had long exercised final authority over all faculty hires, but it typically consulted closely with faculty members before making an offer. In this case, however, Althoff had, as Weber saw it, simply installed his preferred candidate for reasons that had nothing to do with quality and everything to do with the fact that Bernhard's research agenda aligned with the state's material interests.

Even more to Weber's dismay, many academics had supported Althoff. In 1909 Conrad Bornhak, a historian at the University of Berlin, wrote an essay that stressed the importance of hiring university instructors with patriotic views—who else could be trusted to train young people to serve state and church loyally? For conservative academics like Bornhak, there was no tension between patriotism and a stated commitment to the scholarly ideals and virtues of free inquiry. To oppose the state was to oppose reason itself, and to emphasize the state's greatness was to stress what was objectively true.

Weber dismissed such thinking as absurd and dangerous. In response to Bornhak, he wrote that cultivating "political obedience among university students" on behalf of the state was sure to prove catastrophic for German universities and scholarship. Funding and advancing them on such grounds would lead to the "castration" of academic freedom and stunt the "development of a genuine" scholarly character.[47] Universities, he suggested sardonically, may have been better off under the church's influence; at least then they pursued something other than money and power.

What happened next only bore out his fears. Weber had initially been a strong supporter of the war. The day after Germany declared war against Russia on August 1, 1914, he was so excited that he reported for duty to the garrison in Heidelberg where, much to his disappointment, he was judged too old and physically unfit for the battlefield. He accepted a position in the military bureaucracy and sought through his writings to sway Germany's war policy on everything from the occupation of Belgium to the escalation of submarine warfare and voting rights for returning soldiers. Yet by the summer of 1917, he had concluded that the war was essentially lost. The failing that proved to be Germany's undoing was that Germans couldn't think for themselves. "The familiar structure of bureaucratic paternalism," he wrote, had habituated Germans to act as "objects, not agents."[48] Neither the credentialed experts of Germany's sprawling state bureaucracy nor the literary aesthetes of its cultural elite had shown any capacity to grapple intelligently and creatively with the problems of the day, and German education had helped to cause the situation. Emerging from universities that set out to be "sites of real political formation" and moral education, academics, intellectuals, and bureaucrats had all been guilty of an unreflective compliance with the state and its institutions and had directly contributed to the disasters that now faced the country and the German people.

All this must have been very much in the forefront of Weber's and his audience's minds when on November 7, 1917, Weber addressed nearly one hundred students in a small theater connected to the bookshop where the Free Student Alliance met. The year had begun with the "turnip winter," when a root vegetable typically used to feed livestock became a staple of Germans' 1,500-calorie daily ration. Though defeat was by no means a foregone conclusion, a truce was the best that could be hoped for. In the meantime, millions of young men had died, and university enrollments had collapsed. How, in this context, was one to think of the vocation of the scholar? Benjamin and his fellow Wynekians, some of whom were members of the group who had invited Weber to Munich, claimed that the vocation of university students was to be "authors of a transformation" of knowledge, the university, and, ultimately, "humanity."[49] A radical call, but one that evoked and that was indeed rooted in the grand sense of moral purpose that the celebrated architect of the modern German educational system, Wilhelm von Humboldt, had assigned to it some hundred years earlier when he described the university as the "pinnacle" of the nation's moral culture.

Yet Weber, certainly to his audience's dismay, began his lecture not by articulating an ideal but by delving into a frank, empirically based account of the practical risks and liabilities of an academic career. He detailed the ways in which the university, though still heralded as an ideal community, was riddled with structural problems, many of which were getting worse: terrible teaching, workplace discrimination, the adjunctification and exploitation of the labor force, an arbitrary hiring process, and an ever more specialized and businesslike, and thus uninspired, understanding of the scholar's vocation.[50]

Of all of this his audience was certainly aware. Yet Weber offered no suggestions about how to reform academic working conditions or even much hope that the university as an institution could be transformed. He turned instead to the question of whether under these conditions modern scholarship could be a meaningful and sustainable form of life. Germany's "youth," he said, had little hope that it could. They had inverted Plato's cave analogy. Instead of embracing the "truth of scholarship" as that which could compel them to break free of their chains and leave the false shadows of the cave, today's students experienced scholarship and the university as a "play of shadows" that distracted them from life itself even as they longed for their renewal.[51]

As to specialization, Weber presented it as a basic feature of scholarly life. Not only was it here to stay, but he appeared actually to affirm the value of specialized research at the expense of moral formation or *Bildung*. He went so far as to say that specialization was less of a threat to German scholarship than those who used the idealism of the past to call the present order into question.

If before the war Weber had worried about conservative scholarship aligning too closely with the state, now, as Germany's political and social order teetered, he was just as concerned about professors posing as "prophets" trying to shape students' souls in the classroom. Professors who sought to fill a void of meaning from the lectern had found an eager audience in Germany's zealous youth, especially in the university, where, "inspiration" and charisma continued to play an important role in the daily lives of scholars waiting for ideas that arrived on their own time.[52] Professors sermonized and denounced disciplinary boundaries and intellectual fragmentation in the lecture hall in the name of some lost or future harmony and wholeness. In doing so, they were undermining their own authority and the legitimacy of the university itself. They were overreaching. What they sought was simply no longer to be had, and had probably never existed. Expert knowledge had dramatically expanded over the course of the previous century. There were too many disciplinary perspectives and too many competing moral ideals, too much pluralism in too many areas, for any responsible scholar to hold out hope of integrating them all. Weber, in saying this, was effectively declaring that the mission of the neo-humanist, Humboldtian university—to lead people to a higher level of moral consciousness, the mission German scholars had fretted over yet clung to for years—was no longer viable. The students were engaging in a delusion.

What was to be done? To lead the life of the mind within the context of the contemporary university at this particular historical moment, Weber argued, began with a duty that fell particularly to professors, a duty to recognize that universities cannot provide more than a limited "moral instruction" or deliver ready-made comprehensive worldviews. Universities were not institutions for the inculcation of ultimate moral values. Their purpose was to advance scholarship and to educate students in doing so, and they would be "going beyond the boundaries of scholarship if they were to provide not only knowledge and understanding but also beliefs." Scholars had the duty, and Weber considered this an obligation, to exercise self-restraint and instill an unflinching honesty in their students. Anything else would be a violation of scholarly ethics, an abuse and undermining of the legitimacy of academic authority and freedom that would deny students the space they needed to develop their own intellectual and moral capacities and commitments.

A form of asceticism was necessary to sustain the integrity of scholarship and, by extension, the modern university. For Weber this moral asceticism had the force of an obligation, the commitment of faith. Even—indeed, especially—if the choice to follow the scholarly calling couldn't be established through scholarly or rational deliberation alone, a measure of faith was necessary. The moral purpose of the university was to inculcate a distinct character, one forged through scholarly asceticism. Universities were uniquely well equipped to form students into mature, independent, self-reflective subjects with "the capacity to think clearly and 'know what one wants.'" For this reason, too, universities must not tell a student how to live. They could teach students to understand how values conflict with one another, and that acting in accord with their values will have specific social consequences, which is a part of having "genuine character," as Weber had put it in an earlier essay. The "ideals he should serve," the "gods he should bow before," were ultimately a matter for the individual conscience and should come down to where one's passion lies.

## A DISENCHANTED WORLD

It was in this light that Weber introduced his famous and much contested term "the disenchantment of the world."[53] For Weber, this disenchantment was not simply a question of subjective disposition but, more fundamentally, a historical process that stretched over centuries. One might mistakenly think this was a question of the loss of religious belief, that it was another name for what theorists across Europe and North American, in particular, would later in the twentieth century call secularization. But intensely pious Calvinists had already in the sixteenth century begun to help disenchant the world, argued Weber in *The Protestant Ethic*, by denying the Catholic sacraments their "magic."[54] He considered Calvinists' rejection of Catholic sacramental dogma part of an effort to develop their own moral methods and disciplines. It was an example of how humans order their lives by developing habits and ways of living organized around repetition and rules, what Weber called "ascetic rationalization."[55] Rationalization, in this case, did not entail a decline in religious affiliation, belief, or practice, nor did it entail a detachment from or exclusion of divine or transcendent beings or forces. Indeed, one could argue, as Calvin had in *The Institutes of the Christian Religion* (1536), that such regularized piety (and not just belief in things unseen) was "requisite for the knowledge of God."[56] As

Weber understood them, such rationalized, more methodical forms of piety involved a reconfiguration of daily ethical practices and their sources of justification away from transcendent origins and toward more worldly disciplines and structures. Rationalization was regularization.[57] Although these rules could be oppressive, they could also be adaptive, elastic, and supple, pliable to the needs of particular communities and individuals.

In Munich, Weber enjoined his audience to acknowledge that whether or not they believed in magic, ghosts, or supranatural forces, they nonetheless led their lives as though they lived in a disenchanted, rationalized world. To underscore this point, he told his audience, "Those of us who took the streetcar here have no idea how it runs, unless we happen to be engineers or physicists." But his auditors did not need to know. They only needed to know that they could "count on" the streetcar to deliver them punctually and safely to their destination. Although they probably did not consider the streetcar to be laden with moral meaning or a microcosm of a cosmic order, they did "orient" their daily behavior—for example, habitually showing up for the streetcar at the same time every morning—by their implicit trust in the expertise and specialized knowledge that kept the system running. Such quotidian forms of rational trust functioned like practical maxims for daily life. The "savage," in contrast, had not, as Weber wrote elsewhere, been civilized, which Weber understood to mean that he had not been disciplined into this same habituated trust. But for this same reason, the "savage knows incomparably more about his tools" with which he creates his life because he understands, even if only tacitly, how a given object fits into a meaningful whole, how it is part of the cosmos in which he finds himself.[58] The "civilized man," in contrast, exhibits an "inveterate faith" that all the things he relies on in his daily life are the products of human intellectual activity and thus subject to various forms of "knowledge, creation, and control."[59]

Weber thought that these processes of disenchantment and rationalization had historically oftentimes revolved around cultural and religious tensions that had developed when empirical sciences were seen to have reduced the world to a brute causal mechanism. For many people, wrote Weber in 1915, the image of nature presumed by such a causal reduction undercut the ethical postulate that the world was, in fact, "divinely ordered, and thus somehow a cosmos with a meaningful ethical orientation."[60] By refusing to accord explanatory power to forces and powers that on principle could not be known, modern humanities scholarship and the natural and physical sciences act as agents of disenchantment. Modern disciplinary scholarship, whether philology or physics, strips the world of certain forms of magic and mysteries; it de- or unmagics, as the German term *Entzauberung* literally suggests.

"Life," Weber wrote in *The Protestant Ethic*, could be rationalized "under ultimate vantage points that vary considerably from one another and according to very different orientations."[61] These various forms of rationalization referred most importantly to the "diverse array" of intellectual practices for ordering and disciplining human life.[62] They further referred to expansive (if incomplete) changes in authority and trust—in the traditions, institutions, and forms of knowledge that sustained people's daily lives. Weber was pointing out to his audience in Munich that the age of the natural sciences the mandarins of the lab had worked so hard to make seem so natural and inevitable—a world in which human bodies, voices, and words were effortlessly, almost magically transported across cities, continents, and oceans with speed and efficiency[63]—had become ordinary. When Weber contrasted the "magic" of the "savage" to the trust Germany's educated elite placed in modern scholarship and science, he held the former up as a mirror in which the elite might catch a glimpse of who they are.[64] The boundary separating the "savage" from the students was, thus, not a sharp one between reason and nonreason or rationality and irrationality; it was, rather, more circuitous, running among the multivarious disciplines, rationalities, and rules that constituted different ethical traditions and that served as resources for acting and for leading a life.[65]

Weber was aware that the proliferation and transformation of rules that accompanied disenchantment could weigh heavily on the soul. Rational frameworks, such as the taken-for-granted habits that oriented the students' daily lives, could accumulate over time and become entrenched and alien. What were once personally meaningful disciplines or structures for living could become impersonal, meaningless, and simply coercive. It was in this way that modern life could be experienced, as Weber wrote in *The Protestant Ethic*, as a "shell as hard as steel" in which free, conscious, meaningful action was an exceptional achievement.[66] Rationalized forms of life could also deform the lives they were purported to care for. They could fail and harm not because disciplines and rules are necessarily oppressive but rather because instead of helping people and communities shoulder intellectual or moral burdens, disciplines and rules can harden and seem to obviate the need for judgments and exceptions. When they do, reflection on the original reasons for a given rule or why a discipline exists at all becomes nearly impossible, and identification with these forms of life becomes unimaginable. A disenchanted world could be "dark" and "wintry."[67]

Modern humanities scholarship and the sciences had helped to cause a crisis of meaning, and it was this crisis of meaning that was driving the students' yearning for "authentic experience" and their professors to pose as prophets in the classroom. People were in fact trying to reenchant knowledge within the university. Weber spoke of "all the hunting after 'authentic experience'" in academic culture as deriving from "weakness." "For," he went on to say, "it is weakness to be unable to face the destiny of the age head-on."[68] The crisis of shared meaning could not simply be wished away.

In response Weber offered a corrective, a bleak but bracing analysis of the state, purpose, and prospects of higher education and intellectual work in the uncertain modern world. He told his audience that if scholarship and science can do anything, "it is precisely to uproot and destroy the belief that the world has *any such thing* as a 'meaning'!," that purpose and meaning inhered in the world independent of human action. As Freud would in *Civilization and Its Discontents* (1930), Weber urged his audience to come to terms with the challenges of modern life and to avoid actions that would exacerbate them, such as abandoning scholarly integrity. Weber offered his own account of scholarship as a meaningful, deeply moral, and passionate way of life even as he undercut what many saw as the university's moral purpose. Scholarship, too, could be a vocation.

## WEBER AND THE CRISIS OF HUMANIST KNOWLEDGE

The audience who witnessed the lecture is said to have been rapt, riveted, but also repelled by what many considered to be Weber's emptying scholarship of any sense of true meaning and value. For those present, wrote the philosopher Karl Löwith years later, Weber's every word was "haunted by a human gravity that lent him personality. His refusal to offer easy answers was matched only by the acuity of his questions."[69] In recalling his experience as a young student listening to a scholar whose untimely death three years later only burnished the legend of his charismatic personality, Löwith described not just Weber the famed theorist of religion, disenchantment, and rationality but also the ideal of the modern, if German and stereotypically masculine, scholar: biting, critical, and disciplined, yet humane, imaginative, and passionate—devoted to the methodologically informed practice of disciplinary scholarship as well as distinguished by a personality of transformative moral force.[70]

In the summer of 1919, the prestigious Berlin press Duncker and Humblot published *Scholarship as Vocation* alongside the lecture *Politics as Vocation* as two separate volumes. By 1933, over two dozen essays or books responding to the lecture had appeared in print, not to mention countless asides, footnotes, and comments in other texts. Postwar Germany's leading Catholic philosopher and intellectual, Max Scheler, called the published version of the lecture "the most devastating document of an age we have the misfortune to call our own."[71] Like Weber himself, most of his critics were addressing not a general crisis of knowledge but, more particularly, as his friend Ernst Troeltsch put it in 1921, the "crisis of the humanities."[72]

Many were deeply unsettled that a scholar of Weber's prestige could seemingly abandon the triune tradition of *Bildung, Wissenschaft,* and the university. Troeltsch called the lecture a "declaration of war" against universities and scholarship.[73] He and many of his contemporaries thought Weber had offered nothing more than a personal defense of intellectual rectitude and scholarly rigor, hardly a solution for a historical crisis. One critic went so far as to say that Weber had transformed scholarship and university study into "respectable suicide, a path to death that lead through stoic heroism."[74] For most of Germany's cultured elite, Weber's vision of scholarship amounted to either a bleak, existential liberalism, a hopeless capitulation to modernity made up as a heroic realism, or a value-neutral positivism. Weber had poked a hornet's nest that had formed over decades, unleashing a swarm of ideas about rebirth, renewal, and the recovery not just of scholarship and politics but of the ways in which living and working in the modern world could be meaningful.

## THE DREAM OF REENCHANTED KNOWLEDGE

The terms of the debate were quickly established by Weber's most strident critics, who claimed to offer the antithesis of Weber's endorsement of a scholarly asceticism.[75] "We say no!," was the crux of Erich von Kahler's meandering and spirited rejection of what he called "old" knowledge.[76] Like many of those who first responded to Weber, Kahler was a champion of the modern humanities. A young Jewish scholar of literature from a well-to-do Viennese family, he lived and studied in Heidelberg, where he had formed a friendship with Friedrich Gundolf, a literature scholar who was also the editor of the *Jahrbuch für die geistige Bewegung,* a periodical devoted to the esoteric and reactionary politics of the poet Stefan George and the so-called George Circle. Gundolf read Kahler's essay *Der Beruf der Wissenschaft* (The vocation of scholarship) to members of the Circle several times before helping to facilitate its publication with George's publisher, Bondi, in Berlin.[77]

Kahler situated himself and his readers at the far edge of a historical "wasteland" where humankind had been ravaged by death, catastrophe, and, most crucially, the loss of meaning.[78] Behind lay the "old" knowledge; ahead lay the possibility of the "new" knowledge.

Ironically, Kahler associated the "old" knowledge (*Wissenschaft*) and its defenders with the modern world and the forces, processes, and disasters it had fomented. Here, too, the crisis of the humanities was used as an emblem of a perceived crisis of an alienated and compartmentalized social life that had motivated Dilthey decades earlier to envision an alternative to dominant forms of knowledge. Underlying the traditional ideology of knowledge was the presumption of a nominalist reality—one that could not be known or encountered—that aligned with the epistemic limits the scholars of this "old" knowledge now insisted were fixed and unquestionable. Natural scientists and humanities scholars had both assumed the role of priests who mediated access to this realm of knowledge. As the university became a factory, they then remade themselves as masters of cloistered domains whose boundaries they jealously guarded. The world they had formed struck those not wholly at home within it as an ever-changing map where the boundaries and borders served mostly to keep others out and protect those already ensconced within. Most importantly, however, the map of specialized, disciplinary knowledge offered no guidance on how to live; it simply modeled and thus institutionalized the modern university's division of intellectual labor. It represented the well-worn paths of that most unprepossessing of creatures, the "man of modern scholarship."[79]

Although Weber was a dynamic scholar whose work didn't fit particularly well into any single discipline, thanks to the publication of his lecture on scholarship he had become the foremost embodiment of this type. Kahler depicted him not only as an unsparing apologist for the "old" knowledge but also as a callous teacher: when confronted with "youth's bourgeoning discontent," the celebrated professor had just shrugged and admonished his young listeners not to expect too much from their teachers or the university.[80] Kahler, in contrast, claimed to speak for the "youth" and to share their desire for a "new beginning of knowledge."

University-based academic disciplines such as biology, physiology, and psychology, continued Kahler, epitomized how the "old" knowledge reduced life to mere "shadows of reality" and "disenchanted the world." By training those who practiced scholarship endlessly to divide knowledge, theories, concepts, objects, and even other people into "ever-more discrete, internally contained" entities, the university prevented them from asking why and to what end they ought to live. This, according to Kahler, was the lived experience of Weber's account of the "intellectualization of life."[81]

Kahler wrote about modern disciplinary knowledge as if it were a monolithic system that both stood in opposition to "life" and had already infected it. He attempted to bolster his oppositional account with a sweeping historical narrative according to which the kind of natural scientific intellectual and moral formation that the mandarins of the lab had advocated had undone the Platonic (and, more generally, ancient) melding of human flourishing (eudaemonia) with truth. To pursue knowledge at the beginning of the twentieth century was, in a radical inversion of "antiquity," to forsake the notion of philosophy as therapy for the soul and to capitulate to modern university norms about minding boundaries and limits and preparing young people for jobs. It was precisely this sense that knowledge had become detached from life that the students who had invited Weber to speak found "unbearable."[82] As Kahler understood it, Weber's disenchanted world lacked any meaning independent of the rational projections of atomized individuals. Humans were left alone to assert (and fight over) meaning by arbitrarily claiming and conferring values unmoored from any shared and stable truths about life.

It was this "polytheism of values," as Kahler put it, quoting Weber, that was seen as the most catastrophic effect of the "old" knowledge. Modern scholarship had vivisected the good, the true, and the beautiful into discrete objects of study of equal but incommensurable value. This disaggregation was the calamitous effect of the present crisis, whose real causes stretched back millennia as part of the "tragic," "violent" history of the "disenchantment of the world."[83] Seizing on this term of Weber's, Kahler employed it often. Although this historical process reached back to antiquity, he claimed, it had only begun to be fully realized in an early modern period that ran from Occam in the fourteenth century through Hobbes in the seventeenth to Hume in the eighteenth. Occam, Hobbes, and Hume reoriented the nascent methods of natural science from a search for meaningful signs in a divinely created cosmos toward a "substance-less Ratio." It was a German, Immanuel Kant, however, whom Kahler held most responsible for introducing "technical rationality" and with it the image of a natural world denuded of all but the most efficient and immediate of causes.[84]

By narrating the decline of reason, purpose, and the human as a tragic metaphysical loss—the elimination of sacramental presence and the colonization of the real by inauthentic forms of technical rationality—Kahler sought to induce in readers a felt need for a "new" knowledge. His *Der Beruf der Wissenschaft* is filled with incantatory evocations of a still-magical world brimming with the plenitude of meaning as well as refrains offered up to the "unity" of organic forces and the "singularity of existence" (i.e., the idea that "we exist just once").[85] For Kahler the "old" knowledge had not yet fully disenchanted the world, but more significantly, if paradoxically, he contended that this same "old" knowledge could—indeed, would—reenchant it. Every new scientific discovery revealed the "awesome" and inscrutable forces of life. Though they didn't know it, those in thrall to the disenchanting powers of modern rationality were preparing the way for a "new magic."[86] The advent of the "new" knowledge from out of the "old" also portended a return to a world of being in which the gaps between truth, morals, and religion would be closed; different social identities—student, public official, scholar, businessman, politician, husband, wife—fully integrated; conflicting values resolved; and the specialized disciplines of the university made whole again. The true, the good, and the beautiful, now concealed by shadows as though they existed in a world "apart," would finally be unveiled.[87]

Kahler offered little insight into what this future knowledge would entail other than a rejection of the contemporary "state of things." The mechanism of redemption was clear, as was the historical necessity of its advent, but not the actual way forward. The catechism of the "new" knowledge consisted of nothing more than a decline narrative and assertions of the therapeutic value of inscrutable resources: flashes of insight, feeling, and artistic intuition. In this he followed Dilthey, who identified a social "need" and, then, as Kahler enthused, offered a "pioneering and wondrous attempt . . . to see the various expressions of life—such as language, the arts, politics, economics, etc.—as one." The "new" knowledge would be a *"religio,"* a comprehensive form of life.[88]

## THE HUMANITIES AND THE MEANING OF HISTORY

Defenders of what Kahler termed the "old" knowledge typically appealed to the cultural and epistemic authority of the persona of disciplinary knowledge, the ideal scholar, and the institution that formed him, the university. Yet it was just this habitual conflation of authoritative knowledge with the university that in Weber's account at least had driven the current crisis.[89] It represented a refusal on the part of a powerful segment of intellectuals to acknowledge that many people no longer found one of Germany's central institutions compelling and worthy of their trust. Even those who defended Weber adopted not only Kahler's key terms (the "old" versus the "new" knowledge), but also some of his key criticisms, which themselves dated back to Nietzsche and Mommsen if not Diesterweg and other neo-humanist theorists of the 1830s. In Germany, the twilight of the idols included not just the gods of monotheism but those of a proudly modern faith—the university and modern knowledge.

The most persistent epistemological problem German intellectuals and scholars faced with respect to the modern humanities was the lingering question of whether the humanities were ultimately a product of historicism and therefore inextricably bound to and limited by it.[90] In 1922, Troeltsch explicitly identified with the "old" knowledge even as he pointed to Weber's Munich lecture as a key document of the current "crisis of scholarship," a crisis that he further described as a "crisis of historical thought and of the human in general."[91] He tied part of this crisis to the alienating conditions

of the modern university, but like Weber he also believed that these conditions were now the "essence" of the university. The question was what to
do about it. This was why Troeltsch considered historicism to be not just a
theoretical question but also an ethical and pedagogical project.

Troeltsch posited that just as naturalism had developed out of an extreme form of the natural sciences as practiced in universities, so had historicism developed out of an extreme form of history also as practiced in
universities. One discipline led to the "terrifying naturalism and the deso-
lation of all life," the other to a "relativistic skepticism" and the end of the
search for justifications, reasons, and values beyond their specific historical contexts.[92] In the final decades of the nineteenth century, the problem
of historicism had repeated itself across disciplines—in literature as the
attention given to form versus historical context; in philosophy as the value
placed on rigor of argument versus consciousness of the historical development of ideas and concepts; in history itself as the devotion to empirical
facts versus the need for theories to bring those facts together. In the first
two decades of the twentieth century, the epistemological and ethical problems of historicism had morphed into a pervasive cultural anxiety about a
history that was without human agency and thus lacking in any meaning
that was not fixed by the flux of time. Because they had become the sciences
of change, difference, and the particular, the modern humanities were the
primary locus of these anxieties; they had emerged out of the very spirit of
historicism. Troeltsch argued that the only way out of the current crisis was
to transcend history through a "philosophy of history."[93] He turned, that
is, to philosophy, claiming that it was more than an "exact and positive science," more than what Weber had seemed to dismiss as just another "specialized discipline."[94]

Many of the other self-identified defenders of the "old" knowledge shared
Troeltsch's view about Weber's failure to appreciate philosophy. For Weber,
wrote Heinrich Rickert almost plangently in response to the publication
of Weber's lecture, even modern, university-based philosophy maintained
nothing of the "Platonic passion" of ancient Greek philosophy.[95] Rickert
and other neo-Kantians such as Jonas Cohn assumed that philosophy had
(or should have) largely escaped the radical transformations—or deformations—of the modern research university and retained the unique authority
Kant had ascribed to it almost a century earlier. Yet over the course of the
nineteenth century, many German universities and scholars had, in fact,
transformed philosophy into an exacting and, as one scholar put it, "philological" discipline with no relation to, in the ubiquitous term of the day, *life*.

Situated in two of Germany's most prestigious institutions—Rickert
in Heidelberg, where he had assumed the chair that his teacher Wilhelm

Windelband had occupied, and Cohn, who habilitated under Windelband, in Leipzig—the defenders of the "old" knowledge embodied disciplined, university-based philosophy.[96] On the one hand they, like Weber, embraced the authority and legitimacy granted to the hard-won expertise of scholars working in particular disciplines; they thus rejected Kahler's attempt to revolutionize knowledge and the university. Yet on the other hand, they flinched at Weber's identification of philosophy as just another "discipline." Like many other philosophers and philosophically minded German intellectuals and scholars in this period, Rickert and Cohn, too, hoped that philosophy could redeem a culture in crisis.[97] In terms strikingly similar to those used by their philosophical critics, who lamented the reduction of philosophy to epistemological policing and methodological rigor,[98] Rickert and Cohn invoked a *philosophia perennis*, a wisdom that tells humans how to live, that courses through early modern and modern European intellectual history. It was a dream, at once epistemological and ethical, of reason overcoming its social and temporal divisions and realizing a totality, or just what Weber had seemed to reject.

## LIBERALISM, DEMOCRACY, AND THE RISE OF THE ILLIBERAL HUMANITIES

The fervor that Kahler's call for a "new" knowledge elicited certainly signaled not just the desire for different forms of scholarship; it also signaled the waning authority and legitimacy of university-based knowledge generally. The "pillars upon which our culture are thought to rest, in so far as they are based on knowledge have collapsed," wrote the mathematician and strident opponent of any hint of relativism in modern science Hugo Dingler in 1926.[99] Claiming to speak for countless others, Dingler, who joined the National Socialist Party in 1940, demanded to know what Weber's vaunted scholarly virtue—the "rigor, thoroughness, and discipline" of modern scholarship—had to do with art, history, literature, and philosophy as resources for living and not simply as objects of scholarly analysis? Was the insatiable "lust" for facts a desire for knowledge or a manifestation of liberal consumerism?[100] Was the stringent policing of disciplinary borders, boundaries, and domains a jealous hoarding of professional privilege and social status or a desperate means of managing the perceived surfeit of modern knowledge?

In the 1920s many of Weber's critics reformulated decades-old complaints about academic specialization into more pointed attacks on what they considered to be Weber's liberalism. Weber's Heidelberg colleague, the economist and sociologist Arthur Salz, who fled Nazi persecution in 1934 to teach at Ohio State University, described Weber as the consummate "university professor . . . a tolerant and liberal" statesman who felt responsible for a failing institution.[101] In other words Weber was a bourgeois liberal who wanted to maintain order and who evinced the distinctly German "habit" of conflating the university and knowledge, a habit that served liberals like Weber well.[102] Salz thought this explained the relatively unchecked power of the state to control knowledge by supervising the university bureaucracy.[103] On this last point Salz and Weber actually agreed, though Salz continued to expect more from the university.

Over the course of the Weimar Republic, another set of German intellectuals and scholars skeptical of Weber's purported liberalism turned these kinds of critiques into something more blunt and threatening, contending that a number of hostile forces—democracy, liberalism, positivism, specialization, technology—threatened to dissolve or infect what neo-humanists had called the unity-of-knowledge ideal. Instead of casting this unity as an epistemic or ethical norm, however, as most of the early nineteenth-century neo-humanists had done, they sought to ground it in what they asserted was a distinctly Germanic culture and, by the end of the 1920s, *Volk*. These claims were not at all uncommon in the Weimar Republic, when a significant proportion of academics in humanities disciplines were affiliated with or sympathetic to national conservative positions and parties.[104] Academics with liberal sympathies and affiliations, including those identified by the historian Friedrich Meinecke at the time as "republicans of reason," were much less common.[105]

As the National Socialists ascended to power in the early 1930s, many of these same politically conservative scholars repurposed neo-humanist concepts and language for explicitly nationalist and racial ideologies. Looking back in 1934, Ernst Krieck, who two years earlier had joined the Nazi Party and would soon be known as "Hitler's pedagogue," dismissed Weber as the "last hero of liberalism"—the persona of an age and its institutions whose time had passed.[106] For an enemy of liberalism as well as democracy such as Krieck, however, the cancer of academic liberalism had metastasized beyond the university and begun to enfeeble the moral lives of Germany's educated elite. Krieck had been making similar arguments for over a decade. In five different essays published from 1920 to 1922, he had enthusiastically embraced Kahler's call for a "new" knowledge and "a new humanity." Then associated with the *Jungkonservativen*, a group that had formed around the reactionary modernist thinker Arthur Moeller van den Bruck, Krieck illustrated in these early essays how seamlessly the rhetoric of wholeness, unity, and totality could be adapted to political purposes that were "antiliberal, antidemocratic, antiparliamentarian, and anticommunist."[107]

ON THE METHOD AND ETHOS
OF THE MODERN HUMANITIES

The elegiac and then increasingly strident calls among Weber's critics for the convergence or integration of values and worldviews into a universal *Weltbild* and the recovery of a "new humanity" were, in effect if not intent, calls to put an end to the liberal intellectual, moral, and political order that had been central to Germany's educational institutions since at least the 1870s, when Nietzsche had blasted them from Basel. This is why Troeltsch considered Weber's lecture a touchstone in the crisis not only of knowledge as such but the "crisis of the modern humanities" in particular. Despite their own methodological debates and internal transformations, the natural and physical sciences had and would remain largely unaffected by the current crisis, he predicted. As long as they maintained their mutually beneficial and reinforcing relationship with technology and continued to produce economic goods, they would find support both inside and outside the university. In this, he proved correct.

For Troeltsch and many of his contemporaries, however, the current crisis was more existential and ethical than economic or political, and since the late nineteenth century, the modern humanities had claimed such questions and problems as their particular domain. The real crisis, then, reasoned Troeltsch, was to be found in "the modern humanities," because it was here that questions about "the meaning of existence" could be legitimately posed and answered. Given the desperate longing for intellectual wholeness and moral clarity, however, Troeltsch also worried that the "crisis of the humanities" might actually turn out to be a "revolution," one that portended "the beginning of the great world reaction against democracy and socialist enlightenment, against the self-mastery of reason, which boundlessly organizes our existence."[108]

In 1929 Eduard Spranger—who almost three decades earlier had helped reinvent a Humboldtian tradition embraced by students across political divides—confirmed Troeltsch's fears in a speech at the Academy of Sciences in Berlin. In the decade since Weber had "unsettled us" with his claims that "value-generating judgments" had no rightful place in scholarship and that even the modern humanities can legitimately only study "rules or structures or events," he said, a younger "movement" and with it a "new outlook" had arisen in opposition. Although Spranger claimed that he remained committed to the scholarly ideals of the "older generation," he clearly found Weber's younger critics compelling. He believed, as they did, that "forming worldviews and values" constituted the very "roots" of the modern humanities.[109] The concepts and methods of the modern humanities, wrote

Spranger—quoting Erich Rothacker, a philosopher whom he identified as one of the "movement's" exemplary thinkers and who would join the National Socialist Party in 1933—originate from "will and choice."[110] Spranger thought that Rothacker and his contemporaries rightly understood that "the most fruitful instrument of knowledge in the humanities" was neither the epistemology of the neo-Kantians nor the methodological rigor of philology; it was, rather, the simple fact that in the humanities "life and knowledge had grown together."[111] The true "humanities scholar," Spranger concluded, ultimately relies on "a-theoretical or extra-theoretical presuppositions." The modern humanities were grounded not in logical argument, empirical evidence, or the search for causal relations but in the irreducible, often ineffable particularity of a person's life. Instead of grounding the humanities in the arts, practices, methods, and techniques of modern scholarship, Spranger identified them with idiosyncratic lifestyles, what he called the "styles of the humanities." For him, these different "styles" were the spontaneous, nontechnical offshoots of self-contained and self-sustaining views and values.[112]

Spranger was well positioned, then, to enter into discussions of what the humanities are and should do in the here and now. In his 1909 study of Humboldt, he had distinguished "the content" of "our new ideal of humanity" from that of the neo-humanists and their "uomo universal." This content was no longer that of Greek and Roman antiquity but rather "solely that of classical German literature and German idealism."[113] This commitment to a distinctly Germanic mind and spirit—as well as the fact that Spranger was a non-Jewish, nationalist, conservative scholar—made the adoption and adaptation of the modern humanities from *Geisteswissenschaft* (human science) into *Geistesgeschichte* (history of mind or spirit) by the National Socialists so amenable to him as well as other German intellectuals and scholars such as Rothacker, who not only led the "movement" against Weber's purportedly value-free scholarship but also intensified the sense of crisis, opposition, present mindedness, and reaction that had characterized the modern humanities for decades.[114] Like Kahler and even Benjamin's circle, these figures invoked "crisis" as an opportunity to recover the human from the maelstrom of modernity and the cataclysmic forces of rational and scientific organization it had unleashed: alienation, capitalism, technology, bureaucracy, and liberalism. But whereas Benjamin and the Wynekians had invoked ideal or metaphysical notions of wholeness, unity, and life, these right-wing intellectuals imbued these concepts with an antiliberal and antidemocratic force. And they tied them to a "new totality," one all too real—the emergent Nazi regime and its racist and nationalist agenda.[115] They tried to align scholarly rigor with a distinctly Germanic *Geist* and *Volk*.[116] In

1933, just a month after the National Socialists seized power, Spranger not only attacked democracy, pluralism, and Western materialism but also professed his belief that Weber's "polytheism of values" could be transcended through the National Socialist state, *Volk*, and nation.[117]

## THE DISENCHANTED UNIVERSITY AND THE REENCHANTMENT OF THE HUMANITIES

When German universities organized themselves and the cultivation of Germany's youth (or at least the small percentage that became university students) around the division of intellectual labor and upheld the "academic specialist" as the ideal scholar, they transformed themselves and, thus, the central institutions of human formation into bureaucratized capitalist operations. It was this "industrial" character, as Weber put it in 1917, that distinguished German universities from most other educational and knowledge institutions.[118] For Weber the emergence of modern German universities gave an institutional form and educational function to the process of disenchantment in unprecedented ways and with unprecedented effects.

Yet as in other domains, disenchantment had not made meaningful forms of life impossible. It had certainly eroded the demand or expectation that the university reflect a "rational" order, a meaning that inhered in the world itself as before any human self-assertion, that the university be a mirror image or sacramental medium of a cosmic or divinely ordained order. It had also eroded the expectation that disciplinary scholarship offered paths to true being, art, nature, God, or happiness—fullness, plenitude, and unity of knowledge and life. Although these particular paths to transcendence or other desired states had, as Weber put it, been "lost," other paths, whether to transcendence or not, remained possible.[119] And the search for them was a persistent feature of the German philosophical tradition from Kant, who wrote about the metaphysical "need of reason," to Dilthey, who claimed that the modern humanities were a new "bulwark of human freedom."[120]

Weber's history of disenchantment was part of this history. His guiding questions in this regard were not only where and how this felt need persisted but how it had been reshaped and redirected and what future forms it could possibly assume. The need for such a *comprehensive* and *holistic* meaning was not, for Weber, an anthropological feature; it emerged repeatedly in different cultures and through particular historical processes of disenchantment, particularly among intellectuals, who once released from immediate material needs sought systematic, rule-based ways to order their lives. As "magic" is gradually if never fully repressed, wrote Weber in *Wirtschaft und Gesellschaft* (*Economy and Society*), "the intellectual seeks out ways, whose casuistry knows no limits, to give his way of life a holistic meaning, unity with itself, other humans, and the cosmos; it is the intellectual who performs the conception of the 'world' as a problem of meaning."[121] Here as elsewhere, Weber suggests that attempts to disenchant inevitably beget attempts to reenchant.[122] Although he never used the latter term, he explained the enchantment cycle this way: the more a belief in magic is "repressed and the processes of the world are disenchanted and lose their magical meaning, that much more urgent does the demand for the world and a way of leading a life to be meaningfully ordered as a whole become."[123] The modern humanities are a paradigmatic case of this cycle. From their first formulations by Helmholtz and other mid-nineteenth-century intellectuals to those of Weber's critics in the 1920s, intellectuals and scholars invoked "the humanities" as moral compensation for a world experienced as lacking meaning and value. In effect the humanities reenchanted the world.

Accounts of the modern humanities as they developed over the second half of the nineteenth century could also be understood as variations on Immanuel Kant's account of culture as that realm of intellectual activity in which the "beautiful arts and scholarship . . . make humans, if not morally better, at least better mannered for society, very much reducing the tyranny of the sensible tendencies and preparing humans for sovereignty over nature."[124] For Kant and the myriad intellectuals and scholars who embraced a similar faith, culture was the realm through which humans could transcend whatever constrained them and marked them as finite, natural beings. Weber turned this notion of culture—one that over the course of the nineteenth century served as the premise for most every invocation of *Bildung* or the unity-of-knowledge ideal—into an object of study. To study culture was to study this longing to transcend "everyday life" and the various forms it assumed—art for art's sake, naturalism, philosophical systems, religions, and the modern humanities. The modern humanities, the *Geisteswissenschaften*, were, to use Weber's terminology, the result of a long-standing cultural project to solve the theodicy problem or the problem of meaning. Kant called this project pragmatic anthropology; Dilthey called it the *Geisteswissenschaften*; Rickert called it the cultural sciences; twentieth-century Americans, as we shall see in the next chapter, called it the humanities.

## SCHOLARSHIP AS A WAY OF LIFE

Toward the conclusion of *Scholarship as a Vocation*, Weber told the audience of students that "in our current historical situation," scholarship is *specialized* work, done by professional *experts*, in the service of both self-understanding and the knowledge of objective facts—it is not a gift of grace with seers and prophets dispensing holy objects and revelations, nor a part of sages' and philosophers' meditations on the *meaning* of life.[125]

Prophets, as Weber wrote elsewhere, do not "summon the spirit" of the divine; they "bind the people to morality" and tell people how they ought to live.[126] Looking to professors and the university for this "binding power," students ascribed to professors and the university a sacredness and moral autonomy they did not possess. The professor, Weber is saying to his audience, who offers you a vision of complete and universal redemption is misleading you.

Yet Weber understood the students' desires for moral clarity and guidance. He thought that the enormous practical and political problems facing Germans both when he delivered the lecture in 1917 and when it was published in 1919 after the war were also ethical ones. Indeed, how could idealism and realism be combined to realize a better future with ethical and intellectual integrity? Weber addresses the need for ideals as well as an empirically based assessment of the world—for an internal passion and frank account of reality—by adapting a term of religious derivation to modern times, one that appears in the lecture's title, *Beruf*, which can be variously translated as "calling," "vocation," or "work." In order to articulate the paradoxical idea of a true spiritual calling in a time when the gods who might issue it have left, fallen silent, or been drowned out by modernity's rational structures, Weber draws on the analysis of Calvinism he had presented more than a decade earlier in *The Protestant Ethic* but had continued to return to as part of his wide-ranging studies of world religions.

For Weber, "vocation" had two meanings, a traditionally religious one, as in a calling from God, and a professional one, as one's job or employment. Vocation referred to both an individual form of specialization and a social category or form of organization. In the terms of Weber's reading of the sixteenth-century French theologian John Calvin, to fulfill one's calling was to act on an individual belief (that one had been called to do and serve something in particular), but also to fit into an extra-individual and rational organization of the social world. This distinctly Western conception of vocation emerged as a possible solution to the problem of meaning.

For Weber, then, the problem of meaning, or its perceived absence, was not an effect of some grand, inevitable process of secularization or a general atrophy of religious belief and practice. Glossing Calvin's *Institutes of the Christian Religion* (1536), Weber wrote in *The Protestant Ethic*:

To apply the standards of earthly "justice" to [God's] sovereign order is meaningless . . . because he, and he alone, is free, that is, bound to no law, and his decrees are only intelligible to and can only be known by us as he deems it good to share them with us. It is upon these fragments of the eternal truth alone that we can hold ourselves. Everything else—the meaning of our individual fate—is shrouded by dark mysteries, which are impossible and presumptuous to plumb.[127]

With any transcendent life-ordering meaning shrouded in mystery and the free gift of grace wholly independent of human action, Calvinists adapted ancient ascetic ideals and practices to a new order of life: an inner-worldly asceticism whose purpose was not to extract humans from this world but to enable them to actively and faithfully serve God by exercising rational control over and reflection upon one's actions and one's life in this world.

As the grip of Calvinism and Christianity loosened, people across Europe and North America began to use *vocation* to refer to particular ways of ordering a life through activity in the world or in work. Ultimately, vocation became an end in itself. One worked not only to earn money but also to be part of something greater than oneself. The division and specialization of labor were not problems to be solved; they were moral solutions for a new reality. To lead a meaningful life in the modern Western world was to commit to a vocation and be transformed by it. The scholar, to borrow wording Weber used in *Politics as Vocation*, lived not only "from" his vocation, earning a living from it, but also "for" it, deriving meaning and value from the role he served in a social world.[128]

As Weber articulated it, this scholarly vocation was a form of asceticism. Scholarly practice was a distinct ethical tradition with its own "moral powers."[129] To practice it well was not to subordinate scholarship to technical rationalities or a purportedly deeper understanding of life or experience, but to make possible an assessment of current conditions and the possibilities for conducting a life today in light of one's values. The vocation and persona of the scholar consisted in the self-restraining mastery of a specific set of ethical and technical abilities. Pursuing knowledge in this way required students to internalize a distinct character with its own ideals, and values, which Weber summarized as the "only specific scholarly virtue": "intellectual integrity."[130]

In all this, Weber was speaking of scholarship and the university as a whole, as tradition, practice, and institution. Like any other set of modern, university-based disciplines, the modern humanities do not, either directly or indirectly, make students or anyone else good, but neither do they merely produce knowledge that can be technically utilized.[131] Weber defended the goods that scholarship and the university could offer students: specialized knowledge to sustain human dominion over themselves and the earth through calculation; formation and training in different ways of thinking and, thus, accounting for themselves, others, and the world; and, most importantly, "clarity" about themselves, their commitments, and the world in which they found themselves.

The moral task facing professors, Weber told his audience in Munich, is to enable students "to find the perspective from which they can judge" an issue of importance in light of their own ultimate ideals."[132] Universities are in fact uniquely well equipped to form students into mature, independent, self-reflective subjects. They can teach students to understand how values conflict with one another, and that acting in accord with their values will have specific social consequences, which is a part of having "genuine character," as Weber had put it in an earlier essay.[133] Given that moral commitments and values orient and shape human lives, Weber thought they had to be articulated and reflected upon. People had to take responsibility for the things they cared about. Recognizing the amoral actuality of the world—that no natural moral order will be revealed, that no providential good will be made manifest, that no reason will work through history to reconcile moral conflicts—is the beginning of ethical responsibility. Weber considered scholars moral agents in a world where meaning was always questioned and contested. When they understood and committed themselves to the duties entailed by their vocation, they were capable of doing the intellectual work necessary to create and cultivate the rational disciplines, practices, and institutions that could sustain meaningful lives in a modern age. But vocations—distinct, meaning-making orders of life—needed attentive, careful cultivation and devoted resources lest they be completely absorbed by economic and state interests or the pure pursuit of power or prestige.

Animating Weber's concept of vocation was an apparent tension between rule-bound practice and passionate devotion. In an essay published just a few months before he delivered what became *Scholarship as Vocation*, "Der Sinn der 'Wertfreiheit' der soziologischen und ökonomischen Wissenschaften," (The meaning of "value freedom" in the social and economic sciences), he explained how for the scholar this tension manifested itself in the relationship between method and ethos.[134] There he framed his discussion of scholarly method in frankly pedagogical terms: Was the purpose of the university "to educate" and train students in scholarly methods and techniques or "to form" them according to a particular ethical, cultural, or political ethos and set of virtues? By tying the more abstract question of whether a scholar should "profess" a particular value commitment and worldview to the more limited question of whether he should do so within the context of "academic instruction" and, thus, a relationship between a student and a teacher, Weber bound an ostensibly methodological or theoretical question to an ethical one, thereby tying method to ethos.[135] In arguing for value freedom, he addressed scholars as "teachers" whose duty it was to distinguish between the determination facts as products of scholarly method, on the one hand, and their own practical judgment of these facts as "gratifying or not," on the other. When teaching in the university, scholars had a duty to remain faithful to their training in the case of the former and to make reasoned but context-dependent decisions about the latter.

How scholars might reach a decision in any given situation depended on how they understood and related to their vocation. A vocational framework, thought Weber, for example, would help scholars recognize the power differential between themselves and their students. In university classroom settings, especially the lecture halls in which Weber mostly taught, "it's all too easy for a professor to demonstrate the courage of his convictions," he wrote, "where the audience and, perhaps, those who think differently are condemned to silence."[136] Within their shared institution, professors and students occupy different positions of power and, consequently, are accorded different levels of authority and status. It would be "irresponsible," then, for a professor to make certain value judgments in the absence of legitimate and capable critics to challenge and rebut them. There was for Weber a related but more profound difference that characterized the professor-student relationship. Students "desire to know and learn certain things," and so they come to the lecture hall with an expectation that they will be intellectually satisfied and over time make the professor's knowledge their own.[137] The professor-student relationship is, in this sense, also a pedagogical or educational one. If a professor takes a student's desire for knowledge and "transposes" it into an explicitly moral register by making himself an immediate source and exemplar of ultimate moral commitments and values, then the professor fails as a teacher and, thus, for Weber, a scholar. He fails in his responsibility as a scholar to help students gain knowledge and clarity about their own moral commitments. By emphasizing the pedagogical salience of value freedom, Weber acknowledged that the university was not a value-neutral space. It was value laden—full of intellectual and moral desires. For precisely this reason, professors had a responsibility as scholars and teachers to redirect desires for transcendence away from immediate satisfaction in professional personalities and charismatic claims in lecture halls—away from themselves—and toward the intellectual and scholarly goods that they and universities could legitimately provide. They had a responsibility to live and practice scholarly ideals and values.

Weber thought that his account of the scholar's vocation only made sense under the present historical and institutional conditions. He emphasized that over the past "forty years" those conditions had changed dramatically, especially at universities. First, he observed, the university and the broader culture had both been transformed by the heterogeneity of knowledge and values. The conditions of the university of the early twentieth century were defined by the "polytheism of values," the differentiation of knowledge, and the industrialization and bureaucratization of the institution. Second, these new conditions had unleashed desires for transcendence and unity that heretofore had been largely contained by the liberal organization of the university. In contrast, today's universities and scholars, he remarked, are haunted by a "cult of personality," a "self-importance" on the part of professors and a longing among students that cannot be satisfied.[138] Given these particular conditions, Weber made his decision regarding the educational purpose of the university clear: It should no longer aspire to form cultured humans: people who embodied a particular culture's highest ideals and values. Rather, it should focus on forming scholars who were disciplined, committed to method and technique, and distinguished by a singular virtue, "intellectual integrity."[139] This asceticism had for Weber the force of an obligation. The authority and legitimacy of the modern university depended on the types of people it cultivated. Its primary justification was an appeal to ethos.

## ACADEMIC CHARISMA AND THE FATE OF THE HUMANITIES

One of the questions raised in Germany in the 1920s that continued to be debated, and misunderstood, is what Weber meant by the value freedom of scholarship, or what has regularly been poorly translated into English as "value-free" scholarship. American sociologists, led by Talcott Parsons, he of the midcentury project to Americanize Weber, embraced the concept and made Weber its founding figure as they sought to develop a scientific and methodologically rigorous sociology that could serve the modern liberal state.

Max Horkheimer, the German philosopher and leading member of the Frankfurt School, developed a similar reading. Responding to Parsons at a conference in 1962, he described how as a student he had attended both of Weber's vocation lectures and said this about *Politics as Vocation*: "The lecture hall was filled to capacity. And the frustration and disappointment were almost palpable. For two to three hours, we listened to finely balanced definitions of the Russian systems, astutely formulated ideal types of how different kinds of apolitical advisers could be organized. Everything was so precise, so rigorously scholarly, so value-free that we all went dolefully home."[140] Weber's refusal to use his scholarly acumen to construct a better society, Horkheimer continued, was a result of a commitment to value freedom that inhibited his thinking, trapping him in the values of liberal "bourgeois society."

On the other hand, in an influential American critique from the left, that of German émigré Hans Gerth and the young American sociologist C. Wright Mills, Weber was seen as a thinker struggling to overcome his nostalgia. In their introduction to *From Max Weber: Essays in Sociology* (1946), which included the first widely available English translations of Weber's two vocation lectures, Gerth and Mills suggested that Weber had been a reluctant advocate of technical rationality. He was ultimately an "old-fashioned liberal" for whom the "decline of the humanist and ascendency of the expert" were further signs of the "diminished chances of freedom" in "Western" modernity.[141] In 1958 the sociologist and cultural critic Philip Rieff, writing for a special volume of *Daedalus* dedicated to "Science and the Modern World View," introduced an excerpt of Gerth and Mills's translation of *The Scholar's Work*, which they had rendered as "Science as Vocation," thus:

> Weber shared in the scientific imagination of disaster. In this essay, he sketches the model of all our present disasters. Weber was an honest and passionate scientist; when he had finished constructing his model and found himself enclosed in it, he stayed. To his way of thinking there is no way out.[142]

We think that this is all wrong. The vocation of scholarship, including scholarship in the modern humanities, didn't demand the elimination of values from scholarship in the sense of a negative freedom *from* all values; instead; it sought to make possible the "freedom of value judgments" (*Werturteilsfreiheit*)—that is, the freedom that fully scholarly judgments needed. The "freedom of value judgments" might best be understood, in this sense, as a freedom from what Wilhelm Hennis calls the "prejudice of scholarly tutelage."[143] In advocating the "freedom of value judgments," Weber didn't demand that scholars adopt an impossibly neutral stance or a view from nowhere—he ridiculed the idea that one could simply "let the facts speak for themselves."[144] Rather, he warned scholars against looking to scholarship and the university for salvation and ultimate meaning. Weber worried that if students or professors acceded to the demands and longings for a knowledge unconstrained by any disciplined practice, if they overexpected and overpromised, they risked conceding the freedom to practice scholarship and the fragile legitimacy the university still managed to maintain.

What outraged so many of Weber's contemporaries was that he provided

perhaps the most compelling diagnosis of the ethical limits and consequences of the rationalization of human life without offering a satisfactory
therapy.[145] In refusing to provide a solution he foregrounded the "persistent
ambivalence" within the modern humanities surrounding explicit moral
claims and assertions of spiritual value and soul-building capabilities.[146]
As Amanda Anderson rightly notes, this ambivalence comes from the felt
proximity to religious and other domains typically identified with values,
piety, and moral assertions. The modern humanities have regularly been
constrained by an uncomfortable identification with the felt need to return
to the unity of knowledge, humanity or the purity of transcendental inquiry,
or knowledge as an end in itself. The permanent crisis of the humanities
has at least partly consisted in this constant dissatisfaction, in the frustration of failed returns, in the reactive formation at their core: without a theological other against which to define themselves as the *studia humanitatis*
had done, the modern humanities have always been in need of something
against which to define themselves—the natural sciences, politics, instrumental rationality, technology, empiricism, positivism, materialism, and
so forth.

Weber knew that the compulsion to expect too much from the university was particularly strong among those who identified with the modern
humanities. Since at least the late nineteenth century, questions of values,
ideals, and meaning had been partitioned in the university setting from the
natural and physical sciences and thus quarantined in disparate disciplines
such as history, philology, and philosophy.[147] But it was also in these disciplines, once identified as a common project in opposition to the natural
sciences, that meaning was still considered possible in the modern university. For Weber, however, values and moral commitments were not the particular purview of any one domain of knowledge. Moral commitments and
values were everywhere.

Thus, Weber rejected the ideal of consilience.[148] Different disciplines and
different forms of knowledge had different epistemic ideals and goals and
thus their "own character."[149] He also undermined a key premise of the German debate about the boundary between the two classes of disciplinary
knowledge—the assumption that the natural sciences and the modern humanities had developed from a common source: *Wissenschaft*, or reason
itself. According to the histories of knowledge written by Dilthey and those
who followed in his wake, the modern humanities were more developed
because they were, in contrast to the strictly technical natural and physical sciences, capable of reflecting on their own processes and principles.
Weber's rejection of this metaphysically inflected history and the unity-of-
knowledge ideal that it supported also undercut the functional opposition

of the "modern" humanities, which had formed and been justified in the negative, as the not–natural scientific disciplines, as somehow unique to a world purified of the materialist and utilitarian interests of the natural sciences.

The difference between earlier forms of humanist learning, such as the *studia humanitatis*, and the modern humanities was that the former were practiced in relationship to theology (sometimes in a subsidiary role, sometimes in an antagonistic role). According to these earlier forms, knowledge was the product of technical skills, arts, and scholarship, which could be applied to various ends. According to the latter forms, however, knowledge always bore the traces of its higher origins in human mind and reason. For the modern humanities, knowledge was always and continues to be ultimately grounded in the internal principles and processes of human intellection.[150] The human sciences were sciences of the human mind, and this purportedly legitimated their claim to a monopoly over questions of moral concern and meaning. The demand for closure of the gap between method and ethos, *Wissenschaft* and life, then, was an effect of this more fundamental longing for the products of reason to return home to their original unity in human being. The late nineteenth-century histories of science written by figures such as Emil Du Bois-Reymond legitimized such desires but assigned them a circumscribed, secondary status. In their initial reactive formation, the modern humanities functioned as an inchoate repository for these residual, sometimes ornamental concerns, but scholars such as Dilthey gradually claimed responsibility for such concerns, then claimed them as the positive and distinctive domain of the modern humanities.

By rejecting the often obscured metaphysical grounds of the modern humanities, Weber was able to hold the humanities in irresolvable tension. He rejected the conception of the modern humanities as first laid out by early nineteenth-century German intellectuals and scholars as ends in themselves that linked historical forms of humanist knowledge to a metaphysically inflected humanism unbound from theology and juxtaposed to the modern natural sciences. In the modern university, the functions of moral education and knowledge production were in constant conflict. According to Weber's account of the current conditions, there was no immanent secular or religious salvation or resolution, no prospect for a shared, public *religio*. The lacuna the mandarins of the lab had outlined fifty years earlier would remain, and with it the gap between knowledge and life. Weber had condemned as a dangerous delusion the belief that the gaps between what could be known to be true and what was felt to be true could be permanently closed, and he insisted that universities play no part in bridging them. He not only cast into doubt any clear resolution or satisfaction of these longings by the modern humanities, he undercut with forceful clarity their institutional justification. If direct inculcation of ultimate commitments and values within the university was illegitimate (or just practically impossible), then the modern humanities, at least as they were conceived of by Weber's contemporaries, that is as self-sustaining and self-legitimating forms of knowledge and moral value, had no clear place within it.

Reflecting in 1930 on the debate Weber's lecture had provoked over the past decade, the philosopher Erik Wolk described Weber as "the model for the crisis of the modern humanities."[151] Wolk did not mean that Weber had offered an exemplary analysis of the crisis and contradictions; rather, he meant that he *was* "the model." By performing what the modern disciplinary humanities could offer, Weber embodied their "tragically tense ethos"—the desire for a charismatic personality with the commitment to a "depersonalized academic discipline."[152] He had turned disciplined, specialized, and ascetic thinking into a distinctly moral example of how one might choose to live and to commit oneself to intellectual work under the current conditions. He embodied the contradictions of the crisis of the humanities—that they could be justified both as disciplined knowledge and moral formation, as both method and ethos. In this, Weber sharply differed from Spranger and the humanities revolutionaries. He agreed that ultimate values could not be completely rationalized, could not be rendered into an objective, universally accessible form. But he thought that for precisely this reason they needed to be disciplined so that they could become meaningful resources for leading, if not wholly grounding, a life.

As Freud did with modern civilization, Weber called for permanent tension, permanent struggle, in a phrase, permanent crisis—the refusal to assume that a metaknowledge or university-based discourse could provide a unifying, totalizing way of life. That was what it meant to live as an intellectual adult in the modern world. The youth could perhaps be excused for rebelling against the renunciation demanded of them; actual adults—that is, professors—couldn't. Yet for Weber, the permanent crisis of the humanities was not a lament for a lost wholeness; it was an acknowledgment that the need the modern humanities first claimed to address was in fact constitutive: crisis was the justification of the modern humanities.

The permanent crisis persists because it prevents any particular crisis from becoming completely universalized and, thereby, rendered timeless and no longer urgent; the permanent crisis also prevents any particular crisis from becoming particularized and, thereby, rendered contingent and fleeting.[153] Crisis provides a framework for cultured elites and intellectuals to work through intellectual and social change—hence the present mindedness, modernity, or even reactive character of the humanities.

# CHAPTER SEVEN

# Crisis, Democracy, and the Humanities in America

In 1904, while touring the eastern United States, Max Weber encountered an institution that would intrigue him the rest of his life: the American college. Although he was busy finishing *The Protestant Ethic and the Spirit of Capitalism*, he took his time visiting Columbia, Harvard, Haverford, Northwestern, and other schools.[1] On their pretty, well-kept campuses, he was fascinated by the "wild muddle" of education, religion, and socialization.[2] As he saw it, the American college was neither a finishing school for the wealthy nor a training academy for professionals; it was something else entirely, something he had a hard time describing. In subsequent years, in essays and lectures, Weber refined his account of the American college as a unique social-educational institution, repeatedly contrasting it with German institutions of higher education.

In his tour of American postsecondary institutions, Weber saw institutions forming young elite, generally white Protestant men into civic-minded leaders. Originally established by religious sects to train ministers, American colleges had organized themselves around the strict discipline of student life. They required chapel attendance (often multiple times per day), maintained a fixed curriculum, and closely monitored student behavior. This collegiate project of cultivation culminated in a fourth-year moral philosophy course taught by the college president, typically an ordained minister, and designed to ground Protestant morality, character, and dogma in a common reason and shared social commitment. This capstone course showed students how religious doctrine fit with modern knowledge and how both related to life. In its scientific, moral, and religious dimensions, truth was unitary.[3] After visiting Northwestern, Weber wrote to his mother, Helene, describing how "unbelievable" he found the school's compulsory religious observance.[4] Students were required to account for their attendance in a "chapel record"; they *listened* not only to sermons and scripture readings but to the most recent theological scholarship (Harnack's *The His-*

*tory of Dogma* the day Weber visited); and they were dismissed only after the week's football and baseball schedules had been announced. Weber left Evanston impressed by the social life and ethos of American undergraduate education, whose "output," he wrote, was immediately obvious: "endless intellectual stimulation," habituation to hard and serious work, lasting friendships, and enduring forms of sociability. The "college-bred-man," one American businessman assured Weber in Chicago, learned not just to reflect on the world but also to act in it and for it.[5]

Only seven years later, however, Weber gave a different account to an assembly of German university professors and teachers in Dresden. American colleges, he reported, had transformed themselves into universities that in their scope, in what they could teach, and in the competitive focus with which they went about it rivaled even the grandest of German universities.[6] Drawing on his experiences in the United States, Weber explained how these new American institutions had adopted a German university model but adapted it for a different culture and to different ends. They not only shaped students into capitalists of character but had themselves become "industrial enterprises," each led by a president who relentlessly competed for talent, resources, and money.[7] By the time he delivered what became *Scholarship as Vocation* in 1917, he claimed that German universities were becoming "fundamentally Americanized," difficult to distinguish from any other "capitalist operation in which the worker is separated from the means of production."[8]

Weber's scattered observations are further evidence of the transformation of American higher education between 1870 and 1914. The decade or so leading up to the First World War in particular saw the final phase of what Laurence Veysey called "the emergence of the American university," a process that had begun during the Civil War and entailed massive expansion, the rise of research culture, and the introduction of such enduring staples of college education as majors, electives, and general education programs.[9] In 1870 the United States had three hundred colleges and universities whose collective student body numbered fifty-two thousand. By 1910 those figures had grown to 1,690 and 1.4 million, respectively. Older, more established schools like Harvard were no longer what they been: institutions largely devoted to forming the "moral character" of future leaders. Harvard was now a research university whose mission included professional training and the creation of new knowledge.

For many, these changes, driven in part by the demands for new knowledge and more labor resulting from American economic expansion and the quickening pace of industrialization, came at a high price. As different as

German and American universities remained, despite the well-documented modeling of German academia in America, some of the critical responses to the transformation of American higher education echoed early objections to Weber's *Scholarship as Vocation* lecture. For example, faculty, alumni, and occasionally students, too, struggled with what they felt was increasing intellectual fragmentation and the concomitant loss of unity. Quite often at issue was the supplanting of a fixed, common curriculum. In 1922 the debate about a unifying curriculum began to engage the broader public when the *New Republic* published a series of articles on the state of university and college education. Several authors lamented the "centrifugal" forces tearing American universities and colleges apart. Some, such as the president of the University of Michigan, M. L. Burton, blamed Charles Eliot and the system of electives he had introduced at Harvard in the late nineteenth century, which displaced a prescribed and thus common curriculum.[10] Others argued that the curricular confusion of American colleges was ultimately a consequence of the fragmenting effects of modernity, especially those effects related to the ascendancy of the natural sciences.

Alexander Meiklejohn, a philosopher and the president of Amherst College from 1913 to 1924, contended that scientists assumed that "knowledge has no unity" and institutionalized this unfounded presupposition in university curricula and their own scholarship. The sciences, Meiklejohn wrote, "stand upon the ruins of an older scheme which they have smashed. . . . Because another scheme of thought has broken down, they think the schemes of thought are gone forever, that unity in knowledge is a myth."[11] The acceleration of knowledge had overwhelmed the prospect of truth. Resistance, or rather recovery, was possible though. The task of "modern thought," University of North Carolina president and professor of psychology Harry Chase maintained, was to recover the "unification of knowledge."[12] This would be an uphill battle, but it would be worth the effort—the stakes couldn't be higher. Universities, Chase lamented, could come to no "clear conviction of what knowledge is." To replace the nineteenth-century moral theology courses, Chase and others called for a curriculum that aspired to a unified account of knowledge and morality. However, natural scientists were reluctant to offer their research as resources for moral instruction, much less to join together in the name of the unity of knowledge. Faculty members in literature, art, philosophy, and history proved less reluctant. Beginning with the introduction of Columbia University's Contemporary Civilization course in 1919, universities and colleges introduced general education programs in an effort to recapture unity in the pursuit of truth, doing so as a matter both of knowledge and morality.[13] Starting about 1930, literary scholars, philosophers, and historians at dozens of schools banded together to form a new institutional structure that claimed a monopoly over questions of morals and values. They called it "the humanities."

As a coherent set of disciplines institutionalized in universities and colleges, "the humanities" are primarily an invention of American higher education between 1930 and 1950. German intellectuals and scholars, as the previous chapters have detailed, had sought for decades to establish their functional equivalent, the not–natural sciences or what we have termed the *modern humanities*, but it was early twentieth-century Americans who made the term *the humanities* an organizing ideal of their institutions. Importantly, it was also American intellectuals and scholars who untethered "the humanities" from their roots in classical philology and claimed them as a resource for democracy.

The English term *humanities* of course considerably predates early twentieth-century America. It seems to have gained currency in the early nineteenth century as a synonym for classical learning, as an Anglicized form of the *humaniora*, *studia humanitatis*, and related forms of humanist learning and scholarship. In 1819 William Nicholson's *British Encyclopedia* defined *humanities* as a plural noun signifying "grammar, rhetoric, and poetry known by the name of *literae humaniores*; for teaching of which there are professors in the universities in Scotland, called humanists."[14] For most of the nineteenth century, scholars, writers, and institutional leaders continued to use the term *humanities* to refer to the study of classical literature and learning.

Addressing the Phi Beta Kappa Society of Pennsylvania in 1902, Felix E. Schelling, a University of Pennsylvania professor of English and Shakespeare scholar, spoke about the "humanities gone and to come." Whereas past generations had successfully nurtured the classics (by which he meant ancient Greek and Roman literature), present and future generations, Schelling argued, would have to cultivate a "broader conception of the humanities" in order to do battle with an unprecedented threat: "The humanities today are front to front with an attack in comparison with which all previous menaces sink into insignificance." "We are in a struggle for the very principle of liberality in education itself, and, worst of all, our enemy is within," Schelling said. "Practical utility is by far the most insidious enemy of modern education and the chief barrier to the attainment of that higher and spiritual life toward which the nobler members of the race are striving."[15]

For Schelling the gradual but near total triumph of scientific and technical education in American colleges and universities—the dissolution of the classical college curriculum and the ascendance of more "modern" courses in the natural and physical sciences—had introduced a small-hearted disregard for the full capacities of humankind.[16] He conceded that their methods and what he considered their twin, "technical" education, had yielded great practical benefits. (Who didn't appreciate the convenience of a transcontinental railroad?) But they also promoted a utilitarian disposition that threatened to reduce "all things human" to an endless calculation of economic value, thereby rendering all "liberal" pursuits useless and without value.

In language that anticipated the sprawling civilizational-level critiques of modern science and technology by Lewis Mumford, Theodor Adorno, and Max Horkheimer in the 1930s and 1940s, Schelling warned that the technical—by which he meant the combined cultural influence and power of technology and the sciences—was poised to obliterate human nature. More than the mere study of Greek and Roman classics, then, the "humanities to come" stood in for a cultural need to counter this new disposition and maintain the distinction between the human and the technical. In Schelling's usage, the term *humanities* did not refer to distinct forms of knowledge or particular scholarly goods but was instead meant to evoke a social need defined negatively. Echoing Rickert's call for the "not-natural-scientific disciplines" just a few years earlier in Germany, Schelling summoned the not-sciences as a solution to a perceived cultural crisis.

Although he gave the "humanities to come" no specific content, Schelling did characterize them as entailing (and thus rescuing) a liberal attitude, suggesting that in the future, liberal education, an education not dedicated to generating wealth and solving technical problems, would be the exclusive domain of the humanities. By the end of his speech to the Pennsylvania Phi Beta Kappas, he had reduced "science" to instrumental knowledge—the "mechanical skill and technical precision" of engineers. The "humanities to come," Schelling concluded in language that spiraled into ever-greater levels of abstraction, would be "the untechnical studies, the unprofessional studies, be their content . . . what it may." Their role was "to educate, to elevate, and humanize," and in doing so, to negotiate a cultural crisis.[17]

Schelling's rhetoric marked a significant shift in the American context at the beginning of a new century. The discourse of "the humanities" moved away from the more limited and often technical aims of the *studia humanitatis* and philology related to the study of ancient Greek and Roman literature or "the classics" and toward the ideal of the modern humanities as invoked by Dilthey and the German scholars who came after him. In the years following Schelling's talk, the term also acquired new institutional meanings. Scholars, writers, intellectuals, university presidents and deans, leaders of private philanthropic foundations, and even corporate executives began to use *the humanities* in the way Schelling had pioneered it in his Philadelphia speech. They marshaled the term to signify a set of academic disciplines distinct from more technical forms of education and capable of cultivating uniquely human capacities such as autonomy, moral insight, and a liberal disposition.

Although Schelling cast his vision of a "humanities to come" against contemporary crises, Irving Babbitt, a professor of French literature at Harvard, was one of the first to situate such a vision in explicitly institutional terms.[18] In *Literature and the American College*, published in 1908, Babbitt focused on the dramatic rise of the research university in the United States and the related and equally dramatic decline of traditional undergraduate collegiate education. Babbitt called Harvard's Charles Eliot a "pure Rousseauist" for defending his introduction of the elective system on the grounds that "a well-instructed youth of eighteen" is best suited to choose his own course of study because "every youth of eighteen is an infinitely complex organization, the duplicate of which neither does nor ever will exist." In such a system, Babbitt noted sardonically, the "wisdom of all the ages is to be as naught compared with the inclination of a sophomore."[19] The notions of selection and distinction characterized Babbitt's conception of humanism, which bears some affinities with Nietzsche's views on affording students independence at a young age. Babbitt distinguished humanism from humanitarianism, arguing that the latter denoted a sympathy for "mankind in the lump" whereas the former was more "selective in his caresses." "The humanist," he wrote, is concerned with the perfection of the individual, rather than the "elevation of mankind as a whole."[20]

Babbitt even rejected, rightly, the universalizing claim regularly imputed by more contemporary writers to a famous line from the second-century BC Roman playwright Terence: "I am human; nothing human is alien to me" (Humani nihil a me alienum puto).[21] Read without irony and as a motto for a universal humanism—the statement is actually the retort of the play's protagonist to his neighbor's suggestion that he is being nosy—Terence's statement suggests that humanist knowledge lacks the notion of selection.[22] But, observed Babbitt, nowhere are selection, distinction, and taste more important than in sifting and organizing what, with whom, and why to read. As it was for Nietzsche, the problem was that in modern society models abounded, especially bad ones. Particularly threatening was the example set by the specialized scholars who had begun to populate American colleges and universities. "The humanities," Babbitt wrote, "need to be defended today against the encroachments of physical science, as they once needed to be against the encroachment of theology." But he considered the internecine ill of a scientific or specialized disposition to literature, developed through the process of writing a dissertation, an even greater threat: "proof of fitness for a chair in literature is doing more than any one thing to dehumanize literary study and fix our college's philological despotism."[23] Here Babbitt also exhibited affinities with the melancholy mandarins (chap. 2) as well as with the German intellectuals who responded critically to Weber's *Scholarship as Vocation* in the 1920s, describing the state of scholarship and the university more generally as a symptom—and cause—of culture decline. But whereas Weber's critics called for a "new" knowledge, Babbitt wanted to do away with specialized scholarship on the German model, *Wissenschaft*, entirely, at least as it concerned the study of humans whose purposeful activity he thought modern sciences of all kinds either ignored or refuted. He considered the ideal of German research a malign force. This industrial enterprise of erudition "philologized everything"; it reduced literature, history, religion, and other meaningful cultural forms to "the endless accumulation of facts."[24] The humanities were made more necessary than ever by the forces bedeviling them. They were needed "in a quantitative age to produce men of quality." For Babbitt and the New Humanists he inspired, the real failure of the modern university was its abandonment of its selection and filtering purpose, not just of books and ideas, but of people. What was needed was a "religious restraint" that could discipline the base, self-interested passions unleashed by modern cultures and thereby elevate a higher view of the human person as both rational and altruistic.[25] They turned to the humanities to fulfill a function that a nearly desiccated Protestantism no longer could: the maintenance and inculcation of values.

## INSTITUTIONAL FORMATIONS

Actual scholarship in disciplines such as history and literature in the United States continued to evolve in ways Babbitt would have disapproved of. It became more systematic, more specialized, more concerned with method—more German. Yet the way in which intellectuals and scholars sought to justify their own disciplines retained the sense of purpose he had sought to ascribe to the humanities without always retaining the reactionary character of Babbitt's writing. This sense of purpose had institutional consequences. Although scholars had invoked the "humanizing" power of individual disciplines since the end of the nineteenth century,[26] it was not until after the ascendance of the research university and the demise of the classical college curriculum in the United States around 1900 that scholars from previously disparate disciplines—philology, literature, arts, art history, history, philosophy, and religion—joined together to cast "the humanities" as a cultural compensation for the moral and spiritual deprivations of the natural and physical sciences and technology. By the 1930s such scholars had begun to give these claims organizational form in colleges and universities across the United States.[27] Instead of developing a new discourse, American intellectuals and scholars followed their German counterparts, repeating the rhetoric of crisis that cast the humanities as both the imperiled victim and privileged redeemer.

Between 1928 and 1941, American colleges and universities introduced numerous courses and comprehensive programs identified as "humanities."[28] The courses and programs introduced in this period did more than simply revive the study of Greek and Latin language and literature, what Schelling had termed "the humanities gone"; they sought to organize already distinct and specialized disciplines—from art history and English to religion and philosophy—within the context of the modern research university and orient them to a common purpose. These disciplines were said to be united not by a shared set of scholarly methods, epistemic ideals and values, or practices but by their ability to fill a perceived cultural and social need—to provide, as one observer put it in 1941, a "review of human culture and human values in light of modern conditions."[29]

By 1950 many of America's leading universities had institutionalized these promises (and oppositions) in the departmental and divisional structures we know today as "the humanities." Many of the new humanities initiatives were related to long-standing efforts to introduce general education programs whose proponents expressed similar desires for a unity of knowledge, clarity of purpose, moral value, and a regeneration of the uniquely human in the face of the centrifugal pressures of science and technology. As had been the case with general education, the proponents of the humanities characterized them as compensation for something missing from society. Talk of their social value inevitably began with a statement of cultural decline during the period of American history Mark Greif has referred to as the "age of the crisis of man"—a period in which intellectuals and scholars of various political commitments feared that the new technological and social conditions of Western modernity threatened to "snap the long tradition of humanism, the filament of learning, humane confidence, and respect for human capacities."[30] As Schelling had thirty years earlier and Ernst Kahler had in response to Weber in 1920, they worried that the very nature of "man" was being changed.

The "age of the crisis of man," however, was also an age of utopian visions when intellectuals, politicians, scientists, and writers across Europe and the United States championed human dignity, made the case for universal human rights, and continued to pose the question of what it means to be human. Whether in the titles of international conferences, United Nations documents, or curricular reform memos, "modern," "man," "the human," "humanism," and "the humanities" testified not only to the persistence of the question of the human but also to the repeated failure to answer it or even consider what might such an answer require.[31] In 1950 the poet and politician Aimé Césaire, born in Martinique in the French Caribbean, dismissed such projects as a collective "pseudo-humanism" that compelled "not one established writer, not one academic" to reject the colonialism still inflicted under the banner of the human.[32] Despite its interrogative form and claim to curiosity, however, the question, insofar as it was correlated with the rise of the humanities, doubled as an assertion that a limited set of academic disciplines could legitimately claim a monopoly over what counted as a serious answer.

In 1934 the journal *Science* published an article purporting to describe what "the humanities" did. Written by the historian Waldo G. Leland—the secretary and future director of the American Council of Learned Societies—the article was a dense four-page report that detailed the "scope," "task," "ultimate objective," "concern," "principal activities," "principal problems," and "possibilities" of "the humanities." Leland concluded that although "the humanities" had traditionally referred to philological studies, today the "collective term" refers to a "vast and complex group of studies, many of which are highly specialized, but all of which are related by a common ultimate objective—to contribute to the recovery and interpretation of the spiritual experience of mankind." Together with the natural and physical sciences and the social sciences, the humanities "form a triangle" of knowledge, but their legitimacy and significance derives from their ability to address these spiritual "needs of human existence."[33]

Leland considered this tripartite organization of knowledge to be the culmination of a "tendency towards the federation" of existing disciplines and fields into more complex and differentiated institutions. Once institutionalized, each "federation" served a fixed function. But whereas German intellectuals and scholars had since the 1870s described a similarly functionalist system in terms of a natural science–humanities (*die Geisteswissenschaften*) dyad, Leland followed his American colleagues who by 1930 identified economics, psychology, political science, and sociology as social sciences, distinguishing these disciplines collectively from the humanities. The social sciences, wrote Leland, were an "extension" of the humanities; they used "data" from the humanities ("manifestations of the spirit" as found in art, language, and literature) and the natural and physical sciences to study humans in their "association[s]" with each other.[34]

This tripartite division of knowledge was an institutional resolution to early twentieth-century debates over the relationship between scientific knowledge and values. Although German intellectuals and scholars continued their decades-old arguments about scholarship and values throughout the 1920s without a clear resolution,[35] Americans ended theirs, institutionally at least, by imposing—or suffering depending one's position in these debates—a sharply divided intellectual order: the humanities cultivated values, the natural and physical sciences collected and analyzed empirical facts, and the social sciences mediated between the two. This shifting, in-between function made the social sciences an institutional outlet for anxieties and contests about the place of values and norms in the rapidly changing American research university.

The role and function of the humanities in this new institutional order, in contrast, was clearly asserted from the beginning. Although Scripps College had in 1928 introduced a three-year sequence in "The Humanities"— organized around courses titled "The Ancient World," "Western Civilization to 1750," and "The Modern World"—the University of Chicago set a national precedent with its "General Introduction to Humanities" course two years later. Under Robert Maynard Hutchins, a young president recently arrived from Yale, Chicago's faculty approved the "New Plan" in 1930. This extensive curricular reform segmented the arts and sciences faculty into five "juridical units," each led by its own dean—humanities, social sciences, physical sciences, biological sciences, and a college charged with overseeing general education.[36] Each division required undergraduates to take a one-year survey course. The Humanities Division survey course, as the committee of two historians and a linguist tasked with designing it wrote in 1931, would introduce students to "the cultural history of mankind as a continuum and as a whole."[37] In 1933, however, just three years after the faculty approved the reform, Hutchins began to publicly denounce the New Plan, claiming that it suffered from the "information disease" afflicting "all of the modern world": We have confused science with information, ideas with facts, and knowledge with miscellaneous data, and since information, facts, and data have not lived up to our high hopes of them, we are witnessing today a revulsion against science, ideas, and knowledge.[38] Hutchins wanted a "more radical vision" than a survey course on "The Humanities" could offer.[39] A significant part of his curricular reform ideas came from his collaboration with a young philosopher named Mortimer Adler on a "Great Books" honors course. Before his arrival in Chicago (and as he would, for the most part, for the rest of his life), Adler had been devising a methodology and taxonomy for organizing all sciences and fields of knowledge, a project inspired by the metaphysics of Thomas Aquinas. Adler mined Aquinas for permanent, rational categories of knowledge and a timeless conception of human nature. Attracted to these encyclopedic aspirations and Adler's intellectual chutzpah, Hutchins enlisted him in a plan to reinvent liberal undergraduate education for the modern research university by grounding it in a common set of extant truths.

What followed was a highly personal debate about the role of research and modern scholarship in undergraduate education. Even the *Daily Maroon*, the undergraduate newspaper, got involved, mostly by mocking the defenders of the New Plan as mindless positivists while celebrating Hutchins and Adler's "great books" course.[40] Their program set the "greatest books of the western world"—with their purportedly timeless, metaphysically inflected truths—against the dumb empiricism they claimed dominated the natural and physical sciences as well as the social sciences.

The real object of derision, however, was the very idea of specialized scholarship and the concept of knowledge as research—of knowledge not as something that already existed and was to be revealed in a transformative and timeless encounter but as something to be created, unendingly pursued, and always eventually superseded by humans bounded by space and time. Hutchins thought that these two different conceptions of knowledge produced, as he wrote in 1934, an "essential opposition between education and research."[41] Adler and Hutchins believed that undergraduates should be reading what they considered the great books and absorbing their eternal verities without being subjected to the contingent claims of modern science. Adler had outlined a metaphysical plan for the university in the form of a curriculum based on fixed categories he derived from neo-Thomistic principles. Hutchins translated Adler's epistemology into a political imperative. "Unless it is admitted," he wrote, "that the natural moral law underlies the diversity of mores, that the good, the true, and the beautiful are the same for all men, no world civilization is possible."[42] For Hutchins, Chicago's "Great Books" curriculum functioned as the best form of resistance to the positivistic, empiricist, and technological ideologies that plagued modern universities. It provided coherence, certainty, and unity.

## THE BALTIMORES

In the mid-1930s a group of faculty members at Princeton organized what may well have been the first "humanities" program.[43] Dubbed the "Baltimores" because they met regularly in the Baltimore Dairy Lunch, across Nassau Street from Nassau Hall, the group, as historian Bryan McAllister-Grande has detailed, was convened by the classicist, Christian apologist, and editor of the *Nation* Paul Elmer More and included members of the classics, English, and philosophy departments. A nationally known and charismatic leader of the New Humanists, More was a popular figure on the

Princeton campus, but the faculty members who joined him at the Baltimore all shared his sense of civilizational crisis: the leading culprits were, in his view, German research universities and scholars who "pulverized" humanity; Dewey-inspired progressive educators who impiously eschewed the authority of mankind and the divine; and modern science, whose empiricist dogmatism stretched for More across centuries to Bacon.[44] More and his group also shared a desire, as "Baltimore" and philosophy professor Theodore Greene put it in 1942, to create an institutional "counterbalance" to the departments, schools, and "legion of individual courses" that stifled any sense of the unifying "vital interests and achievements of mankind."[45]

The Baltimores had advocates in the administration, as McAllister-Grande notes, including Christian Gauss, who held one of Princeton's first chairs in modern languages and served as dean of the college from 1929 to 1946. Gauss was a personal friend of More, and like More, he attached great importance to the compensatory function of teaching and scholarship that self-consciously identified itself as belonging to the humanities. "Devotees of science tell us that if the humanities were only willing to recognize the importance of the specialized branches of science, physics, chemistry, biology," Gauss wrote in the early 1940s, "we would soon realize that nothing had been lost and much gained in the reconstruction of the modern course of study."[46] But the sciences had little to say about justice, beauty, or the value of democracy; it had also exposed "modern man" to unprecedented "possibilities for destruction," by which Gauss meant not only technical destruction but also the destruction of the Christian ideals and beliefs that he claimed supported the nation. Only a revival of the humanities and what he called the "humanistic attitude," he implied, could place a moral restraint on science's unceasing disruptions.

Initially called the Divisional, the Special Program in the Humanities (SPH) welcomed its first cohort of undergraduate majors at Princeton in 1936 and for twenty-eight years awarded roughly sixteen bachelor's degrees annually.[47] A faculty committee drawn from various departments oversaw the program and enticed undergraduate SPH majors with intensive individual advising and teaching. The committee also organized a lecture and seminar series and served as an "evangelist of the humanities" within the broader university.[48] In his autobiography, the literary scholar Edward Said, who graduated from Princeton in 1957 with a bachelor's degree from SPH, described his humanities courses as "unreflectingly historical in organization" and as having introduced him to the texts that "formed the foundation of everything" he would go on to write and teach as a scholar.[49] When Princeton set out to redesign its undergraduate curriculum and introduce the increasingly standard threefold divisional structure (natural sciences, social sciences, and humanities) in 1943, five SPH faculty served on the Humanities Council, which had been charged with overseeing the organization of the humanities division.[50] These five faculty members helped ensure that those who advocated on behalf of the humanities at Princeton understood their ultimate function to be a moral one. As president Harold Dodds wrote in 1942 to the Rockefeller Foundation, SPH's primary benefactor, the humanities were the last defense of "human values" and the human as such against the tyranny of "technology and mechanism."[51]

In 1938 Princeton University hosted five scholars over three weeks to lecture on "The Meaning of the Humanities." The event was a "catalyst" for the articulation and success of the humanities as an institutional and ideological force in American higher education in subsequent decades.[52] Although the lecturers drew on their own disciplines, from philosophy and theology to art history and history, they all focused, as one observer put it, on the "nature and value of the Humanities . . . in a world of ever-increasing social regimentation and scientific mechanization."[53] In his response to the lectures, Theodore Greene, who in addition to being a Baltimore was also an SPH cofounder, argued that the humanities were "not academic luxuries" but rather "vital forces" for the defense of "human freedom, dignity, and worth."[54] Harvard philosophy professor Randolph Barton Perry noted how American colleges and universities had for some time grouped particular courses and subjects "under departments" but only recently had established the practice of grouping these departments within "divisions," the most common arrangement being "physical science, biological science, social science—*and* 'the humanities.'" Conflating liberal, nonutilitarian learning with "the humanities," Perry worried that this new organization of knowledge—what he dismissed as a vestigial "groping for unity"—reduced real, liberal learning to "only one-quarter of the whole."[55] The other speakers, who included the famed art historian (and German émigré) Erwin Panofsky, offered similar arguments: the modern humanities continued a well-established tradition of Renaissance humanism; they synthesized specialized knowledge and satisfied social needs that other, especially scientific, forms of knowledge could not. For each of the speakers, "the humanities" were much more than a set of methods. They represented a commitment to a cultural ideal; they constituted an attitude.

Both during and after World War II, American intellectuals and scholars continued to promote the humanities, but with greater urgency because of the acute sense that the war had exacerbated the institutional and, in the language of the day, "civilizational" plight of liberal education. They did so in the face of suspicions that the humanities were not an urgent social need. "The immediate necessity is to win this war," said secretary of war Henry

Stimson in 1942, "and unless we do that there is no hope for liberal education in this country." This remark appears as a comment in a *New York Times*
piece titled "New Plans Suspend Liberal Education."[56]

Despite such opposition, but also because of it, the humanities continued to assume new and greater institutional forms. In the fall of 1942
Stanford University professors in the departments of classics, Germanic
languages, religion, Romantic languages, Slavic languages, history, philosophy, and music helped establish the "School of the Humanities."[57] The
school was an undergraduate division established, as Stanford president
Ray Lyman Wilbur said in 1941, to balance "the pressure for early specialization and the need for a coherent view of human activities."[58] Lewis Mumford moved to Palo Alto in 1942 to become the school's first director. He
described the purpose of the humanities as the "deep regeneration and renewal . . . of human civilization."[59] The humanities provided "a fighting generation . . . an appreciation of all the things that are worthwhile living for,
struggling for, fighting for, and, if need be, dying for."[60]

After the war and through the early 1950s, Princeton, Yale, Harvard, and
Johns Hopkins similarly established "the humanities" as a comprehensive
divisional category or, as in Harvard's case, a set of required courses.[61] In
postwar America, with the financial support and programmatic encouragement of private foundations, the still-emerging institutional structures
known as the humanities were put to increasingly civic and explicitly state-
defined ends by university administrators. In a series of monographs and
committee reports that transformed arguments for the humanities into a
genre of bureaucratic and institutional high-mindedness—including the
Rockefeller Foundation's *The Rebirth of Liberal Education* (1945), Stanford's
*The Humanities Look Ahead* (1943), and the American Council of Learned
Societies' *Liberal Education Re-examined: Its Role in a Democracy* (1943)—
the humanities were celebrated as a necessary and necessarily democratic
"movement" surpassing the more aristocratic intentions of the prewar New
Humanists.[62]

As early as 1935 the trustees of the Rockefeller Foundation voted to expand the mandate of its humanities division, which had been created only
seven years earlier in 1928, from supporting individual scholarship focused
on philology and archaeology to include support of libraries, museums,
drama, radio programming, and related endeavors that participated in
the "new renaissance of the human spirit." A year earlier, a special committee had proposed doing just this, but only after suggesting that a "program in the humanities, based on a cloistered kind of research," was no
longer aligned with the broader goals of the foundation.[63] Whatever their
differences, these reports and declarations invariably cast the humanities

as a unifying inquiry into and concern with human being that transcended mere method and technique.

In *General Education in a Free Society* (1945), a committee of Harvard faculty maintained that American education was in "supreme need . . . of a unifying purpose and idea."[64] They concluded that given the "varieties of faith and even of unfaith" in postwar America, religion and, thus, an explicitly religious basis for an undergraduate curriculum, was no longer possible. These "centrifugal forces" were further amplified by the prevalence and power of specialists in all areas of postwar American society. So instead of forming Christian gentleman through a prescribed and generally Protestant-based curriculum, American colleges and universities should form liberal moral agents capable of distinguishing "the expert from the quack, and the better from the worse expert."[65] The role of the humanities in such a project, wrote the committee, was to enable young Harvard undergraduates to understand "man in relation to himself" by "stirring the imagination with ideals" and "explor[ing] the realm of value." The committee contrasted this moral task with the strictly epistemological one—to judge simply between "true and false statements"—they ascribed to the natural and physical sciences. The humanities inspire and seek out value; the sciences serve "a harsh master—brute facts of physical reality." The committee echoed Leland's description of the social sciences' mediating role, claiming that they combined the methods of the natural sciences and the humanities in order to explain as well as to evaluate and, in the context of undergraduate education, to prepare students for the "task of citizenship."[66]

By 1945, however, Leland's "triangle," despite the Harvard's committee's suggestion that the social sciences borrow equally from the humanities and the natural and physical sciences, resembled more an isosceles triangle than an equilateral one. With their functionalist disposition, uncompromising embrace of quantitative methods, and "engineering conception" of knowledge, social scientists considered themselves the equals of natural and physical scientists in terms of method, social utility, and opposition to the valorization of interpretation and values in modern science.[67] Whether natural, physical, or social, "science" both inside and outside the university named a type of knowledge that reduced any commitment or thing of interest, as Andrew Jewett writes, to "a matter of cold, amoral, facts."[68] With *General Education*, which sold over forty thousand copies in its first five years in print, Harvard faculty members, however inadvertently, had reinforced the tripartite framework within which the sciences were largely an undifferentiated, blunt instrument that experts could use to achieve the moral ends deposited in and refined by the humanities.[69]

Four years after Harvard president James Bryant Conant established his institution's committee on general education in 1943, MIT's faculty appointed the Committee on Educational Survey in 1947 to reexamine whether the university's educational principles continued to be "applicable to the conditions of a new era emerging from social upheaval and the disasters of war." In its report (1950), the committee alluded to "forces" that threatened American democracy and the "initiative and individuality" of its people. More profound and more "subtle" than even the threat of atomic warfare, wrote the committee, was the "persistent tendency [in American society] to growth and centralization of control in all organizations and institutions, industrial, financial, educational, and labor." This "tendency," continued the report, had been institutionalized in MIT's undergraduate curriculum, which was deemed too rigid, unimaginative, impersonal, and illiberal. In order to counter the technical and utilitarian disposition that characterized both the university and its students, the committee argued that MIT should commit itself to "liberal education."[70] The best way to accomplish this was to increase the number of courses required in "the humanities" and to establish a school of humanities and social sciences.

This institutional movement culminated on a federal level in 1965 when Congress voted to establish the National Endowment for the Humanities, whose founding legislation juxtaposed the humanities with "science and technology" and included the somewhat ominous assertion that the humanities were what would make humans "masters of their technology and not its unthinking servants."[71]

In 1948 almost fifty years after Schelling spoke of a "humanities to come," another professor and institutional leader, Wesleyan's Cornelius Kruse, who had recently stepped down as executive director of the American Council of Learned Societies, attested to the humanities' arrival or, at least, to the resilience of their promise. The occasion was the seventy-fifth anniversary of Ohio State University in Columbus, where over two days some of America's corporate and cultural elite spoke about big social ideas: General Motors' vice president on "Science and Technology—Servants of Man"; an original member of the US Atomic Energy Commission on "Education for Survival"; and the theologian Reinhold Niebuhr on "Our Pilgrimage from a Century of Hope to a Century of Perplexity." Kruse, a professor of philosophy who struggled for decades to complete a philosophical refutation of pessimism, delivered a now-forgotten lecture, "On Humanity's Need for the Humanities." It was nonetheless an address that clarified the normative function of the humanities at the middle of the century—culturally, institutionally, politically, and socially.

Reprising Schelling's rhetorical model, Kruse diagnosed a cultural crisis, inveighed against the moral poverty of modernity, argued that humane and liberal learning were under threat, and exhorted the audience to embrace the humanities in order to "save humanity."[72] The humanities, Kruse told his audience, had always been guided by the "humanistic creed" that placed "man and his spirit in the forefront of interest."[73] To embrace the humanities by studying different cultures and languages here at a public university in central Ohio was not only to encounter this "spirit" but also to act in its defense. Like Schelling before him, Kruse highlighted the humanities' therapeutic effects — "serenity, stability, and mutual appreciation" — for an entire culture confronted with the tumult of scientific and technological change.[74] The rhetorical force of Kruse's speech relies on an identification on the part of an audience member or reader with Kruse's diagnosis of cultural decline that threatens *the human* (and not just a particular culture) and also from a promise that *the human* could be recovered and regenerated. Kruse induces audience members and readers to participate in the humanities as both an individual and species-level project of redemption. What was — and is — needed was the right set of disciplines and the institutional space to practice them. In fields across the university, scholars acknowledged the limited goods of the sciences and looked to the humanities — especially, as we shall see, what many only then began to refer to as the art and literature of "Western Civilization" and "The Great Books" — as a remedy for a scientific and technical age.[75]

## THE HUMANISMS OF THE EUROPEAN ÉMIGRÉS

The desire for unity, coherence, and a countervailing force to the centrifugal powers of modernity — technology, capitalism, information, science — that characterized formative humanities discourse in the United States in the first half of the twentieth century echoed the debates in Germany about the crises of knowledge, history, the university, and the humanities. Between the two world wars many European intellectuals sought a new humanism. Like Kahler's call for a new knowledge, however, beyond that initial invocation of the human they rarely shared much more than a diagnosis of cultural decline and the expectation that the future would bring redemption. Catholics (themselves split among traditionalists, modernists, and ultramodernists), communists, Protestants, Dadaists, futurists, and liberals were pulled by very different epistemological, ethical, political, and social orientations even though, as Stefanos Geroulanos has shown, each claimed to possess the one form of knowledge or practice that could rescue *the human* from the enervation, superficiality, decadence, and general soullessness of modernity.[76]

As German-Jewish scholars began to flee Nazi Germany in the early 1930s, European and American humanisms sometimes converged.[77] The various humanisms of American intellectuals and scholars, however, remained enmeshed with continued anxieties about the institutional authority and legitimacy of the humanities in universities and among reading publics, either external or adjacent to an institution that was becoming with each passing decade more specialized and professional. The concerns of American intellectuals and scholars didn't always register with German émigrés. The story of Kahler is exemplary in this regard. In 1938 Kahler, the same German-Jewish literary scholar who had responded to Max Weber's *Scholarship as Vocation* in 1920, escaped to the United States. Five years later, he published *Man the Measure*, an attempt, he explained, "to re-interpret history, not by discussing, but by re-telling it, by allowing interpretations to arise spontaneously from the arrangement of facts," and so "to write history, not write about history."[78] Kahler concluded his nearly seven-hundred-page plod through the history of "man" with a worn complaint about the fate of "the humanities" in a world where, he wrote, "empirical facts rule indiscriminately" even though they are "in themselves senseless and worthless until they are interpreted and linked together from a guiding view of the whole." The sorry state of the humanities—their incoherence and lack of "public support" (by whom Kahler didn't specify)—was "a symptom of the dangerous condition of our civilization. In this gravest of human crises," he insisted, "nothing is more urgent, nothing more vital" than the unifying knowledge they could provide.[79]

In 1957 a group of faculty members at Ohio State nominated Kahler for the inaugural Ralph D. Mershon professorship, a new visiting professorship funded as part of a seven-million-dollar gift from an alumnus who was a former commanding officer of the Ohio National Guard.[80] Writing to their dean, they presented Kahler as an internationally recognized scholar of the humanities and one of the few "humanists" who could help transform Ohio State into an "important center of theoretical and applied interdisciplinary research in the nature and history of culture."[81] The dean eventually agreed, and Kahler served as one of the first two Mershon visiting professors between 1959 and 1961, leading a "Faculty seminar in the humanities" and delivering lectures.

By the middle of the twentieth century, Ohio State had established itself as a well-functioning midwestern public university that had made good on the promise of the 1862 Morrill Act—the congressional legislation that helped states establish new universities or expand existing ones—to bring practical and liberal education to communities across the country.[82] But Ohio State was not an internationally recognized research university like its neighbor to the north, the University of Michigan. This was especially the case for departments such as German, history, philosophy, and English. The faculty members who pushed for Kahler's appointment—for example, Roy Harvey Pearce, a scholar of American literature and author of the anti–New Criticism manifesto "Historicism Once More"—wanted an eminent scholar who could expose them to advanced scholarly techniques and methods particular to the humanities.[83] In 1959 Pearce and some of his more research-oriented colleagues sought to use Kahler's visit to gain administrative support for a humanities institute. In a memorandum titled "Proposal for Support of a Mershon Institute for Humanistic Studies," Pearce defined the humanities as "a group of subjects devoted to the study of man as a being other than a biological product and different from a social or sociological entity." He concluded not only by claiming they were in crisis but offering a possible solution: "The crisis in humanistic studies today is not only in the weakening of their role in society, but in their being unable to develop rapidly enough the modes and methods whereby they maintain that role, should it again be granted them."[84]

Not surprisingly, Kahler rejected Pearce's premise that "the crisis" in the humanities could be overcome through method and disciplinary knowledge. In fact, as David Kettler notes, he expressed little interest in Pearce's plans to use the presence of the German émigré to bolster the scholarly legitimacy and prestige of Ohio State's fledgling humanities departments. In one of his final communications with the members of his faculty seminar from 1961, which he had organized around the theme of "crisis," Kahler chided them for allowing "over-meticulous terminological disputes" and a compulsion to focus on "specific books" to distract them from their "ultimate common purpose"—the "human crisis of the era."

A crisis is a final breaking point, the overpowering of the controlling form by the discontinuous multitude of life. At such a point only a fundamentally broadening re-organization, reformation of the system, of its frame and means of control, may be able to cope with the anarchical situation and put an end to the crisis. To be sure, we find crises occurring all along in human history . . . [but they] lacked the present panicky simultaneity and therefore immediate universality and comprehensiveness of crisis, which is mainly due to the technological unification of our world, the rapidity of world-wide communication, the crowding of events and reactions to events. The incessant advances of our technology and science have, moreover, brought about an inner crisis of man, by promoting conformity and standardization, by alienating individuals from each other and from themselves by besetting human consciousness with continuous material changes, by sweeping away traditions and memories and thus endangering personal and communal identity.[85]

In his response to Weber in 1920, Kahler had identified specialized scholarship as the primary cause of the crisis then facing Germany and with it all of humankind. Here, in his 1961 memorandum, he identified technology and science as causal agents and emphasized how they had transformed discrete crises into a "general human crisis." In order to gain a "comprehensive picture" of this crisis, he wrote, faculty members needed "discipline." But, as he had done in response to Weber, Kahler dissociated discipline from the specialized knowledge of modern universities; he judged as inadequate to the present crisis a disciplinary, historicizing knowledge oriented toward ideals of method and rigor—what in 1920 he had termed the "old" knowledge. Just as he had called for a "new" knowledge to address the crisis then, he called, again, for a new, transformative knowledge that would recover the unity of humankind. He offered few details, however, about this humanities of the future other than to describe it as a not-specialized, not-"mechanical" knowledge that would allow scholars to "accept the phenomenal world as the reality that is given to us."[86]

Almost forty years earlier, Max Scheler, Germany's leading Catholic philosopher, had dismissed Kahler's call for a new knowledge in response to Weber's statements about the "meaninglessness" of modern knowledge. He agreed with Weber's diagnosis even if he drew sharply different conclusions about a way forward. In calling for a "new" knowledge, Kahler had sought to "revolutionize" something, wrote Scheler, that had developed over "two thousand years of the history of the West: disciplinary knowledge was in its foundations and methods rational, inductive or formal-deductive, and free of presuppositions." This intellectual and moral learning process had now in the early twentieth century reached its apogee in what Germans termed *Wissenschaft*. Unlike Kahler, however, Scheler rejected the notion that this particular "Western" history represented a stage in a universal learning process: "What we today call '*Wissenschaft*' is itself the product of just one worldview, namely, that of the West; *Wissenschaft* is only possible when and where this worldview retains its authority."[87] Kahler had never conceded or understood this. Whether in 1920s Germany or 1950s America, Kahler, like the neo-humanists who preceded him, longed for a knowledge that transcended the historically particular practices, ideals, and virtues of a Weltanschauung. He refused to see specialized, disciplinary knowledge, *Wissenschaft*, especially as it had been institutionalized in research universities across Germany and the United States, as an incomplete, partial development of reason itself. Echoing the metaphysical and world-historical aspirations of the young student-leader Walter Benjamin, Kahler thought that the only way "to keep the world human" was to recover this history in its fullness, which meant its future consummation as well as its past.[88] That Kahler's "revolution" was actually a restoration project makes the enthusiastic embrace of him at Ohio State especially ironic. Although Kahler longed to transcend the specialized scholarship of the research university without entirely abandoning its ethos, his Columbus faculty colleagues identified him as the ideal research scholar, an authoritative figure who could legitimize their attempts to institutionalize the modern humanities at Ohio State.

American apologists for the humanities also sought historical legitimacy, and by midcentury many of them embraced the Italian Renaissance as the fount of the modern humanities' "essential nature."[89] In his speech at Ohio State in 1948, Kruse had drawn an unbroken line between fourteenth- and fifteenth-century traditions of the *litterae humaniores* to the postwar American humanities. Whether in fifteenth-century Florence or twentieth-century Columbus, "the humanities," he argued, have always been bound by the "humanistic creed" that placed "man and his spirit in the forefront of interest."[90] He described the humanities as shared "human enterprises which lie closest to the hearts of men when they feel themselves to be truly men[,] . . . the expression in manifold form . . . of man's intrinsic values." The humanities as found in twentieth-century American universities and colleges were and always had been a form of humanism, not just a curricular order but a unifying and irreducibly human endeavor.

Whereas early modern scholars turned to the literature of antiquity to liberate the human spirit from an overbearing and stultifying church (or so claimed many twentieth-century scholars), postwar American scholars invented the humanities to free themselves from the monstrosities of mechanism and tyrannies of technology. Not merely a "class name for certain divisions of knowledge," as Ralph Barton Perry claimed in 1938, the humanities provided the moral resources that made possible "a certain condition of freedom" under otherwise increasingly inhuman conditions.[91] The origins of this "condition," he continued, were to be found in Italian Renaissance humanism, which "signified the emancipation of the human faculties from the restraints of religious zeal, preoccupation or authority; the reinstatement of natural and secular values after their disparagement by the cult of other-worldliness."[92] Sustained by its purported universality and continuity, Renaissance humanism could be "transferred to any time and place" whenever and wherever the "gift of freedom" was needed. Embedded within the humanities, then, was a history of perpetual threats and attempts, as Perry had put it, to "thwart" its essential purpose: to resist the "dehumanizing influences" of any given time and place. The most immediate threat, however, was institutional: "the ascendance in American higher education of technique, the multiplication of accessory disciplines, and vocational utility."[93]

## KRISTELLER AND RENAISSANCE REVISIONISM

In the decades after World War II, scholars of the Renaissance, especially those who studied fourteenth- and fifteenth-century Italian history, literature, and philosophy, began to engage the widespread efforts in American academia to justify the modern humanities by tracing their history back over the centuries. Historians such as the German-Jewish émigré Paul Oskar Kristeller and Eugenio Garin, an Italian, helped reveal what motivated these twentieth-century attempts to establish (or reject) the continuity of the Renaissance humanistic knowledge and the modern humanities. In a scholarly relationship that extended over fifty years (from 1937 to 1994), Kristeller and Garin not only debated interpretations of humanism, they showed how the problem of Renaissance humanism had become the problem of the modern humanities—the mixing of a commitment to method and a desire for moral transformation.[94] On one end of the spectrum, Garin, a historian who devoted most of his career to establishing a unique Italian contribution to modern philosophy, depicted the two centuries between Petrarch and Bruno (roughly 1350–1550) as the period when an "entirely changed human attitude" found expression in a new "philosophical method" that embraced historical and philological insights in order to identify exemplary forms of human life as lived in the world. Humanism was a new attitude that ushered in a radically "modern thought" and enabled a fuller appreciation of human becoming, of the human as a profoundly historical being.[95] Garin saw, as James Hankins writes, a genetic connection extending from the Italian, Latinate work of Pico della Mirandola through the neo-humanist, philhellenic German writings of Kant, Hegel, Nietzsche, and Heidegger.[96] On the other end of the spectrum, Kristeller emphasized the discontinuity of modern philosophical humanisms with Renaissance forms of humanistic knowledge such as the *studia humanitatis*. He argued that "most of the works of the humanists have nothing to do with philosophy even in the vaguest possible sense of the term." The Italian humanists of the fourteenth and fifteenth centuries were "neither good nor bad philosophers, but no philosophers at all."[97]

Kristeller certainly considered his circumscription of Renaissance humanism to a limited set of epistemic practices and the *studia humanitatis* to a technical curriculum to be correctives to bad scholarship. Scattered throughout his countless essays are idiomatic markers of a highly disciplined scholarly ethos: "modern scholarship has been far too much influenced by all kinds of prejudices"; "complete objectivity may be impossible to achieve, but it should remain the permanent aim and standard of the historian as well as of the philosopher and scientist."[98] He considered such constraints manifestations of virtues characteristic of the ideal Renaissance scholar as well as modern humanities scholar. Whereas Garin's Renaissance humanists (in fifteenth-century Italy or twentieth-century Germany) conducted a "moral kind of inquiry to be practiced and advanced among men for the sake of men,"[99] Kristeller's practiced philology and history as the "ancestors" of modern humanistic scholars.[100]

Just as Kahler had articulated his longing for a "new" knowledge before leaving Germany, Kristeller began to develop his more chastened account of Renaissance humanism long before receiving tenure at Columbia University in 1948. A student of, among others, Martin Heidegger, Werner Jaeger, and Ulrich von Wilamowitz-Moellendorff in Germany, Kristeller had been educated in the tradition of *Wissenschaft* and exposed to the sense of crisis that permeated German universities in the early twentieth century. He certainly knew of the various humanisms that had been drafted to address it.[101] After fleeing Germany in 1934 and then working in Italy, Kristeller eventually landed a permanent position in the United States. It was in America that he sought to distinguish between "the philological, literary, and rhetorical humanism he saw in the Renaissance and the unhistorical and often politicized interpretations of humanisms he saw multiplying around him." He developed a "contempt for American humanism."[102] Instead of a "humanist creed" or a "humanist faith," as American academics such as Kruse and Greene respectively put it, the *studia humanitatis*, and thus the most likely precedent to the modern humanities, were, argued Kristeller, a loosely related set of practices that flourished in a range of communities and institutional settings. Kristeller historicized humanism not only in order to distinguish Renaissance humanism as scholarly practice from other, less historically informed accounts but also to counter what he considered the "instrumentalized interpretations" then rampant in the United States.[103]

Kristeller's humanists—more historical than philosophical, more technically skilled than theoretically ambitious—had no clear institutional home in twentieth-century American universities. The "so-called humanities," he wrote in 1961, were an invention of twentieth-century American universities in which the predominant classification of knowledge is "taken for granted in public discussions on matters of learning and education: we are accustomed to speak of the natural sciences, the social sciences, and the humanities."[104] Such an organization juxtaposed humanistic with scientific knowledge and created confusions about what disciplines such as

literature, the arts, music, philosophy, linguistics, archaeology, and classical philology actually did. Did they create knowledge? Did they claim objectivity? Did they undercut the sciences? Did they make truth claims? Or did
they offer moral succor?

Kristeller thought that the discipline of history exemplified the "precarious" and confounding place of the humanities in the American "scheme" of
university-based knowledge. "Most of us," he wrote,

> would admit that [historical] disciplines contain elements of valid and
> verified empirical knowledge. On the other hand, English and American
> usage does not seem to sanction the application of the term "science" to
> historical knowledge. Yet I cannot see how it is possible to avoid one of
> the following alternatives: either we must agree to extend the term "sci-
> ence" to include historical knowledge, and to speak of the "historical sci-
> ences"; or we must admit that there is a body of valid empirical knowl-
> edge that is not "scientific" in the usual sense of the word.[105]

The ambiguous epistemological status of history exemplified the situation
of the modern humanities more broadly. Kristeller concludes that given
the uncertain position of those disciplines that had only recently come to
be known collectively as the humanities, their American defenders inevitably failed to articulate the humanities' "status as branches of knowledge."
Rather, they resorted to emphasizing the humanities' "educational value in
a rather hazy fashion." In contrast to this American tendency, Kristeller af-
firms the epistemic goods and virtues of humanistic knowledge (if not "the
humanities"), which he associates in this context primarily with the discipline of history. "The aim of historical method remains always the same: to
establish the events of the human past on the basis of available evidence.
The rigor with which this task is being pursued represents a wholesome
intellectual and moral discipline, for the scholar engaged in this work, and
for the student and reader who becomes an indirect participant in it."[106]
The immediate aims of the early humanists from Italy to Germany were
more quotidian, more technical than those Kruse and his contemporaries
cared to admit.[107]

Yet Kristeller acknowledged that humanist practices could and certainly
had been put to various ends. He even offered his own account of the ends
to which humanist scholarly practice could be put in what he called, echoing Weber, a "personal confession":

> I am convinced that the concern with history, and especially with cul-
> tural and intellectual history, is based on a kind of faith, a faith which

I fully share: the works of art and literature, the philosophical and scientific ideas, even the political actions and social institutions that are contained in the human past represent a realm of essences in which we may participate. We are called upon to preserve, appropriate, and transmit it, not because it happens to be there, but because it is valuable and meaningful.[108]

Kristeller reveals his dual commitment as a scholar. Methodologically he is a modern and, thus, empirical scholar. Philosophically he is a Platonist, and, thus, one who maintains a faith in the existence of an external, stable reality "on which humans base their truth claims."[109] Kristeller's dual commitment fit well within a hierarchy of knowledge—itself extending from Greek antiquity to early eighteenth-century Germanophone lands—that ordered rational, deductive thought above the study of particular events or objects. Kristeller understood the former to be philosophy and the latter to be history or *historia*. On his account, the vocation of humanist scholars such as himself was to contribute to an empirically accurate and ultimately comprehensive account of a given phenomenon or historical period of time. History aspires to philosophy—it strives to give an account of the whole. By participating in this endless pursuit of the whole and true, the individual scholar becomes "part of a continuous tradition . . . by contributing to it." Unlike Kahler, Kristeller remained committed to the "old" knowledge, its neo-humanist ideals, and disciplinary, university-based knowledge: the unity-of-knowledge ideal, research as an endless pursuit of truth, and the belief that the search for knowledge should be joined with the process of individual moral formation. "I hopefully believe," wrote Kristeller in reference to his American colleagues, "that this is what is meant by the frequently shallow talk we hear about the liberal arts and the humanities."[110] Like Weber, he considered scholarship, *Wissenschaft*, a vocation and a testament to "human dignity."[111]

Kahler and Kristeller were not alone in their struggles to come to terms with the legacy of the (for them, German) research university. In 1936, three years before he immigrated to the United States, Thomas Mann criticized the "bifurcation between *Wissenschaft* and *Bildung*" and the reduction of *Bildung* to the "cultivation of the humanities," and by 1945 American intellectuals and scholars were celebrating Mann as the "re-creator and re-inspirer of the idea of humanity emanating from the 'spirit of the age of Goethe.'"[112] In 1944, just over a decade after debating Martin Heidegger in Davos on what it is to be a human and then fleeing the Nazi regime in 1933, the German philosopher Ernst Cassirer identified the same problem and offered roughly the same response in the text that introduced him to a new, American audience: his *Essay on Man*. "The real crisis of the problem of man," he wrote, manifested itself only after any legitimate authority by which humans could order their lives ceased to exist. But this crisis could be resolved with the knowledge that humans could order their own lives and liberate themselves through culture—the process of humankind's self-liberation through art, literature, religion, and even science.[113] American audiences welcomed Cassirer's claim, recalling Du Bois-Reymond's arguments for the limits of natural science, that in asserting an absolute monopoly of knowledge within the domain of matter, scientists had denied it "access, insight, or authority over the great aspect of totality of being, of genuine reality."[114] In 1952 Erich Auerbach, then teaching at Yale after having fled Germany in 1935 and living in Istanbul for a decade, lamented how "human life has become standardized" while also observing that modern scholarship, "the only system of thought left with universal validity," had "become our new mythology."[115] His response was to call for a reorientation of philology to the human. What bound many of these German émigrés in the United States together, in addition to their native language, was their desire for a humanistic knowledge that superseded the disciplinary forms into which they had been trained, for a new scholarship that nevertheless remained, like Nietzsche's gay science, *Wissenschaft*.

In the postwar United States, intellectuals, writers, and academics were just as receptive to such humanisms as were their counterparts in Europe. The proliferation of humanisms represented possibilities for mitigating the effects of what David Hollinger describes as the "absorption into the academic humanities of more and more of the nation's learned conversation" about literature, philosophy, art, and domains and questions considered largely outside the natural and physical sciences.[116] By 1960 many of those who had crafted a new form of literary, cultural, and political criticism in the small magazines of the 1930s, 1940s, and 1950s—such as the *Partisan Review*, the *Kenyon Review*, and the *Paris Review*—had become academics and were thus subject to the epistemic and ethical ideals of institutions that had been utterly transformed over the previous half century. During this extended postwar period, American academic culture, especially fields identified as part of the modern humanities, was carried by institutional inertia through a passage from "range to rigor," methodological ambiguity to clarity, synthetic sweep to analytical precision.[117] Yet that crucial practice of the humanities, its self-reckoning and reflections on the value of its own practice and sense of purpose, didn't evolve in the same way. The story of Pearce and Kahler talking past each other at Ohio State using similar key terms highlights the complex and, for some, maddening situation of the humanities in postwar American institutions. There the abstract discourses around conflicting imperatives and justifications (like Pearce's and Kahler's) often overlapped, conveying just how muddled the self-understanding of those purporting to defend the humanities was. This is what frustrated—indeed, infuriated—Kristeller. In these situations, the appeal to crisis was an expression of a desire to recover, return, and reinvent, and thus remember a calling whose echo had faded.

### THE POSTDISCIPLINED HUMANITIES

Despite its centripetal force and increasing monopoly over what counted as authoritative and expert knowledge, however, the research university never fully captured what the modern humanities claimed as their own: the faith and hope people placed in art, literature, and philosophy. People continued to read, write, and think about books and other cultural objects not only in relation to "professional desires" and according to disciplinary, academic ideals but also in settings where, for example, "undisciplinary and undisciplined" ways of reading flourished.[118] The persistence of reading practices not wholly determined by the disciplining power of professional humanities scholars—in institutional and social spaces parallel or adjacent to the established order of knowledge within universities—is not in itself surprising. Yet the rhetorical power and intellectual and affective force of the discourse of the modern humanities has often obscured these possibilities.

On June 23, 1954, a group of twenty middle managers from AT&T, all men, and their families celebrated the completion of a ten-month training program with a cake decorated with one candle and a message:

With Love and Kisses

to

"The Humans"

Class of 1954

As E. Digby Baltzell reported in a 1955 *Harper's* article, the men had just completed a course of study at AT&T's Institute for Humanistic Studies for Executives at the University of Pennsylvania, where they worked their way through a curriculum of courses in philosophy, literature, arts, and science in addition to a full schedule of guests lectures and museum outings.[119] Here the humanities were framed as a "bulwark," to use Dilthey's metaphor, against the purportedly narrow technical knowledge of middle managers in America's leading corporations. They were just the countervailing force "organization man" so desperately needed.[120] Like the general education projects before and contemporary with them, the AT&T program for executives sought to convey a common knowledge. The humanities stood in for a desire; the corporation, writes Timothy Aubry, considered the humanities an "antidote to social fragmentation and institutional specialization, promoting both a unified self of democratic values [and a] capacity among students for independent thought."[121]

AT&T's humanities institute was not the first program to bring businessmen and big books together. In 1947, the same year that he successfully introduced an almost entirely general education curriculum at the University of Chicago, Robert Hutchins, along with Mortimer Adler, founded the Great Books Foundation with the intention of spreading their faith in "great books" beyond the university. The foundation helped establish reading groups across the country, published inexpensive paperback editions, and in 1952 with Encyclopedia Britannica published *Great Books of the Western World*, a fifty-four-volume set containing 443 "great books." With a research staff of ninety graduate students and over seven years, Adler oversaw the production of the encyclopedia's first two volumes titled *A Syntopicon of Great Books of the Western World*. Part encyclopedia and part index, the *Syntopicon* had 102 chapters, each devoted to one "great idea," from "Angel" to "World," and consisting of an essay, outline, references, and additional reading suggestions. The references, over 162,000 in total, pointed to the particular volume and page number where readers could find and then join the "discussion" on any given subject. The *Syntopicon*, wrote Adler, was an "intellectual instrument" that not only allowed readers to participate in an ongoing discussion stretching across millennia; it also revealed the "internal structure" and unity of that "living organism" known as the "tradition of western thought."[122]

One of earliest initiates to Adler and Hutchins' great books scheme was Walter Paepcke, president of the Container Corporation of America and a University of Chicago trustee, who along with his wife Elizabeth, a connoisseur of European modernist art and design, attended a great books course taught by Hutchins in downtown Chicago for trustees, businessmen, and their wives. In 1947 Hutchins proposed that Paepcke sponsor a bicentennial celebration of the Goethe's birth. Paepcke agreed, and the Goethe Bicentennial Convocation and Music Festival was held for three weeks beginning on June 27, 1949, in Aspen, Colorado, then a small mining town perched at just under eight thousand feet in the Rocky Mountains, where he and his wife had just bought an old Victorian house. Encouraged by the event's success and its celebration of grand cosmopolitan ideas such as *Bildung*, world literature (*Weltliteratur*), humanity, and universal communication, Paepcke founded the Aspen Institute for Humanistic Studies in 1950. Within a year— and at the encouragement of media magnate Henry Luce—he decided to focus the institute's programs on American business, cultural, and government leaders and to establish what would become the centerpiece of its brand, the executive seminar. An alpine and more aristocratic version of the great books courses he attended in Chicago, the seminar became a retreat into the humanities but one designed to meld high-minded conversation around art, literature, and philosophy with the cultivation of common moral commitments among America's leading experts and decision makers. The Aspen Institute used the humanities to pursue a postwar liberal consensus and legitimate the melding of high culture and industrial capitalism.[123] By gathering the (mostly) men who managed managers, it also helped make the modern humanities a central element in the postwar administration and management of human well-being by experts and what C. Wright Mills in 1956 termed the "power elite."[124]

Although the immediate aims of these humanities-focused executive humanities seminars, reading groups, and institutes varied, they shared a common premise: undisciplined, unmediated encounters with certain books and ideas could transform everyone. Limiting access to universal ideas and reason itself to scholars and universities was an artificial and ultimately irrational effort to control a common gift. Yet efforts to democratize higher education and literary culture through the great books idea was undercut by the same premise that lent the idea its ostensible coherence. What made certain books great and others simply good (or irrelevant) was their capacity to bring both disciplined and undisciplined readers into the presence of a truth presumed to transcend space and time. Although Adler and other advocates of the great books idea sought to democratize access to truth, they had little interest in democratizing truth itself in regarding truth not as a transcendent reality but as the conflicted, endless product of democratic deliberation.

Whether in executive training programs, universities, or government agencies, in the midst of civilizational crisis the humanities were pictured as an urgent project for the continuity of humanism, human capacities, and human nature. Even in their postdisciplinary form, the modern humanities served a similar social function.

They represented a confrontation with the specters that have long haunted melancholy moderns — capitalism, technology, science, or whatever new force threatens to pervert the human. The modern humanities did so not only as part of the modern university but also alongside and tangential to it by adopting criticisms of scholarly specialization and research that dated back to the 1830s in Prussia, turn-of-the-century America, and postwar literary culture even as they took advantage of the fruits that same scholarship continued to share.[125]

After their high period from the 1930s to the 1960s, the humanities faced new challenges and opportunities: the increasing professionalization of criticism and American letters, the continued influx of federal funding to fields in the sciences and engineering, feminism, affirmative action, demographic change. After the post–World War II boom funded in part by the GI Bill and increased state support, postsecondary enrollment rates stabilized in the 1970s only to resume their "upward advance" in the 1980s and 1990s, reaching 65 percent of the population aged eighteen to twenty-one.[126] With the advent of Cold War with the Soviet Union and "globalized nationalism," the explicitly universal aspirations and earnest humanisms of the immediate postwar years largely disappointed.[127] But the humanities as institutionalized between 1930 and 1950 remained largely intact and served analogous institutional and social functions. Whereas they had been invoked immediately after World War II to defend universal values against the "mechanism, militarism, and mammonism" of the contemporary world, in the 1960s and into the 1970s their function was to provide a (distinctly American) moral and political check against the communism and technorationality of the Soviet Union as well as the tumult of postcolonial nationalisms.[128]

The arrival of poststructuralist theory in American universities in the 1970s, for example, didn't undo their institutional stability and organizing force. In some ways it solidified it by sharpening the already established divisions between the humanities and the sciences within universities and by reaffirming the modern categories its theorists (or as was more often the case, their American acolytes) sought to supersede. Even many of the key figures of late twentieth-century and early twenty-first-century "theory" framed their work in these same oppositional terms, pitting the utilitarian, technical, and vocational rationality of the sciences against the disinterested, liberal, and critical humanities. Michel Foucault understood his project as an enlightenment one—the critique of the limits of the human in order "to go beyond them," as if to liberate the human again and again.[129] Jacques Derrida invoked "the new Humanities," describing them as a philosophical discipline that allowed for an unconditional capacity for critique and juxtaposing them to "science and technology" that allowed for positivism, utility, and the perpetuation of given authority.[130] More recently, scholars have identified the "Anthropocene" as the ultimate challenge to the order of the humanities. But like his predecessors, historian Dipesh Chakrabarty frames what is perhaps humankind's and the planet's greatest current challenge—artificially induced climate change—as making "moral demands" on humans and ultimately reaffirms the humanities as the "domain for discussion" of moral issues. On the one hand, Chakrabarty suggests that the centuries-old separation "between our moral and animal (i.e. biological) lives" must be questioned, rightly recognizing that it has long buttressed the division between the humanities and the sciences. In this sense, he argues, climate change represents "a critical turning point" for the humanities. On the other hand, Chakrabarty insists that climate change demands abilities and capacities, such as empathy, that only "the humanities can foster."[131] The "new" humanities for the Anthropocene would, so it seems, not be all that new. They would seek to maintain the monopoly over moral concerns that characterized the modern humanities since the late nineteenth century. Their defenders would continue to insist on the humanities' "monopoly on meaning."[132] As Dilthey formulated it more than a century ago, only the modern humanities enable humans to understand their world, not merely to explain it.

Louis Menand has claimed that between 1970 and 1990 "the humanities experienced a revolution," expanding to include as part of research agendas and undergraduate curricula questions about the "significance of gender and racial difference" among other concerns.[133] But their defining characteristic—the dispositional crisis sensibility and reactive self-understanding—remained however much scholars across literature, philosophy, gender studies, and ethnic studies did to contribute to deep and important intellectual and institutional changes. The capture of these new forms of knowledge within the modern humanities helped introduce new communities of previously excluded scholars to American universities, but it also compelled many of these same scholars to account for themselves and their concerns in terms inherited from the modern humanities—their epistemic ideals, functionalist self-understanding, and crisis thinking. For decades, the humanities have arrogated to themselves critique and critical thinking, and thus they asserted a privileged capacity to demystify, unmask, reveal, and, ultimately, liberate the human from history, nature, or other humans. Whether as Judith Butler's high-theory posthumanism or Stephen Greenblatt's new historicist communion with the dead, the humanities have claimed sole possession of critique and cast themselves as custodians of human value.[134] In order to legitimize such claims and such a self-understanding, the modern humanities needed the "disenchantment of the world" and needed as well to hold the sciences responsible for this moral catastrophe. Only then could their defenders position themselves as the final guardians of meaning, value, and human being.

Similarly, the canon wars of the 1980s and 1990s reaffirmed the basic logic of the high period of the humanities. Amid the postwar demographic expansion of American universities, both multicultural critics and conservative defenders of the Western canon affirmed not only the value of the humanities but also their distinctly social functions—the battles would not have been as fierce if not for the broad agreement that our moral and democratic development depended on the result. In all these attempts to re-imagine the humanities, the "obligation," as Mark Greif puts it, to speak of the human remains, as does the institutional organization of any possible answer.[135] Meanwhile, the humanities live on even if the mid-twentieth-century attempts to establish them as the de facto core of common culture and liberal education dissolved into the cafeteria-style curricula of distri-bution requirements that were already becoming present in the 1960s.[136]

# Conclusion

Advocates of the humanities, from Adolph Diesterweg, Friedrich Nietzsche, and Matthew Arnold to Allan Bloom and Wendy Brown, have proven adept at identifying basic tensions between the instrumental logic governing modern societies and the noninstrumental openness that humanities scholarship and teaching have been thought to require. These advocates have been less energetic in reflecting on the discourse of crisis and decline they have participated in—particularly on its tensions and effects. Scholars have largely overlooked both the continuities in the talk of the modern humanities' decline and the extent to which the practices and very self-conception of the modern humanities emerged from and have sustained themselves through this crisis discourse in Germany and perhaps even more so in the United States. Crisis has not only been variously invoked to describe the plight of the humanities—crisis has also been the humanities' rationale.[1]

The persistence of this crisis discourse, then, should not be dismissed as "humanities hypochondria," to paraphrase David Bell, or as "Cassandraism," to quote Stefan Collini.[2] Talk of crisis was an integral feature of the modern humanities as they developed in Germany and, subsequently, in the United States. Such talk has been as crucial to the humanities' self-understanding and sense of purpose, as much a constitutive element, as the methods that scholars such as Rens Bod and James Turner have recently pointed to in their attempts to identify a coherent tradition of humanities scholarship that spans cultures and stretches across centuries.[3] We are not saying that this crisis discourse should be embraced or even accepted as necessary. But we do think that reckoning seriously with this discourse and its complexities is necessary to understanding the formation, evolution, and possible futures of the modern humanities.

The historian Daniel Rogers observes that crisis does not typically beget, as Jacob Burckhardt hoped it would in nineteenth-century Basel, new

ideas and ways of engaging with the world. In periods of crisis and transformation, people tend to "fall back on inherited and instinctive values in
an effort to cope."[4] A permanent crisis, then, can lead to a state of endless
repetition. To an important extent, this has been the case for the permanent crisis of the humanities. Despite the catastrophic loss of human life
and ways of living caused by world wars, genocide, and colonialism, the
discourse of the modern humanities as first propounded around 1900 in
Germany and then expanded in the United States has remained remarkably
stable. Turn-of-the-century thought experiments anticipating the advent of
the "not-natural-scientific disciplines" or the "humanities to come" began
with cultural critique and concluded with the modern humanities as the
much-needed solution. They also identified the ideals and sensibilities that
are said to distinguish the humanities to this day: a preference for qualitative reasoning over quantitative; suspicion of methodology; celebration of
interpretation; rejection of positivism; concern with the subject of knowledge, not just the object of knowledge; valuation of the particular over the
general.[5] Here, a sense of crisis helped transform disparate disciplines and
forms of knowledge into a cultural project now known as the modern humanities. But crisis discourse has also trapped self-identified humanities
scholars, such as ourselves, in inherited contradictions, oppositions, and
presumptions. It has also blinded humanities scholars to the paradoxical
relationships, competing goods, and varied ends that have characterized
the creation and transmission of knowledge for centuries and that the most
trenchant crisis thinking has frankly confronted.

First, crisis discourse has encouraged negative justifications and self-
conceptions of the modern humanities. As we have shown throughout this
book, many of the most significant attempts to define or defend the modern humanities have been not only oppositional but also defensive, pitting
them against various threats: the sciences, the Soviet Union, technology,
utility, the practical or vocational, authority, religion. Such thinking, of
course, has its own benefits, such as uncovering oppressive power structures or revealing the effects of ideas in this world. The very notion of the humanities that we work with today derives directly from it. But oppositional
thinking can also generate unhelpful distinctions that wipe away historical
traditions of learning and scholarship and the complex ways in which they
have always been wrapped up with the very things they only recently were
purported to oppose. Technical knowledge and skills, practical wisdom and
training, professional and vocational training, and the history of the sciences have long been important elements, for example, of any philological
and reading practices. The institutional division of episteme and techne
is one of the more deleterious consequences of the success of the modern

humanities, obscuring just how contingent and, ultimately, unstable the boundaries between forms of knowledge can be.[6] Similarly, religious practices and traditions, institutions, and communities have for centuries been deeply interwoven with humanist, philological, and scientific knowledge practices and traditions.

Second, crisis discourse obscures how difficult it can be to adapt older, largely Western humanist traditions to more contemporary, egalitarian, and democratic ends. These underlying tensions are especially important in light of the prominence of arguments about the unique capacity of the humanities to form democratic citizens.[7] In his trilogy on the history and future of American universities, Christopher Newfield consistently sought to recover an older concept of *Bildung* for the sake of mass education, assuming that contemporary forms of democracy and *Bildung* are compatible, with the latter powerfully reinforcing the former. Describing a lecture he delivered in 2019, he wrote, "I noted that none of these working-class students at working-class colleges mentioned that pecuniary metric du jour, upward mobility. They focused on *Bildung*, a word nobody used. It is mass *Bildung*: arguably the core higher ed goal is *Bildung* for all."[8] Worried not simply about irrelevance or marginalization but rather about budgetary oblivion, progressive defenders of the humanities have been eager to avoid implying that there is any significant tension between the humanities' promise of self-development and democratic values. But there are in fact deep and persistent tensions, incompatibilities even, between *Bildung* and democracy, and progressive defenders of liberal education should face them honestly rather than dismiss them as the stock response of conservative reactionaries and elitists.

For Wilhelm von Humboldt and the fellow German neo-humanists who made *Bildung* a basic aim of university study, *Bildung* was never simply self-development (despite what bad translations have suggested). It always implied a *Bild*, an image beyond the self to which a person submitted himself. No person could simply form himself. Such a process required authoritative texts, images, models, traditions, and practices in terms of which one was formed. It presupposed models—*Vorbilder*—that could be trusted and that were worthy of critical engagement. The process of formation was both active and passive. Liberation required subordination and, to use one of Humboldt's key terms, *restriction*.

The institutionalization of *Bildung* at German universities was a project that drew on democratic thinking about the self in basic ways. Writing at the beginning of the nineteenth century, Humboldt stressed that anyone could, theoretically, unfold himself to his "full humanity" through humanist education. But it was clear to him and his contemporaries that most people—that is, most young men—would have neither the opportunity nor the mettle to succeed. Nor could the *Bildung*-fostering university, as Humboldt imagined it, accommodate masses of students. The humanist education envisioned by Humboldt—and by centuries of humanist learning—was based on intimate practices of intellectual and moral apprenticeship. In the German research university, these practices were adopted and adapted in the necessarily exclusive and intimate setting of the research seminar. A higher freedom—as manifested by "the autonomous individual or personality," as he put it—was certainly the goal, but Humboldt, a master at integrating opposing programs (e.g., the social utility and the autonomy of the research university), thought it could be achieved only through the cultivation of ideals and virtues that did not necessarily accord with democratic values. In this tradition, the ideal scholar was both critical of and awed by intellectual traditions that had preceded him. While Humboldt wanted the university to produce independent minds, he thought that *Bildung* was not just a sharpening and disciplining of an individual's unique mental powers. Indeed, the character of the person who would ultimately emerge from the process was never certain. *Bildung*, as Hegel wrote, was an "ordeal." It demanded supreme commitment and entailed existential risk, both for the person undergoing it and the community responsible for overseeing it. There was, for Hegel and Humboldt alike, a necessary duration to the formation of the self. *Bildung* could—should—have its joyful moments, but it could not be had without intense struggle and certainly not on the quick.

As we discussed in chapter 3, Friedrich Nietzsche delivered a scathing rebuke of Prussia's attempts to democratize Humboldt's humanist education system, and not just on antiegalitarian grounds. He claimed that mass *Bildung* was an oxymoron that would routinize *Bildung* and sacrifice great human potential in order serve the immediate interests of a state in need of highly skilled but tractable citizens. The émigré German philosopher Hannah Arendt argued something similar in her 1958 essay "The Crisis in Education." "Exactly for the sake of what is new and revolutionary in every child," she wrote, "education must be conservative." Instead of "instructing in the art of living," which Arendt saw as the misguided aim of her American colleagues, teachers of the humanities should lead young minds to a formative awareness of their place in the "old world" in which they find themselves, a journey requiring rigorous learning about that world.[9] Especially in the modern world, an education that forgoes "either authority or tradition" does its students a grave disservice, Arendt wrote. Similarly, Lionel Trilling maintained that the German ideal of *Bildung* entailed "strict sanctions and required submission."[10] It signified fashioning, forming, and cultivating, but also being fashioned, formed, and cultivated. Writing on the state of liberal education in the 1970s, Trilling had come to think that what stood in the way of *Bildung* in the United States—and he used the German term—was not only a native attachment to autonomy but also an unwilling-ness to commit to just one self and its development. Americans, he claimed, wanted to have multiple selves and the attendant feelings of possibility.

For Newfield, *Bildung* of the transformative kind seems to happen merely through the teaching of critical analytical skills—in which the practical and the liberal attain proximity—a process that neatly aligns with democratic values of autonomy, self-expression, and individual creativity and with the postwar golden age of American public higher education.[11] But if Hum-boldt, Nietzsche, and Arendt are right, there are other virtues necessary for *Bildung*: humility and a willingness to be formed by something greater than the self. These virtues can seem not just antiquated but authoritarian as well in an American culture that celebrates individualism, self-reliance, and autonomy. The promise of democracy certainly does not obviate the possi-bility of drawing distinctions and exercising judgment. Yet those who argue that *Bildung* can be greatly scaled up and that it is essentially compatible with democracy should recognize that they are working against the moral and philosophical grain of the tradition they are appropriating for their own very different vision of the humanities.

There is another, related problem with attempts to rehabilitate *Bildung* for contemporary purposes. A central feature of this tradition, as adopted and adapted from Hegel to Du Bois-Reymond and the young Benjamin to Habermas, was the belief that reason and its others (feeling, irrationality, myth, religion) would be reconciled through an intellectual, moral, and so-cial learning process (or *Bildung*). Although participants in this tradition ar-gued about the particular forms and variations this historical process would assume, they all presumed that its ultimate outcome would be a distinctly and identifiably European or Western modernity. This developmental his-torical account legitimated the norms, ideals, and practices for which they argued, including the necessity of the modern humanities. Over the course of the nineteenth century, the research university and disciplinary knowl-edge were cast, on both sides of the Atlantic, as primary agents of a univer-sal learning process. It is unclear to us how a coherent and fruitful concept of *Bildung* can be decoupled from this inheritance in which one form of hu-man being and institutional life are consistently presumed to be necessary and universal.

Finally, the crisis discourse in the humanities has promoted overpromis-ing—the framing of the modern humanities as the redemptive solution to a larger crisis routinely referred to as modernity. In the confrontation with the loss of meaning, the degradation of human being, even existential threats to the continuation of life on earth, the scholarly way of life to which Max Weber confessed can seem small minded, quietist, and, well, less than fully human. In his 1983 book *The World, the Text, and the Critic*, the literary scholar Edward Said laments the "specialization" and "division of intellectual labor" endemic to contemporary literary criticism and condemns the "pernicious effect" of the "cult of professional expertise" with its jargon-ridden theory, obsession with method, and aloofness from the world. As an antidote to pedantic expertise, Said proposes a "secular criticism" capable of reintegrating world, text, and critic.[12] It would be "skeptical," "reflectively open to its own failings," and ultimately "oppositional . . . reducible neither to a doctrine nor to a political position on a particular question, and if it is to be in the world and self-aware simultaneously, then its identity is its difference from other cultural activities." Said's "secular criticism" reproduces many of the basic features of the discourse of permanent crisis pervading the modern humanities: a cultural critique expressing a general unease with expertise, method, and the division of labor; a negative, defensive self-definition; a claim to continuity and tradition; a desire not to "lose touch" with life as lived.[13] Its most salient component, however, is the messianic purpose Said envisions for it. Moving from an account of how a secular scholar ought to read a text to, as Michael Allan describes it, one of the "consciousness necessary" to be recognized as a legitimate and, thus, secular scholar,[14] Said writes that the "secular critical consciousness" is "life-enhancing and constitutively opposed to every form of tyranny, domination, and abuse; its social goals are noncoercive knowledge produced in the interests of freedom."[15] The "secular," "noncoercive" humanities will set us free if only we allow them to transform us first.

How exactly would a "secular" humanities accomplish this liberation? Said casts Erich Auerbach, a German philologist whose essay "Philology of World Literature" was translated by Said and his wife, Maire Said, in 1969, as the exemplary "secular" scholar. In his celebrated work *Mimesis: Representations of Reality in Western Literature* (1946), which he wrote during World War II while in exile in Istanbul, Auerbach claims that he could not have written the book had he not left Germany. What Auerbach means, writes Said, is that in exile he lost "the authentic presence of the culture, as symbolized materially by libraries, research institutes, other books and scholars," and became "an outcast from sense, nation, and milieu."[16] But Auerbach's cultural disorientation also freed him from "that grid of research techniques and ethics" that business as usual would have imposed.[17] By liberating Auerbach from the norms of university-based scholarship, exile made *Mimesis* an undisciplined or even supradisciplinary book. "Secular criticism," Said suggests, would reproduce Auerbach's experience by resisting and opposing any such cultural impositions. Secular criticism or the secular humanities would liberate without the coercive force of discipline, expertise, method, and technique. The properly "secular" scholar can relate autonomously and immediately to a text and the world and is thus equipped to pursue the work of liberating the mind.

Said criticizes the "Eurocentric" character of canons and curricula of literature departments and the "Eurocentric humanities" generally, but he does not do the same with certain other of his categories, such as "literature," "the humanities," "the humanist," and "the humanistic scholar." And throughout "Secular Criticism," the university remains almost unmentioned. Secular criticism seems to have no particular culture, no requisite *religio* of its own. Said's primary concern is to contest which texts are included and excluded—represented—in these fixed categories and within that purportedly stable institution known as the university. In the closing chapter of *The World, the Text, and the Critic*, "Religious Criticism," Said contrasts "secular criticism" with "religion," "culture," and "Orientalism," Allan observes.[18] Each of these latter three phenomena is, for Said, "an agent of closure, shutting off human investigation, criticism, and effort in deference to the authority of the more-than-human, the supernatural, the other-worldly."[19] Said ultimately defines his secular humanities, then, not against the natural sciences, technology, or capitalism but against religion and cultural imperialism. He transforms historically theological and religious questions into questions for the humanities. When practiced well, the humanities push back against religion rather than occupy the space created by its absence.

In this way, Said's "secular" criticism claims to accomplish what the modern humanities have been said to do for over a century now—to operate as a moral force in the face of grave challenges. Whether in the form of Said's "secular criticism," Dilthey's *Geisteswissenschaften*, or Felix Schelling's "humanities to come," the modern humanities have consistently been presented as the locus of moral education and meaning in higher education.

In *Permanent Crisis* we have been concerned with *the humanities* as a key discursive element in broad but historically bounded intellectual, moral, political, and social projects. *The modern humanities* have stood in for a shared set of sensibilities, narratives, and ends and the attempt to institutionalize them in colleges and universities. From this we do not conclude that recent attempts to stretch their history over centuries and across cultures are necessarily misguided or wrong. But we do think that the humanities as they are conceived of today are both more recent and more particular than the regular invocations of *the human* or humanism made on their behalf or the attempts to identify examples of *humanistic* scholarship across cultures and time might suggest. They continue to bear the marks of their relatively few and recent places of origin. The formation of the modern humanities and their underlying sensibilities and presuppositions about the history and ends of knowledge coincides with the rise of the modern research university in Germany and the United States. Like the institution from which they emerged, the modern humanities arose as an effect of a particular time and world — not as an effect of history, reason itself, or a self-evident and stable humanism.

What lends the modern humanities their universal or, at least, global force is not the human or some grand historical process; it is the more contingent and more recent research university and disciplinary knowledge. Echoing the melancholy mandarins from Diesterweg and Nietzsche to Bloom and William Deresiewicz, Said's lament about "specialization" and "expertise" and their alienating effects is an expression of disappointment with what has (again) become of the mandarins' project: its capture by a bureaucratic machine called the modern university. This is the disenchanted world of Said's "secular" humanities, one bound in space and time and, more particularly, bound to an institution. "The notorious unevenness and multiplicity of the secular, the modern, and the West," writes Tomoko Masuzawa, "presents an intriguing contrast with the relatively even and uniform spread of the modern university" from nineteenth-century Germany to the United States and throughout the world today.[20] Despite the important local differences and adaptations to be found in universities from Berlin to Baltimore to Beijing, the university as reinvented in late nineteenth-century Germany and the United States of the early twentieth century has been adopted and adapted around the world. The ubiquitous power of the modern research university to shape sensibilities and sustain norms is nowhere more evident than in disavowals such as Said's, which have always accompanied the exercise of this power.

"Only in the West does disciplinary, specialized knowledge exist at the stage of development that is today recognized as legitimate" wrote Max Weber in 1919. For Weber, this observation did not mean that bureaucracy, empirical observation, mathematics, medicine, or science only existed in or at higher levels in Western cultures. These and myriad other forms of rational knowledge had long flourished elsewhere, especially, he thought, in China, India, and Egypt. For almost a decade he had been studying these cultures of knowledge while writing a sociology of five world religions — Buddhism, Christianity, Confucianism, Judaism, Hinduism — as "systems for the regulation of life." Each system represented distinct cultures of calculation and rationalization replete with their own "schools of higher learning" in which young people were inculcated into a particular culture's highest practices, ideals, and virtues. What distinguished Western, and especially German, cultures of knowledge and rationality, he wrote, was the degree to which "professionalization and specialization have attained such a culturally dominant meaning"; they had become "the cornerstone" of both the economy and the state. Weber's word for this distinct culture and its dominant ethic was *capitalism*—"the most fateful power of our modern life."[21]

Like Weber, we think that the modern research university epitomizes this ethic, especially the value it accords to professionalization and specialization as unrivaled forms of authority and legitimacy. It does so by joining the objective, material forms of knowledge (printed books, instruments, laboratories) with the subjective development of people. The research university creates knowledge and forms people, sustaining a distinct set of sensibilities, categories, practices, and virtues. It cultivates an ethos in those who have been disciplined into it. Indeed, the humanities embody the research university as much as the sciences.

Yet the terms under which the epistemic and ethical organization of the modern research university was settled—buttressed and justified, as we detailed in the preceding chapters, with elaborate histories, epistemologies, and institutional politics—ensured that its conflicts over ends and values would primarily be the burden of the humanities: therapeutic value versus epistemic value; liberal value versus utility and practical value; moral formation versus method; knowledge versus information. The natural and physical sciences largely excused themselves from questions of moral concern and formation, ideals of liberal education, and any bad conscience about their utility to industry and the state. What Weber called the spirit of capitalism transformed universities and intellectual life most profoundly not by introducing an ethic of greed and endless striving for knowledge, prestige, or profit but rather by turning moral interest and reflection into a particular, specialized function called the modern humanities.

How might we break out of this tiresome rehearsal of predetermined roles? At the conclusion of a story recounting versions of the same conflict, it might seem, well, repetitive to look for answers in two texts we have already discussed and whose tone has long been associated with a grim, even demoralizing resignation. But that it is what we propose to do by returning to Weber's *Scholarship as Vocation*.

As we noted in chapter 6, after the publication of Weber's vocation lectures in 1919, Germany's cultured elite largely discounted his vision of politics and scholarship as a bleak liberalism, a hopeless capitulation to modernity dressed up to look like a heroic realism or a soulless technical rationality. In the following decades, the Max Weber constructed on both sides of the Atlantic—from Talcott Parsons's embrace of Weber as the methodologically rigorous, value-neutral ur-sociologist to Max Horkheimer's rejection of the same—matched the image first crafted by his Weimar critics. In America, as in Germany, Weber was portrayed as the austere advocate of dispassionate, disinterested scholarship utterly lacking in what German intellectuals called "engagement." Even Weber's more sympathetic readers—such as Hans Gerth and C. Wright Mills, who authored the first widely available English translations of the vocation lectures—did not consider the notion of value freedom a statement of Weber's methodological commitments; rather, they considered it an attempt to salvage traditional and now-imperiled liberal goods, such as academic freedom.

There is certainly something to the idea that with his concept of value freedom, Weber sought to preserve endangered freedoms—more on that below. But all of these readings fall short, or, rather, fail to recognize what we contend is a path out of the permanent crisis of the humanities, a path that Weber could only point to. In saying this, we don't mean to suggest that Weber figured out how to overcome the material and cultural conditions that continue to fuel crisis talk and are likely to intensify as colleges and universities navigate the effects of a global pandemic and economic crisis. We also don't mean to suggest that the path we describe is the only way out of a tradition of crisis talk that played a productive part in the initial development of the modern humanities in Germany and the United States but has long since lost its generative force. Such talk is freighted with defensiveness and overpromising and is burdened with blind spots that are, as we have shown, political, historical, epistemological, and, finally, ethical. The crisis of the humanities is, impossibly, always new, but also always the same. Its permanence has normalized ideas that have undermined the credibility of scholars and universities and the most charismatic believers in the humanities' false prophets. It is an all too common vanity to assume that universities and the academic humanities, in particular, have a near monopoly on intellectual work.

Over the course of the last century, advocates of the humanities have clung to crisis rhetoric, engaging in overpromising that became more extreme as the moral scaffolding and cultural authority on which it based its claims of soul building and secular transformation receded into the past. In so doing, these advocates have largely avoided a basic question that scholars who urge the decolonization of particular disciplines and the university in general have forcefully and justifiably insisted on: How do the modern humanities make certain concepts and institutional forms seem necessary and universal, thereby obscuring their colonial legacies and reinforcing an uncritical use of inherited concepts?[22] Or, to put the question in terms of our argument in the present volume, *How do the modern humanities reinforce what turns out to be an inherited and limited set of positions and conflicts whose value and function have already been determined by the permanent crisis of the humanities?*

Those who read Weber in the standard ways laid out above misunderstand the tension at the center of the vocation lectures: the double bind that is both the burden and the possibility of living in a disenchanted world. In a world permeated with values and moral claims, intellectual work is of paramount importance. The purpose of intellectual work is to help make possible meaningful forms of life for this world.

Paradoxically, a form of moral asceticism was needed to protect the particular moral education that could sustain the scholar's calling within the modern university. One of Weber's names for this asceticism was "value freedom." Often translated as "value neutrality," the term has since Weber's day been used, mistakenly in our view, as evidence that he was an epistemologically naive positivist. Yet Weber dismissed the notion that a scholar could ever simply let the facts speak for themselves or muster complete disinterest. Scholarship required particular ideals, values, and virtues. In fact, the values that Weber identified as essential for scholarship turn out to resemble the ones that today's advocates of moral education tend to foreground as a counterpoise to research training: inclusiveness, intellectual integrity, courage, and a principled commitment to intellectual and value pluralism, among others.

In Weber's view, universities should impart those values, which are at once scholarly and moral. He thought universities were uniquely well equipped to form students into mature, independent, self-reflective subjects with "the capacity to think clearly and 'know what one wants.'"[23] As we suggested at the end of chapter 2, universities shouldn't shy away from values; rather, they should induce students to reflect conscientiously on the values they presume to be their own. They should teach students to understand how their own moral claims and values will inevitably conflict with those of others, and that acting in accord with their values will have specific social consequences. For this teaching to happen in a scholarly way, students and university faculty alike need "value freedom." As Weber understood it, value freedom had the effect of an imperative to take responsibility for one's freedom and, thus, one's own ultimate commitments and values. Neither specialized scholarship nor the modern, disciplinary university could ground and sustain one's highest ideals and loves. The "ideals" students "should serve," "the gods he should bow before," are for Weber ultimately a matter students must figure out for themselves and should come down to where their passions lie.[24] Even—indeed, especially—the choice to follow the scholarly calling and adopt its ideals and values can't be justified through scholarly deliberation alone. A measure of faith is necessary.

As the twentieth century began, Weber was trying to figure out how politicians and scholars should understand their institutions and lives together in light of their responsibility to a future that seemed highly uncertain. A hundred years later, the questions he faced are still with us. Our own liberal institutions and democracies have proven not to be as robust as many had presumed, with ascendant far-right movements, intensifying inequality, endless war, and feckless cultural and political elites undermining confidence in the inevitability of liberal democracy. And now, as we write this conclusion, a global pandemic spreads not only disease and death but epistemic and existential uncertainty among even the most stable of societies. The invisible hand of history, the market, or reason have failed to guide us to universal health, peace, and prosperity. To read Weber's vocation lectures today is to be reminded of the moral urgency of sober, unglamorous, disciplined thinking in times of crisis. It is to be reminded, as Weber put it, that ethics can be and often are "used in morally disastrous ways" in both the academic and political spheres, ways that preclude an honest and responsible reckoning with the world in which we find ourselves.

In *Scholarship as Vocation*, Weber does not suggest, much less promise, that the conditions of intellectual life all too familiar to his Munich audience in 1917 can be radically improved. Whereas critics have often interpreted Weber's apparent disinclination to do so to be an expression of his resignation, we see a more future-oriented and hopeful call for productive unburdening that is as appropriate in 2021 as it was in 1917, possibly more so. Weber's ultimate concern was not with the restoration of a declining institution or the restoration of a particular form of cultural authority. He was not interested in recovering a mythical university or a form of knowledge so bound up with a particular cultured class and set of self-identified intellectuals. Weber's ultimate concern, rather, was with the conditions of intellectual life and the possibility of trustworthy knowledge. He wanted to understand and help create the conditions under which scholarship, education, and intellectual work more generally could be protected from real threats and flourish, one of the most important of these threats being the unreflective responses they elicited from scholars—their crisis talk. This is our desire as well.

# Acknowledgments

The collaborative aspect of this book extends well beyond the fact of its co-authorship. At every turn, and there were many of them, we received vital feedback and support from fellow humanities scholars. Our goal here isn't to determine whether or not the humanities are in crisis, but we will say that we are fortunate to have so many brilliant and generous colleagues and to be working at a time when there is so little methodological sectarianism in the humanities and so much open-minded exchange.

*Permanent Crisis* benefited just as much from the skill, insight, and psychological acumen of editors. We first presented some of the thinking at the center of the book in essays published in the *Hedgehog Review*, where B. D. McClay, Leann Davis Alspaugh, and Jay Tolson helped us craft our initial intuitions into more coherent ideas. We also drew on our thinking for the book in writing the introductions for two separate volumes in the New York Review Books Classics Series (*Anti-Education* and *Charisma and Disenchantment: The Vocation Lectures*), and we are very glad to have had the opportunity to work with Edwin Frank, the series editor, who combines a poet's sense of rhythm and verbal nuance with a philosopher's devotion to logic and rigor. Elizabeth Branch Dyson, our editor at the University of Chicago Press, was part of this project from the beginning, helping us frame and reframe it, and then reframe it again. It is no exaggeration to say that if it weren't for her encouragement and insight, there would be no *Permanent Crisis*. We thank Steve LaRue and Vince Ercolano for making our prose clearer, and Mollie McFee and Christine Schwab for making the journey through the production process smooth and pleasant.

# Notes

INTRODUCTION

1. See Reinhart Koselleck, "Krise," in *Geschichtliche Grundbegriffe: Historisches Lexikon zur politisch-sozialen Sprache in Deutschland*, ed. Otto Brunner, Werner Conze, and Reinhart Koselleck (Stuttgart: Kotta, 1982), 3:617–50; Reinhart Koselleck and Michaela W. Richter, *Journal of the History of Ideas* 67, no. 2 (April 2006): 357–400.

2. Karl Marx, "Address to the Communist League, 1850," in *Two Speeches by Karl Marx* (Vancouver: Historical Research Bureau, 1923), 5.

3. Jacob Burckhardt, *Weltgeschichtliche Betrachtungen* (Berlin: W. Spemann, 1905), 192.

4. Benjamin Schmidt, "The Humanities Are in Crisis," *Atlantic*, August 23, 2018.

5. Stefan Collini, *Speaking of Universities* (London: Verso, 2017), 1–25.

6. Collini, *Speaking of Universities*, 87.

7. Kyla Wazana Tompkins, "Are You Okay Tobe White: Some Comments on the 'Race' Keyword at the MLA Plenary Session for the Literature of People of Color," *Professor Tompkins Is Out of Order* (blog), January 14, 2020, https://outoforder.sub stack.com/p/are-you-okay-tobe-white. On crisis consensus, see Abigail Boggs and Nick Mitchell, "Critical University Studies and the Crisis Consensus," *Feminist Studies* 44, no. 2 (2018): 436.

8. "Other disciplines offer knowledge about things, the humanities offer knowledge about human beings." Geoffrey Harpham, *The Humanities and the Dream of America* (Chicago: University of Chicago Press, 2011), 17.

9. *The Report of the Commission on the Humanities* (1964) describes the humanities as useful to the nation and individuals in need of marketable skills. See https://publications.acls.org/NEH/Report-of-the-Commission-on-the-Humanities-1964.pdf. The Commission on the Humanities, sponsored by the Rockefeller Foundation and established in 1978, wrote *The Humanities in American Life* (1980), extolling the "different skills" the humanities convey. Commission on the Humanities, *The Humanities in American Life* (Berkeley: University of California Press, 1980). The American Academy of Arts and Sciences, *The Heart of the Matter* (Cambridge, MA: American Academy of Arts and Sciences, 2013), plainly states that the humanities are needed to create "an adaptable and creative workforce" (https://www.humani tiescommission.org/_pdf/hss_report.pdf).

10. See, for example, Talbot Brewer, "The Coup That Failed: How the Near-

Sacking of a University President Exposed the Fault Lines of American Higher Education," *Hedgehog Review* 16, no. 2 (2014), https://hedgehogreview.com/issues/mind ing-our-minds/articles/the-coup-that-failed-how-the-near-sacking-of-a-university -president-exposed-the-fault-lines-of-ameri.

11. See Helen Small, *The Value of the Humanities* (Oxford: Oxford University Press, 2013), 29; Eric Hayot, "What Happens to Literature if People Are Artworks?" *New Literary History* 48, no. 3 (2017): 460.

12. Wilhelm Dilthey, *Wilhelm Dilthey Gesammelte Schriften* [*WDGS*], 26 vols. (Stuttgart: B. G. Teubner, 1961–1966), 1:6.

13. Helge Jordheim, "Dealing with Contingency: Progress, Crisis, and the Role of the Humanities" (unpublished lecture), Beirut, September 2019.

14. This was the premise of the First International Conference on the History of the Humanities, held October 23–25, 2008, University of Amsterdam Doelenzaal, Singel 425, Amsterdam, http://www.historyofhumanities.org/wp-content/uploads /2015/07/mohamsterdam2008.pdf. See also Rens Bod, *A New History of the Humanities: The Search for Principles and Patterns from Antiquity to the Present* (Oxford: Oxford University Press, 2014).

15. See Juliette A. Groenland, "Humanism in the Classroom," in *The Making of the Humanities*, ed. Rens Bod, Jaap Maat, and Thijs Weststeijn (Amsterdam: Amsterdam University Press, 2010), 1:199–229; Ian Hunter, "The Mythos, Ethos, and Pathos of the Humanities," *History of European Ideas* 40, no. 1 (2014): 11–36.

16. Jacob Burckhardt, *The Civilization of the Renaissance in Italy*, trans. S. G. C. Middlemore (New York: Macmillan, 1904), 300.

17. See Brian Stock, *Ethics through Literature: Ascetic and Aesthetic Reading in Western Culture* (Lebanon, NH: University Press of New England, 2007), 26–29. For a more detailed account of the history of reading suggested in this and the following paragraphs, see Chad Wellmon, "Sacred Reading from Augustine to the Digital Humanists," *Hedgehog Review* 17, no. 2 (Fall 2015): 70–84.

18. Francesco Petrarca, *Letters from Petrarch*, trans. Morris Bishop (Bloomington: Indiana University Press, 1966), 49.

19. Ibid., 51.

20. Christopher S. Celenza, *Petrarch: Everywhere a Wanderer* (London: Reaktion Books, 2017), 205.

21. Celenza, *Petrarch*, 199, 205.

22. Paul F. Grendler, *The Universities of the Italian Renaissance* (Baltimore: Johns Hopkins University Press, 2004), 205; Celenza, *Petrarch*, 205.

23. Francesco Petrarca, "On His Own Ignorance and That of Many Others," in *The Renaissance Philosophy of Man*, trans. Hans Nachod, ed. Ernst Cassirer, Paul Oskar Kristeller, and John Randall Jr. (Chicago: University of Chicago Press, 1956), 72.

24. Ian F. McNeely and Lisa Wolverton, *Reinventing Knowledge: From Alexandria to the Internet* (New York: W. W. Norton, 2008), 79.

25. Alex J. Novikoff, *The Medieval Culture of Disputation: Pedagogy, Practice, and Performance* (Philadelphia: University of Pennsylvania Press, 2013).

26. For a detailed account of the university from 1200 to 1800, see William Clark, *Academic Charisma and the Origins of the Research University* (Chicago: University of Chicago Press, 2006), here 34–38.

27. Christopher S. Celenza, *The Intellectual World of the Italian Renaissance: Language, Philosophy, and the Search for Meaning* (Cambridge: Cambridge University Press, 2018), 94.

28. Salutati, *Epistolario*, quoted in Celenza, *Intellectual World*, 55, 57.

29. Walter Rüegg, "Das Aufkommen des Humanismus," in *Geschichte der Universität Europa*, ed. Walter Rüegg (Munich: C. H. Beck, 1993), 1:394.

30. Paul Oskar Kristeller, "Humanism and Scholasticism," in *Renaissance Thought and Its Sources*, ed. Michael Mooney (New York: Columbia University Press, 1979), 85–105, 99; see also Grendler, *Universities of the Italian Renaissance*, 209.

31. Augusto Campana, "The Origin of the Word 'Humanist,'" *Journal of the Warburg and Courtauld Institutes* 9 (1946): 61.

32. Martha Nussbaum, *Not for Profit: Why Democracy Needs the Humanities* (Princeton, NJ: Princeton University Press, 2010), 55. Gayatri Chakravorty Spivak, "Critical Intimacy: An Interview with Gayatri Chakravorty Spivak," interview by Steve Paulson, *Los Angeles Review of Books*, July 29, 2016, https://lareviewofbooks.org/article/critical-intimacy-interview-gayatri-chakravorty-spivak.

33. On the variety of uses to which ancient knowledge was put in the Renaissance, see Gerhard Oestreich, "Die antike Literatur als Vorbild der praktischen Wissenschaften im 16. und 17. Jahrhundert," in *Classical Influences on European Cultures A.D. 500–1500*, ed. R. R. Bolgar (Cambridge: Cambridge University Press, 1971), 315–24.

34. Leonardo Bruni, "The Study of Literature," in *Humanist Educational Treatises*, ed. and trans. Craig W. Kallendorf (Cambridge, MA: Harvard University Press, 2002), 103.

35. Kristeller, "Humanism and Scholasticism," 22.

36. See Notker Hammerstein, *Bildung und Wissenschaft vom 15. bis 17. Jahrhundert* (Munich: Oldenbourg, 2010), 103. For a more recent assessments of Kristeller's basic definition, see, for example, Christopher S. Celenza, "Humanism and the Classical Tradition," *Annali d'italianistica* 26 (2008): 25–44, and Douglas Biow, *Doctors, Ambassadors, Secretaries: Humanism and the Professions in Renaissance Italy* (Chicago: University of Chicago Press, 2002).

37. Kristeller, "Humanism and Scholasticism," 89.

38. James Hankins, "Two Twentieth-Century Interpreters of Humanism: Eugenio Garin and Paul Oskar Kristeller," *Comparative Criticism* 23 (2001): 4.

39. Anthony Grafton and Lisa Jardine, *From Humanism to the Humanities: Education and the Liberal Arts in Fifteenth and Sixteenth-Century Europe* (Cambridge, MA: Harvard University Press, 1986), 68–71.

40. See Brian P. Copenhaver and Lodi Nauta, introduction to *Lorenzo Valla: Dialectical Disputations* (Cambridge, MA: Harvard University Press, 2012), 1:xv–xvii.

41. Lorenzo Valla, *Elegances*, quoted in Celenza, *Intellectual World*, 184.

42. Grafton and Jardine, *From Humanism to the Humanities*, 124.

43. See Grafton and Jardine, *From Humanism to the Humanities*.

44. Walter J. Ong, *Ramus: Method and the Decay of Dialogue* (Cambridge, MA: Harvard University Press, 1983), 313.

45. Anthony Grafton, *Defenders of the Text: The Traditions of Scholarship in an Age of Science, 1450–1800* (Cambridge, MA: Harvard University Press, 1991), 8.

46. See Chad Wellmon, *Organizing Enlightenment: Information Overload and the*

*Invention of the Modern Research University* (Baltimore: Johns Hopkins University Press, 2015), 45–76.

47. Hunter, "The Mythos, Ethos, and Pathos of the Humanities," 16.

48. Ibid., 14.

49. *Oxford English Dictionary*, s.v. "humanity," sec. 2a, "Caxton tr. J. de Voragine Golden Legende 121 a/2. He floured in double science . . . that is to saye dyuynyte and humanyte." For this example and for the broader account, we are indebted to Ann Blair, "Disciplinary Distinctions before the 'Two Cultures,'" *European Legacy* 13, no. 5 (2008): 577–88.

50. Erasmus, "On the Method of Study," in *Collected Works of Erasmus*, ed. Craig R. Thompson, *Literary and Educational Writings 2* (Toronto: University of Toronto Press, 1978), 24:683. See Rüegg, "Das Aufkommen des Humanismus," 392; Grafton and Jardine, *From Humanism to the Humanities*, 147–49.

51. Mary J. Caruthers, *The Book of Memory: A Study of Memory in Medieval Culture* (Cambridge: Cambridge University Press, 1990), 156. Augustine, *On Christian Doctrine* (Oxford: Oxford University Press, 1997), 9. See Jean Leclercq, *The Love of Learning and the Desire for God: A Study of Monastic Culture* (New York: Fordham University Press, 1982).

52. Stock, *Ethics through Literature*, 39.

53. David Lines, "Humanism and Italian Universities," in *Humanism and Creativity: Essays in Honor of Ronald G. Witt*, ed. Christopher S. Celenza and Kenneth Gouwens (Leiden: Brill, 2006), 338–39; Grendler, *Universities of the Italian Renaissance*, 229.

54. Walter Rüegg, "Themen, Probleme, Erkenntnisse," in *Von der Reformation bis zur Französischen Revolution (1500–1800)*, Geschichte der Universität in Europa 2, ed. Walter Rüegg (Munich: C. H. Beck, 1993): 50; Grendler, *Universities of the Italian Renaissance*, 229–36. For a different but historically parallel account of the institutionalization of the *studia humanitatis* by sixteenth-century Jesuits, see John W. O'Malley, *The First Jesuits* (Cambridge, MA: Harvard University Press, 1993).

55. On this gap, see Robert Black, *Humanism and Education in Medieval and Renaissance Italy: Tradition and Innovation in Latin Schools from the Twelfth to the Fifteenth Century* (Cambridge: Cambridge University Press, 2001).

56. Grendler, *Universities of the Italian Renaissance*, 248.

57. Clark, *Academic Charisma*, 34–43.

58. Franz Eulenburg, *Die Frequenz der deutschen Universitäten von ihrer Gründung bis zur Gegenwart* (Leipzig: Teubner, 1904), 205, 309–14; Peter A. Vandermeersch, "Die Universitätslehrer," in *Von der Reformation zur Französischen Revolution (1500–1800)*, Geschichte der Universität Europa 2 (Munich: C. H. Beck, 1993), 199.

59. *Grosses vollständiges Lexicon aller Wissenschaften und Künste* (Leipzig and Halle: Zedler, 1739), 13:1155–56.

60. Cicero, "Pro Archia Poeta," in *Cicero*, vol. 11, Loeb Classical Library 158 (Cambridge, MA: Harvard University Press, 1923), pt. 1, chap. 3, pp. 2, 8.

61. Gellius, *Noctes Atticae*, 13.17, http://penelope.uchicago.edu/Thayer/E/Roman/Texts/Gellius/13*.html.

62. See Grafton and Jardine, *From Humanism to the Humanities*, 219.

63. *Grosses vollständiges Lexicon*, 1155.

64. All Kant citations refer to the Akademie Ausgabe: Immanuel Kant, *Gesammelte Schriften*, ed. Königlich Preussischen Akademie der Wissenschaften, 29 vols. to date (Berlin: Walter de Gruyter, 1902-). Hereafter, all citations will include a short title followed by volume and page number. See also Kant, *Kritik der Urteilskraft*, 5:433.

65. Kant, *Streit der Fakultäten*, 7:22, 19. See also Hunter, "The Mythos, Ethos, and Pathos of the Humanities."

66. F. A. Wolf, *Prolegomena to Homer*, trans. Anthony Grafton, Glenn W. Most, and James E. G. Zetzel (Princeton, NJ: Princeton University Press, 1985), 55-56.

67. See, for example, Wellmon, *Organizing Enlightenment*, 101-7, 108-122; Multigraph Collective, *Interacting with Print: Elements of Reading in the Era of Print Saturation* (Chicago: University of Chicago Press, 2018), 243-59.

68. Wilhelm Schlegel, "Vorlesungen über schöne Literatur und Kunst" [Lectures on literature and art], in *Vorlesungen über Ästhetik I: (1798–1803)*, ed. Ernst Behler (Paderborn: Ferdinand Schöningh, 1989), 484.

69. Friedrich I. Niethammer, *Der Streit des Philanthropinismus und Humanismus in der Theorie des Erziehungs-Unterrichts unsrer Zeit* (Jena: Frommann, 1808), 9.

70. Ibid., 36.

71. Ibid., 72.

72. Review, *"Der Streit des Philanthropinismus und Humanismus in der Theorie des Erziehungs-Unterrichts unsrer Zeit*, dargestellt von Friedrich Niethammer," *Allgemeine Literatur-Zeitung*, September 1, 1808, 3.

73. Niethammer, *Der Streit*, 15, 17.

74. Ibid., 16.

75. Ibid., 59, 76.

76. Ibid., 8.

77. Ibid., 357.

78. *WDGS*, 1:3.

79. Odo Marquard, "Über die Unvermeidlichkeit der Geisteswissenschaften," in *Apologie des Zufälligen: Philosophische Studien* (Stuttgart: Philip Reclam, 1986), 98-116, 105. Marquand's articulation of the *Kompensationstheorie* of the humanities or *Geisteswissenschaften* is an elaboration of Joachim Ritter, "Die Aufgabe der Geisteswissenschaften in der modernen Gesellschaft" (1962), in *Subjektivität: Sechs Aufsätze* (Frankfurt am Main: Suhrkamp, 1974), 105-40.

80. Simon During, "Losing Faith in the Humanities," *Chronicle Review*, December 18, 2019, https://www.chronicle.com/interactives/20191218-During.

81. F. A. W. Diesterweg, *Ueber das Verderben auf den deutschen Universitäten* (Essen: Baedecker, 1836), 52.

82. Eduard Spranger, "Der Sinn der Voraussetzungslosigkeit in den Geisteswissenschaften," in *Eduard Spranger: Gesammelte Schriften* (Tübingen: Max Niemeyer, 1980), 6:155.

83. Ibid., 155, 152.

84. Ibid.

85. Ibid., 180.

86. Harpham, *Humanities and the Dream*, 22 (see n. 8).

87. On philology as an object of theoretical inquiry, see Pascale Hummel, "History of History of Philology: Goals and Limits of an Inquiry," in *Metaphilology: His-*

*tories and Languages of Philology*, ed. Pascale Hummel (Paris: Philologicum, 2009), 7–28.

88. See, for example, *The Trans-Saharan Book Trade: Manuscript Culture, Arabic Literacy and Intellectual History in Muslim Africa*, ed. Graziano Krätli and Ghislaine Lydon (Leiden: Brill, 2011); *The Transmission of Learning in Islamic Africa*, ed. Scott Reese (Leiden: Brill, 2004).

89. Rajeev Kinra, "Cultures of Comparative Philology in the Early Modern Indo-Persian World," *Philological Encounters* 1, nos. 1–4 (2016): 225–87.

90. See, for example, Sheldon Pollock, Benjamin A. Elman, and Ku-ming Kevin Chang, eds., *World Philology* (Cambridge, MA: Harvard University Press, 2015). For a more programmatic and, to our minds, helpfully critical account of Pollock's broader project, see Islam Dayeh, "The Potential of World Philology," *Philological Encounters* 1 (2016): 396–418.

91. Sheldon Pollock, "Future Philology? The Fate of a Soft Science in a Hard World," *Critical Inquiry* 35, no. 4 (2009): 932.

CHAPTER ONE

1. Hugo Münsterberg, "The St. Louis Congress of Arts and Sciences," *Atlantic Monthly* 91 (1903): 671–84.

2. Dewey and James quoted in Julie Reuben, *The Making of the Modern University: Intellectual Transformation and the Marginalization of Morality* (Chicago: University of Chicago Press, 1996), 91.

3. Ibid., 17–35.

4. Peter Galison, "Introduction: The Context of Disunity," in *The Disunity of Science: Boundaries, Context, and Power*, ed. Galison and David Stump (Stanford, CA: Stanford University Press, 1996), 1.

5. Lorraine Daston, "The Academies and the Unity of Knowledge: The Disciplining of the Disciplines," *Differences: A Journal of Feminist Cultural Studies* 10, no. 2 (1998): 68.

6. Ibid., 81.

7. Friedrich Schelling, "Lectures on the Method of Academic Study," in *The Rise of the Research University: A Sourcebook*, ed. Louis Menand, Paul Reitter, and Chad Wellmon (Chicago: University of Chicago Press, 2017), 87.

8. Quoted in Jordi Cat, "The Unity of Science," in *The Stanford Encyclopedia of Philosophy* (Fall 2017 ed.), ed. Edward N. Zalta, https://plato.stanford.edu/archives/fall2017/entries/scientific-unity/.

9. See Roger Chickering, *Karl Lamprecht: A German Academic Life* (Leiden: Brill, 1993), 120.

10. R. Steven Turner, "The Prussian Universities and the Research Imperative, 1806–1848" (PhD diss., Princeton University, 1973), 331–41.

11. Cited in Turner, "Prussian Universities," 338.

12. See Thomas Albert Howard, *Protestant Theology and the Making of the Modern German University* (New York: Oxford University Press, 2005), 139, 170–72; Theodore Ziolkowski, *German Romanticism and Its Institutions* (Princeton, NJ: Princeton University Press, 1990), 253–54. In some of the classic German texts on German universities—for example, Friedrich Paulsen's *Deutsche Universitäten und*

*Universitätsstudium* (1903)—the unity of knowledge is more a cherished ideal than an object of inquiry.

13. Theodor Adorno, *Minima moralia* (Frankfurt: Suhrkamp, 1969), 128.

14. Theodor Adorno and Max Horkheimer, *Dialektik der Aufklärung: Philosophische Fragmente* (Frankfurt am Main: Fischer, 1988).

15. Adorno, *Minima moralia*.

16. Anne Harrington, *Reenchanted Science: Holism in German Culture from Wilhelm II to Hitler* (Princeton, NJ: Princeton University Press, 1996). The Goethe quotation cited here occurs on page 5. See pages 175–85 for Harrington's main discussion of Nazism and German holism.

17. Charles McClelland, *Berlin: Mother of All Research Universities, 1860–1918* (Lanham, MD: Lexington Books, 2017), 113.

18. Quoted in Fritz Ringer, *The Decline of the German Mandarins: The German Academic Community, 1890–1933* (Hanover, NH: Wesleyan University Press, 1990), 189.

19. Michael André Bernstein, *Foregone Conclusions: Against Apocalyptic History* (Berkeley: University of California Press, 1994).

20. Anthony La Vopa, "Specialists against Specialization: Hellenism as Professional Ideology in German Classical Studies," in *German Professions, 1800–1950*, ed. Geoffrey Cocks and Konrad Jarausch (Oxford: Oxford University Press, 1990), 37. On the discourse of modernity as diseased, see Michael Cowan, *The Cult of the Will: Nervousness and German Modernity* (University Park: Pennsylvania State University Press, 2008).

21. Jean-François Lyotard, *The Postmodern Condition: A Report on Knowledge*, trans. Geoff Bennington and Brian Mussimi (Minneapolis: University of Minnesota Press, 1984), 33, 34. Originally published as *La condition postmoderne: Rapport sur le savoir* (Paris: Minuit, 1979).

22. Frederick Beiser, *After Hegel: German Philosophy 1840–1900* (Cambridge, MA: Harvard University Press, 2014), 15.

23. Chad Wellmon, *Organizing Enlightenment: Information Overload and the Invention of the Modern Research University* (Baltimore: Johns Hopkins University Press, 2015), 123–50.

24. The philologist F. A. Wolf's influential *Outline of Classical Studies* (1807) is but one example. Friedrich August Wolf, *Darstellung der Altertumswissenschaft*, vol. 1 of *Museum der Alterthums-Wissenschaft*, ed. F. A. Wolf and P. Buttmann (Berlin, 1807), 1–145.

25. Cited in Rüdiger Safranski, *Schiller oder die Erfindung des deutschen Idealismus* (Munich: DTV, 2004), 307.

26. Kant, "Idee zu einer allgemeinen Geschichte," 8:29.

27. Friedrich Schiller, "What Is Universal History and Why Study it? An Inaugural Academic Lecture," in Menand, Reitter, and Wellmon, *Rise of the Research University*, 33.

28. Jürgen Habermas incisively discusses Schiller's reckoning with the issue of what would later be called instrumental logic in *Der philosophische Diskurs der Moderne* (Frankfurt: Suhrkamp, 1985), 59–64. For a contextualizing reading of Schiller's lecture, see Peter-André Alt, *Friedrich Schiller: Leben, Werk, Zeit* (Munich: C. H. Beck, 2000), 604–13.

29. Schiller, "What Is Universal History," 33.

30. Ibid.

31. Wellmon, *Organizing Enlightenment*, 184-85.

32. Schiller, "What is Universal History," 37.

33. Ibid., 35, 37.

34. Ibid., 37.

35. Safranski, *Schiller*, 315.

36. Schiller, "What Is Universal History," 43.

37. William Clark, *Academic Charisma and the Origins of the Research University* (Chicago: University of Chicago Press, 2006), 85, 378-80.

38. Friedrich Gedike, "Report to King Friedrich Wilhelm II of Germany," in Menand, Reitter, and Wellmon, *Rise of the Research University*, 15.

39. Schiller, "What Is Universal History," 34.

40. Karl Marx, *Zur Judenfrage* (Berlin: Rowohlt, 1919), 9.

41. Schiller, "What Is Universal History," 42.

42. Compare to Kant's claim that the "idea" of a cosmopolitan history "consoles" in "Idee zu einer allgemeinen Geschichte," 8:30, 29.

43. Ziolkowski, *German Romanticism and Its Institutions*, 240.

44. La Vopa compares Schiller's notion of intellectual wholeness to Fichte's, and here, too, he frames the neo-humanist notion of intellectual wholeness as backward looking, as seeing modernity as an obstacle to wholeness, rather than as something that makes it possible, if not easy. La Vopa, *Fichte: The Self and the Calling of Critical Philosophy, 1762-1799* (Cambridge: Cambridge University Press, 2001), 220-22.

45. See also Ziolkowski, *German Romanticism and Its Institutions*, 246.

46. "Editor's Preface," in *Fichte: Early Philosophical Writings*, ed. and trans. Daniel Breazeale (Ithaca, NY: Cornell University Press, 1988), 138.

47. Ibid.

48. Fichte, "A Plan, Deduced from First Principles, for an Institution of Higher Learning to Be Established in Berlin, Connected to and Subordinate to an Academy of Science," in Menand, Reitter, and Wellmon, *Rise of the Research University*, 70.

49. See La Vopa, *Fichte*, 341-44.

50. Geoffrey Galt Harpham, *What Do You Think, Mr. Ramirez? The American Revolution in Education* (Chicago: University of Chicago Press, 2017), xiii.

51. Fichte, "A Plan," 75.

52. Schelling, "Lectures on the Method of Academic Study," 89. In *German Philosophy 1760-1860: The Legacy of Idealism* (Cambridge: Cambridge University Press, 2014), Terry Pinkard offers a particularly lucid account of this aspect of Schelling's work; see esp. 175-80.

53. Pinkard, *German Philosophy*, 177.

54. Schelling, "Lectures on the Method of Academic Study," 92.

55. Ibid., 100.

56. Wellmon, *Organizing Enlightenment*, 162-69.

57. In 1802 the Prussian royal adviser Karl von Beyme began entertaining proposals for an institution of higher learning in Berlin. See Rudolf Köpke, *Die Gründung der königlichen Universität zu Berlin* (Berlin: Gustav Schade, 1860), 145. In

1807, Beyme circulated a call for proposals, contacting the philologist Friedrich Wolf and other luminaries.

58. Schelling, "Lectures on the Method of Academic Study," 86.

59. Ibid.

60. Chad Wellmon, "Touching Books: Diderot, Novalis and the Encyclopedia of the Future," *Representations* 114, no. 1 (2011): 65–102.

61. Schelling, "Lectures on the Method of Academic Study," 87.

62. Ibid.

63. Ibid., 97.

64. Ibid., 102.

65. Ibid.

66. Ibid., 103, 104.

67. For more on this local infrastructure and how Humboldt and colleagues conceived of the university as an organizing medium, see Wellmon, *Organizing Enlightenment*, 218–20.

68. Schleiermacher, "Occasional Thoughts on German Universities in the German Sense," in Menand, Reitter, and Wellmon, *Rise of the Research University*, 62.

69. Richard Crouter, *Friedrich Schleiermacher: Between Enlightenment and Romanticism* (Cambridge: Cambridge University Press, 2005), 146.

70. Schleiermacher, "Occasional Thoughts," 54.

71. Ibid., 48.

72. Quoted in Crouter, *Friedrich Schleiermacher*, 145.

73. Schleiermacher, "Occasional Thoughts," 61.

74. Ibid., 49, 52, 53, 54.

75. Ibid., 48, 49.

76. Schleiermacher, "Occasional Thoughts," 66.

77. Ibid., 53.

78. Ibid., 55.

79. Ibid., 60.

80. See, in particular, Peter Moraw, *Gesammelte Beiträge zur deutschen und europäischen Universitätsgeschichte* (Leiden: Brill, 2008), 3–54.

81. Schleiermacher, "Occasional Thoughts," 60.

82. See Schleiermacher, *Hermeneutik und Kritik* (Frankfurt am Main: Suhrkamp, 1990), 75–98.

83. Schleiermacher, "Occasional Thoughts."

84. Wilhelm von Humboldt, "On the Internal Structure of the University in Berlin and Its Relationship to Other Organizations," in Menand, Reitter, and Wellmon, *Rise of the Research University*, 108.

85. See, for example, Mitchell G. Ash, ed., *Mythos Humboldt: Vergangenheit und Zukunft der deutschen Universitäten* (Vienna: Böhlau, 1999).

86. See Rüdiger vom Bruch, "Langsamer Abschied von Humboldt? Etappen deutscher Universitätsgeschichte 1810–1945," in Ash, *Mythos Humboldt*, 29–57.

87. Humboldt, "On the Internal Structure of the University in Berlin," 109, 110.

88. Ibid., 109.

89. Humboldt, "Memorandum," in Menand, Reitter, and Wellmon, *Rise of the Research University*, 116–19.

90. Quoted in Reinhold Steig, *Heinrich von Kleist's Berliner Kämpfe* (Berlin: W. Spemann, 1901), 301. For a further discussion, see Wellmon, *Organizing Enlightenment*, 151.

CHAPTER TWO

1. For a discussion of the term *mandarin*, see chapter 4. See Matthew Arnold, *Schools and Universities on the Continent* (London: Macmillan, 1868) and *Culture and Anarchy: An Essay in Political and Social Criticism* (London: Smith, Elder, 1869). See also Victor Cousin, *État de l'instruction primaire dans le royaume de Prusse à la fin de l'année 1831* (Paris: F. G. Levrault, 1833); *Denkschrift über den Gymnasialunterricht im Königrreich Preussen, nebst des Verfassers Leben und einer allgemeinen Übersicht der Preussischen und Sächischen Unterrichtsanstalten*, ed. and trans. J. Kröger (Altona: Hammerich, 1837).

2. Tappan, "On German Universities," in *The Rise of the Research University: A Sourcebook*, ed. Louis Menand, Paul Reitter, and Chad Wellmon (Chicago: University of Chicago Press, 2017), 151.

3. See, for example, Adolph Diesterweg's review in *Diesterweg: Sämtliche Werke*, ed. Hans Ahrbeck et al. (Berlin: Volk und Wissen Volkseigener, 1959), 3:3–22.

4. Quoted in Jeffrey L. Sammons, *Heinrich Heine: A Modern Biography* (Princeton, NJ: Princeton University Press, 1979), 79.

5. Rahel Levin Varnhagen, *Rahel Bibliothek: Gesammelte Werke*, ed. Konrad Feilchenfeldt et al. (Munich: Matthes & Seitz, 1983), 2:609.

6. F. A. W. Diesterweg, "Über die Lehrmethode Schleiermachers," in *Diesterweg: Sämtliche Werke*, pt. 1 ed. Hans Ahrbeck et al. (Berlin: Volk und Wissen Volkseigenerverlag, 1959), 3:267.

7. F. A. W. Diesterweg, *Ueber das Verderben auf den deutschen Universitäten* (Essen: Baedeker, 1836), iv. Our translation of the title is somewhat liberal; a more literal one would be "On the ruin at German universities."

8. Allan Bloom, *The Closing of the American Mind: How Higher Education Has Failed Democracy and Impoverished the Souls of Today's Students* (New York: Simon and Schuster, 2012), 346.

9. Diesterweg's book appeared as the third installment of a trilogy of works to which he gave the heading "Life and Death Questions of Civilization."

10. Nearly every professor Diesterweg names in his book, which purports to be about German universities in general, worked or had worked at the University of Berlin (e.g., Schleiermacher, Hegel, and Friedrich Benecke).

11. For a useful account of Diesterweg's life and work, see Horst Rupp, *F.A.W. Diesterweg: Pädagogik und Politik* (Göttingen: Muster-Schmidt, 1989).

12. Diesterweg, *Ueber das Verderben*, vii.

13. Johan Östling tracks the continuity of these ideals amid the diversity of appropriation in the German context in *Humboldt and the Modern German University: An Intellectual History* (Lund: Lund University Press, 2018).

14. See the introduction to Menand, Reitter, and Wellmon, *Rise of the Research University*.

15. See Wendy Brown, "The End of Educated Democracy," *Representations* 116, no. 1 (Fall 2011): 19–41, and Christopher Newfield, "What Are the Humanities For?

Rebuilding the Public University," in *A New Deal for the Humanities: Liberal Arts and the Future of Public Higher Education*, ed. Gordon Hunter and Feisal Mohamed (New Brunswick, NJ: Rutgers University Press, 2015), 160–78.

16. Newfield, "What Are the Humanities For?," 162; Geoffrey Galt Harpham, *What Do You Think, Mr. Ramirez? The American Revolution in Education* (Chicago: University of Chicago Press, 2017), xiii.

17. Harpham, *What Do You Think, Mr. Ramirez?*, xv.

18. Ibid., xiii.

19. See Danielle Allen, *Education and Equality* (Chicago: University of Chicago Press, 2016); Martha Nussbaum, *Not for Profit: Why Democracy Needs the Humanities* (Princeton, NJ: Princeton University Press, 2010); Helen Small, *The Value of the Humanities* (Oxford: Oxford University Press, 2013); Stefan Collini, *Speaking of Universities* (London: Verso, 2017); and Andrew Delbanco, *College: What It Was, What It Is, and What It Should Be* (Princeton, NJ: Princeton University Press, 2012).

20. Small, *Value of the Humanities*, 174–83.

21. Cathy Davidson, *The New Education: How to Revolutionize the University and Prepare Students for a World in Flux* (New York: Basic Books, 2017).

22. We offer an account of the characteristics of this literature in Chad Wellmon and Paul Reitter, "Melancholy Mandarins: Bloom, Weber, and Moral Education," *Hedgehog Review* 19, no. 3 (Fall 2017), http://iasc-culture.org/THR/THR_article_2017_Fall_ReitterWellmon.php.

23. Cited in Heinz-Dieter Meyer, *The Design of the University: German, American, and "World Class"* (New York: Routledge, 2016), 23.

24. Ibid.

25. Friedrich Gedike, "Report to King Friedrich Wilhelm II of Germany," in Menand, Reitter, and Wellmon, *Rise of the Research University* 21.

26. Cited in Rudolf Köpke, *Die Gründung der königlichen Friedrich Wilhelms Universität zu Berlin* (Berlin: Schade, 1860), 49.

27. See Chad Wellmon, *Organizing Enlightenment: Information Overload and the Invention of the Modern Research University* (Baltimore: Johns Hopkins University Press, 2015), 162–69.

28. J. G. Fichte, "A Plan, Deduced from First Principles, for an Institution to Be Established in Berlin, Connected to and Subordinate to an Academy of Sciences," in Menand, Reitter, and Wellmon, *Rise of the Research University*, 72.

29. See Schleiermacher, "Occasional Thoughts," in Menand, Reitter, and Wellmon, *Rise of the Research University*, 54.

30. Perhaps the clearest expression of Humboldt's admiration for Greek culture can be found in *Wilhelm von Humboldt: Briefe an Friedrich August Wolf*, ed. Philip Mattson (Berlin: Walter de Gruyter, 1990), 122.

31. On this point, see Meyer, *Design of the University*, 39–58. See also Wilhelm von Humboldt, "On the Internal Structure of the University in Berlin and Its Relationship to Other Organizations," in Menand, Reitter, and Wellmon, *Rise of the Research University*.

32. Kant, *Streit der Fakultäten*, 7:17–28.

33. Paul Sweet, *Wilhelm von Humboldt: 1808–1835* (Columbus: Ohio State University Press, 1978), 60.

34. Quoted in Heinz-Elmar Tenorth, "Studenten, Studium und Lehre," in *Ge-*

*schichte der Universität Unter den Linden: Gründung und Blütezeit der Universität zu Berlin 1810–1918*, 6 vols., ed. Charles McClelland and Heinz-Elmar Tenorth (Berlin: Akademie, 2010–2013), 1:227. However, this formulation was considerably more liberal than the line defining the mission of Prussian universities in the Prussian Legal Code of 1794—to convey "useful knowledge" to students. We are very grateful to Charles McClelland and Heinz-Elmar Tenorth for discussing their research with us.

35. Cited in McClelland and Tenorth, *Geschichte der Universität unter den Linden*, 1:7.

36. The term used at the time was *allgemeine wissenschaftliche Bildung*, by which was meant, generally speaking, what "liberal higher education" signifies today.

37. Cited in Tenorth, "Studenten, Studium und Lehre," 234.

38. Such an attitude was expressed in a discussion of dissertation requirements at an 1836 meeting of the university's philosophical faculty: phil Fac N 102 Litt. S. n 7, Humboldt University Universitätsarchiv. The University of Berlin required a PhD candidate to be present for an oral exam at the end of the process and to submit a printed dissertation in Latin. At "PhD factories" such as Jena, students could receive the doctor title remotely by mailing a handwritten dissertation in German. Because salaries at the University of Berlin were higher than at Jena, it was easier for professors there to take the pedagogical high road.

39. R. Steven Turner, "Justus Liebig versus Prussian Chemistry: Reflections on Early Institute-Building in Germany," *Historical Studies in the Physical Sciences* 13, no. 1 (1982): 129–62.

40. The term *Bildung* eventually came to connote "liberal education," its counterpart being *Ausbildung*, which signified professional training. One complication that occasioned much hand-wringing was that *Bildung* was in fact professional for students intending to devote their lives to scholarship.

41. Prussian universities were greatly affected by the climate of suspicion during the restoration era. Fraternities were banned, government representatives or "plenipotentiaries" were charged with supervising universities, which lost their exemption from censorship in 1819, and professors who showed any enthusiasm for the students' movement for national unity were harassed by the authorities.

42. Tenorth, "Studenten, Studium und Lehre," 249–51.

43. Ibid., 246.

44. Cited in Anthony Grafton, "Polyhistor into *Philolog*: Notes on the Transformation of German Classical Scholarship, 1780–1850," *History of Universities* 3 (1983): 169.

45. Humboldt, "On the Internal Structure," 110.

46. Boeckh's line about no question being too small is cited in Lorraine Daston, "The Academies and the Unity of Knowledge: The Disciplining of the Disciplines," *differences: A Journal of Feminist Critique* 10, no. 2 (1998): 174.

47. See Sebastiano Timpanaro, *The Genesis of Lachmann's Method*, ed. and trans. Glenn Most (Chicago: University of Chicago Press, 2006).

48. Quoted in ibid., 88.

49. See Hayden White, *Metahistory: The Historical Imagination in Nineteenth-Century Europe* (Baltimore: Johns Hopkins University Press, 1973), 165; August

Boeckh, *Encyclopädie und Methodologie der philologischen Wissenschaften von August Boeckh*, ed. Ernst Bratuscheck (Leipzig: Teubner, 1877).

50. Friedrich Schelling, "Lectures on the Method of Academic Study," in *The Rise of the Research University: A Sourcebook*, ed. Louis Menand, Paul Reitter, and Chad Wellmon (Chicago: University of Chicago Press, 2017), 87.

51. Peter Galison, "Introduction: The Context of Disunity," in *The Disunity of Science: Boundaries, Context, and Power*, ed. Galison and David Stump (Stanford, CA: Stanford University Press, 1996), 1.

52. Rudolf Virchow, *Die Gründung der Berliner Universität und der Übergang aus dem philosophischen in das naturwissenschaftlichen Zeitalter* (Berlin: Becker, 1893), 18.

53. Wilhelm von Humboldt, *Schriften zur Politik und zum Bildungswesen*, ed. Andreas Flintner and Klaus Giel (Darmstadt: Wissenschaftliche Buchgesellschaft, 2010), 579.

54. The student was Georg Andreas Gabler (1786–1853), whose appointment was surely the highpoint of an otherwise undistinguished career. See Herbert Schnädelbach, "Philosophie auf dem Weg von der System- zur Forschungswissenschaft. Oder: Von der Wissenschaftslehre zur Philosophie als Geisteswissenschaft," in McClelland and Tenorth *Geschichte der Universität Unter den Linden*, 4:183.

55. Hans Joaquim Schoeps, ed., "Ein Gutachten des Kultusministers von Altenstein," *Zeitschrift für Pädagogik* 12 (1966): 262.

56. Henrich Steffens, *Was Ich Erlebte: Aus der Erinnerung Niedergeschrieben* (Breslau: Josef Mar, 1844), 8:290.

57. "Rundschreiben des Kultusministers Karl Friedrich Eichhorn an die Kuratoren und Fakultäten der preußischen Universitäten, Berlin, 17. April 1844," in *Acta Borussica: Das Kultusministerium auf seinen Wirkungsfeldern Schule, Wissenschaft, Kirchen, Künste und Medizinalwesen* (Berlin: Akademie, 2010), 379.

58. See R. Steven Turner, "The Growth of Professorial Research in Prussia, 1818–1848—Causes and Context," *Historical Studies in the Physical Sciences* 3 (1971): 177–78, and Theodor Caplow and Reece McGee, *The Academic Marketplace* (New York: Transaction, 2001).

59. The theory that competition among universities played a key part in the formation of research universities is most closely associated with the work of Joseph Ben-David, *Centers of Learning: Britain, Germany, France, and the United States* (New York: Routledge, 2017), first published in 1977.

60. See Alexander Busch, *Die Geschichte des Privatdozenten: Eine soziologische Studie zur großbetrieblichen Entwicklung der deutschen Universitäten* (Stuttgart: Enke, 1959).

61. See Köpke, *Die Gründung*, 296–98.

62. Erich Hahn, "The Junior Faculty in 'Revolt': Reform Plans for Berlin University in 1848," *American Historical Review* 82, no. 4 (October 1977): 875–95.

63. Conrad Varrentrapp, *Johannes Schulze und das höhere preußische Unterrichtswesen in seiner Zeit* (Leipzig: Teubner, 1889), 488.

64. A. von S. (August Jäger), *Felix Schnabel's Universitätsjahre* (Stuttgart: Balz, 1835), 47. Diesterweg uses *Bildung* and *Ausbildung* interchangeably.

65. Diesterweg, *Ueber das Verderben*, 2, 4.

66. Ibid., 2.

67. Ibid., 23.

68. Ibid., 6.

69. Ibid., 35.

70. See, for example, Jürgen Oelkers, "Bildung und Gerechtigkeit: Zur historischen Vergewisserung der aktuellen Diskussion," in *Wann ist Bildung gerecht? Ethische und theologische Beiträge im interdisziplinären Kontext*, ed. Hans Münk (Bielefeld: Bertelsmann, 2008), 24.

71. Diesterweg, *Ueber das Verderben*, 70–71.

72. Ibid., 50, 51.

73. Ibid., 56–57.

74. Ibid., 44.

75. Ibid.

76. In 1830s Prussia, professors were subject to censorship in their writings much more than in the classroom.

77. Diesterweg, *Ueber das Verderben*, 31.

78. The German conception of academic freedom entailed breaking it down into different categories, *Lehrfreiheit* and *Lernfreiheit*, the freedom of professors to teach what and how they wanted to and the freedom of students to study what they wanted to.

79. Richard Hofstadter and Walter Metzger, *The Development of Academic Freedom in the United States* (New York: Columbia University Press, 1955), 387.

80. Diesterweg, *Ueber das Verderben*, 10, 18.

81. William Deresiewicz, *Excellent Sheep: The Miseducation of the American Elite and the Way to a Meaningful Life* (New York: Free Press, 2014); Daniel Bell, *The Reforming of General Education* (New York: Columbia University, 1966).

82. Steven Pinker, "The Trouble with Harvard," *New Republic*, September 4, 2014, https://newrepublic.com/article/119321/harvard-ivy-league-should-judge-st udents-standardized-tests.

83. Deresiewicz responded to Pinker in "The Neoliberal Arts: How College Sold Its Soul to the Market," *Harper's Magazine*, September 2015, 25–32, https://harpers .org/archive/2015/09/the-neoliberal-arts/.

84. Deresiewicz, *Excellent Sheep*, 62.

85. Max Weber, "Die Lehrfreiheit der Universitäten" in *Max Weber Gesamtausgabe* (hereafter *MWG*), ed. Horst Baier et al. (Tübingen: J. C. B. Mohr, 1984–), 1.13: 133.

86. Deresiewicz, "Neoliberal Arts," 26.

87. Max Weber, *Wissenschaft als Beruf*, *MWG*, 1.17:103.

88. Edward Said, "Identity, Authority, and Freedom: The Potentate and the Traveler," in *The Future of Academic Freedom*, ed. Louis Menand (Chicago: University of Chicago Press, 1998), 215.

89. Joan W. Scott, "Academic Freedom as an Ethical Practice," in Menand, *Future of Academic Freedom*, 166.

90. Kerr, "The Idea of a Multiversity," in *The Uses of the University* (Cambridge, MA: Harvard University Press, 2001): 12.

91. Cited in Laurence Veysey, *The Emergence of the American University* (Chicago: University of Chicago, Press, 1970), 70.

92. Willa Cather, *The Professor's House* (New York: Merchant Books, 2012), 83.

93. See John Guillory, "Who's Afraid of Marcel Proust? The Failure of General Education in the American University," in *The Humanities and the Dynamics of Inclusion since World War II*, ed. David Hollinger (Baltimore: Johns Hopkins University Press, 2006), 41.

94. https://www.harvard.edu/president/speech/2016/2016-commencement-speech.

95. William Rainey Harper, "The University and Democracy," in Menand, Reitter, and Wellmon, *Rise of the Research University*, 220.

96. Quoted in Newfield, *The Great Mistake: How We Wrecked Public Universities and How We Can Fix Them* (Baltimore: Johns Hopkins University Press, 2016), 30.

97. Andrew White, "The Relation of the National and State Governments to Advanced Education," in Menand, Reitter, and Wellmon, *Rise of the Research University*, 210.

98. Diesterweg, *Ueber das Verderben*, 71, 72.

99. Joseph E. Davis, "A Conversation with Andrew Delbanco," *Hedgehog Review* 15, no. 1 (2013), https://iasc-culture.org/THR/THR_article_2013_Spring_Interview_Delbanco.php.

100. Brad Gregory, *The Unintended Reformation* (Cambridge, MA: Harvard University Press, 2012), 303.

101. Thomas Pfau, "History without Hermeneutics: Brad Gregory's Unintended Modernity," *Immanent Frame*, November 6, 2013, https://tif.ssrc.org/2013/11/06/history-without-hermeneutics-brad-gregorys-unintended-modernity/.

102. Diesterweg, *Ueber das Verderben*, 74.

103. Deresiewicz, *Excellent Sheep*, 194, 198.

## CHAPTER THREE

1. An early version of this chapter appeared as "How the Philologist Became a Physician of Modernity: Nietzsche's Lectures on German Education," *Representations* 129, no. 2 (Summer 2015): 68–104.

2. Ritschl quoted in Lionel Gossman, *Basel in the Age of Burckhardt: A Study in Unseasonable Ideas* (Chicago: University of Chicago Press, 2000), 413.

3. Friedrich Nietzsche, *Nietzsches Briefwechsel: Kritische Gesamtausgabe*, ed. Giorgio Colli and Mazzino Montinari, 24 vols. in 4 parts (Berlin: Walter de Gruyter, 1975–2004), 2.1:155.

4. The *Realschule* was more practical and vocational than the *Gymnasium*. Until the late nineteenth century, the only path to university study was the *Gymnasium*, and getting through it entailed a nine-year course of study that included Greek, Latin, religion, physics, history, literature, mathematics, and natural history. The *Gymnasium* culminated with the *Abitur*—a comprehensive examination that determined university entrance and placement.

5. James Porter, *Nietzsche and the Philology of the Future* (Stanford, CA: Stanford University Press, 2000).

6. Friedrich Nietzsche, *Anti-Education*, ed. Paul Reitter and Chad Wellmon, trans. Damion Searls (New York: New York Review Books, 2016), 45.

7. This is why some scholars have developed convincing readings of the lectures

to the effect that their ethos is democratic while others have persuasively stressed their authoritarian-elitist content. For an example of the democratic interpretation, see Jeffrey Church, *Nietzsche's Culture of Humanity: Beyond Aristocracy and Democracy in the Early Period* (Cambridge: Cambridge University Press, 2015), 175. For an example of the authoritarian interpretation, see Robert Holub, *Nietzsche in the Nineteenth Century: Social Questions and Philosophical Interpretations* (Philadelphia: University of Pennsylvania Press, 2018), 19–74.

8. Several of Nietzsche's proposals were in fact accepted, such as the textbook he recommended for all forms (Ernst Koch's *Griechische Schulgrammatik*, 1869), and his suggestion that Greek be mandatory for all students.

9. Nietzsche, *Briefwechsel*, 1.2:248.

10. Rüdiger Safranski, *Nietzsche: A Philosophical Biography*, trans. Shelley Laura Frisch (New York: Granta, 2003), 53.

11. Ibid., 56.

12. Nietzsche, *Briefwechsel*, 1.2:81.

13. On Nietzsche's complex relationship to Schopenhauer, see Christian J. Emden, *Nietzsche and the Politics of History* (Cambridge: Cambridge University Press, 2008), 46–50.

14. Nietzsche, *Briefwechsel*, 1.2:184.

15. Tamsin Shaw, *Nietzsche's Political Skepticism* (Princeton, NJ: Princeton University Press, 2007), 46.

16. Friedrich Nietzsche, *Nachgelassene Fragmente Sommer 1872 bis Ende 1874*, in *Werke: Kritische Gesamtausgabe* (New York: Walter de Gruyter, 2003), 3.4:141.

17. Shaw, *Nietzsche's Political Skepticism*, 49–52.

18. Nietzsche, *Briefwechsel*, 1.2:184. He is quoting from Lange, *Geschichte des Materialismus und Kritik seiner Bedeutung in der Gegenwart* (Iserlohn: Baedeker, 1866), 269.

19. Nietzsche, *Briefwechsel*, 1.2:299.

20. Cited in Safranski, *Nietzsche*, 64.

21. Cosima von Bülow quoted in Nietzsche, *Briefwechsel*, 2.2:140.

22. Nietzsche, *Briefwechsel*, 2.1:65–66.

23. Quoted in George S. Williamson, *The Longing for Myth in Germany* (Chicago: University of Chicago Press, 2004), 234.

24. Nietzsche, *Briefwechsel*, 2.1:155.

25. Friedrich Nietzsche, *Unzeitgemässe Betrachtungen*, in Friedrich Nietzsche, *Kritische Studienausgabe*, ed. Giorgio Colli and Mazzino Montinari, 15 vols. (Berlin: Walter de Gruyter, 1999), 1:365. For an excellent discussion of Nietzsche's concern with the state's instrumentalization of cultural and educational institutions, see Hugo Drochon, *Nietzsche's Great Politics* (Princeton, NJ: Princeton University Press, 2016), 60–64.

26. As rector of the University of Berlin during unification, Du Bois-Reymond celebrated the event by describing the professoriate as the new empire's "intellectual bodyguard."

27. In May 1872 the Prussian parliament passed legislation placing all schools under state supervision. Several months later, Adalbert Falk, the Prussian minister of education, promulgated the May Laws, which effectively put all public aspects of Catholic life, including the training of theologians, under state control.

28. Burckhardt quoted in Carl Schorske, "Science as a Vocation in Burckhardt's Basel," in *The City and the University: From Medieval Origins to the Present*, ed. Thomas Bender (New York: Oxford University Press, 1988), 198.

29. Martin A. Ruehl, *The Italian Renaissance in the German Historical Imagination, 1860–1930* (Cambridge: Cambridge University Press, 2015), 70.

30. Nietzsche, *Unzeitgemässe Betrachtungen*, 260–61.

31. Nietzsche, *Anti-Education*, 93.

32. Friedrich Meinecke, *Zur Geschichte der Geschichtsschreibung*, ed. Eberhard Kessel (Munich: R. Oldenbourg, 1968), 196.

33. Heinrich von Treitschke, *Die Zukunft des deutschen Gymnasiums* (Leipzig: Hirzel, 1890), 8.

34. Ibid., 6–7.

35. Ibid.

36. Ibid., 8, 10.

37. Nietzsche, *Anti-Education*, 19.

38. Ibid., 18.

39. Ibid.

40. Ibid., 14, 19.

41. Ibid., 91.

42. The German educational system clearly failed to live up to the ideals of inclusiveness established by its nineteenth-century architects, who claimed to believe that everyone would benefit from classical study and that merit, much more than means, should determine who has access to elite education.

43. Johannes Conrad, *Universitätsstudium in Deutschland während der letzten 50 Jahre: Statistische Untersuchungen* (Jena: Fischer, 1884). On the 1859 regulations, see Bärbel Holtz and Christina Rathgeber, "Zwischen Bildungskonzept und Bildungsweg—Lokale Schulhoheit und Intensivierung des Staatsdurchgriffs (1817 bis 1866)," in *Acta Borussica: Das preußische Kultusministerium als Staatsbehörde und gesellschaftliche Agentur (1817–1934)*, ed. Wolfgang Neugebauer, vol. 2, pt. 1. (Berlin: Akademie, 2010), 52–54.

44. Quoted in James C. Albisetti, *Secondary School Reform in Imperial Germany* (Princeton, NJ: Princeton University Press, 1983), 174–75.

45. On Nietzsche's gross generalizations about the philological establishment, see Anthony Grafton, *Bring Out Your Dead: The Past as Revelation* (Cambridge, MA: Harvard University Press, 2002).

46. Quoted in Fritz Blättner, *Das Gymnasium: Aufgaben der höheren Schule in Geschichte und Gegenwart* (Heidelberg: Quelle und Meyer, 1960), 170.

47. Nietzsche, *Anti-Education*, 15.

48. Ibid., 41.

49. Ibid., 19.

50. Ibid., 16.

51. Ibid.

52. Quoted in *The Rise of the Research University: A Sourcebook*, ed. Louis Menand, Paul Reitter, and Chad Wellmon (Chicago: University of Chicago Press, 2017), 310.

53. For a wide-ranging anthology of views related to this debate, see Arthur Kirchoff, ed., *Die akademische Frau: Gutachten hervorragender Universitätsprofes-*

*soren, Frauenleher, und Schriftsteller über die Befähigung der Frauen zum wissen-schaftlichen Studium und Beruf* (Berlin: Steinik, 1897).

54. Johannes Conrad, *Das Universitätsstudium in Deutschland während der letzten 50 Jahre* (Jena: Fischer, 1884), 5, 1, 136, 140, respectively.

55. Nietzsche, *Unzeitgemässe Betrachtungen*, 4.

56. Nietzsche, *Anti-Education*, 35, 38.

57. Andrew Delbanco, *College: What It Was, What It Is, and What It Should Be* (Princeton, NJ: Princeton University Press, 2012), 43. Compare, for example, Mark Edmundson, *The Heart of the Humanities: Reading, Writing, Teaching* (New York: Bloomsbury, 2018).

58. Delbanco, *College*, 143.

59. Nietzsche, *Anti-Education*, xxii.

60. Ibid., 33.

61. Ibid., 36.

62. Nietzsche, *Unzeitgemässe Betrachtungen*, 366.

63. See Ian Hunter, "Secularization: The Birth of a Modern Combat Concept," *Modern Intellectual History* 12, no. 1 (2015): 1–32.

64. Nietzsche writes this in an explicit comparison of the cultures of Alexandrian-Roman antiquity and late nineteenth-century Germany in *Die Geburt der Tragödie*, in Colli and Montinari, *Kritische Studienausgabe*, 1:148–49.

65. See, for example, Glenn W. Most, "On the Use and Abuse of Ancient Greece for Life," *Cultura tedesca* 20 (2000): 31–53.

66. Nietzsche, *Anti-Education*, 31.

67. See, for example, Wilhelm von Humboldt, "Über das Studium des Altertums und des griechischen inbesondere" (1793), in *Wilhelm von Humboldts Gesammelte Schriften*, ed. Bruno Gebhardt, 17 vols. (Berlin: B. Behr, 1968), 1:255–81. On Humboldt's Greek classicism, see Suzanne L. Marchand, *Down from Olympus: Archaeology and Philhellenism in Germany, 1750–1970* (Princeton, NJ: Princeton University Press, 1996).

68. Nietzsche, "Homer's Wettkampf," in Colli and Montinari, *Kritische Studienausgabe*, 1:783–92.

69. Nietzsche, *Anti-Education*, 38.

70. Humboldt, "Theorie der Bildung des Menschen," in *Wilhelm von Humboldts Gesammelte Werke*, 1:282–87.

71. Nietzsche, *Anti-Education*, 26, 27.

72. Nietzsche, *Also Sprach Zarathustra*, in Colli and Montinari, *Kritische Studienausgabe*, 4:16–17.

73. Tamsin Shaw, "The 'Last Man' Problem: Nietzsche and Weber on Political Attitudes to Suffering," in *Nietzsche as Political Philosopher*, ed. Barry Stocker and Manuel Knoll (Berlin: Walter de Gruyter, 2014), 345–80.

74. Friedrich Nietzsche, "Notizen zu 'Wir Philologen," in Colli and Montinari, *Kritische Studienausgabe* (Munich: Walter de Gruyter, 1999), 8:46.

75. For an overview of the "concept of genius" in Kant and nineteenth-century German culture, see Hans-Georg Gadamer, *Wahrheit und Methode: Grundzüge einer philosophischen Hermeneutik* (Tübingen: Mohr Siebeck, 1990), 48–94.

76. Nietzsche, *Anti-Education*, 42.

77. Ibid., 85.

78. Ibid.

79. We are drawing here and below on Shaw, *Nietzsche's Political Skepticism*, 19–40 (see n. 15).

80. Nietzsche, *Unzeitgemässe Betrachtungen*, 389.

81. Peter Sloterdijk, *Du mußt dein Leben ändern: Über Anthropotechnik* (Frankfurt am Main: Suhrkamp 2009), 58.

82. Nietzsche, *Anti-Education*, 78.

83. Nietzsche, "Notizen zu 'Wir Philologen,'" 21.

84. Ibid., 20.

85. Friedrich Nietzsche, *Nachgelassene Fragmente, 1869–1874*, in Colli and Montinari, *Kritische Studienausgabe*, 7:613.

86. Mommsen to Wilamowitz, letter 393, February 25, 1894, in *Theodor Mommsen und Friedrich Althoff Briefwechsel 1882–1903*, ed. Stefan Rebenich and Gisa Franke (Munich: Oldenbourg, 2012).

87. Mommsen, *Reden und Aufsätze* (Berlin: Weidmann, 1905), 69.

88. *Sitzungsberichte der Königlich Preussischen Akademie der Wissenschaften zu Berlin* (Berlin: Königlichen Akademie der Wissenschaften, 1900), pt. 1, 667.

89. Mommsen, "Ansprache am Leibnizschen Gedächtnistag" (1895) in *Reden and Aufsätze*, 197.

90. Ibid., 198.

91. *Theodor Mommsen und Friedrich Althoff Briefwechsel 1882–1903* (Munich: Oldenbourg, 2012), 309.

92. Erich Rothacker, ed., *Briefwechsel zwischen Wilhelm Dilthey und dem Grafen Paul Yorck von Wartenburg, 1877–1897* (Bremen: Europäischer Hochschuleverlag, 2011), 181.

93. Mommsen, review of *Geschichte der Römer* (1851) in *Gesammelte Schriften* (Berlin: Weidmannsche Buchhandlung, 1910), 6:653.

94. Quoted in Schorske, "Science as a Vocation in Burckhardt's Basel," 204.

95. Lionel Gossman *Orpheus Philologus: Bachofen versus Mommsen on the Study of Antiquity* (Philadelphia: American Historical Society, 1983), 21.

96. Mommsen, in *Theodor Mommsen: Tagebuch der französisch-italienischen Reise 1844/45*, ed. Gerold Walser (Frankfurt am Main: H. Lang, 1976), 239.

97. Hans-Georg Kolbe, ed., *Wilhelm Henzen und das Institut auf dem Kapitol: Eine Auswahl seiner Briefe an Eduard Gerhard* (Mainz: Philipp Von Zabern, 1984), 338.

98. Mommsen, *Reden und Aufsätze*, 38.

99. Nietzsche, *Unzeitgemässe Betrachtungen*, 327.

100. Nietzsche, "Notizen zu 'Wir Philologen,'" 20.

101. See, in particular, Friedrich Schlegel, *Über das Studium der griechischen Poesie* (Munich, 1985).

102. Nietzsche, "Notizen zu 'Wir Philologen,'" 69, 80.

103. Ibid., 14.

104. Ibid., 37.

105. Friedrich Nietzsche, *Zur Genealogie der Moral*, in Colli and Mazzino Montinari, *Kritische Studienausgabe*, 5:335–37.

106. Nietzsche, *Unzeitgemässe Betrachtungen*, 327.

107. Ibid., 243.

108. Nietzsche, "Notizen zu 'Wir Philologen,'" 30.

109. Ibid., 123.

110. For this and the following paragraph, we are indebted to discussions with and the work of Joshua Billings, especially "Nietzsche and the Philology of the Present" (unpublished manuscript).

111. Billings, "Nietzsche and the Philology of the Present," 8–9.

112. Nietzsche, *Jenseits von Gut und Böse*, in Colli and Mazzino Montinari, *Kritische Studienausgabe*, 5:230.


CHAPTER FOUR

1. Wilhelm Dilthey, *Wilhelm Dilthey Gesammelte Schriften*, [*WDGS*], 26 vols. (Stuttgart: B. G. Teubner, 1961–1966), 1:1.

2. Francis Bacon, *The New Organon* (Cambridge: Cambridge University Press, 2000), 10, 221.

3. David Cahan, introduction to *Science and Culture: Popular and Philosophical Essays* (Chicago: University of Chicago Press, 1995), xi.

4. *Fragmente aus den Naturwissenschaften: Vorlesungen und Aufsätze*, trans. A. H., with a foreword and additions by Hermann Helmholtz (Brunswick: Friedrich Vieweg, 1874).

5. Andreas Daum, *Wissenschaftspopularisierung im 19. Jahrhundert* (Munich: R. Oldenbourg, 2002), 435–36.

6. Helmholtz, "Ueber das Streben nach Popularisierung der Wissenschaft: Vorrede zu der von Tyndall's 'Fragments of Science' 1894" in Hermann Helmholtz, *Vorträge und Reden* (Berlin: Vieweg & Sohn, 1903), 2:422.

7. Helmholtz, "Die Tatsachen in der Wahrnehmung," in *Vorträge und Reden* (Berlin: Vieweg & Sohn, 1903), 2:216. Cited hereafter as "Facts.".

8. Ibid., 2:218.

9. Ibid.

10. Ibid.

11. Ibid., 2:245.

12. Massimo Mezzanzanica, "Philosophie der Erfahrung und Erneuerung des Apriori: Dilthey und Helmholtz," in *Recent Contributions to Dilthey's Philosophy of the Human Sciences*, ed. Hans Ulrich Lessing (Stuttgart: Fromann-Holzboog, 2011): 59–82.

13. *WDGS*, 1:188.

14. The *Geisteswissenschaften* are more often translated as "the human sciences" or even "the social sciences." For reasons that should become clear in this chapter, we have chosen "the modern humanities" while acknowledging how unusual this translation might strike some readers as being. For a brief note on why "the social sciences" does not, to our minds, work well, see chapter 7, note 35.

15. Fritz Ringer, *The Decline of the German Mandarins: The German Academic Community, 1890–1933*, (Cambridge, MA: Harvard University Press, 1969).

16. Rudolf Virchow, *Die Gründung der Berliner Universität und der Uebergang aus*

*dem philosophischen in das naturwissenschaftliche Zeitalter* (Berlin: Julius Becker, 1893).

17. Ibid. Alexander von Humboldt was the younger brother of Wilhelm von Humboldt. All references to "Humboldt" without use of a first name in this chapter are to Wilhelm von Humboldt.

18. The desire for unity also found form in, for example, the ethnological museum of Berlin and its attempt to account for an ideal human unity in the tradition of Alexander von Humboldt's work. See H. Glenn Penny, "Bastian's Museum: On the Limits of Empiricism and the Transformation of German Ethnology," in *Worldly Provincialism*, ed. H. Glenn Penny and Matti Bunzl (Ann Arbor: University of Michigan Press, 2003), 86–126.

19. Ibid., 26, 27–28.

20. Friedrich Nietzsche, *Unzeitgemässe Betrachtungen*, in Friedrich Nietzsche, *Kritische Studienausgabe*, ed. Giorgio Colli and Mazzino Montinari, 15 vols. (Berlin: Walter de Gruyter, 1999), 1:366.

21. Heinrich Rickert, *Kulturwissenschaft und Naturwissenschaft* (Tübingen: Mohr, 1910), 1.

22. Joseph Ben-David, "Scientific Productivity and Academic Organization in Nineteenth Century Medicine," *American Sociological Review* 25, no. 6 (1960): 828–43.

23. Emil Du Bois-Reymond, *Gedächtnissrede auf Johannes Müller* (Berlin: Akademie der Wissenschaften, 1860), 69. See Gabriel Finkelstein, *Emil Du Bois-Reymond: Neuroscience, Self, and Society in Nineteenth-Century Germany* (Cambridge, MA: MIT Press, 2013), 44–45; Laura Otis, *Müller's Lab* (Oxford: Oxford University Press, 2007), 17–18.

24. See Müller's inaugural lecture at Bonn University in 1824, "Ueber das Bedürfnis der Physiologie nach einer philosophischen Naturbetrachtung," published as the introduction to Johannes Müller, *Zur vergleichenden Physiologie des Gesichtssinnes des Menschen und der Thiere* (Leipzig: K. Knobloch, 1826).

25. Du Bois-Reymond was enrolled in the university, but Helmholtz and Virchow were students at the Friedrich-Wilhelm medical institute. On these complicated relationships with their teacher, see Frederic Holmes, "The Role of Johannes Müller in the Formation of Helmholtz's Physiological Career," in *Universalgenie Helmholtz: Rückblick nach 100 Jahren*, ed. Lorenz Krüger (Berlin: Akademie, 1994).

26. Emil Du Bois-Reymond describes his first microscope in letters to Hallmann, August 19 and December 26, 1840, in *Jugendbriefe von Emil Du Bois-Reymond an Eduard Hallmann*, ed. Estelle Bu Bois-Reymond (Berlin: Reimer, 1918), 66, 79.

27. Otis, *Müller's Lab*, 76–189.

28. Du Bois-Reymond, *Gedächtnissrede*, 87–88, 92.

29. Rudolf Virchow, "Ueber die Reform der pathologischen und therapeutischen Anschauungen durch die mikroskopischen Untersuchungen," *Archiv für pathologische Anatomie und Physiologie und für klinische Medicin* 1 (1847): 213.

30. Helmholtz, "Das Denken in der Medicin," in Hermann Helmholtz, *Vorträge und Reden* (Brunswick: Vieweg & Sohn, 1903), 2:181. See Otis, *Müller's Lab*; Michael Hagner and Bettina Wahrig-Schmidt, eds., *Johannes Müller und die Physiologie* (Berlin: Walter de Gruyter, 1995). Despite the often dismissive attitude of Du

Bois-Reymond and, to a lesser extent, Helmholtz toward what they regarded as Müller's commitment to *Lebenskraft*, Müller himself was at least open to the more experimental and physicalist direction his students took. In a letter to the Prussian Ministry of Culture recommending them both for a professorship in Königsberg in 1849, he extolled their exceptional talent as practitioners of an experimental physiological method improved by a deep knowledge of physics. Wilhelm Haberling, *Johannes Müller: Das Leben der rheinischen Naturforschers* (Leipzig: Akademische, 1924), 329.

31. Helmholtz, "Das Denken in der Medicin," 181.

32. Helmholtz, "Über das Verhältniss der Naturwissenschaften zur Gesammtheit der Wissenschaft," in *Vorträge und Reden*, 3rd ed. (Brunswick: Vieweg & Sohn, 1884), 1:128.

33. Rudolf Virchow, "Was die 'medicinische Reform' will," in *Die medicinische Reform*, no. 1. (July 10, 1848): 2.

34. Werner Siemens, *Das Naturwissenschaftliche Zeitalter* (Berlin: Carl Heymann, 1886), 9.

35. Rudolf Virchow, "Empirie und Transscendenz," in *Archiv für pathologische Anatomie und Physiologie und für klinische Medicin* 7 (Berlin: Georg Reimer, 1854), 28.

36. Ringer, *Decline of the German Mandarins*.

37. Weber, *Die Wirtschaftsethik der Weltreligionen: Konfuzianismus und Taoismus*, *MWG*, 1.19:302–4.

38. Ringer, *Decline of the German Mandarins*.

39. See Edward Jurkowitz, "Helmholtz and the Liberal Unification of Science," and Heinrich Schipperges, "Einheitsbestrebungen auf der Naturforschungsversammlung im 19. Jahrhundert," *Sudhoff's Archiv* 61, no. 4 (1977): 313–30.

40. Kant, *Kritik der Urteilskraft*, 5:431, 433.

41. Emil Du Bois-Reymond, *Culturgeschichte und Naturwissenschaft* (Leipzig: Veit, 1878), 35.

42. Keith M. Anderton, "The Limits of Science: A Social, Political, and Moral Agenda for Epistemology in Nineteenth-Century Germany" (PhD diss., Harvard University, 1993), 188n139.

43. Helmholtz, "Über das Verhältniss," 140, 142.

44. Anderton, "Limits of Science," 188n193.

45. Johann Gustav Droysen, *Historik: Vorlesungen über Enzyklopädie und Methodologie*, ed. Rudolf Hübner (Munich: Oldenbourg, 1974), 18.

46. On the continued influence of Hegel, see Herbert Schnädelbach, "Philosophie auf dem Weg von der System- zur Forschungswissenschaft," in *Geschichte der Universität Unter den Linden: Gründung und Blütezeit der Universität zu Berlin 1810–1918*, 6 vols., ed. Charles McClelland and Heinz-Elmar Tenorth (Berlin: Akademie, 2010–2013), 4:180–183.

47. Ulrich Dierse, "Das Begriffspaar Naturwissenschaften-Geisteswissenschaften bis zu Dilthey," in *Kultur Verstehen*, ed. Kühne-Bertram Gudrun, Hans-Ulrich Lessing, and Volker Steenblock (Würzburg: Könighausen and Neumann, 2003), 15–34.

48. Droysen, *Historik*, 3.

49. Johann Eduard Erdmann, *Vorlesungen über akademisches Leben und Studium* (Leipzig: Carl Geibel, 1858), 276, 279.

50. Heinrich A. Oppermann, *Enzyclopädie der Philosophie* (Hannover: Hahn'schen Hofbuchhandlung, 1844), 51.

51. Droysen, *Historik*, 378.

52. Andreas Ludwig Kym, *Die Weltanschauungen und deren Consequenzen* (Zurich: S. Hoehr, 1854), 12.

53. Carl Heinrich Schultz-Schultzenstein, *Die Bildung des menschlichen Geistes durch Kultur der Verjüngung seines Lebens in Hinsicht auf Erziehung zur Humanität und Civilization* (Berlin: August Hirschwald, 1855), 928.

54. Kym, *Die Weltanschauungen*, 12–14.

55. Ibid., 25.

56. Ibid., 12.

57. Johannes Emil Kuntze, *Der Wendepunkt der Rechtswissenschaft: Ein Beitrag zur Orientirung über den gegenwärtigen Stand- und Zielpunkt derselben* (Leipzig: J. C. Hinrich, 1856), 2.

58. David Cahan, "Helmholtz and the Civilizing Power of Science," in *Hermann von Helmholtz and the Foundations of Nineteenth-Century Science*, ed. David Helmholtz (Berkeley: University of California Press, 1993), 244–45; Helmholtz, "Über das Verhältniss," 125.

59. Helmholtz, "Über das Verhältniss," 120.

60. Ibid., 122.

61. Ibid., 122, 131, 132, 133.

62. Ibid., 137; Cahan, *Helmholtz*, 248.

63. Helmholtz, "Über das Verhältniss," 137.

64. Ibid., 133, 138.

65. For an excellent overview of the vast literature on gender studies of science and women in science, see Erika Lorraine Milam and Robert A. Nye, "An Introduction to Scientific Masculinities," *Osiris* 30 (2015): 1–14.

66. Virchow, *Die Gründung*, 25, 29.

67. Helmholtz, "Ueber das Streben nach Popularisierung der Wissenschaft: Vorrede zu der von Tyndall's 'Fragments of Science' 1894," in *Vorträge und Reden*, vol. 2 (Berlin: Vieweg & Sohn, 1903): 424, 426.

68. Weber, *Wissenschaft als Beruf, MWG*, 1.17:86–87.

69. Helmholtz, "Über das Verhältniss," 135.

70. Du Bois-Reymond, "Der physiologische Unterricht sonst und jetzt," in *Reden von Emil Du Bois-Reymond* (Leipzig: Veit, 1887), 379.

71. Rudolf Virchow, "Die naturwissenschaftliche Methode und die Standpunkte in der Therapie," *Archiv für pathologische Anatomie und Physiologie und für klinische Medicin* 2 (1849): 12.

72. Helmholtz, "Über das Verhältniss," 138.

73. Helmholtz quoted in *Dokumente einer Freundschaft: Briefwechsel zwischen Hermman von Helmholtz und Emil Du Bois-Reymond (1846–1894)*, ed. Christa Kirsten (Berlin: Akademie, 1986), 55.

74. Helmholtz, "Ueber das Streben nach Popularisierung," 426.

75. See Otto Brüggemann, *Naturwissenschaft und Bildung: Die Anerkennung des Bildungswertes der Naturwissenschaften in Vergangenheit und Gegenwart* (Heidelberg: Quelle und Meyer, 1967).

76. Our comparison is one of historical perception and degree. For example, as

290 | NOTES TO PAGES 129-134

recent work on early modern philology has shown, scholars have long worked with technologies of all sorts, the printed book being just one. For an overview of some of the more recent work, see Alberto Cevolini, ed., *Forgetting Machines: Knowledge Management Evolution in Early Modern Europe* (Leiden: Brill, 2016).

77. Otis, *Müller's Lab*, 94.

78. Du Bois-Reymond, "Der physiologische Unterricht sonst und jetzt," in *Reden von Emil Du Bois-Reymond* (Leipzig: Veit, 1887), 364.

79. Ibid., 373. We draw here on Otis, *Müller's Lab*, 92–93, and Christian Emden, *Nietzsche's Naturalism: Philosophy and the Life Sciences in the Nineteenth Century* (Cambridge: Cambridge University Press, 2014), 53.

80. Finkelstein, *Emil Du Bois-Reymond*, 171–72.

81. Virchow, *Die Gründung*, 24.

82. Helmholtz, "Das Denken in der Medicin," 181.

83. Du Bois-Reymond, "Der physiologische Unterricht," 379.

84. Du Bois-Reymond quoted in Finkelstein, *Emil Du Bois-Reymond*, 190; Du Bois-Reymond, "Der physiologische Unterricht," 363–64.

85. Virchow, "Die naturwissenschaftliche Methode und die Standpunkte," 17, 19.

86. Emil Du Bois-Reymond, *Ueber Neo-Vitalismus* (Brackwede: Breitenbach, 1913), 10.

87. Emil Du Bois-Reymond, *Untersuchungen über thierische Elektricität* (Berlin: Georg Reimer, 1848), 1:xxix.

88. Ibid., xxvi–xxvii.

89. Paul Foreman, "The Primacy of Science in Modernity, of Technology in Post-modernity, and of Ideology in the History of Technology," *History and Technology* 23, no. 1/2 (2007): 1–152.

90. On this broader dynamic, see Sven Dierig, *Wissenschaft in der Maschinen-stadt: Emil Du Bois-Reymond und seine Laboratorien in Berlin* (Göttingen: Wallstein, 2006), 126.

91. Justus von Liebig, *Der Zustand der Chemie in Preußen* (Brunswick: Bieweg, 1840), 12.

92. Ibid., 13.

93. M. Norton Wise, *Aesthetics, Industry, and Science: Hermann Helmholtz and the Berlin Physical Society* (Chicago: University of Chicago Press, 2018), 197.

94. Ibid., 197, 236.

95. Helmholtz, "Über das Verhältniss," 135.

96. Ibid., 135, 137.

97. Virchow, "Die naturwissenschaftliche Methode und die Standpunkte," 3; David Cahan, "Helmholtz and the Civilizing Power of Science," in *Hermann von Helmholtz and the Foundations of Nineteenth-Century Science*, ed. David Helmholtz (Berkeley: University of California Press, 1993), 559–601.

98. See Daum, *Wissenschaftspopularisierung im 19. Jahrhundert*, 51–64.

99. Helmholtz, "Über das Verhältniss," 141.

100. For an account of Helmholtz's "liberalism," see Cahan, *Helmholtz*, 249–50; for Du Bois-Reymond, see Finkelstein, *Emil Du Bois-Reymond*, 22, 62.

101. Kant, "Beantwortung der Frage: Was ist Aufklärung?," 8:33.

102. Helmholtz, "Über das Verhältniss," 138.

103. Ibid., 130, 135, 138, 142, 144.

104. Ibid., 139, 140, 143.

105. Ibid., 139.

106. Ibid., 141.

107. Ibid., 123.

108. For a Kantian like Helmholtz, spontaneity was a property reserved strictly for reason or mind. See Helmholtz, "Ueber das Ziel und Fortschritt der Naturwissenschaft," in *Vorträge und Reden*, vol. 1 (Braunschweig: Vieweg & Sohn, 1896).

109. Rudolf Virchow, "Über den Fortschritt in der Entwicklung der Humanitäts-Anstalten," in *Amtlicher Bericht über die Fünf und Dreissigste Versammlung Deutscher Naturforscher und Ärzte, in Königsberg Preussen, September 1860* (Königsberg: Hartungsche, 1861), 41.

110. Emil Du Bois-Reymond, "Über die Grenzen des Naturerkennens," in *Über die Grenzen des Naturerkennens und die Sieben Welträthsel: Zwei Vorträge*, 3rd ed. (Leipzig: Veit, 1891).

111. Finkelstein, *Du Bois-Reymond*, 191, 203.

112. Quoted in ibid., 272.

113. Du Bois-Reymond, *Über die Grenzen des Naturerkennens*, 37.

114. Ibid., 39.

115. Ibid., 45.

116. Emil Du Bois-Reymond, *Hr. Rothstein und der Barren: Eine Entgegnung* (Berlin: Georg Reimer, 1863), 4.

117. See Kurt Bayertz, "'Das Rätsel gibt es nicht': Von Emil Du Bois-Reymond über Wittgenstein zum Wiener Kreis," in *Der Ignorabimus-Streit*, ed. Kurt Bayertz, Myriam Gerhard, and Walter Jaeschke (Hamburg: Felix Meiner, 2007), 185.

118. Du Bois-Reymond, *Culturgeschichte und Naturwissenschaft*, 14.

119. Ibid., 35.

120. Ibid., 35; Du Bois-Reymond, "Über die Geschichte der Wissenschaft," in *Reden* (Leipzig: Veit, 1887), 2:354.

121. Du Bois-Reymond's account echoes Nicolas de Condorcet, *Esquisse d'un tableau historique des progrès de l'esprit humain* (1795), and more immediately, Henry Thomas Buckle, *The History of Civilization in England* (London: Parker and Son, 1858).

122. Du Bois-Reymond, *Culturgeschichte und Naturwissenschaft*, 54.

123. Ibid., 30, 54.

124. Ibid., 42, 43, 44.

125. Helmholtz, *Über die Erhaltung der Kraft: Eine physikalische Abhandlung* (Berlin: Reimer, 1847), 7.

126. Christoph Gradmann, "Naturwissenschaft, Kulturgeschichte und Bildungsbegriff bei Emil Du Bois-Reymond," *Tractrix* 5 (1993): 14–15.

127. See James C. Albisetti, "The Decline of the German Mandarins after Twenty-Five Years," *History of Education Quarterly* 34, no. 4 (1994): 454.

128. Virchow, "Die naturwissenschaftliche Methode und die Standpunkte," 9.

129. Lorraine Daston, "When Science Went Modern," *Hedgehog Review* 18, no. 3 (Fall 2016), https://hedgehogreview.com/issues/the-cultural-contradictions-of-modern-science/articles/when-science-went-modern.

130. Du Bois-Reymond, *Culturgeschichte und Naturwissenschaft*, 54.

131. Ibid.

132. Ibid., 58.

133. Ibid., 51.

134. Du Bois-Reymond, "Die Sieben Welträthsel," in *Über die Grenzen des Natur-erkennens und die Sieben Welträthsel: Zwei Vorträge*, 3rd ed. (Leipzig: Veit, 1891), 62.

135. Here we draw directly from Kurt Bayertz "Einleitung," in *Der Ignorabimus-Streit*, ed. Kurt Bayertz, Myriam Gerhard, and Walter Jaeschke (Hamburg: Felix Meiner, 2012), xxi–xxvi.

136. Daum, *Wissenschaftspopularisierung im 19. Jahrhundert*, 33–42, 85–89.

137. See Finkelstein, *Emil Du Bois-Reymond*, 269–72.

138. Robert J. Richards, *The Tragic Sense of Life: Ernst Haeckel and the Struggle over Evolutionary Thought* (Chicago: University of Chicago Press, 2008), 1.

139. Ernst Haeckel, *Anthropogenie, oder Entwicklungsgeschichte des Menschen* (Leipzig, 1874), xii.; Haeckel, *Ueber die Entwicklungstheorie Darwin's* in *Vorträge aus dem Gebiete der Entwicklungslehre* (Bonn: Emil Strauss, 1878), 24–25.

140. Haeckel, *Freie Wissenschaft und freie Lehre* (Leipzig: Kröner, 1908), 73, 82.

141. Roberts, *Tragic Sense of Life*, 124.

142. Todd H. Weir, *Secularism and Religion in Nineteenth Century Germany: The Rise of the Fourth Confession* (Cambridge: Cambridge University Press), 67.

143. Title page, *Kosmos* 1, no. 1 (April–September 1877).

144. Ibid., 3.

145. In the journal's opening essay, one of the editors called for a "new reunification" of philosophy and natural science. Otto Caspari, "Die Philosophie im Bund mit der Naturforschung," *Kosmos* 1, no. 1 (April–September 1877): 4–16.

146. This is a sample of titles from volumes 1 (1877) to 6 (1879).

147. Eduard von Hartmann, "Anfänge naturwissenschaftlicher Selbstkenntnisse," in *Der Ignorabimus-Streit*, ed. Kurt Bayertz, Myriam Gerhard, and Walter Jaeschke (Hamburg: Felix Meiner, 2012), 35.

148. Quoted in Frederick Beiser, *After Hegel: German Philosophy 1840–1900* (Cambridge, MA: Harvard University Press, 2014), 118.

149. Carl von Nägeli, "Ueber die Schranken der Naturwissenschaftlichen Erkenntnis," in *Der Ignorabimus-Streit*, ed. Kurt Bayertz, Myriam Gerhard, and Walter Jaeschke (Hamburg: Felix Meiner, 2012), 150, 151.

150. Ottokar Lorenz, "Die 'bürgerliche' und die naturwissenschaftliche Geschichte," *Historische Zeitschrift* 39, no. 3 (1878): 485. On Lorenz, Irmline Veit-Brause makes this same point in "Scientists and the Cultural Politics of Academic Disciplines in Late 19th-Century Germany: Emil Du Bois-Reymond and the Controversy over the Role of the Cultural Sciences," *History of the Human Sciences* 14, no. 4 (2001): 47.

151. Virchow, "Über den Fortschritt," 41.

152. Rudolf Virchow, *Die Freiheit der Wissenschaft im modernen Staat* (Berlin: Wiegandt, Hempel, & Parey, 1877), 22.

153. Ibid., 9.

154. Ibid., 23.

155. Ibid., 24.

156. Ibid., 7, 24, 29. Du Bois-Reymond, *Über die Grenzen des Naturerkennens*, 45.

157. Virchow, *Die Freiheit der Wissenschaft*, 29.

158. Ernst Haeckel, *Die heutige Entwickelungslehre im Verhältnisse zur Gesammtwissenschaft* (Stuttgart: E. Schwiezerbart'sche, 1878), 16.

159. Ernst Haeckel, *Freie Wissenschaft und freie Lehre* (Leipzig: Alfred Kröner, 1908), 32.

160. Ibid., 33, 82.

161. Haeckel, *Die heutige Entwicklungslehre*, 6.

162. Ibid., 6–7.

163. Ibid., 10.

164. Helmholtz, *Über die Akademische Freiheit der deutschen Universitäten* (Berlin: Hirschwald, 1878), 30.

165. Jessica Riskin, *The Restless Clock: A History of the Centuries-Long Argument over What Makes Living Things Tick* (Chicago: University of Chicago Press, 2016), 261.

166. Ibid., 256–57.

167. Virchow, "Empirie und Transscendenz," 27 (see n. 35).

168. Virchow, *Die Freiheit der Wissenschaft*, 29.

169. Bayertz, "Das Rätsel gibt es nicht," 187 (see n. 117).

170. Emil Du Bois-Reymond, *Goethe und kein Ende* (Leipzig: Veit, 1882), 10, 29.

171. See Charles Taylor, *A Secular Age* (Cambridge, MA: Harvard University Press, 2007), 26–27.

172. Odo Marquard, "Über die Unvermeidlichkeit der Geisteswissenschaften," 98 (see n. 79).

173. *WDGS*, 1:22.

174. August Wilhelm Hofmann, *Die Frage der Theilung der philosophischen Facultät* (Berlin: F. Dümmler, 1881), 80.

CHAPTER FIVE

1. Wilhelm Dilthey, *Wilhelm Dilthey Gesammelte Schriften* [*WDGS*], 26 vols. (Stuttgart: B. G. Teubner, 1961–1966), 1:3.

2. Ibid., 1:21.

3. *WDGS*, 11:239.

4. Helmholtz, "Die Tatsachen in der Wahrnehmung," in *Vorträge und Reden* (Berlin: Vieweg & Sohn, 1903), 2:365.

5. Ibid., 2:284.

6. Riskin, *The Restless Clock*, 257.

7. Dilthey, *Der junge Dilthey: Ein Lebensbild in Briefen und Tagebüchern*, ed. Clara Misch-Dilthey (Stuttgart: Teubner, 1960), 284.

8. *WDGS*, 5:353, 355.

9. *WDGS*, 1:113.

10. Ibid., 1:xix.

11. *WDGS*, 5:357.

12. Ibid. See also *WDGS*, 1:365, 367, 368, 371.

13. Helmholtz, "Die Tatsachen in der Wahrnehmung," 13, 14.

14. Heinrich Rickert, *Kulturwissenschaft und Naturwissenschaft* (Tübingen: Mohr, 1910), 1.

15. *WDGS*, 1:13.

16. For an account of how Dilthey's basic concepts changed over time, see Frederick C. Beiser, *The German Historicist Tradition* (Oxford: Oxford University Press, 2011), 322–64. In the following paragraphs, we draw on Beiser's argument about Dilthey's ultimate failure to present a salient difference between the two classes of knowledge on methodological, ontological, or epistemic grounds (325–331).

17. *WDGS*, 1:10–13.

18. Ibid., 1:6.

19. Ibid., 1:9.

20. Ibid., 1:11.

21. Ibid., 1:11–13.

22. Ibid., 1:xvii.

23. Ibid., 1:36.

24. Ibid.

25. Ibid., 1:15.

26. Ibid., 1:15.

27. Ibid, 1:6.

28. *WDGS*, 7:199.

29. *WDGS*, 1:20.

30. Ibid., 1:11.

31. Ibid., 1:4.

32. Ibid., 1:355, 356.

33. Ibid.

34. Ibid., 1:129, 133.

35. Ibid., 1:113, 125–126.

36. Ibid., 1:125. See also *WDGS* 7:191–294, 217, 218.

37. *WDGS*, 7:218.

38. *WDGS*, 1:124, 276, 330, 352.

39. Ibid., 1:352.

40. Ibid.

41. Ibid., 1:375.

42. Ibid., 1:374.

43. Ibid., 1:375; see also 28.

44. Ibid., 1:377.

45. Ibid., 1:384.

46. *WDGS*, 5:193.

47. Beiser, *Historicist Tradition*, 333.

48. *WDGS*, 5:158, 165.

49. Ibid., 5:172.

50. Ibid., 5:226. See Beiser, *Historicist Tradition*, 333.

51. *WDGS*, 5:153.

52. Ibid., 5:215–216.

53. *WDGS*, 1:144. See also *WDGS*, 5:144.

54. *WDGS*, 1:384.

55. Ibid., 1:138, 385.

56. Ibid., 1:385.

57. Ibid., 1:137, 385.

58. Dilthey compares his concept of religious "experience" to Schleiermacher's account of religion as "das schlechthinige Abhängigkeitsgefühl." See *WDGS*, 1:139n1, and *WDGS*, 6:288–305.

59. *WDGS*, 1:11–12, 15.

60. See Chad Wellmon, *Organizing Enlightenment: Information Overload and the Invention of the Modern Research University* (Baltimore: Johns Hopkins University Press, 2015), 234–61; William Clark, "On the dialectical Origins of the Research Seminar," *History of Science* 27 (1989): 111–54; Kathryn Olesko, *Physics as Calling: Discipline and Practice in the Königsberg Seminar for Physics* (Ithaca, NY: Cornell University Press, 1991).

61. Roger Chickering, *Karl Lamprecht: A German Academic Life* (Leiden: Brill, 1993), 27.

62. For an extensive account of the halting introduction of the "doctor of philosophy," see William Clark, *Academic Charisma and the Origins of the Research University* (Chicago: University of Chicago Press, 2006), 183–238.

63. Hans Joaquim Schoeps, ed., "Ein Gutachten des Kultusministers von Altenstein," *Zeitschrift für Pädagogik* 12 (1966): 262.

64. See Thomas Albert Howard, *Protestant Theology and the Making of the Modern German University* (New York: Oxford University Press, 2005), 284.

65. Karl Marx, *Zur Judenfrage* (Berlin: Rowohlt, 1919), 173, 216.

66. Karl Ludwig Michelet, *Entwicklungsgeschichte der neuesten deutschen Philosophie* (Berlin: Duncker & Humblot, 1843), 305, 400.

67. See, for example, August Boeckh, "Über das Verhältniss der Wissenschaft zum Leben," in *August Boeckh's Gesammelte kleine Schriften*, vol. 2, *Boeckh's Reden Gehalten auf der Universität und in der Akademie der Wissenschaften zu Berlin* (Leipzig: Teubner, 1877).

68. August Wilhelm Hofmann, *Die Frage der Theilung der philosophischen Facultät* (Berlin: F. Dümmler, 1881), 24.

69. Fritz Ringer, *The Decline of the German Mandarins: The German Academic Community, 1890–1933*, (Cambridge, MA: Harvard University Press, 1969), 282–94.

70. W. Lexis, "Vorwort" in *Die Deutschen Universitäten*, ed. W. Lexis, vol. 1 (Berlin: A. Ascher, 1893).

71. Friedrich Paulsen, "Wesen und geschichtliche Entwicklung der deutschen Universitäten," in ibid., 1:104.

72. Paulsen, "Wesen," in Lexis, *Die Deutschen Universitäten*, 1:105, 106, 108.

73. Ibid., 1:109.

74. Ibid.

75. Quoted in Hofmann, *Die Frage*, 8–9.

76. *WDGS*, 11:242.

77. For an introduction and key source texts, see Kurt Bayertz, ed., *Der Materialismus-Streit* (Berlin: Meiner, 2012).

78. Dilthey quoted in "Vorbericht des Herausgebers" in *WDGS*, 5:lxxiv.

79. Dilthey, "Die Wissenschaften vom handelnden Menschen," in *WDGS*, 18:19.

80. Julian Hamann, "The Making of the *Geisteswissenschaften: A Case Study of Boundary Work?*," FIW Working Paper, June 2017, 15.

81. Herbert Schnädelbach, *Philosophie in Deutschland 1831–1933* (Frankfurt

am Main: Suhrkamp, 1983), 89ff; "Philosophie auf dem Weg von der System- zur Forschungswissenschaft. Oder: Von der Wissenschaftslehre zur Philosophie als Geisteswissenschaft," in *Geschichte der Universität Unter den Linden: Gründung und Blütezeit der Universität zu Berlin 1810–1918*, 6 vols., ed. Charles McClelland and Heinz-Elmar Tenorth (Berlin: Akademie, 2010–2013), 4:192.

82. Klaus Köhnke, *Entstehung und Aufstieg des Neukantianismus: Die deutsche Universitätsphilosophie zwischen Idealismus und Positivismus* (Frankfurt am Main: Suhrkamp, 1993); Frederick C. Beiser, *The Genesis of Neo-Kantianism, 1796–1880* (Oxford: Oxford University Press, 2014).

83. For a comparable analysis of the role of neo-Kantianism in these debates, to which we are indebted, see Hamann, "The Making of the *Geisteswissenschaften*," 15.

84. Windelband, "Was Ist Philosophie?," in *Präludien* (Tübingen: Mohr, 1924), 1:2, 24, 25, 33.

85. Windelband, "Kritische oder genetische Methode," in *Präludien*, 2:123.

86. Ibid.

87. Stephan Roscher, *Die Kaiser-Wilhelms-Universität Straßburg 1872–1902: Geisteswissenschaftler zwischen Reichsidee und Regionalismus* (Frankfurt am Main: Peter Lang, 2006).

88. Wilhelm Dilthey, "Entwurf zu einem Gutachten über die Gründung der Universität Straßburg," in *Die Erziehung: Monatsschrift für den Zusammenhang von Kultur und Erziehung in Wissenschaft und Leben* 16 (1941): 81–85.

89. Horst Gundlach, *Wilhelm Windelband und die Psychologie: Das Fach Philosophie und die Wissenschaft Psychologie im Deutschen Kaiserreich* (Heidelberg: University of Heidelberg Press, 2017), 119.

90. Wilhelm Windelband, *Geschichte und Naturwissenschaft* (Straßburg: Heitz, 1894), 21, 22.

91. Ibid., 40.

92. Ibid., 22, 26, 28–29, 30.

93. Eric Hayot, "What Happens to Literature If People Are Artworks?," *New Literary History* 48, no. 3 (2017): 458.

94. Windelband, *Geschichte und Naturwissenschaft*, 25.

95. Ibid., 31–34.

96. Ibid., 36, 40.

97. Ibid., 40.

98. Windelband, "Kulturphilosophie und transzendentaler Idealismus," in *Präludien*, 2:279–94. Quoting and drawing on Beiser, *Historicist Tradition*, 391–92.

99. Beiser, *Historicist Tradition*, 391. Rickert, *Kulturwissenschaft und Naturwissenschaft*, 12.

100. See Beiser, *Historicist Tradition*, 394–442.

101. Heinrich Rickert, *Kulturwissenschaft und Naturwissenschaft* (Freiburg: Mohr, 1899), 5.

102. We are quoting from the second version published as Heinrich Rickert, *Kulturwissenschaft und Naturwissenschaft* (Tübingen: Mohr, 1910), "Vorwort."

103. Rickert, *Kulturwissenschaft und Naturwissenschaft* (1910), 1.

104. Ibid., 5–6, 7, 1.

105. Ibid., 51, 13.

106. Beiser, *Historicist Tradition*, 382.

107. Rickert, *Kulturwissenschaft und Naturwissenschaft* (1910), 17–19, 20.

108. Ibid., 40, 41, 109.

109. Ibid., 44.

110. Windelband, *Geschichte und Naturwissenschaft*, 40.

111. We borrow this phrase from Henry M. Clowes, "History Naturalized," *Historical Studies in the Natural Sciences* 47, no. 1 (2017): 107–16.

112. Emil Du Bois-Reymond, *Über die Grenzen des Naturerkennens und die Sieben Welträthsel: Zwei Vorträge*, 3rd ed. (Leipzig: Veit, 1891), 44.

113. Max Verworn, "Die Frage nach den Grenzen der Erkenntnis: Ein Vortrag," in *Der Ignorabimus-Streit*, ed. Kurt Bayertz, Myriam Gerhard, and Walter Jaeschke (Hamburg: Felix Meiner, 2012), 287.

114. Emil Du Bois-Reymond, "Darwin vs. Galiani" (1876), in *Reden von Emil Du Bois-Reymond* (Leipzig: Veit, 1912), 1:561–62.

115. Du Bois-Reymond, "Darwin vs. Galiani," 563.

116. Rickert, *Kulturwissenschaft und Naturwissenschaft* (1910), 125.

117. Walter Rathenau, "Ignorabimus," in *Der Ignorabimus-Streit*, ed. Kurt Bayertz, Myriam Gerhard, and Walter Jaeschke (Hamburg: Felix Meiner, 2012), 234.

118. Ibid., 3:236.

119. Ibid., 3:238, 239.

120. Ibid., 3:250–51.

121. Lorraine Daston, "When Science Went Modern," *Hedgehog Review* 18, no. 3 (Fall 2016), https://hedgehogreview.com/issues/the-cultural-contradictions-of-modern-science/articles/when-science-went-modern.

122. Siemens, *Das Naturwissenschaftliche Zeitalter*, 8, 13.

123. Daston, "When Science Went Modern."

124. Heinrich Rickert, *Die Grenzen der naturwissenschaftlichen Begriffsbildung* (Tübingen: Mohr, 1929), 7.

125. Rickert, *Die Grenzen*, xxv, xxiii.

126. Rickert, *Kulturwissenschaft und Naturwissenschaft* (1910), 148.

127. Ibid., 149.

128. Ibid.

129. Rickert, *Die Grenzen*, 536–37.

130. Weber, *Wissenschaft als Beruf*, MWG, 1.17:101, 103.

131. See Hayot, "What Happens to Literature."

132. Compare to Amanda Anderson, *Psyche and Ethos: Moral Life after Psychology* (Oxford: Oxford University Press, 2018).

133. Helen Small, *The Value of the Humanities* (Oxford: Oxford University Press, 2013), 29.

## CHAPTER SIX

1. Spranger, "Leben und Wissenschaft," in *Eduard Spranger: Gesammelte Schriften* (Tübingen: Max Niemeyer, 1980), 6:91, 100.

2. Konrad H. Jarausch, *Students, Society, and Politics in Imperial Germany* (Princeton, NJ: Princeton University Press, 1982), 23–113.

3. The Wittenberg Program quoted in Friedrich Schulze und Paul Ssymank, *Das*

*deutsche Studententum von den aeltesten Zeiten bis zum Weltkriege* (Leipzig: R. Voigt-länder 1918), 363.

4. Jarausch, *Students*, 282–83.

5. Ssymank, *Das Deutsche Studententum*, 365; See also Jarausch, *Students*, 280.

6. Felix Behrend, *Der freistudentische Ideenkreis* (Munich: Bavaria, 1907).

7. Ibid., 13.

8. Quoted in Ssymank, *Das Deutsche Studententum*, 402.

9. Charles E. McClelland, "Studium und Studenten," in *Geschichte der Universität Unter den Linden: Gründung und Blütezeit der Universität zu Berlin 1810–1918*, 6 vols., ed. Charles McClelland and Heinz-Elmar Tenorth (Berlin: Akademie, 2010–2013), 1:516.

10. Hartmut Titze, *Wachstum und Differenzierung der deutschen Universitäten 1830–1945* (Göttingen: Vandenhoeck & Ruprecht 1995), 91.

11. Peter Lundgreen, "Studium zwischen Forschungsorientierung und Berufs-konstruktion," in *Die Berliner Universität im Kontext der deutschen Universitätsland-schaft*, ed. Rüdiger vom Bruch (Munich: Oldenbourg, 2010), 111–127.

12. See Heinz-Elmar Tenorth, "Transformation der Wissensordnung," in McClelland and Tenorth, *Geschichte der Universität Unter den Linden*, 5:19. For an overview of similar patterns at other universities, see Titze, Wachstum, 91. Uwe Meves, "Die Gründung germanistischer Seminare an den preußischen Universi-täten (1875–1895)" (1987), in *Ausgewählte Beiträge zur Geschichte der Germanistik und des Deutschunterrichts im 19. und 20. Jahrhundert*, ed. Uwe Meves (Hildesheim: Weidmann, 2004), 279–327.

13. Andrew Abbott, *Chaos of Disciplines* (Chicago: University of Chicago Press, 2001).

14. Weber, "Rezension von: Eulenburg, Die Entwicklung der Universität Leipzig," *MWG*, 1.13:170.

15. Bruno Gebhardt, *Wilhelm von Humboldt als Staatsmann*, 2 vols. (Stuttgart: Cotta, 1896–1899).

16. Rüdiger vom Bruch, "Langsamer Abschied von Humboldt?" in *Mythos Hum-boldt: Vergangenheit und Zukunft der deutschen Universitäten*, ed. Mitchell G. Ash (Vienna: Böhlau, 1999), 29–58.

17. Harnack, "Zur Kaiserlichen Botschaft vom 11. Okt. 1910: Begründung von Forschungsinstituten," in *Adolf von Harnack als Zeitgenosse*, ed. Kurt Nowack (Ber-lin: Walter de Gruyter, 1996), 2:1026–49.

18. Harnack, "Wissenschaft als Großbetrieb," in Nowack, *Adolf von Harnack als Zeitgenosse*, 2:1004.

19. Quoted in Jarausch, *Students*, 289.

20. Behrend, *Der Freistudentische Ideenkreis*, 33.

21. Karl Korsch, "Rechtsformen für die Verwicklichung freistudentischer Ideen," *Akademische Rundschau* 14, no. 1 (1912): 7, quoted in Hans Harald Müller, *Intellek-tueller Linksradikalismus in der Weimarer Republik* (Kronberg: Scriptor, 1977), 30.

22. Kranold, "Der Werdegang des Freistudententums," in *Freistudententum: Ver-such einer Synthese der freistudententischen Ideen*, ed. Hermann Kranold (Munich: Max Steinbach, 1913), 17, 19.

23. Benjamin, "Ziele und Wege der studentisch-pädagogischen Gruppe an

reichsdeutschen Universitäten," in *Walter Benjamin Gesammelte Schriften*, ed. Rolf Tiedemann and Hermann Schweppenhäuser (Frankfurt am Main: Suhrkamp, 1972), 2.1:64.

24. Hilde Benjamin quoted in Howard Eiland and Michael W. Jennings, *Walter Benjamin: A Critical Life* (Cambridge, MA: Harvard University Press, 2014), 36–37.

25. Meißnerformel of 1913 as reprinted in *Hoher Meissner 1913: Der Erste Freideutsche Jugendtag in Dokumenten, Deutungen und Bildern*, ed. Winfried Mogge and Jürgen Reulecke (Cologne: Wissenschaft und Politik, 1988), 34.

26. Ibid.

27. Walter Benjamin, "Das Leben der Studenten," in *Walter Benjamin Gesammelte Schriften*, ed. R. Tiedemann and H. Schweppenhäuser (Frankfurt am Main: Suhrkamp, 1972), 2.1:82, hereafter *WBG*; *Walter Benjamin Gesammelte Briefe*, 6 vols., ed. Christoph Gödde and Henri Lonitz (Frankfurt am Main: Suhrkamp, 1995–2000), 1:175.

28. See Benjamin, *Gesammelte Briefe*, 1:160.

29. Benjamin, "Ziele und Wege der studentisch-pädagogischen Gruppen," 61.

30. Ibid., 65.

31. Ibid., 61.

32. See Barbara Stambolis and Jürgen Reulecke, eds., *100 Jahre Hoher Meißner (1913–2013): Quellen zur Geschichte der Jugendbewegung* (Göttingen: V & R Unipress, 2014).

33. Benjamin, "Die Jugend schwieg," in *WBG*, 2.1:66. See Eiland and Jennings, *Walter Benjamin*, 62–63.

34. Benjamin, "Das Leben der Studenten," *WGB*, 2.1:82, 77, respectively.

35. Benjamin, "Bericht über den ersten Freideutschen Jugendtag," in *WBG*, 2.3:913.

36. Hans Reichenbach, "Die Idee des Freistudententums," in Kranold, *Freistudententum*, 7.

37. Benjamin, "Die freie Schulgemeinde," *Der Anfang* 4 (1911): 80.

38. See Ulrich Linse, "Hochschulrevolution! Zur Ideologie und Praxis sozialistischer Studentengruppen während der deutschen Revolutionszeit 1918/19," *Archiv für Sozialgeschichte* 14 (1974): 9.

39. Birnbaum quoted in Müller, *Intellektueller Linksradikalismus*, 31.

40. *Der Aufbruch: Monatsblätter aus der Jugendbewegung* (1915).

41. Benjamin, Letter to Ernst Schoen, May 23, 1914 in *Gesammelte Briefe*, 1:231.

42. Letter of October 25, 1914, *Gesammelte Briefe*, 1:257.

43. Here and in the following sections, we draw on our introduction in *Charisma and Disenchantment: The Vocation Lectures*, ed. Paul Reitter and Chad Wellmon (New York: New York Review Books, 2020).

44. More of a liberal social democrat, Birnbaum had joined the FSA in Munich in 1913/14, become a leader, joined the SPD in 1917, and in the spring of 1919 sought to mediate between student revolutionaries and university leaders in Munich.

45. Franz Schwab, "Beruf und Jugend," *Die weißen Blätter* 4, no. 5 (May 1917): 103.

46. Birnbaum, "Nachwort," in Max Weber, *Wissenschaft als Beruf* (Munich: Duncker & Humblot, 1919), 38.

47. Weber, "Die Lehrfreiheit der Universitäten," *MWG*, 1.13:133.

48. Weber, *Parlament und Regierung im neugeordneten Deutschland: Zur politischen Kritik des Beamtentums und Parteiwesens*, *MWG*, 1.15:593.

49. Benjamin, "Das Leben der Studenten," *WBG*, 2.1:75.

50. Weber, *Wissenschaft als Beruf*, *MWG*, 1.17:72-74.

51. Ibid., 89.

52. Ibid., 84.

53. For a recent overview of the literature on disenchantment, see Hans Kippenberg, "Dialektik der Entzauberung: Säkularisierung aus der Perspektive von Webers Religionssystematik," in *Alte Begriffe—Neue Probleme Max Webers Soziologie im Lichte aktueller Problemstellungen*, ed. Thomas Schwinn and Gert Albert (Tübingen: Mohr Siebeck, 2016), 81-116.

54. Weber, *Die Protestantische Ethik und der Geist des Kapitalismus*, *MWG*, 1.9:398.

55. Ibid., 1.9:342.

56. Calvin, *Institutes of the Christian Religion*, trans. Ford Lewis Battles, 2 vols. (Louisville, KY: Westminster John Know, 2006), vol. 1, chap. 2. sec. 1.

57. Wilhelm Hennis, *Max Weber: Essays in Reconstruction*, trans. Keith Tribe (London: Allen & Unwin, 1988), 42.

58. Weber, *Wissenschaft als Beruf*, *MWG*, 1.17:86.

59. Ibid. See also "Ueber einige Kategorien der verstehenden Soziologie," in Max Weber, *Gesammelte Aufsätze zur Wissenschaftslehre* (Tübingen: Mohr 1922), 449.

60. Weber, *Die Wirtschaftsethik der Weltreligionen: Vergleichende religionssoziologische Versuche*, *MWG*, 1.19:102.

61. Weber, *Die protestantische Ethik*, *MWG*, 1.9:177.

62. Hunter, "Science as Vocation, Philosophy as Religion," *Sociologica* 12, no. 1 (2018): 137-53. See also Hennis, *Max Weber*, esp. 38-46.

63. Werner Siemens, *Das Naturwissenschaftliche Zeitalter* (Berlin: Carl Heymann, 1886), 6.

64. Weber, "Ueber einige Kategorien," 449.

65. For related discussions of magic and rationality, see Simon During, *Modern Enchantments: The Cultural Power of Secular Magic* (Cambridge, MA: Harvard University Press, 2004), and Emily Ogden, *Credulity: A Cultural History of Mesmerism* (Chicago: University of Chicago Press, 2018).

66. Weber, *Die protestantische Ethik*, *MWG*, 1.18:487.

67. Weber, *Politik als Beruf*, *MWG*, 1.17:251.

68. Ibid., 101.

69. Karl Löwith, *Mein Leben in Deutschland vor und Nach 1933* (Stuttgart: J. B. Metzler, 2007), 16-17.

70. Erik Wolk, "Max Webers ethischer Kritizismus und das Problem der Metaphysik," *Logos* 19 (1930): 360.

71. Max Scheler, "Weltanschauungslehre, Soziologie, und Weltanschauungssetzung," in *Kölner Vierteljahreshefte für Sozialwissenschaften* 2 (1922): 18-33.

72. Ernst Troeltsch, *Die Revolution in der Wissenschaft* (Munich: Duncker & Humblot, 1921), 67-68.

73. Ibid., 83.

74. Werner Holz, "Die Lage der Studentenschaft," *Die Hochschule* 3, no. 8 (1919): 230.

75. Krieck, "Vom Sinn der Wissenschaft," *Der neue Merkur* 5 (1921): 512; Arthur Salz, *Für die Wissenschaft: Gegen die Gebildeten unter ihren Verächtern* (Munich: Drei Masken, 1921), 18.

76. Erich von Kahler, *Der Beruf der Wissenschaft* (Berlin: Georg Bondi, 1920), 31.

77. Richard Pohle, *Max Weber und die Krise der Wissenschaft: Eine Debatte in Weimar* (Göttingen: Vandenhoeck & Ruprecht, 2009), 41–43.

78. Kahler, *Der Beruf der Wissenschaft*, 32.

79. Ibid., 21.

80. Ibid., 7.

81. Ibid., 10, 18.

82. Ibid., 71.

83. Ibid., 15.

84. Ibid.

85. Ibid., 34.

86. Ibid., 49, 50.

87. Ibid., 42, 78.

88. Ibid., 79, 99.

89. Salz, *Für die Wissenschaft*, 15, 29.

90. Alwin Diemer, "Die Differenzierung der Wissenschaften in die Natur- und die Geisteswissenschaften und die Begründung der Geisteswissenschaften als Wissenschaft," in *Beiträge zur Entwicklung der Wissenschaftstheorie im 19. Jahrhundert*, ed. Alwin Dieter (Meisenheim am Glan: Anton Hain, 1968): 214.

91. Ernst Troeltsch, *Der Historismus und Seine Probleme* (Aalen: Scientia, 1961), 1, 3.

92. Ibid., 108.

93. Ibid., 772.

94. Troeltsch, *Die Revolution in der Wissenschaft* (Munich: Duncker & Humblot, 1921), 89, and Weber, *Wissenschaft als Beruf, MWG*, 1.17:104.

95. Heinrich Rickert, "Max Weber und seine Stellung zur Wissenschaft," *Logos* 15, no. 2 (1926): 234.

96. On neo-Kantianism, see Klaus Christian Köhnke, *The Rise of Neo-Kantianism: German Academic Philosophy between Idealism and Positivism*, trans. R. J. Hollingdale (Cambridge: Cambridge University Press, 1991).

97. Albert Dietrich, "Wissenschaftskrisis," in *Die Neue Front*, ed. Arthur Moeller van den Bruck (Berlin: Paetel, 1922), 171.

98. Edmund Husserl, "Philosophie als strenge Wissenschaft," *Logos* 1 (1910/1911): 289–341.

99. Hugo Dingler, "Der Zusammenbruch der Wissenschaft und der Primat der Philosophie" (1926), quoted in Eduard Spranger, "Der Sinn der Voraussetzungslosigkeit in den Geisteswissenschaften" in *Eduard Spranger: Gesammelte Schriften* (Tübinben: Max Niemeyer, 1980), 6:157n.

100. Dietrich, "Wissenschaftskrisis," 154, 167.

101. Salz, *Für die Wissenschaft gegen die Gebildeten unter ihren Verächtern* (Munich: Drei Masken, 1921), 14, 30.

102. Quoted in Troeltsch, *Die Revolution in der Wissenschaft*, 90.

103. Salz, *Für die Wissenschaft*, 58.

104. See, for example, Michael Grüttner, "Die nationalsozialistische Wissenschaftspolitik und die Geisteswissenschaften," in *Literaturwissenschaft und Nationalsozialismus*, ed. Dainat and Danneberg (Tübingen: Niemeyer, 2003), 13–39.

105. See, Gisela Bock and Daniel Schönpflug, eds. *Friedrich Meinecke in seiner Zeit: Studien zu Leben und Werk* (Stuttgart: F. Steiner, 2006).

106. Ernst Krieck, "Das Ende einer Wissenschaftsideologie," *Deutsches Recht* 4 (1934): 297–300. Krieck also wrote "The Racial-Völkisch-Political Conception of History" (1934).

107. Jan Eckel, *Geist der Zeit: Deutsche Geisteswissenschaften seit 1870* (Göttingen: Vandenhoeck & Ruprecht 2008), 54.

108. Troeltsch, *Die Revolution in der Wissenschaft*, 67–68, 93.

109. Spranger, "Der Sinn," 151, 152.

110. Ibid., 153. Spranger is quoting from Erich Rothacker *Logik und Systematik der Geisteswissenschaften* (1926).

111. Ibid., 157–60.

112. Ibid.

113. Eduard Spranger, *Wilhelm von Humboldt und die Humanitätsidee* (Berlin: Reuther & Reichard, 1909).

114. D. Timothy Goering, "Einleitung," in *Ideengeschichte Heute: Traditionen und Perspektiven* (Bielefeld: Transcript, 2017), 16–24.

115. Krieck, "Vom Sinn der Wissenschaft," *Der neue Merkur* 5 (1921): 511.

116. Spranger made *Geisteswissenschaften* into what Max Horkheimer called an "Unbegriff." Horkheimer, "Geisteswissenschaften," *Gesammelte Schriften*, vol. 14, *Nachgelassene Schriften 1949–1972* (Frankfurt am Main: Suhrkamp, 1988), 385.

117. Eduard Spranger, "März 1933," *Die Erziehung: Monatsschrift für den Zusammenhang von Kultur und Erziehung in Wissenschaft und Leben* 8, no. 7 (April 1933): 402–8.

118. Weber, *Wissenschaft als Beruf*, MWG, 1.17:80.

119. Ibid., 92.

120. Kant, *Kritik der reinen Vernunft*, 451/B479; WDGS, 1:6.

121. Weber, *Wirtschaft und Gesellschaft*, MWG, 1.22.2:273, 269–70.

122. See Jason A. Josephson-Strom, *The Myth of Disenchantment: Magic, Modernity, and the Birth of the Human Sciences* (Chicago: University of Chicago Press, 2017), 290–96.

123. Weber, *Religiöse Gemeinschaften*, MWG, 1.22.2:273.

124. Kant, *Kritik der Urteilskraft*, 5:433.

125. Weber, *Wissenschaft als Beruf*, MWG, 1.17:105.

126. Weber, *Die Wirtschaftsethik der Weltreligionen*, MWG, 21.2:642–43.

127. Weber, *Die protestantische Ethik*, MWG, 1.9:257.

128. Weber, *Politik als Beruf*, MWG, 1.17:170.

129. Weber, *Wissenschaft als Beruf*, MWG, 1.17:104.

130. Max Weber, "Der Sinn der 'Wertfreiheit' der soziologischen und ökonomischen Wissenschaften," in *Gesammelte Aufsätze zur Wissenschaftslehre* (Tübingen: Mohr 1922), 178.

131. Jürgen Habermas, in *Max Weber and Sociology Today*, 59.

132. Weber, *Wissenschaft als Beruf*, *MWG*, 1.17:103.

133. Weber, "Die Lehrfreiheit der Universitäten," *MWG*, 1.13:133.

134. Weber, "Der Sinn der 'Wertfreiheit,'" 451–502. We translate *Wertfreiheit* as "value freedom." Although the usual English translation is "value neutrality," for reasons that we make clear in the following paragraphs we have chosen a more literal translation.

135. Weber, "Der Sinn der 'Wertfreiheit,'" 453, 451.

136. Weber, *Wissenschaft als Beruf*, *MWG*, 1.17:103.

137. Amia Srinivasan, "Sex as Pedagogical Failure," *Yale Law Journal* 129 (2020): 1118–19.

138. Weber, "Der Sinn der 'Wertfreiheit,'" 456.

139. Weber, *Wissenschaft als Beruf*, *MWG*, 1.17:97.

140. Horkheimer, "Einleitung zur Diskussion," in Otto Stammer, ed., *Max Weber und die Soziologie heute: Verhandlungen des 15. Deutschen Soziologentages in Heidelberg 1964* (Tübingen: Mohr Siebeck, 1965), 65–66.

141. Gerth and Mills, "Introduction: The Man and His Work," in *From Max Weber: Essays in Sociology*, ed. Hans H. Gerth and C. Wright (New York: Oxford University Press, 1946), 73.

142. Rieff, "Introduction: Max Weber," in "Science and the Modern World View," *Daedalus* 87, no. 1 (Winter 1958): 111.

143. Hennis, *Max Weber*, 52 (see n. 57).

144. Weber, *Wissenschaft als Beruf*, *MWG*, 1.17:97.

145. Erik Wolf made this point in "Max Webers ethischer Kritizismus und das Problem der Metaphysik," *Logos* 19 (1930): 363.

146. Amanda Anderson, *Psyche and Eros: Moral Life after Psychology*, Clarendon Lectures in English (Oxford: Oxford University Press, 2018), 88.

147. Riskin, *The Restless Clock*, 256–7.

148. Jonathan Kramnick, "The Interdisciplinary Fallacy," *Representations* 140, no. 1 (2017): 67–83.

149. Weber, "'Energetische' Kulturtheorien," in *Gesammelte Aufsätze zur Wissenschaftslehre* (Tübingen: Mohr, 1922), 389.

150. Ian Hunter, "The Mythos, Ethos, and Pathos of the Humanities," *History of European Ideas* 40, no. 1 (2014): 16–17.

151. Wolk, "Max Webers ethischer Kritizismus," 360.

152. Ernst Curtius, "Max Weber über die Wissenschaft als Beruf," *Arbeitsgemeinschaft: Monatsschrift für die gesamte Volkshochschulwesen* 1 (1920): 203.

153. Eckel, *Geist der Zeit*, 136.

## CHAPTER SEVEN

1. Lawrence A. Scaff, *Max Weber in America* (Princeton, NJ: Princeton University Press, 2011), 48–52.

2. Max Weber to Helene Weber, letter from September 19 and 20, 1904, *MWG*, 2.4:292.

3. See Julie Reuben, *The Making of the Modern University: Intellectual Transformation and the Marginalization of Morality* (Chicago: University of Chicago Press, 1996), 17–35.

4. Weber, letter September 19 and 20, *MWG*, 2.4:292.

5. Ibid., *MWG*, 2.4:292, 294, 295.

6. Max Weber, "Die von den deutschen abweichenden Einrichtungen an den nordamerikanischen Hochschulen," *MWG*, 1.13:397–410.

7. Ibid., *MWG*, 1.13:402.

8. Weber, *Wissenschaft als Beruf*, *MWG*, 1.17:74.

9. Laurence Veysey, *The Emergence of the American University* (Chicago: University of Chicago, Press, 1970).

10. M. L. Burton, "The Undergraduate Course," *New Republic*, October 25, 1922, 9–11.

11. Alexander Meiklejohn, "The Unity of the Curriculum," *New Republic*, October 25, 1922, 2–4.

12. H. W. Chase, "The Problem of Higher Education," *New Republic*, October 25, 1922, 4–5.

13. For an extended discussion from which we draw here, see Chad Wellmon, "Whatever Happened to General Education?," *Hedgehog Review* 19, no. 1 (2017): 93–105.

14. "Humanities," in William Nicholson, *British Encyclopedia, or, Dictionary of Arts and Sciences*, American ed., vol. 6 (Philadelphia: Mitchell, Ames, and White, 1819–1821).

15. Felix E. Schelling, "The Humanities Gone and to Come: Read Before the Phi Betta Kappa Society at the University of Pennsylvania," June 18, 1902, 11.

16. Ibid.

17. Ibid., 12, 16.

18. J. David Hoeveler Jr., *The New Humanism: A Critique of Modern America: 1900–1940* (Charlottesville: University Press of Virginia, 1977), 118.

19. Irving Babbitt, *Literature and the American College* (Washington, DC: National Humanities Institute, 1986), 96.

20. Ibid., 74.

21. Terence, *Heauton Timorumenos*, 1.1.77.

22. Babbitt, *Literature and the American College*, 75.

23. Ibid., 87, 147.

24. Ibid., 138.

25. Ibid., 8, 117. See, Andrew Jewett, *Science, Democracy, and the American University* (Cambridge: Cambridge University Press, 2012), 199–200. See also, J. David Hoeveler, *The New Humanism: A Critique of Modern America, 1900–1940* (Charlottesville, VA: University of Virginia Press, 1977).

26. Consider, for example, Thomas Fitz-Hugh, whose book *The Philosophy of the Humanities* (Chicago: University of Chicago Press, 1897) invokes "the humanities" only to focus on what he calls the "Latin Humanities" and their "humanizing" effects, 10–12. Jon H. Roberts and James Turner provide an excellent account of such late nineteenth-century invocations in *The Sacred and Secular University* (Princeton, NJ: Princeton University Press, 2000), esp. 73–106.

27. Geoffrey Harpham offers a similar dating but few details in *The Humanities and the Dream of America* (Chicago: University of Chicago Press, 2011), 14.

28. See, Patricia Beesley, *The Revival of the Humanities in American Higher Education* (New York: Columbia University Press, 1942).

29. Ibid., 128. See also Reuben, *Modern University*, 226.

30. Mark Greif, *The Age of the Crisis of Man: Thought and Fiction in America 1933–1973* (Princeton, NJ: Princeton University Press, 2015), 3.

31. Stefanos Geroulanos, *An Atheism That Is Not Humanist Emerges in French Thought* (Palo Alto, CA: Stanford University Press, 2010), 209–15.

32. Aimé Césaire, *Discourse on Colonialism* (New York: Monthly Review Press, 2000), 37, 39.

33. Waldo G. Leland, "Recent Trends in the Humanities," *Science* 79, no. 2048 (March 30, 1934): 281–82.

34. Ibid., 281, 283.

35. Compare the institutional settlement in the United States with the fate of the so-called classical tradition of sociology, which never gained institutional footing in German universities. There were no chaired professorships in sociology and, thus, no distinct institutional locations for sociology or Leland's "federation" of social sciences in Germany until after World War I. Following an intense debate on the institutional place of sociology in 1919, however, several universities finally established chairs in sociology, such as Hamburg in 1927, Leipzig in 1925, and Aachen in 1926. In this light, it is important to note that Max Weber was not, as Talcott Parsons claimed in 1937, the author of a "generalized theoretical system of social action" and, thus, the founding father of sociology. As far as his position in the university was concerned, Weber was an economist and had actually been trained in law. "In Germany," as A. Salomon put it in 1945, "there is no sociology, only sociologists." In contrast, sociology in the United States was already well established by the turn of the century with departments at both the University of Chicago and Columbia University as well as a journal, the *American Journal of Sociology* (1895). The Social Science Research Council was founded in 1923–1924. Talcott Parsons, *The Structure of Social Action* (New York: McGraw Hill, 1937), 686. See also Lawrence Scaff, "Weber's Reception in the United States, 1920–1960," in *Das Faszinosum Max Weber: Die Geschichte seiner Geltung*, ed. Karl-Ludwig Ay and Knut Borchardt (Konstanz: UVK, 2006), 55–89; A. Salomon, "German Sociology," in *Twentieth-Century Sociology*, ed. G. Gurvitch and W. E. Moore (New York: Philosophical Library, 1945), 587.

36. John W. Boyer, *The University of Chicago: A History* (Chicago: University of Chicago Press, 2015), 229.

37. "Preliminary Report of the Committee in Charge of the General Courses in the Humanities," April 1931, quoted in John W. Boyer, *A Twentieth-Century Cosmos: The New Plan and the Origins of General Education at Chicago*, Occasional Papers on Higher Education 16 (Chicago: College of the University of Chicago, [2007?]), 12.

38. Robert Maynard Hutchins, *No Friendly Voice* (Chicago: University of Chicago Press, 1936), 24–25.

39. Boyer, *University of Chicago*, 244.

40. Ibid., 242–52.

41. Hutchins, *No Friendly Voice*, 176.

42. Quoted in Greif, *Age of the Crisis of Man*, 30.

43. Harpham, *Humanities and the Dream of America*, 14. We draw here and in the following paragraphs on Princeton and the Baltimores directly on Bryan

McAllister-Grande, "The Inner Restoration: Protestants Fighting for the Unity of Truth, 1930–1960" (PhD. diss., Harvard University, 2017).

44. See Theodore M. Greene, "Christian Education and Democracy," *Christian Education* 23, no. 3 (February 1940): 154.

45. Hinds quoting Greene in a letter from June 1942 as quoted in Wallace Irwin Jr., "The Legacy of SPH: How a Small Program in the Humanities Changed Princeton's Entire Curriculum," *Princeton Alumni Weekly*, January 14, 1987, 14; Greene, introduction to *The Meaning of the Humanities* (Princeton, NJ: Princeton University Press, 1938), xxx.

46. Christian Gauss, "Peace at Gettysburg," quoted in McAllister-Grande, "The Inner Restoration," 33. McAllister-Grande dates the essay to the early 1940s.

47. Irwin, "Legacy of SPH."

48. Ibid., 13.

49. Edward W. Said, *Out of Place: A Memoir* (New York: Alfred A. Knopf, 1999), 277.

50. Irwin, "Legacy of SPH," 15.

51. Dodds quoted in Irwin, "Legacy of SPH," 16.

52. Laurence Veysey, "The Plural Organized Worlds of the Humanities," in *The Organization of Knowledge in Modern America, 1860–1920*, ed. Alexandra Oleson and John Voss (Baltimore: Johns Hopkins, 1979), 56.

53. *Princeton Alumni Weekly*, April 8, 1938, 595.

54. Theodore Greene quoted in ibid.

55. Ralph Barton Perry, "A Definition of the Humanities," in *The Meaning of the Humanities*, ed. Theodore Meyer Greene (Princeton, NJ: Princeton University Press, 1938), 31, 32.

56. Quoted in V. R. Cardozier, *Colleges and Universities in World War II* (Westport, CT: Praeger, 1993).

57. Charles Dorn, "Promoting Public Welfare in Wartime: Stanford University during World War II," *American Journal of Education* 112 (2005): 111.

58. Quoted in ibid., 116.

59. Lewis Mumford, *The Condition of Man* (New York: Harcourt, Brace, and World, 1944), 376.

60. Mumford quoted in Donald L. Miller, *Lewis Mumford: A Life* (Pittsburgh: University of Pittsburgh Press, 1992), 410. See also Mumford, "The Humanities Look Ahead," in *Report of the First Annual Conference of the Stanford School of the Humanities* (Palo Alto, CA: Stanford University Press, 1943).

61. Beesley, *Revival of the Humanities*, 3; Harpham, *Humanities and the Dream of America*, 14.

62. Carl E. Schorske, "The New Rigorism in the Human Sciences," *Daedalus* 126, no. 1 (Winter, 1997): 303.

63. Both reports are quoted in Raymond B. Fosdick, *The Story of the Rockefeller Foundation* (New York: Harper & Brothers, 1952), 240–41.

64. *General Education in a Free Society: Report from the Harvard Committee* (Cambridge, MA: Harvard University Press, 1950), 43.

65. Ibid., 53–54, 76.

66. Ibid., 59, 60, 61, 178. See Jewett, *Science, Democracy, and the American University*, 332.

67. Dorothy Ross, "Changing Contours of the Social Science Disciplines," in *The Cambridge History of Science: The Modern Social Sciences*, ed. Theodore M. Porter and Dorothy Ross (Cambridge: Cambridge University Press, 2003), 219.

68. Jewett, *Science, Democracy, and the American University*, 206–16, 233.

69. Harvard's then president James Bryant Conant, a chemist whose term lasted from 1933 to 1953, generally endorsed such claims. In a series of more public-facing, polemical publications, however, he also argued that the natural and physical sciences were deeply human, even humane activities in which individuals sought not only to control nature but also (and more importantly) to understand it. Like art and literature, science was a creative and imaginative human activity. See, for example, James B. Conant, *On Understanding Science* (New Haven, CT: Yale University Press, 1947); *Science and Common Sense* (New Haven, CT: Yale University Press, 1951); and *Modern Science and Modern Man* (New York: Columbia University Press, 1952). See also Jewett, *Science, Democracy, and the American University*, 315–17, and Christopher Hamlin, "The Pedagogical Roots of the History of Science: Revisiting the Vision of James Bryant Conant," *Isis* 107, no. 2 (2016): 282–308.

70. *Report of the Committee on Educational Survey* (Cambridge, MA: Technology Press, MIT, 1949), 3, 4, 94.

71. National Foundation on the Arts and Humanities Act of 1965 (Pub. L. No. 89–209), https://www.neh.gov/about/history/national-foundation-arts-and-humanities-act-1965-pl-89-209.

72. Cornelius Kruse, "On Humanity's Need for the Humanities," in *History of the Ohio State University*, vol. 6, *State University: Addresses and Proceedings of the Seventy-Fifth Anniversary 1948–49* (Columbus: Ohio State University Press, 1951), 62.

73. Ibid., 55–56.

74. Ibid., 64.

75. See, Joan Shelley Rubin, "The Scholar and the World: Academic Humanists and General Readers" in *The Humanities and the Dynamics of Inclusion Since World War II*, ed. David A. Hollinger (Baltimore: Johns Hopkins University Press, 2006), 73–103.

76. Geroulanos, *An Atheism* (see n. 31).

77. Mark Greif, *Age of the Crisis of Man*, 45–46.

78. Erich von Kahler, *Man the Measure: A New Approach to History* (New York: George Braziller, 1956), 25.

79. Ibid., 637–39.

80. We draw here on the source material as collected and quoted in David Kettler, "The Symbolic Use of Exile: Erich Kahler at the Ohio State University," in *Exile and Otherness: New Approaches to the Experience of the Nazi Refugees*, ed. Alexander Stephan (Bern: Peter Lang, 2005), n21.

81. Roy Harvey Pearce and colleagues to Dean J. Osborn Fuller (October 17, 1957), quoted in Kettler, "Symbolic Use of Exile."

82. "The Morrill Act," in *The Rise of the Research University: A Sourcebook*, ed. Louis Menand, Paul Reitter, and Chad Wellmon (Chicago: University of Chicago Press, 2017), 167.

83. Roy Harvey Pearce, "Historicism Once More," *Kenyon Review* 20, no. 4 (1958): 554–91.

84. *Faculty Seminar Report: 1959*, quoted in Kettler, "Symbolic Use of Exile," 26–27.

85. Kahler to Ohio State Seminar, March 1961, as quoted in Kettler, "The Symbolic Uses of Exile."

86. Kahler quoted in David Kettler, *The Liquidation of Exile: Studies in the Intellectual Emigration of the 1930s* (New York: Anthem Press, 2011), 187n.

87. Max Scheler, "Weltanschauungslehre, Soziologie und Weltanschauungssetzung," *Kölner Vierteljahreshefte für Sozialwissenschaften* 2, no. 1 (1922): 22, 23, 25.

88. Kahler quoted in Gerhard Lauer, "The Empire's Watermark: Erich Kahler and Exile," in *Exile, Science, and Bildung: The Contested Legacies of German Émigré Intellectuals*, ed. David Kettler and Gerhard Lauer (New York: Palgrave Macmillan, 2005): 68.

89. Kruse, "On Humanity's Need for the Humanities," 55–56.

90. Ibid.

91. Perry, "Definition of the Humanities," 3, 30.

92. Ibid., 16–17.

93. Ibid., 22, 33, 41.

94. James Hankins, "Garin and Paul Oskar Kristeller: Existentialism, Neo-Kantianism, and the Post-War Interpretation of Renaissance Humanism," in *Eugenio Garin: Dal Rinascimento all'illuminismo*, ed. Michele Ciliberto (Rome: Edizioni di Storia e Letteratura), 481–505.

95. Eugenio Garin, *Italian Humanism: Philosophy and Civic Life in the Renaissance*, trans. Peter Munz (Oxford: Blackwell, 1965), 3, 5, 220–21. See Christopher S. Celenza, *The Lost Italian Renaissance: Humanists, Historians, and Latin's Legacy* (Baltimore: Johns Hopkins University Press, 2006), 30–36.

96. James Hankins, "Two Twentieth-Century Interpreters of Renaissance Humanism: Eugenio Garin and Paul Oskar Kristeller," *Comparative Criticism* 23 (2001): 6.

97. Paul Oskar Kristeller, "Humanism and Scholasticism," in *Renaissance Thought and Its Sources*, ed. Michael Mooney (New York: Columbia University Press, 1979), 91.

98. Ibid., 105.

99. Rocco Rubini, *The Other Renaissance: Italian Humanism between Hegel and Heidegger* (Chicago: University of Chicago Press, 2014), 348.

100. Kristeller, "Humanism and Scholasticism," 89.

101. Hankins, "Garin and Paul Oskar Kristeller"; Kay Schiller, "Paul Oskar Kristeller, Ernst Cassirer and the 'Humanistic turn' in American Emigration," in *Exile, Science and Bildung: The Contested Legacies of German Intellectual Figures* (Basingstoke: Palgrave Macmillan, 2005), 125–38.

102. Hankins, "Twentieth-Century Interpreters," 11.

103. Ibid.

104. Paul Oskar Kristeller, "Some Problems of Historical Knowledge," *Journal of Philosophy* 58, no. 4 (1961): 85, 86.

105. Ibid., 86.

106. Ibid., 97.

107. See Notker Hammerstein, *Bildung und Wissenschaft vom 15. bis 17. Jahrhundert*, Enzyclopädie deutscher Geschichte 64 (Munich: Oldenbourg, 2010), 103.

108. Paul Oskar Kristeller, "Studies on Renaissance Humanism during the Last Twenty Years," *Studies in the Renaissance* 9 (1962): 16–17.

109. Celenza, *Lost Italian Renaissance*, 41.

110. Kristeller, "Some Problems of Historical Knowledge," 109.

111. Paul Oskar Kristeller, "The Dignity of Man," in Mooney, *Renaissance Thought and Its Sources*, 181.

112. Thomas Mann, *Gesammelte Werke* (Frankfurt am Main: S. Fischer, 1974), 10:346.

113. Ernst Cassirer, *Essay on Man* (New Haven, CT: Yale University Press, 1972), 21, 228.

114. Ernst Cassirer, *Determinism and Indeterminism in Modern Physics*, trans. O. Theodor Benfey (New Haven, CT: Yale University Press, 1956), 4.

115. Erich Auerbach, "Philologie der Weltliteratur," in *Weltliteratur: Festgabe für Fritz Strich zum 70. Geburtstag*, ed. Walter Muschg and E. Staiger (Bern: Francke, 1952), 41.

116. David A. Hollinger, introduction to *The Humanities and the Dynamics of Inclusion since World War II*, ed. David A. Hollinger (Baltimore: Johns Hopkins University Press, 2006), 4.

117. Schorske, "The New Rigorism in the Human Sciences," 295 (see n. 62).

118. Rachel Sagner Buurma and Laura Heffernan, "The Common Reader and the Archival Classroom: Disciplinary History for the Twenty-First Century," *New Literary History* 43, no. 1 (Winter 2012): 113. See also Merve Emre, "Post-Disciplinary Reading and Literary Sociology," *Modernism/Modernity*, vol. 3, cycle 4, February 1, 2019, https://modernismmodernity.org/forums/posts/post-disciplinary-reading-and-literary-sociology.

119. E. Digby Baltzell, "Bell Telephone's Experiment in Education," *Harper's Magazine*, March 1, 1955, 73–77.

120. William H. Whyte, *Organization Man* (New York: Simon and Schuster, 1956).

121. Timothy Aubry, "Humanities, Inc.," *American Studies* 53, no. 4 (2014): 12.

122. *The Great Ideas: A Syntopicon of Great Books of the Western World*, vol. 1, ed. Mortimer Jerome Adler (Chicago: Encyclopedia Britannica, 1952), xv, xi, xiv. See Tim Lacy, *The Dream of a Democratic Culture: Mortimer J. Adler and the Great Books Idea* (New York: Palgrave Macmillan, 2013).

123. See, Justus Nieland, *Happiness by Design: Modernism and Media in the Eames Era* (Minneapolis: University of Minnesota Press, 2019); James Sloan Allen, *The Romance of Commerce and Culture: Capitalism, Modernism, and the Chicago-Aspen Crusade for Cultural Reform* (Chicago: University of Chicago Press, 1983).

124. C. Wright Mills, *The Power Elite* (Oxford: Oxford University Press, 1956).

125. For an account of how literature in particular "mattered" beyond the university in the 1940s and was supported by more than just wealthy, powerful elites but also by the US military, public libraries, and the paperback explosion, see George Hutchinson, *Facing the Abyss: American Literature and Culture in the 1940s* (New York: Columbia University Press, 2018), 15–35.

126. Claudia Goldin and Lawrence F. Katz, "The Shaping of Higher Education: The Formative Years in the United States, 1890 to 1940," *Journal of Economic Perspectives* 13, no. 1 (1999): 37–62.

127. Samuel Moyn, "The Universal Declaration of Human Rights of 1948 in the History of Cosmopolitanism," *Critical Inquiry* 40, no. 4 (2014): 378.

128. Lewis Mumford, "The Unified Approach to Knowledge and Life," in *Values for Survival: Essays, Addresses, and Letters on Politics and Education* (New York: Harcourt, Brace, 1946), 189.

129. Michel Foucault, "What Is Enlightenment?," in *The Foucault Reader*, ed. Paul Rabinow (New York: Pantheon Books, 1984).

130. Jacques Derrida, "The University without Condition," in *Without Alibi*, ed. and trans. Peggy Kamuf (Stanford, CA: Stanford University Press, 2002), 202–37; Derrida, "Of the Humanities and the Discipline of Philosophy," *Surfaces* 4 (1994): 5–21.

131. Dipesh Chakrabarty, "Humanities in the Anthropocene: The Crisis of an Enduring Kantian Fable," *New Literary History* 47, no. 2/3 (2016): 378.

132. John Durham Peters, *The Marvelous Clouds* (Chicago: University of Chicago Press, 2015), 379.

133. Louis Menand, *The Marketplace of Ideas: Reform and Resistance in the American University* (New York: W. W. Norton, 2010), 91.

134. Steven Connor, "Decomposing the Humanities," *New Literary History* 47, no. 2/3 (2016): 281.

135. Greif, *Age of the Crisis of Man*, 328 (see n. 30).

136. John Guillory, "Who's Afraid of Marcel Proust: The Failure of General Education in the American University," *The Humanities and the Dynamics of Inclusion since World War II*, ed. David Hollinger (Baltimore: Johns Hopkins University Press, 2006), 25–72.

## CONCLUSION

1. Geoffrey Galt Harpham, "Beneath and beyond the 'Crisis in the Humanities,'" *New Literary History* 36, no. 1 (Winter 2005): 36.

2. David A. Bell, "Reimagining the Humanities: Proposals for a New Century," *Dissent*, Fall 2010, https://www.dissentmagazine.org/article/reimagining-the-humanities-proposals-for-a-new-century; Stefan Collini, *Speaking of Universities* (London: Verso, 2017).

3. Rens Bod, *A New History of the Humanities* (Oxford: Oxford University Press, 2013), and James Turner, *Philology: The Forgotten Origins of the Modern Humanities* (Princeton, NJ: Princeton University Press, 2014). Both authors highlight methodological continuities as a way of defining what the humanities are. The focus on method as a way of understanding cultural artifacts means that key aspects of the humanities—their claims to shape character and function as a social good, for example—go largely unexamined.

4. Daniel T. Rogers, *Atlantic Crossings: Social Politics in a Progressive Age* (Cambridge, MA: Harvard University Press, 1998), 413.

5. Helen Small, *The Value of the Humanities* (Oxford: Oxford University Press, 2013), 29.

6. For an excellent and historically rich explication of this point, see Jennifer J. Summit, "Renaissance Humanism and the Future of the Humanities," *Literature Compass* 9 (2012): 665–78.

7. Martha Nussbaum, *Not for Profit: Why Democracy Needs the Humanities* (Princeton, NJ: Princeton University Press, 2010); Danielle Allen, *Education and Equality* (Chicago: University of Chicago Press, 2016); Christopher Newfield, *The Great Mistake* (Baltimore: Johns Hopkins University Press, 2017).

8. Christopher Newfield, "The Crisis of Higher Ed Realpolitik: A Visit to Connecticut," Remaking the University, https://utotherescue.blogspot.com/2019/04/the-crisis-of-higher-ed-realpolitik.html.

9. Hannah Arendt, "The Crisis in Education," in *Between Past and Present* (New York: Penguin, 2006), 189.

10. Lionel Trilling, "The Uncertain Future of the Humanistic Educational Ideal," *American Scholar* 44, no. 1 (Winter 1974/1975), 62.

11. Christopher Newfield, *The Great Mistake: How We Wrecked Public Universities and How We Can Fix Them* (Baltimore: Johns Hopkins University Press, 2018).

12. Edward W. Said, *The World, the Text, and the Critic* (Cambridge, MA: Harvard University Press, 1983), 2, 24.

13. Ibid., 26.

14. Michael Allan, *In the Shadow of World Literature: Sites of Reading in Colonial Egypt* (Princeton, NJ: Princeton University Press, 2016), 36.

15. Said, *The World*, 26, 29.

16. Ibid., 6.

17. Ibid., 9.

18. Allan, *In the Shadow of World Literature*, 36.

19. Said, *The World*, 290.

20. Tomoko Masuzawa, "Secular by Default? Religion and the University before the Post-Secular," in *The Post-Secular Question: Religion in Contemporary Society*, ed. Philip Gorski et al. (New York: New York University Press, 2012), 187.

21. Weber, "Vorbemerkung," *MWG*, 1.18:101,104, 105.

22. The literature on decolonizing scholarship and the university is vast. See, for example, Kwasi Wiredu, "Toward Decolonizing African Philosophy and Religion," *African Studies Quarterly* 1, no. 4 (1998): 17–46; Mahmood Mamdani, "The African University," *London Review of Books* 40, no. 14 (July 19, 2008), https://www.lrb.co.uk/the-paper/v40/n14/mahmood-mamdani/the-african-university; *Decolonising the University*, ed. Gurminder K. Bhambra, Kerem Nişancıoğlu, and Dalia Gebrial (London: Pluto Press, 2018).

23. Weber, *Wissenschaft als Beruf, MWG*, 1.17:103.

24. Ibid., 84.

# Index

humanities (*continued*)
  temptations of, 4–5, 19–20, 79–80,
    183–85, 217–20, 225–26, 229–31, 236,
    247–52, 257–58; postwar capitalism
    and, 248–50; social sciences and,
    231, 235; theology's relation to, 11,
    16, 258–59. *See also* knowledge; lib-
    eral learning; not-natural-scientific
    disciplines; spontaneity; unity-of-
    knowledge ideal; vocationalism
"Humanities Are in Crisis, The"
  (Schmidt), 2
*Humanities in American Life, The* (Commission on the Humanities), 267n9
*Humanities Look Ahead, The* (Stanford),
  234
Humboldt, Wilhelm von: academic
  freedom and, 71–72; *Bildung* and,
  37, 57, 255, 257; death of, 54; moral
  formation and, 48–52; natural scientists' uses of, 117–18; Nietzsche and,
  99–105; Schleiermacher and, 48–49;
  unity-of-knowledge ideal and, 19,
  25, 28–29, 38, 59–60, 121, 185, 255–
  56; University of Berlin and, 49–50,
  60–64; university reform and, 43–
  44
Hutchins, Robert Maynard, 230–31,
  248

idealism (German): natural sciences
  and, 123–28, 132–41; neo-humanism
  and, 43–48; part-whole relationships and, 30–35, 38–40, 47–48, 59–
  60, 159; unity-of-knowledge thesis
  and, 23; university organization and,
  36–42. *See also specific philosophers*
*Ideas for a Philosophy of Nature* (Schelling), 38
industrialization, 6–7, 16, 153–54, 193,
  236–37. *See also* capitalism; modernity and modernization; technology
*Institutes of the Christian Religion, The*
  (Calvin), 197–98, 212
instrumental logic, 15, 30–35, 41–42,
  46, 273n28. *See also* rationalization

(institutional); utilitarianism (in university education)
*Introduction to the Humanities* (Dilthey), 113, 116–17, 122, 153–65, 170–
  71, 173

Jaeger, Werner, 243
*Jahrbuch für die geistige Bewegung*,
  201
James, William, 22–23
Jardine, Lisa, 10
Jaspers, Karl, 188
"Jewishness in Music" (Wagner), 85
Johns Hopkins University, 234
*Journal for the Advancement of Industry*,
  62

Kahler, Erich von, 201–2, 204, 206, 228,
  237–41, 243, 245–47
Kaiser Wilhelm Society, 189
Kant, Immanuel, 13–17, 26–30, 37, 39,
  60, 64, 69, 121, 158, 170–71, 180, 203,
  211, 242, 271n64
*Kenyon Review*, 246
Kerr, Clark, 74
knowledge: alienating pursuits of, 16,
  39, 41, 102, 116, 150–57, 201–4, 209,
  239, 260; as erudition, 11, 41–42,
  141, 219; human needs and, 159–62;
  instrumental logic regarding, 4,
  30–35, 46–48, 56–58, 97–98, 104–5,
  131–32, 138–42, 178–79, 213–14, 224–
  25, 241–42, 253–55, 273n28; liberal
  learning and, 13–18, 56–58, 90–94,
  191; life's connection to, 35–45, 59,
  68–69, 86–90, 108–12, 163–84, 202–
  3, 209; morality and, 76–80, 99–105,
  108–12, 125–28, 211; reenchantment
  of, 201–4; sociability and, 44–48,
  168–69, 188–89, 243; specialization
  and fragmentation in, 96–99, 125–
  28, 131–51, 165–70, 182–87, 193–207,
  218, 223–27, 237–46, 250–52, 258–
  61; state interest in, 43–52, 59–60,
  62–65, 71–76, 87–94, 99–108, 193–
  94, 213–14, 256; unity aspirations